Human Trafficking

Human Trafficking

Suman Kakar
Associate Professor
Department of Criminal Justice
Florida International University

Carolina Academic Press
Durham, North Carolina

Library of Congress Cataloging-in-Publication Data

Names: Kakar, Suman, 1953- author.
Title: Human trafficking / Suman Kakar.
Description: Durham, North Carolina : Carolina Academic Press, [2017] | Includes bibliographical references and index.
Identifiers: LCCN 2017005003 | ISBN 9781611637564 (alk. paper)
Subjects: LCSH: Human trafficking. | Social media. | Human trafficking (International law)
Classification: LCC HQ281 .K35 2017 | DDC 306.3/62--dc23
LC record available at https://lccn.loc.gov/2017005003

eISBN 978-1-53100-439-2

Carolina Academic Press, LLC
700 Kent Street
Durham, North Carolina 27701
Telephone (919) 489-7486
Fax (919) 493-5668
www.cap-press.com

Printed in the United States of America
2021 Printing

Contents

Human Trafficking

Chapter 1

Understanding Trafficking in Persons

Chapter Objectives

This chapter provides a comprehensive understanding of the following:

- What is Human Trafficking?
- Trafficking in Persons: Global Crime
- Trafficking Case Involving US Citizens as Perpetrators
- Fact Check on Trafficking
    - Trafficking Victims are not Only Foreigners
    - Trafficking is the not Same as Illegal Migration, Forced Migration or Smuggling
    - All Victims of Trafficking Are not Poor Foreigners
    - Persons Claiming to be Victims of Trafficking are not Employees Who Consented to be Employed in the Professions They are in—They are Victims
    - Illegal Underground Industries are not the Only Industries Involved in Human Trafficking
- Human Trafficking: Human Rights Violations
    - The Cyrus Cylinder
    - The Magna Carta
    - Universal Declaration of Human Rights
    - Human Trafficking Prosecution Unit
    - Human Trafficking and the United States Criminal Code, Title 18, Chapter 77
- Human Trafficking: Business

  - Traditional Professions Such as Teaching and Medicine are also Part of the Trafficking Business
  - Differences and Similarities: Human Trafficking and Slavery
- Bondage
- Bonded Labor and Debt Bondage among Migrant Laborers
- Forced Labor
- Sex Trafficking

Introduction: What Is Human Trafficking?

Human trafficking has been called by different names and synonymously used with terms such as "slavery," "modern slavery," "illegal migration," "smuggling," "under-age prostitution of foreigners," "facilitated irregular migration," "sex-slavery," "servitude," and "child labor," among other terms. Often these terms are used interchangeably, confounding the manner in which victims, perpetrators, and communities understand it. This understanding of the issue, in turn, affects how policy makers address human trafficking.

This chapter presents a detailed overview of human trafficking. It reviews various terms confused with human trafficking. It discusses differences and similarities between human trafficking, slavery, illegal immigration, and smuggling. Human trafficking is discussed as a process and in terms of a human rights violation. The chapter discusses the economics of human exploitation for the purposes of commercializing humans for labor, sex, organs, and other profit-producing practices. To facilitate understanding of what human trafficking is, this chapter provides examples of cases to analyze. The case analyses demonstrate the necessary elements that have to be present in a human trafficking case to distinguish it from other cases that may be very similar to human trafficking, such as "illegal migration," "smuggling," "under-age prostitution of foreigners," "facilitated irregular migration," "sex-slavery," "servitude," and "child labor." Such an introduction provides a broader understanding of human trafficking.

Trafficking in Persons: Global Crime

Trafficking in persons is a global crime—ubiquitous in nature—affecting nearly all countries in every region of the world. It is a crime that ruthlessly exploits women, children, and men for numerous purposes including forced labor and sex. This global crime generates billions of dollars in profits for traffickers. The International Labor Organization estimates that 20.9 million people are victims of forced labor—in terms of sex and labor trafficking globally.[1] This estimate also includes victims of human trafficking for labor and sexual exploitation. There are vast numbers of local, national and regional interpretations and responses to this crime, and an immense number of stake-holders involved in addressing it. According to the United Nations definition, human trafficking can be understood as a process by which people are recruited in their community and exploited by traffickers using deception and/or some form of coercion to lure and control them.[2]

"The exploitation of one human being by another is the basest crime. Still trafficking in persons remains all too common, with all too few consequences for the perpetrators ..."[3]

Trafficking in persons is conceptualized, described, and understood differently in different contexts. It is only recently that there is some consensus on what human trafficking is and the term "Trafficking in Persons" has been recognized as a term on its own. The first-ever agreed upon definition of trafficking, now known as Protocol to Prevent, Suppress and Punish Trafficking in Persons, was incorporated in 2000, which supplemented the United Nations Convention against Transnational Organized Crime.[4] The United Nations criminalized human trafficking under the protocols of Transnational Organized Crime in 2000 and adopted the United Nations Protocol to Prevent, Suppress and Punish Trafficking in Persons, Especially Women and Children.

On November 15, 2000, the United Nations General Assembly passed Resolution 55/25, adopting the Convention against Transnational Organized Crime and its supplemental protocols. The Protocol to Prevent, Suppress and Punish Trafficking in Persons, especially Women and Children—a protocol against Transnational Organized Crime—was adopted by the United Nations General Assembly in 2000 and entered into force on December 25, 2003. As of June 2015, it has been ratified by 167 parties.[5]

Article 3, paragraph (a) of the Protocol to Prevent, Suppress and Punish Trafficking in Persons defines Trafficking in Persons:

> as the recruitment, transportation, transfer, harboring or receipt of persons, by means of the threat or use of force or other forms of coercion, of abduction, of fraud, of deception, of the abuse of power or of a position of vulnerability or of the giving or receiving of payments or benefits to achieve the consent of a person having control over another person, for the purpose of exploitation. Exploitation shall include, at a minimum, the exploitation of the prostitution of

> others or other forms of sexual exploitation, forced labor or services, slavery or practices similar to slavery, servitude or the removal of organs (UNDOC.ORG, 2014).[6]

Trafficking in Persons Protocol (Article 3) provided uniformity in describing the phenomenon of trafficking in persons. It also provided elements that clearly distinguished it from other crimes that may look and sound similar, such as smuggling and illegal immigration, but are legally different. It provides a clear and consistent overview of elements that must be present to consider it a crime. It is not limited to crossing borders—it occurs both across and within the borders of a country. In addition to sexual exploitation, it covers a wide variety of exploitative purposes. Victims are not only women or adults but include children, women, and men. In some cases, it may involve organized crime groups and others it may be an individual, a small group, or a family operation. Article 5 of Trafficking in Persons Protocol recommends that the conduct set out in Article 3 be criminalized in domestic legislation. The Trafficking in Persons Protocol requires criminalization of:

- Attempts to commit a trafficking offense
- Participation as an accomplice in such an offense
- Organizing or directing others to commit trafficking

According to this definition, the elements of human trafficking include act, means, and purpose. The "recruitment, transportation, transfer, harboring, or receipt of persons" refer to the act; the "threat or use of force or other forms of coercion, of abduction, of fraud, of deception, of the abuse of power or of a position of vulnerability, or of the giving or receiving of payments or benefits" refer to the means; and the activities "to achieve the consent of a person having control over another person, for the purpose of exploitation" refer to what finally facilitates accomplishment of the process of human trafficking. These various elements of human trafficking have been presented in Figure 1.

The three elements of human trafficking are act, means, and purpose. The **act** refers to the activities that are necessary elements of human trafficking. These include: recruitment, transportation, transfer, harboring, or receipt of persons. The **means** refer to the use of threats, force, coercion, fraud, deception, abuse of power, or any other means used to conduct the activities. To achieve the consent of a person having control over another person refers to the **purpose**, and the **process** refers to the methods used to carry out the human trafficking activities. These specifically refer to the threat or use of force,

Figure 1: The Elements of Human Trafficking

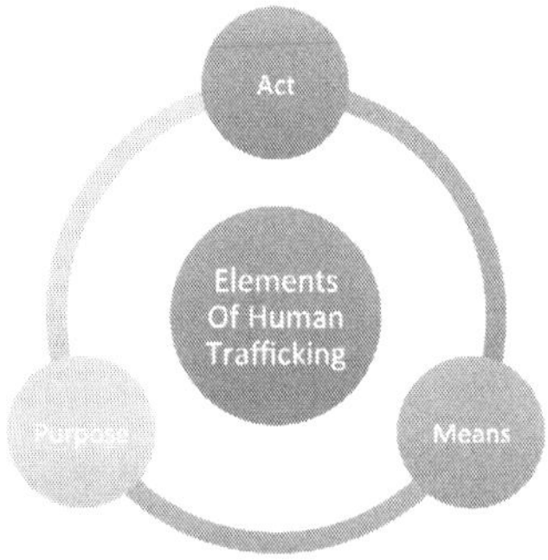

Adapted from https://www.unodc.org/unodc/en/human-trafficking/what-is-human-trafficking.html.

coercion, abduction, fraud, deception, abuse of power or vulnerability, or giving payments or benefits to a person in control of the victim. The **purpose** refers to the reasons for engaging in activities that are classified as human trafficking. The Protocol to Prevent, Suppress and Punish Trafficking in Persons identifies exploitation as the purpose—which includes forced prostitution, sexual exploitation, forced labor, slavery or similar practices, and the removal of organs.

To ascertain whether a particular circumstance constitutes trafficking in persons, consider the definition of trafficking in the Trafficking in Persons Protocol and the constituent elements of the offense, as defined by Florida Statutes.

For example, according to the Florida Statutes 787.06, "human trafficking is a form of modern-day slavery. Victims of human trafficking are young children, teenagers, and adults. Thousands of victims are trafficked annually across international borders worldwide. Many of these victims are trafficked into this state. Victims of human trafficking also include citizens of the United States and those persons trafficked domestically within the borders of the United States."[7] According to the Florida Statutes 787.06, "victims of human trafficking are subjected to force, fraud, or coercion for the purpose of sexual exploitation or forced labor."[8]

Trafficking Case Involving U.S. Citizens as Perpetrators

Below is an actual case of human trafficking—involving United States citizens and foreigners—that occurred on United States soil.

Box 1: Kil Soo Lee and the Case of the Samoan Sweatshop

Consider the case of **Kil Soo Lee** (shown in the above picture), convicted of enslaving more than 250 garment workers in his factory in American Samoa.

In the late 1990s, Mr. Kil Soo Lee crafted a ruthless business plan to mass produce clothes for top U.S. retailers.

Mr. Lee built his factory on a remote island of American Samoa, an unincorporated U.S. territory 2,300 miles south of Honolulu. Since the business is conducted on the U.S. territorial land, he could use the "Made in America" label on his clothes but not draw attention to his operation.

He recruited more than 250 skilled garment workers from Vietnam and China, mostly young women, enticing them with promises of a steady job that could help support their children and families back home. To guarantee this new job in America, he demanded an exorbitant down payment of as much as $6,000 from each worker.

When the employees arrived, he placed them on grueling schedules in horrid conditions and paid them next to nothing. Then, he kept the workers in line through threats, beatings, starvation, false arrests, sexual assaults, debt repayment schemes, deportation, and other tactics—all enforced by security guards appointed by him in a gated compound.

Adapted from https://www.fbi.gov/news/stories/2004/july/kilsoolee_071904.

Dissect the case to determine whether you can identify the elements and purpose of human trafficking in this case.

Case Analysis

A careful analysis of this case demonstrates all the elements (act, means, and purpose) and the process of human trafficking.

- Mr. Lee building a factory on a remote island of American Samoa and recruiting more than 250 skilled garment workers from Vietnam and China, mostly vulnerable young women, by enticing them with promises of a steady job, refers to the "act."
- Mr. Lee demanding a down payment of $6,000 from each worker to guarantee a job in America and placing the employees on grueling schedules in horrid conditions and paying minimal to no wages, refers to the "means."
- Mr. Lee threatening the employees with beatings, starvation, false arrests, sexual assaults, debt repayment schemes, deportation, and other tactics enforced by security guards in a gated compound refers to the "process."
- Mr. Lee's desire to use this location of the factory to use the "Made in America" label on his clothes but not draw attention to his operation, exploit the employees' vulnerability to place them on grueling schedules in horrid conditions and deny remuneration, threaten with physical harm and deportation, etc. in order to make exorbitant profits refers to "purpose."

We just analyzed a case to understand the definitional elements of human trafficking. Now let us dissect it a step further to fully understand the key features of the 2000 Protocol to Prevent, Suppress and Punish Trafficking in Persons.

- A general perception of trafficking is in terms of sexual exploitation of young girls and women. Often trafficking is equated to sexual exploitation and prostitution. However, the definition of human trafficking provided in the Protocol to Prevent, Suppress and Punish Trafficking in Persons makes it abundantly clear that trafficking involves a wide variety of exploitative practices much beyond prostitution and sexual exploitation of young girls and women. It equally affects women, men, and young boys and girls.
- It is generally believed that trafficking involves traveling and transportation, especially crossing international borders. The definition of human trafficking provided in the Protocol to Prevent, Suppress and Punish Trafficking in Persons states that trafficking **does not require any travel**, let alone travel across international borders. Human beings can be traf-

ficked within the same neighborhood and community, city, town, state, across the state and/or provincial lines and borders, as well as international borders.
- It is also a common perception that trafficking victims want to enter the criminal enterprise by crossing the borders and actually participate in the act voluntarily—implying that the victims willingly and knowingly enter the exploitative situations and have an opportunity to leave the situation as and when they decide. The definition clarifies that victims do not have control over their exploitation and have no opportunity to "consent" and, in fact, cannot give consent to trafficking. The definition specifies deception, coercion, force, and fraud as "means" of duping trafficking victims into agreeing to be placed in exploitative situations and as a matter of fact, the victims have no ability to consent.

According to the US Department of State,[9] the United States is a destination country for thousands of men, women, and children trafficked from all areas of the world. These victims are trafficked for the purposes of sexual and labor exploitation. Many of these victims are lured from their homes with false promises of well-paying jobs, romance, and marriage. In many instances, young women and girls—desirous of a high standard of living, upscale lifestyle, expensive clothes, jewelry, and upward mobility eagerly search for opportunities that will take them to their desired end. They become easy targets for exploitation. Traffickers take advantage of their eagerness to leave their homes and start their glamorous—but often imaginary—lives. As soon as they arrive at their destinations, their identification documents are confiscated, they are isolated, and forced or coerced into prostitution, domestic servitude, farm or factory labor, or other types of forced labor. For traffickers, it has become the most lucrative illicit form of business with very little investment. Victims often find themselves in a foreign country. They do not understand or speak the language. Traffickers often strip victims of their identities by taking away their travel and identity documents, telling them that if they attempt to escape, they themselves and/or their families back home will be harmed, and the victims' families will assume their debt.[10]

Human Trafficking and Smuggling— What Are the Differences?

Generally, trafficking is used as an alternate term for smuggling and human trafficking is understood to be the same as illegal migration, forced migration, or smuggling. This is an erroneous classification of human trafficking and smuggling. The definition of human trafficking provided in the Protocol to

Prevent, Suppress and Punish Trafficking in Persons clarifies the difference between human trafficking and smuggling. This protocol defines trafficking differently from smuggling of migrants or illegal migration. According to this protocol, human trafficking focuses on exploitation of human beings' mind and body through force, fraud, or coercion while smuggling focuses on profit only. In human trafficking, the person involved does not participate willingly. There is use of "force, fraud, or coercion" (actual, perceived, or implied), unless the individual is under 18 years of age and involved in commercial sex acts. In the case of smuggling, the person being smuggled is a willing participant and cooperates with the smuggler voluntarily, while in trafficking, victims are forced to cooperate or duped into cooperation. Persons who are trafficked are victims while the smuggled persons are complicit in the smuggling crime. They are not necessarily victims of the crime of smuggling (though they may become trafficking victims depending on the circumstances in which they were smuggled). Rather, they are perpetrators as they willingly violate international law by crossing international borders illegally.

While smuggling and illegal migration involve illegal and facilitated movement across an international border for profit and may involve deception and/or abusive treatment, the main objective of smuggling is to profit from the act of facilitating crossing the border (generally an international border) not the exploitation. The act of smuggling may eventually turn into the act of trafficking, but that generally is not the intended purpose of the initial act. Table 1 describes the similarities and differences between human trafficking and smuggling.

Fact Check on Human Trafficking

A general misperception is that trafficked persons are only foreign nationals. Only illegal and undocumented immigrants from other countries (mainly poverty-stricken citizens of developing nations) end up as victims of human trafficking. The facts are very different from this perception. Both US citizens and foreign nationals (illegal or legal) can be and are found to be the victims of trafficking. Both are protected under the federal trafficking statutes since the TVPA of 2000. Human trafficking encompasses both transnational trafficking that involves crossing transnational borders and domestic or internal trafficking that occurs within a country without crossing any transnational borders.

Human Trafficking Victims are not Only Foreigners

Contrary to the general belief, human trafficking can, but does not necessarily have to, involve some form of travel, transportation, or movement across state

Table 1: Differences between Human Trafficking and Smuggling

TRAFFICKING	SMUGGLING
The person does not participate willingly. There is use of force, fraud, or coercion (actual, perceived, or implied), unless under 18 years of age and involved in commercial sex acts.	The person being smuggled is generally cooperating. Thus, person is a willing participant in the violation of international law.
Forced labor and/or exploitation.	There is no actual or implied coercion.
Persons trafficked are victims.	Persons smuggled are complicit in the smuggling crime; they are not necessarily victims of the crime of smuggling (though they may become victims depending on the circumstances in which they were smuggled).
Victims do not have much freedom of movement. They are isolated and watched. Their identifying documents are confiscated.	Persons are free to leave, change jobs, etc.
Does not necessarily involve the actual movement of the victim from one place to another.	Facilitates the illegal entry of person(s) from one country into another.
Victims do not have to cross an international border.	Smuggling always involves crossing an international border.
Person must be involved in labor/services or commercial sex acts, i.e., must be "working."	Person must only be in country or attempting entry illegally.

Adapted from US Department of State, "Fact Sheet: Distinctions between Human Smuggling and Human Trafficking," January 1, 2006.

or national borders. While it is true that sometimes victims are transported from other countries and that may involve crossing borders, trafficking victims do not necessarily have to be transported across borders. Trafficking can take place within the same city and state. When victims do not need to be transported from a different country and the act does not involve crossing of any international borders, the act is known as **domestic human trafficking**.

It is also true that victims—domestic or international—may often be transported and housed in strange and isolated places to keep them dependent on the perpetrator for their survival. However, this is not an essential element of trafficking. Transporting victims to undisclosed locations makes it easier for the perpetrators to manipulate them and take advantage of their naivety, ignorance, and their unfamiliarity with their surroundings. This tactic increases the victims' probability of compliance with the perpetrators' demands. As demonstrated in the case of Kil Soo Lee (discussed earlier), any noncompliance results in threats, beatings, starvation, false arrests, sexual assaults, debt repayment schemes, deportation, and other tactics. The victims begin to believe that the only surety of their continuation in the job, escape from physical beatings and other forms of punishment, and in fact survival is dependent upon their full compliance with all the demands of their employers—including exploitation.

Trafficking Is not the Same as Illegal Migration, Forced Migration, or Smuggling

Most often human trafficking is understood to be the same as illegal migration, forced migration, or smuggling. This is an erroneous classification of human trafficking. (This is discussed more in detail later in the book). Human trafficking is exploitation of human beings' mind and body through force, fraud, or coercion. It is a form of involuntary servitude, or "compelled service" where a victim has no freedom to choose what she/he will and can do or think. Rather all actions are chosen for the victim. For survival, the victim is left with no choice but to comply. Any deviation will result in sanctions—such as physical beatings or worse, death—which generally are not limited to the victims only but also extended to their family members, friends, and loved ones.

Another common misperception purports that trafficking is a foreign country's issue and it does not happen in the United States, and if it does then it is only because foreigners arrive here illegally and try to find jobs. In that case, the employers who hire them have every right to pay them less than the legal citizens. The employers are actually trying to be humanitarians in helping these illegals survive. In any case, the job, salary, and working and living conditions that these illegals have are a way better than the circumstances they left at home.

All Victims of Trafficking Are not Poor Foreigners

It is also commonly believed that human trafficking victims are all very poor and they willingly come and take up the jobs offered to them, knowing very well what they are getting into. They happily sign contracts and in fact many times even pay and beg employers to hire them. So, what is the big fuss? There is no exploitation—rather it is an economic and business decision made by both parties—employees and employers.

The fact is that although it may involve foreigners and may happen more in other countries, yet it is as much a domestic issue as it is an international issue. It happens in the United States more than most people are willing to admit. Undoubtedly, foreigners arriving from other countries legally or illegally may have a higher probability of being trafficked and exploited than the indigenous people. However, indigenous people are equally vulnerable to exploitation and trafficking. In fact, according to the Department of State (2015),[11] US citizens in every state in the nation are equally vulnerable and fall prey to the greed of traffickers at an alarming rate. Without regard to nationality of victims and with greed as their motivation, traffickers seek to exploit those who are most vulnerable—the young and the desperate who can be easily manipulated.[12]

Although poverty increases persons' vulnerability to exploitation and decreases their resistance to manipulation and trafficking, all victims are not poor. The data from various sources, including the Department of State, show that trafficking victims come from a variety of socioeconomic levels, and many may come from families with higher socioeconomic status and higher education levels.

Persons Claiming to be Victims of Trafficking are not Employees Who Consented to be Employed in the Professions They are in—They are Victims

There is a general belief that if the persons claiming to be victims consented to be employed and were informed about what type of work they would be doing or that commercial sex would be involved, then it cannot be a case of human trafficking or against their will because they "knew better." It is believed that the employees who consented to the work and willfully signed the contract cannot claim to be "victims" and look for assistance from laws of the destination country because they willingly accepted the job without any pressure from the employers. The employers who provided jobs cannot be called traffickers. They are employers like any other business entrepreneurs engaged in business. They followed the rules—explained to the potential employees about the kind of work they would be doing and the employees consented before accepting employment. The so called "victims" are "paid employees." This is a specious belief misleading the general public.

The fact is that a victim cannot consent to human trafficking. Initial consent to commercial sex or a labor setting prior to acts of force, fraud, or coercion (or if the victim is a minor in a sex trafficking situation), which may have been given or obtained using manipulation, false promises, and or other tactics such as playing on the victims' desperate situation, is not relevant to the crime, nor is the payment.

Illegal Underground Industries are not the Only Industries Involved in Human Trafficking

Another common misperception is that human trafficking only occurs in illegal underground industries. The fact is that trafficking can and does occur in legal and legitimate business settings as well as underground markets. Elements of human trafficking can be identified whenever the means of force, fraud, or coercion induce a person to provide services in any form or industry including labor and sex.

The next section demonstrates the nexus between human trafficking and human rights. It exhibits how the very core of human trafficking is a gross violation of human rights and thus, human trafficking should be addressed as a crime not only against the victim but also against humanity.

Human Trafficking: Human Rights Violations

The Cyrus Cylinder

The history of human rights can be traced back to 539 B.C. when the armies of Cyrus the Great, the first king of ancient Persia, conquered the city of Babylon and freed all slaves, declared that all people had the right to choose their own religion, and established racial equality. His decrees related to human rights were recorded on a baked-clay cylinder known today as the Cyrus Cylinder. This perhaps can be considered the world's first charter of human rights. The first four articles of the Universal Declaration of Human Rights (UDHR) are parallel to the provisions of this Cyrus Cylinder. In the contemporary world, the proclamation and adoption of the Universal Declaration of Human Rights (UDHR) on December 10, 1948, marked the real beginning of the momentous international journey towards ensuring that human rights are protected universally by the rule of law.[13]

The Magna Carta

The Magna Carta (1215), the Petition of Rights (1628), the US Constitution (1787), the French Declaration of the Rights of Man and of the Citizen (1789), and the US Bill of Rights (1791) are some of the main written precursors to many of today's human rights documents.

Universal Declaration of Human Rights

The proclamation and adoption of the Universal Declaration of Human Rights (UDHR) on December 10, 1948, acknowledged the essential need to protect human rights through the rule of law and announced that the international laws unequivocally guarantee universal basic human rights protection to all the citizens of the world and are not restricted by any boundaries.[14]

Human Trafficking Prosecution Unit

Since this proclamation and adoption of the UDHR, human rights have undergone an evolution at an exponential rate. In 2007, the Human Trafficking Prosecution Unit (HTPU) was created within the Criminal Section the Civil Rights Division. This HTPU consolidates the expertise of some of the nation's top human trafficking prosecutors and these prosecutors work closely with Assistant United States Attorneys (AUSAs) and law enforcement agencies to streamline fast-moving trafficking investigations.

Human rights law prohibits discrimination on the basis of race and sex; it demands equal or at least certain key rights for non-citizens; it decries and outlaws arbitrary detention, forced labor, debt bondage, forced marriage, and sexual exploitation of children and women; and it has been a champion of freedom of movement and right to leave and return to one's own country.

Given this understanding of human rights, trafficking in persons is not only a crime but also a gross violation of basic human rights that brings in exorbitant profits to the offenders through exploitation of the victims. Human beings are recruited, transported, bought, and sold as commodities. Their services are exploited in labor and their bodies are bartered for prostitution, sexual exploitation, or servitude. They are forced to live under horrific conditions and provide services as needed and dictated by the people who have a complete hold on their minds and bodies. Traffickers instill fear of starvation, torture, and death not only to the captives but also to their families. Victims are traded as commodities and discarded as and when their services are no longer profitable. They are truly "disposable people" as Kevin Bales (1999, 2012) describes in his book *Disposable People: New Slavery in the Global Economy*.[15] Apart from being an illegal activity, it is a multi-faceted human rights issue. Various human rights violations occur at different stages of the trafficking cycle.[16]

Human Trafficking and the United States Criminal Code, Title 18, Chapter 77

The term "human trafficking" is commonly used to describe many forms of exploitation of human beings and evokes images of poor foreigners, especially young girls and women, being smuggled across international borders for sexual exploitation. At every stage of the trafficking venture, human rights violations occur. Undoubtedly it should be considered as a multi-faceted human rights issue.

In reality, the term "human trafficking" has a different and highly specific meaning. The United States Criminal Code, Title 18 and Chapter 77, defines human trafficking as acts that compel or coerce a person to perform and provide labor, services, or commercial sex. The coercion can be subtle or blatant, physical or psychological, but it must be used to force a victim into performing labor, services, or commercial sex acts. These statutes are rooted in the prohibition against slavery and involuntary servitude guaranteed by the Thirteenth Amendment to the United States Constitution. The United States' Department of Justice and the Civil Rights Division collaborate in enforcing these statutes. All agencies that fall under the authority of the United States Department of Justice, the Office of the United States Attorney General, and the Civil Rights Division, as well as all law enforcement agencies work together to address human trafficking.[17] Just a simple analysis of the human trafficking definition demonstrates that the very core of trafficking is entrenched in human rights violations. Human trafficking cannot take place without exploitation and denial of basic rights of an individual. Consequently, human trafficking is steeped in human rights violations and should be addressed as such.

According to the Human Rights and Human Trafficking Fact Sheet No. 36, "violations of human rights are both a cause and a consequence of trafficking in persons."[18] In essence, the act of trafficking in persons is a severe violation of human rights. Thus, discussion of human rights should be the central issue when discussing any issue related to human trafficking—be it the definition of human trafficking, causes, consequences, or devising strategies and policies to control and prevent trafficking.[19] A careful analysis of the historical discussions about human trafficking, beginning in 1910 and continuing through the TIP Report in July 2015, makes it crystal clear that trafficking must be addressed in conjunction with human rights.

In 1949, the UN Convention for the Suppression of the Trafficking in Persons and of the Exploitation of the Prostitution of Others declared trafficking a human rights violation incompatible with human dignity and worth. A similar statement is repeated in the 2015 TIP Report. While presenting the TIP Report in July 2015, the United States' secretary of state (2015)[20] proclaimed that

> Trafficking in persons is an insult to human dignity and an assault on freedom. Whether we are talking about the sale of women and children by terrorists in the Middle East, the sex trafficking of girls lured from their homes in Central Europe, the exploitation of farm workers in North America, or the enslavement of fishermen in Southeast Asia, the victims of this crime each have a name. And they each have been robbed of their most basic human rights.[21]

A similar statement was given by the United Nations Secretary-General during the 13th United Nations Congress on Crime Prevention and Criminal Justice—Doha 12–19 April 2015.

> Human trafficking is one of the world's most shameful ills—a heartless violation of human rights in which lives are traded, sold, exploited, abused and ruined. No country is immune, and millions of lives are at stake. We must take a united stand, shine a spotlight on the issue, put traffickers behind bars and give protection and support to victims and vulnerable people.

In general—the poor, the young, the desperate, and the easily manipulated become easy targets for exploitation and are subjected to deprivation of human rights.[22] Poor and marginalized people such as women, minorities, and children are often subjected to human rights violations. Victims fall easy prey to exploitation. Their own insecurity about themselves and their marginalized status in the society, their desire to attain a glamorized status as depicted in movies, as well as false promises by the perpetrators assuring them of having such coveted status and life within an easy reach facilitate and complement perpetrators' tactics of manipulation. The root causes of human rights deprivations and violations are precursors of trafficking.

The phenomenon of trafficking in persons comprises a range of human rights violations. The most common ones are the right to personal autonomy, the right not to be held in slavery or servitude, the right to liberty and security of person, the right to be free from cruel or inhumane treatment, the right to safe and healthy working conditions, and the right of freedom of movement.[23] Human trafficking is condemned as a violation of human rights by international conventions. In addition, human trafficking is subject to a directive in the European Union.[24]

Human Trafficking: Business

The next section discusses human trafficking as business. It provides a brief overview of how a business model based on the minimum input and the maximum output is a prototype for exorbitant profits.

Trafficking in persons and illicit drugs are two of the most heinous forms of transnational organized crime.[25] Human trafficking has been recognized as an extremely profitable business venture. In this business, human beings are obtained and held to provide services as desired by the person, agency, business, or the state that is holding them. These services may vary from highly skilled and technical work to basic manual labor, house work, or sex. Since profits at the minimum cost of production are considered the leading indicators of the highest productivity, human trafficking becomes one of the most worthwhile ventures.

By some estimates, it is an international business enterprise that rakes in $31.6 billion per annum, involving 161 countries—including the United States.[26] It is thought to be one of the fastest-growing activities of trans-national criminal organizations.[27] Although, in general, there is more awareness regarding sex trafficking and it is believed that sex trafficking is more prevalent, 68 percent of the trafficking victims are victims of forced labor practice.[28] The global illicit flow of goods, guns, people, and natural resources is estimated at approximately $650 billion. Despite the scarcity of the official data, it is generally accepted that illicit drug trafficking and counterfeiting are the two most valuable markets.[29] Trafficking is among the fastest-growing criminal activities, involving exploitation of thousands of women, men, and children for sex and labor. Networks operate smoothly across borders, easily adapting to changing ground conditions and circumventing national law enforcement intended to blunt their efforts.[30]

In 2006, Schauer and Wheaton reported that, "within the next 10 years, crime experts expect human trafficking to surpass drug and arms trafficking in its incidence, cost to human well-being, and profitability to criminals" (164–165).[31] The most recent report (2012) issued by the International Labor Organization (ILO) estimated that three out of every 1,000 people worldwide are trapped in jobs into which they were coerced or deceived and which they cannot leave.[32] According to the same report there are nearly 21 million people who are victims of forced labor across the world. So long as businesses place profit ahead of human wellbeing, trafficking may continue to prosper.

Wheaton et al. (2010) hypothesize "human trafficking as a monopolistically competitive industry in which traffickers act as intermediaries between vulnerable individuals and employers by supplying differentiated products to employers."[33] They purport that all of us who consume products of that exploited labor actually are the "employers" of trafficked labor and the "products" are human beings.

Traditional Professions such as Teaching and Medicine Are Also Part of the Trafficking Business

One of the non-governmental organization (NGO) representatives at the International Human Trafficking and Forced Labor Hearing in 2012 stated that there has been a rapid increase in the cases of trafficked immigrant teachers, nurses, construction, and service workers—who all hold valid visas—in the United States, Europe, and Japan. The fact that these professionals who actually hold valid visas are victims of trafficking is indicative of the structural failures within economic and employment systems of these first-world countries. Multinational corporations, employers, businesses, labor recruiters, and others exploit these failures.[34] Such incidents make it evident that human trafficking is not only a big business but is becoming increasingly a legitimate business.

For example, the United States currently has two guest worker programs under which employers are authorized to import unskilled labor for temporary or seasonal work lasting less than a year: The H-2A program for agricultural work and the H-2B program for non-agricultural work. Review the following case to understand these two types of visas.

The next section of the chapter provides an overview of differences and similarities between human trafficking and slavery, smuggling, and bondage.

Differences and Similarities: Human Trafficking and Slavery

Technically speaking there are some slight differences in the legal definitions of slavery and trafficking. For example, during the 1927 Slavery Convention slavery was defined as "... the status or condition of a person over whom any or all of the powers attaching to the right of ownership are exercised."[35]

"Slavery is an institution in which the slave master's exercise of the rights of ownership destroys the human personality—the person as a bearer of rights—and reduces the slave to chattel, without rights."[36]

Table 2 describes the similarities and differences between human trafficking and slavery.

Table 2 presented differences in "trafficking" and "slavery's" six main elements—ownership, profits, availability, relationship, responsibility, and

Box 2: Guest-Worker Teachers Defrauded in International Labor Trafficking Scheme

Hundreds of Filipino guest workers lured to teach in Louisiana public schools were cheated out of tens of thousands of dollars and forced into exploitative contracts by an international trafficking ring run by labor contractors, according to a class action lawsuit filed today by the Southern Poverty Law Center (SPLC), the American Federation of Teachers (AFT) and Covington & Burling LLP.

The federal lawsuit was filed on behalf of more than 350 Filipino teachers working in Louisiana under the federal H-1B guest worker program. It accuses officials of two labor contractors—Universal Placement International, based in Los Angeles, and its sister organization, Manila-based PARS International Placement Agency—of human trafficking, racketeering, and fraud. The suit also names the East Baton Rouge Public School System, several school district officials, and a California lawyer, Robert Silverman, based on their roles in the fraudulent trafficking scheme.

"The outrageous conduct by the companies that recruited these teachers and those who assisted them in carrying out their scheme is part of a larger pattern of exploitation that we've documented in guest-worker programs," said SPLC Legal Director Mary Bauer,* author of the 2007 report *Close to Slavery: Guestworker Programs in the United States*. "It's clear that the very structure of the program lends itself to pervasive worker abuse. Guest worker programs should not be the model for immigration reform."

About 200 of the teachers were assigned to the East Baton Rouge school system; others were spread among the Caddo Public School District, Jefferson Parish Public School System, and the Recovery School District as well as other school districts in Louisiana. Only the East Baton Rouge district was named as a defendant.

The teachers began arriving in the United States in 2007 after each paid about $16,000, several times the average household income in the Philippines, to obtain the jobs. The H-1B guest-worker program, administered by the Department of Labor, permits foreign nationals with special skills to work in the United States for a period of up to six years.

"These teachers have been victimized in ways reminiscent of the worst abuses students learn about in history class: labor contracts signed under duress and arrangements that remind us of indentured servitude," said AFT President Randi Weingarten.** "The goal of this lawsuit is to put an end to this exploitation, which should have no place in 21st-century America."

Adapted from the Southern Poverty Law Center, August 4, 2010.

* Bauer, Mary. "Close to slavery, guest worker programs in the United States." The Southern Poverty Law Center. (2007).

** Bauer, Mary. "Close to slavery, guest worker programs in the United States." The Southern Poverty Law Center. (2007).

discrimination. In 2000 during the United Nations Convention against Transnational Organized Crime (UNTOC) the UN Trafficking Protocol defined trafficking as described earlier in the chapter.[37]

Table 2: Differences between Human Trafficking and Slavery

TRAFFICKING	SLAVERY
Ownership: No legal ownership.	Ownership: Legal ownership; it's documented.
Cost: Low to no cost of purchase and maintenance.	Cost: High cost of purchase and maintenance.
Profits: Very high.	Profits: Average.
Availability: Easy to obtain. Always a surplus.	Availability: Difficult to obtain. Always a shortage.
Relationship: Almost none and if any, very short lived.	Relationship: Almost permanent and long-term.
No discrimination: All races and ethnicities equally vulnerable.	Very discriminatory and limited to minorities.
Responsibility: No responsibility. Individuals are disposable.	Responsibility: Responsible for the upkeep.

Many academicians and clinicians alike believe that slavery is "a vestige of the past" and vehemently deny that the vile practices of historic slavery continue into this century.[38] However, even a cursory look at the political or economic system of any country illuminates its persistence and pervasiveness, making it apparent that historic slavery has metamorphosed itself into a new type of slavery known as human trafficking. This new type of slavery is not confined to one nation or one part of the world. It is not restricted to one race, ethnicity, or color. It is omnipresent and indiscriminately affects all people in all corners of the world. It takes different forms and exists in all kinds of professions and anybody can be enslaved or be a slave driver. Trafficking has been facilitated and accelerated through recent industrialization and urbanization along with "the rapid economic globalization, the increased flow of capital and people, and the extension of production and distribution networks around the world."[39]

Different forces of globalization such as trade and transactions, capital and investment movements, migration and movement of people, and dissemination of knowledge have facilitated this metamorphosis. The new form actually exceeds the old form in inequality and oppression. The new from is difficult to identify as it exists everywhere and it is forbidden everywhere. It exists in "Orwellian doublespeak" as its practices are rampant yet it is illegal everywhere. Everyone practices it or at least is a consumer of it but no one admits its existence. The old slavery was justified and considered legal as it was perceived necessary and beneficial, as compared to the new form where everyone admits it is an abomination and illegal and proposes its eradication but enjoys the benefits of its existence.

Patterson (1982) defined slavery throughout history as "the permanent, violent domination of natally alienated and generally dishonored persons."[40] There is a widespread agreement among scholars and legislators that violence or the threat of violence for the control of another person is the central element of slavery. This violence supports a relation of domination,[41] an extreme power differential marked by decentralized violence.[42] Natal alienation refers to the forced loss of ties of birth and blood to both ascending and descending generations. As cited by Quirk, "Patterson (1982) refers to slavery as 'an exceptional level of personalized control, ii) social and genealogical isolation, and iii) distinctive forms of socio-political dishonor.'[43] All rights and claims of heritage are severed, as the slave becomes a socially dead person who 'ceases to belong in his own right to any legitimate social order.' "[44]

Bales (2007) defines contemporary slavery similarly—more in contemporary or modern terms, where people are forced to work through violence for the most minimum or no pay. Bales maintains that the most significant difference between contemporary and historical slavery is that slavery is no longer legal.[45] Fueled by overpopulation, primarily in the Global South, the historical shortage of slaves has been replaced with a surplus labor (potential slaves). This increased supply of labor has resulted in a decrease in their value and cost; slaves are cheaper today. The duration of enslavement has decreased. For example, historically most slaves were bound for a lifetime, but the bondage of contemporary slaves is temporary, perhaps as short as between two and five years.[46] The greater availability and decreased cost of slaves has resulted in a disincentive for the slaveholder to maintain the health and survival of the slave. A decrease in the cost of procuring and maintaining slaves has resulted in an increase of the profits they generate. Economic vulnerability puts individuals at a greater risk for slavery than racial or ethnic differences. Where ethnic differences exist in modern slavery, they often reflect deeper economic disparities. However, whereas historical slavery existed primarily in the context of racism, modern slavery is less tied to race and color and more to economic deprivation and vulnerability.[47]

The fact is that the nineteenth century abolition of trans-Atlantic slavery never fully abolished slavery. Slavery morphed itself into human trafficking, which has re-emerged only in the sense that it has re-entered public consciousness. Slavery has always been a part of human existence and was not eliminated by the nineteenth century abolition of trans-Atlantic slavery. In the United

States, the Immigration and Customs Enforcement (ICE), the largest investigative agency within the Department of Homeland Security, enforces a wide range of crimes related to border security, including investigations of human smuggling and human trafficking. In fact, ICE is one of the primary federal agencies responsible for combating human trafficking.

Bondage

Another common form of slavery is debt bondage. The UN Supplementary Convention Article 1 on the Abolition of Slavery, the Slave Trade, and Institutions and Practices Similar to Slavery includes debt bondage as a practice similar to slavery. One form of coercion is the use of a bond, or debt. Debt bondage arises from a pledge by a debtor of his personal services or of those of a person under his control as security for a debt, "if the value of those services as reasonably assessed is not applied towards the liquidation of the debt or the length and nature of those services are not respectively limited and defined."[48]

It is referred to as "bonded labor" or "debt bondage," the practice has long been prohibited under US law by its Spanish name, peonage, and the Palermo Protocol calls for its criminalization as a form of trafficking in persons. Workers around the world fall victim to debt bondage when traffickers or recruiters unlawfully exploit an initial debt the worker assumed as part of the terms of employment. Workers may also inherit intergenerational debt in more traditional systems of bonded labor.[49]

Bonded Labor and Debt Bondage among Migrant Laborers

Abuses of contracts and hazardous conditions of employment for migrant laborers do not necessarily constitute human trafficking. However, the burden of illegal costs and debts on these laborers in the source country, often with the support of labor agencies and employers in the destination country, can contribute to a situation of debt bondage. This is often exacerbated when the worker's status in the country is tied to the employer in the context of employment-based temporary work programs and there is no effective redress for abuse.[50]

Forced Labor

Forced labor is the same as involuntary servitude. It is a form of exploitation in which "unscrupulous employers exploit workers made more vulnerable by high rates of unemployment, poverty, crime, discrimination, corruption, political conflict, or even cultural acceptance of the practice."[51] Female victims of forced or bonded labor, especially women and girls in domestic servitude, are often sexually exploited as well. Sometimes forced labor is equated to contract slavery. As Free the Slaves, a nonprofit advocacy, anti-abolitionist organization founded in 2000 states, contract slavery refers to the contract in which employees are deceived into slavery through false employment contracts. The contracts serve as lures because it gives an impression of the promise of genuine employment.

Sex Trafficking

Sex trafficking is when an adult is coerced, forced, or deceived into prostitution—or maintained in prostitution—through coercion. Sex trafficking involves recruiting, transporting, harboring, receiving, or obtaining the person for sex, prostitution, and sex slavery. Sex trafficking can also occur within debt bondage, as women and girls are forced to continue in prostitution through the use of unlawful "debt" purportedly incurred through their transportation, recruitment, or even their crude "sale," which exploiters insist they must pay off before they can be free.

The United States Department of State (2015), states that a person's initial consent to participate in prostitution is not legally determinative, especially if an individual is thereafter held in service through psychological manipulation or physical force.[52]

Chapter Review

In this chapter we have discussed what human trafficking is. We learned various aspects of trafficking to develop an understanding of human trafficking in our contemporary world. In essence, we discussed the following:

- Historical Perspective on Human Trafficking
- Definitions of Human Trafficking
- Human Trafficking: A Process

- Human Trafficking: Human Rights Violation
- Trafficking: A Business and Market
- Differences and Similarities: Human Trafficking and Slavery
- Human Trafficking and Smuggling
- Bondage
- Debt Bondage
- Bonded Labor and Labor Trafficking
- Bondage and Sex Trafficking
- Sexual Slavery

Discussion Questions

1) What are the differences and similarities between human trafficking and modern day slavery?

2) List three examples that describe the differences between trafficking, smuggling, and slavery.

3) Discuss three elements of human trafficking. How do these three elements of human trafficking explain the human trafficking cases you read?

4) Review newspapers for a month and identify the news that is related to human trafficking.

5) Search literature and identify two human trafficking cases—one labor and one sex. Discuss similarities and differences in these cases.

References

Androff, David K. "The Problem of Contemporary Slavery: An International Human Rights Challenge for Social Work." *International Social Work* 54, no. 2 (2011): 209–222.

Bales, Kevin. *Disposable people: New slavery in the global economy*. Univ. of California Press, 2012.

Bales, Kevin. *Ending slavery: How we free today's slaves*. Univ. of California Press, 2007.

Bauer, Mary. "Close to Slavery: Guestworker Programs in the United States." The Southern Poverty Law Center. 2007.

Crawford, Mary, and Michelle R. Kaufman. "Sex Trafficking in Nepal: Survivor Characteristics and Long-Term Outcomes." *Violence Against Women* 14, no. 8 (2008): 905–916.

Florida Statutes. Title XLVI: Chapter 787.06. Online Sunshine, 2016. http://www.leg.state.fl.us/Statutes/index.cfm?App_mode=Display_Statute.

Glendon, Mary Ann. "The Rule of Law in the Universal Declaration of Human Rights." *Northwestern Journal of International Human Rights* 67 (2004).

Haken, J. *Transnational Crime in the Developing World*. Washington, DC: Global Financial Integrity, 2011.

Human Rights Center (HRC). *Freedom Denied: Forced Labor in California*. Berkeley, CA: University of California, 2005.

International Labour Office, Special Action Programme to Combat Forced Labour (SAP-FL). *ILO Global Estimate of Forced Labour: Results and Methodology*. Geneva: ILO, 2012.

Jordan, Ann. "Slavery, Forced Labour, Debt Bondage and Human Trafficking: From Conceptual Confusion to Targeted Solutions." *Issue Paper* 2 (2012).

Lyons, Karen. "Globalization and Social Work: International and Local Implications." *British Journal of Social Work* 36, no. 3 (2006): 365–380.

Organisation for Economic Co-Operation and Development. *Annual Report 2008*. Paris: OECD Publications, 2008.

Patterson, Orlando. *Slavery and Social Death*. Harvard University Press, 1982.

Schauer, Edward J., and Elizabeth M. Wheaton. "Sex Trafficking into the United States: A Literature Review." *Criminal Justice Review* 31, no. 2 (2006): 146–169.

Shelley, Louise I. *Human Smuggling and Trafficking into Europe: A Comparative Perspective*. Transatlantic Council on Migration, Migration Policy Institute, 2014.

Tsutsumi, Atsuro, Takashi Izutsu, Amod K. Poudyal, Seika Kato, and Eiji Marui. "Mental Health of Female Survivors of Human Trafficking in Nepal." *Social Science & Medicine* 66, no. 8 (2008): 1841–1847.

United Nations Human Rights Office of the High Commissioner. Supplementary Convention on the Abolition of Slavery, the Slave Trade and Institutions and Practices Similar to Slavery. http://www.ohchr.org/EN/ProfessionalInterest/Pages/SupplementaryConventionAbolitionOfSlavery.aspx.

United Nations Human Rights Office of the High Commissioner. "Who We Are." 2014. http://www.ohchr.org/EN/AboutUs/Pages/WhoWeAre.aspx.

United Nations Office on Drugs and Crime (UNODC). *Global Report on Trafficking in Persons*. Vienna: United Nations, 2012.

United Nations Office on Drugs and Crime (UNODC). *Global Report on Trafficking in Persons, 2014*. Vienna: United Nations, 2014.

United Nations Office on Drugs and Crime (UNODC). *Protocol to Prevent, Suppress, and Punish Trafficking in Persons, Especially Women and Children.* Supplement to United Nations Convention against Transnational Organized Crime. New York, NY: United Nations, 2004.

United Nations Organization. International Human Trafficking and Forced Labor Hearing. 2012.

United States Department of State. *Trafficking in Persons Report 2015*. Washington, DC: US Department of State, July 2015.

United States Department of State. "What Is Modern Slavery?" 2015. http://www.state.gov/j/tip/what/.

United States Immigration and Customs Enforcement (ICE). "Human Trafficking: A Global Problem." https://www.ice.gov/human-trafficking.

Wheaton, Elizabeth M., Edward J. Schauer, and Thomas V. Galli. "Economics of Human Trafficking." *International Migration* 48, no. 4 (2010): 114–141.

Further Suggested Readings

Glendon, Mary Ann. *A World Made New: Eleanor Roosevelt and the Universal Declaration of Human Rights* Random House, 2001.

Human Rights Watch (HRW). *The Small Hands of Slavery*. New York: Human Rights Watch, 1996.

International Labour Office (ILO). *Global Estimate of Forced Labour: Results and Methodology*. Special Action Programme to Combat Forced Labour (SAP-FL). Geneva: ILO, 2012.

International Labour Organization (ILO). *A Global Alliance against Forced Labour.* Geneva: ILO, 2005.

International Labor Organization (ILO). *Training Manual to Fight Trafficking in Children for Labour, Sexual, and Other Forms of Exploitation: Textbook 2—Advocacy against Child Trafficking at Policy and Outreach Levels.* Geneva: ILO, 2009.

International Organization for Migration (IOM). *Data and Research on Human Trafficking: A Global Survey.* Geneva: IOM, 2005.

Smuggling, H., & Center, T. "Fact Sheet: Distinctions between Human Smuggling and Human Trafficking." Washington, DC: US State Department, 2006.

United Nations Office on Drugs and Crime (UNODC). *Global Report on Trafficking in Persons*. Vienna: United Nations, 2006.

United Nations Office on Drugs and Crime (UNODC). *Global Report on Trafficking in Persons*. Vienna: United Nations, 2009.

United States Department of Health and Human Services. *Factsheet: HHS Fights to Stem Human Trafficking*. 2006. http://www.hhs.gov/news/factsheet/humantrafficking.html.

United States Government Accountability Office (USGAO). *Human Trafficking: Better Data, Strategy, and Reporting Needed to Enhance US Antitrafficking Efforts Abroad*. Washington, DC: USGAO, 2006.

Waltz, Susan. "Reclaiming and Rebuilding the History of the Universal Declaration of Human Rights." *Third World Quarterly* 23, no. 3 (2002): 437–448.

Notes

1. United Nations Office on Drugs and Crime (UNODC). (2012). *Global report on trafficking in persons*. Vienna: United Nations.

2. United Nations Office on Drugs and Crime (UNODC). (2012). *Global report on trafficking in persons*. Vienna: United Nations.

3. United Nations Office on Drugs and Crime (UNODC). (2014). *Global report on trafficking in persons*. Vienna: United Nations.

4. United Nations Office on Drugs and Crime (UNODC). (2004). *Protocol to prevent, suppress, and punish trafficking in persons, especially women and children*. Supplement to United Nations Convention against Transnational Organized Crime. New York, NY: United Nations.

5. United Nations Office on Drugs and Crime (UNODC). (2014). *Global report on trafficking in persons*. Vienna: United Nations.

6. United Nations Office on Drugs and Crime (UNODC). (2014). *Global report on trafficking in persons*. Vienna: United Nations.

7. Florida Statutes. (2016). Title XLVI: Chapter 787.06. Online Sunshine. http://www.leg.state.fl.us/Statutes/index.cfm?App_mode=Display_Statute.

8. Florida Statutes. (2016). Title XLVI: Chapter 787.06. Online Sunshine. http://www.leg.state.fl.us/Statutes/index.cfm?App_mode=Display_Statute.

9. US Department of State. Annual. *Trafficking in persons report*. Washington, DC: US Department of State.

10. US Immigration and Customs Enforcement (ICE). *Human trafficking*. https://www.ice.gov/human-trafficking.

11. US Department of State, Office to Monitor and Combat Trafficking in Persons. (2015).What is modern slavery? http://www.state.gov/j/tip/what/.

12. US Department of State, Office to Monitor and Combat Trafficking in Persons. (2015). What is modern slavery? http://www.state.gov/j/tip/what/.

13. Glendon, M. A. (2004). The rule of law in the Universal Declaration of Human Rights. *Northwestern Journal of International Human Rights*, 67.

14. Glendon, M. A. (2004). The rule of law in the Universal Declaration of Human Rights. *Northwestern Journal of International Human Rights*, 67.

15. Bales, K. (2012). *Disposable people: New slavery in the global economy*. Berkeley and Los Angeles: University of California Press.

16. Organization for Economic Co-Operation and Development. (2008). *Annual report*.

Paris. https://www.oecd.org/newsroom/40556222.pdf.

17. US Department of State, Office to Monitor and Combat Trafficking in Persons. (2015). What is modern slavery? http://www.state.gov/j/tip/what/.

18. United Nations Human Rights Office of the High Commissioner (2014). Human Rights and Human Trafficking, Fact Sheet No. 36. http://www.ohchr.org/Documents/Publications/FS36_en.pdf.

19. United Nations Human Rights Office of the High Commissioner.(2014). Who we are. http://www.ohchr.org/EN/AboutUs/Pages/WhoWeAre.aspx.

20. US Department of State, Office to Monitor and Combat Trafficking in Persons. (2015). What is modern slavery? http://www.state.gov/j/tip/what/.

21. US Department of State. (2015, July). *Trafficking in persons report.* Washington, DC: US Department of State.

22. US Department of State. (2008). Trafficking in Persons Report. https://www.state.gov/j/tip/rls/tiprpt/2008/.

23. The Organization for Economic Co-operation and Development (OECD). (2015). https://www.oecd.org/unitedstates/.

24. Commission Implementing Regulation (EU) No 577/2011 of 16 June 2011 amending for the 149th time Council Regulation (EC) No 881/2002 imposing certain specific restrictive measures directed against certain persons and entities associated with Usama bin Laden, the Al-Qaida network, and the Taliban.

25. United Nations Sixty-Seventh General Assembly, Third Committee, Seventh Meeting. (2012). A/RES/67/1.

26. Haken, J. (2011, February). *Transnational crime in the developing world.* Washington, DC: Global Financial Integrity.

27. Shelley, L. I. (2014). *Human smuggling and trafficking into Europe: A comparative perspective.* Washington, DC: Migration Policy Institute, Transatlantic Council on Migration.

28. International Labour Organization. (2012). *ILO global estimate of forced labour: Results and methodology.* Geneva: ILO, International Labour Office, Special Action Programme to Combat Forced Labour (SAP-FL).

29. Haken, J. (2011, February). *Transnational crime in the developing world.* Washington, DC: Global Financial Integrity.

30. United Nations Sixty-Seventh General Assembly, Third Committee, Seventh Meeting. (2012). A/RES/67/1.

31. Schauer, E. J., & Wheaton, E. M. (2006). Sex trafficking into the United States: A literature review. *Criminal Justice Review, 31*(2), 146–169.

32. International Labour Organization. (2012). *ILO global estimate of forced labour: Results and methodology.* Geneva, ILO, International Labour Office, Special Action Programme to Combat Forced Labour (SAP-FL).

33. Wheaton, E. M., Schauer, E. J., & Galli, T. V. (2010). Economics of human trafficking. *International Migration, 48*(4), 114–141.

34. Misra, Neha Human Trafficking: A Big Business Built on Forced Labor (2013). http://www.huffingtonpost.com/neha-misra/human-trafficking-a-big-b_b_2602398.html.

35. Slavery Convention: Signed at Geneva on 25 September 1926 Entry into force: 9 March 1927, in accordance with article 12. http://www.ohchr.org/EN/ProfessionalInterest/Pages/SlaveryConvention.aspx.

36. Jordan, A. (2011, February). Slavery, forced labour, debt bondage and human traf-

ficking: From conceptual confusion to targeted solutions. *Issue Paper, 2.*

37. United Nations Office on Drugs and Crime (UNODC). (2004). *Protocol to prevent, suppress, and punish trafficking in persons, especially women and children.* Supplement to United Nations Convention against Transnational Organized Crime. New York, NY: United Nations.

38. Androff, D. K. (2011). The problem of contemporary slavery: An international human rights challenge for social work. *International Social Work, 54*(2), 209–222.

39. Lyons, K. (2006). Globalization and social work: International and local implications. *British Journal of Social Work, 36,* 365–80.

40. Patterson, O. (1982). *Slavery and social death: A comparative study.* Cambridge, MA: Harvard University Press.

41. Patterson, O. (1982). *Slavery and social death: A comparative study.* Cambridge, MA: Harvard University Press.

42. Bales, K. (2007). *Ending slavery: How we free today's slaves.* Berkeley, CA: University of California Press.

43. Patterson, O. (1982). *Slavery and social death: A comparative study.* Cambridge, MA: Harvard University Press.

44. Quirk, J. (2008). Unfinished Business: A comparative survey of historical and contemporary slavery. *African Diaspora Archaeology Newsletter, 11*(4), 20. Patterson, O. (1982). *Slavery and social death: A comparative study.* Cambridge, MA: Harvard University Press.

45. Bales, K. (2007). *Ending slavery: How we free today's slaves.* Berkeley, CA: University of California Press.

46. This endnote has three references:

1) Crawford, M., & M. Kaufman. (2008). Sex trafficking in Nepal. *Violence Against Women, 14*(8), 905–16.
2) Human Rights Center (HRC). (2005). *Freedom denied: Forced labor in California.* Berkeley, CA: University of California.
3) Tsutsumi, A., T. Izutsu, A. Poudyal, S. Kato, & E. Marui. (2008). Mental health of female survivors of human trafficking in Nepal. *Social Science and Medicine, 66,* 1841–7.

47. Bales, K. (2007). *Ending slavery: How we free today's slaves.* Berkeley, CA: University of California Press.

48. United Nations Human Rights Office of the High Commissioner. (1956, April 30). *Supplementary convention on the abolition of slavery the slave trade, and institutions and practices similar to slavery.* http://www.ohchr.org/EN/ProfessionalInterest/Pages/SupplementaryConventionAbolitionOfSlavery.aspx.

49. US Department of State, Office to Monitor and Combat Trafficking in Persons. (2015). What is modern slavery? http://www.state.gov/j/tip/what/.

50. US Department of State, Office to Monitor and Combat Trafficking in Persons. (2015). What is modern slavery? http://www.state.gov/j/tip/what/.

51. US Department of State, Office to Monitor and Combat Trafficking in Persons. (2015). What is modern slavery? http://www.state.gov/j/tip/what/.

52. US Department of State, Office to Monitor and Combat Trafficking in Persons. (2015). What is modern slavery? http://www.state.gov/j/tip/what/.

Chapter 2

Trafficking in Persons: Historical and Global Perspectives

Chapter Objectives

This chapter provides a comprehensive understanding of the following:

- Human Trafficking—Historical and Global Perspectives
- The United States Constitution and Outlaw of Slavery
- The United States and Human Trafficking
    - History of Human Trafficking Legislation
    - Human Trafficking across Borders
        - Human Trafficking: A Transnational Crime
        - Origin and Destination Countries: Trafficking in Persons is Ubiquitous in Nature
    - Human Trafficking Profits
    - Global Poverty, Homelessness, Unemployment, and Human Trafficking
    - Human Trafficking: A Global Health Issue
    - Human Trafficking: Individual Enterprise or Organized Business?
    - Profits and Human Trafficking

Introduction: Human Trafficking—Historical and Global Perspectives

Human trafficking has often been equated to slavery and modern slavery.[1] Sometimes it is referred to as slavery while other times modern slavery. According to the 2014 Global Slavery Index (2015), modern slavery is a hidden crime and it takes many forms, such as slavery, forced labor, or human trafficking. Regardless of the form, "it involves one person depriving another person of their freedom: their freedom to leave one job for another, their freedom to leave one workplace for another, their freedom to control their own body."[2]

However, compared to slavery, "Trafficking in Persons" in its present form, has a much shorter history. Slavery dates back to the prehistoric hunting societies. It has survived throughout the history of mankind as a universal institution. Although slaves have always been subjected to physical and sexual exploitation, discussion of human trafficking in the context of exploitation and equivalence to slavery has begun fairly recently. That perhaps is the reason why human trafficking is often perceived in the context of slavery. According to the 2014 Global Slavery Index (2015), slavery involves one person possessing or controlling another person to significantly deprive that person of their individual liberty, with the intention of exploiting that person through their use, management, profit, transfer, or disposal.[3]

This chapter presents an overview of human trafficking from historical and global perspectives. This chapter examines conception and evolution of human trafficking legislation, policies, and programs. It addresses discussions about human trafficking in terms of "slavery" and "modern slavery" so as to facilitate understanding of human trafficking in its present form.

The United States Constitution and Outlaw of Slavery

The Declaration of Independence—one of the founding documents of the United States—proclaims "that all men are created equal [and] that they are endowed by their Creator with certain unalienable rights." The right to be free from slavery and involuntary servitude is among those unalienable rights. This founding document recognizes the inherent dignity and worth of all people. Based on the essence of this document, in 1865, the United States acknowledged slavery and involuntary servitude as evil institutions. Consequently, slavery and involuntary servitude were abolished by law in the United States in 1865.

The United States and Human Trafficking

The 106th Congress in 2000 reported that the current practices of sexual slavery and trafficking of women and children are similar to slavery and involuntary servitude and are similarly abhorrent to the principles upon which the United States was founded. The Congress also affirmed that such practices are in direct contradiction to the unalienable rights provided to all. The Congress demanded that such abhorrent practices must be stopped.

History of Human Trafficking Legislation

White-Slave Traffic Act (The Mann Act)

As far as it can be determined, first law prohibiting transporting women from one state to another for the purposes of sex work is the **White-Slave Traffic Act**, also known as the **Mann Act**. This act is the first federal human trafficking law in the United States, and was passed on June 25, 1910. Prior to the criminalization of human trafficking in 1910, international conferences against white slavery were organized in 1899 and 1902. In 1904, the International Agreement for the Suppression of the "White Slave Traffic," the first international agreement on human trafficking, was signed.[4]

This agreement was designed to ensure repatriation of the victims. The criminalization of white slavery did not occur until the signing of the International Convention for the Suppression of the White Slave Trade (the Mann Act) in 1910. The Mann Act criminalized transportation of women across state lines "for the purpose of prostitution or debauchery, or for any other immoral purpose." The main objective of this act was to combat forced prostitution. However, the law is broadly worded and courts have used it to criminalize many other forms of consensual sexual and other illegal activities.

The First Formal Human Trafficking Task Force (1923)

The Mann Act was followed by the establishment of the first formal task force in 1923, to investigate and submit a formal report on trafficking in women and children. Prior to the establishment of the first human trafficking task force, the League of Nations was established in 1920. Its primary goals included preventing wars through collective security and disarmament and settling international disputes through negotiation and arbitration. It included treaties addressing labor conditions, just treatment of native inhabitants, human and drug trafficking, arms trade, global health, prisoners of war, and protection of minorities in Europe. This was the first time that human trafficking was formally addressed at an international level.

It stated:

> Subject to and in accordance with the provisions of international conventions existing or hereafter to be agreed upon, the Members of the League:
>
> (a) will endeavor to secure and maintain fair and humane conditions of labor for men, women, and children, both in their own countries and in all countries to which their commercial and industrial relations extend, and for that purpose will establish and maintain the necessary international organizations ...[5]

All the elements of trafficking—such as slavery and involuntary servitude, violence against women, forced labor, forced marriages, and other forms of inhuman behavior—have repeatedly been condemned by the international community through declarations, treaties, and United Nations resolutions and reports. Below is a brief history of such efforts.

The **American Declaration of the Rights and Duties of Man**, also known as the Bogota Declaration, was the world's first international human rights instrument of a general nature, predating the Universal Declaration of Human Rights by less than a year. The declaration was adopted by the nations of the Americas at the Ninth International Conference of American States in Bogotá, Colombia, in April 1948.[6] The same meeting adopted the Charter of the Organization of American States and thereby created the Organization of American States, known as OAS.

In 1957, the Abolition of Forced Labor Convention—also known as Convention concerning the Abolition of Forced Labor (No. 105) was held. This is one of the eight ILO fundamental conventions of the International Labor Organization, which cancels certain forms of forced labor still allowed under the Forced Labor Convention of 1930, such as punishment for strikes and as a punishment for holding certain political views.[7] In order to implement the 1930 Forced Labor Convention and the 1957 Abolition of Forced Labor Convention, the Special Action Program to Combat Forced Labor was set up.

The Universal Declaration of Human Rights (UDHR), drafted by representatives with different legal and cultural backgrounds from all regions of the world, was proclaimed by the United Nations General Assembly at the Palais de Chaillot in Paris on December 10, 1948, (General Assembly Resolution 217 A) as a common standard of achievements for all peoples and all nations.[8] The declaration arose directly from the experience of the Second World War and represents the first global expression of what many people believe to be the rights to which all human beings are inherently entitled. It sets out, for the first time, fundamental human rights to be universally protected.[9]

The fundamental rights afforded to all human beings outlined in the United Nations Universal Declaration of Human Rights offer some protection to trafficked persons, such as the right to freedom from slavery and servitude, freedom of movement, and freedom from inhuman or degrading treatment.[10] Through this declaration and that of the Council of Europe Convention on Action Against Trafficking in Human Beings, human trafficking has been seen as a violation of human rights.

Below are the relevant UDHR articles.

> **Article 1** of UDHR states that:
>
> > All human beings are born free and equal in dignity and rights. They are endowed with reason and conscience and should act towards one another in a spirit of brotherhood.
>
> **Article 3** of UDHR states that:
>
> > Everyone has the right to life, liberty and security of person.
>
> **Article 4** of UDHR states that:
>
> > No one shall be held in slavery or servitude; slavery and the slave trade shall be prohibited in all their forms.[11]

The 1956 Supplementary Convention on the Abolition of Slavery, the Slave Trade, and Institutions and Practices Similar to Slavery was adopted by a Conference of Plenipotentiaries convened by Economic and Social Council Resolution 608 (XXI) of April 30, 1956, done at Geneva on September 7, 1956, and entered into force on April 30, 1957, in accordance with Article 13. This declared that no one shall be held in slavery or servitude and that slavery and the slave trade shall be prohibited in all their forms.

> **Section I. Institutions and practices similar to slavery, Article 1** states that
>
> Each of the States Parties to this Convention shall take all practicable and necessary legislative and other measures to bring about progressively and as soon as possible the complete abolition or abandonment of the following institutions and practices, where they still exist and whether or not they are covered by the definition of slavery contained in article 1 of the Slavery Convention signed at Geneva on 25 September 1926:

(a) Debt bondage, that is to say, the status or condition arising from a pledge by a debtor of his personal services or of those of a person under his control as security for a debt, if the value of those services as reasonably assessed is not applied towards the liquidation of the debt or the length and nature of those services are not respectively limited and defined;

(b) Serfdom, that is to say, the condition or status of a tenant who is by law, custom or agreement bound to live and labor on land belonging to another person and to render some determinate service to such other person, whether for reward or not, and is not free to change his status;

(c) Any institution or practice whereby:

(i) A woman, without the right to refuse, is promised or given in marriage on payment of a consideration in money or in kind to her parents, guardian, family or any other person or group; or

(ii) The husband of a woman, his family, or his clan, has the right to transfer her to another person for value received or otherwise; or

(iii) A woman on the death of her husband is liable to be inherited by another person;

(d) Any institution or practice whereby a child or young person under the age of 18 years, is delivered by either or both of his natural parents or by his guardian to another person, whether for reward or not, with a view to the exploitation of the child or young person or of his labor.

Section II. The slave trade, Article 3 declared that

1. The act of conveying or attempting to convey slaves from one country to another by whatever means of transport, or of being accessory thereto, shall be a criminal offence under the laws of the States Parties to this Convention and persons convicted thereof shall be liable to very severe penalties.

2. (a) The States Parties shall take all effective measures to prevent ships and aircraft authorized to fly their flags from conveying slaves and to punish persons guilty of such acts or of using national flags for that purpose.

(b) The States Parties shall take all effective measures to ensure that their ports, airfields and coasts are not used for the conveyance of slaves.

> 3. The States Parties to this Convention shall exchange information in order to ensure the practical co-ordination of the measures taken by them in combating the slave trade and shall inform each other of every case of the slave trade, and of every attempt to commit this criminal offence, which comes to their notice.[12]

The **International Covenant on Civil and Political Rights** (ICCPR)—a multilateral treaty—was adopted by the United Nations General Assembly on December 16, 1966. The ICCPR has been in force since March 23, 1976. According to this covenant, all parties must respect the civil and political rights of individuals, including the right to life, freedom of religion, freedom of speech, freedom of assembly, electoral rights, and rights to due process and a fair trial. Currently, the covenant has 74 signatories and 168 parties. The ICCPR is part of the International Bill of Human Rights, along with the International Covenant on Economic, Social and Cultural Rights (ICESCR), and the Universal Declaration of Human Rights (UDHR) (The United Nations Human Rights, The Office of the High Commissioner).[13]

Human Trafficking as a Human Rights Violation

Human Trafficking Declared a Human Rights Violation (1949)

In 1921, following the establishment of the Covenant of the League of Nations, 33 countries at a League of Nations international conference signed the International Convention for the Suppression of Trafficking in Women and Children. At this time, human trafficking only covered trafficking for the purposes of sexual exploitation and prostitution.

United Nations Protocol to Prevent, Suppress and Punish Trafficking in Persons, Especially Women and Children (2000)

More than half a century (51 years) after the UN Convention for the Suppression of the Trafficking in Persons and of the Exploitation of the Prostitution of Others declared human trafficking a human rights issue, the United Nations criminalized human trafficking under the protocols of Transnational Organized Crime in 2000 and adopted the United Nations Protocol to Prevent, Suppress and Punish Trafficking in Persons, Especially Women and Children.[14]

On November 15, 2000, the United Nations General Assembly passed Resolution 55/25 adopting the Convention against Transnational Organized Crime and its supplemental protocols. The Protocol to Prevent, Suppress and Punish Trafficking in Persons, Especially Women and Children was adopted by the United Nations General Assembly in 2000 and entered into force on December 25, 2003. As of June 2015, it has been ratified by 167 parties. This protocol is also known as Palermo Protocol.[15]

It was the first agreement that acknowledged modern-day slavery, as well as the possibility of men being victims of human trafficking. During the 51 years between the 1949 convention and the adoption of the United Nations protocol in 2000, other forms of exploitation, such as organ harvesting, slavery, and forced labor migration, were added to the definition.

Trafficking Victims Protection Act (2000)

Following the adoption of the Protocol to Prevent, Suppress and Punish Trafficking in Persons, in 2000, the United States Congress passed a federal statute—the Trafficking Victims Protection Act (TVPA)—into a law, offering protections for persons who may be illegally in the country and victims of human trafficking. Public Law 106–386, 114 Stat. 1465, was passed in 2000:

1) to combat trafficking in persons, especially into the sex trade, slavery, and involuntary servitude,
2) to reauthorize certain federal programs to prevent violence against women, and for other purposes.

Under this public law, the Trafficking Victims Protection Act of 2000 was established. The purposes of this division are to combat trafficking in persons, a contemporary manifestation of slavery whose victims are predominantly women and children, to ensure just and effective punishment of traffickers, and to protect their victims. Public Law 106–386 was passed based on the findings of the 106th Congress.[16] Some selected findings of the Congress are reported below.

Congress finds that:

> (1) As the 21st century begins, the degrading institution of slavery continues throughout the world. Trafficking in persons is a modern form of slavery, and it is the largest manifestation of slavery today. At least 700,000 persons annually, primarily women and children, are trafficked within or across international borders. Approximately 50,000 women and children are trafficked into the United States each year.

(2) Many of these persons are trafficked into the international sex trade, often by force, fraud, or coercion. The sex industry has rapidly expanded over the past several decades. It involves sexual exploitation of persons, predominantly women and girls, involving activities related to prostitution, pornography, sex tourism, and other commercial sexual services. The low status of women in many parts of the world has contributed to a burgeoning of the trafficking industry.
(3) Trafficking in persons is not limited to the sex industry. This growing transnational crime also includes forced labor and involves significant violations of labor, public health, and human rights standards worldwide.
(5) Traffickers often transport victims from their home communities to unfamiliar destinations, including foreign countries away from family and friends, religious institutions, and other sources of protection and support, leaving the victims defenseless and vulnerable.
(6) Victims are often forced through physical violence to engage in sex acts or perform slavery-like labor. Such force includes rape and other forms of sexual abuse, torture, starvation, imprisonment, threats, psychological abuse, and coercion.
(10) Trafficking also involves violations of other laws, including labor and immigration codes and laws against kidnapping, slavery, false imprisonment, assault, battery, pandering, fraud, and extortion.
(11) Trafficking exposes victims to serious health risks. Women and children trafficked in the sex industry are exposed to deadly diseases, including HIV and AIDS. Trafficking victims are sometimes worked or physically brutalized to death.
(12) Trafficking in persons substantially affects interstate and foreign commerce. Trafficking for such purposes as involuntary servitude, peonage, and other forms of forced labor has an impact on the nationwide employment network and labor market. Within the context of slavery, servitude, and labor or services which are obtained or maintained through coercive conduct that amounts to a condition of servitude, victims are subjected to a range of violations.
(13) Involuntary servitude statutes are intended to reach cases in which persons are held in a condition of servitude through nonviolent coercion. In *United States v. Kozminski*, 487 U.S. 931 (1988), the Supreme Court found that section 1584 of title 18, United States Code, should be narrowly interpreted, absent a definition of involuntary servitude by Congress. As a result, that section was interpreted to criminalize only servitude that is brought about through use or threat-

ened use of physical or legal coercion, and to exclude other conduct that can have the same purpose and effect.

(22) One of the founding documents of the United States, the Declaration of Independence, recognizes the inherent dignity and worth of all people. It states that all men are created equal and that they are endowed by their Creator with certain unalienable rights. The right to be free from slavery and involuntary servitude is among those unalienable rights. Acknowledging this fact, the United States outlawed slavery and involuntary servitude in 1865, recognizing them as evil institutions that must be abolished. Current practices of sexual slavery and trafficking of women and children are similarly abhorrent to the principles upon which the United States was founded.

(23) The United States and the international community agree that trafficking in persons involves grave violations of human rights and is a matter of pressing international concern. The international community has repeatedly condemned slavery and involuntary servitude, violence against women, and other elements of trafficking, through declarations, treaties, and United Nations resolutions and reports, including the Universal Declaration of Human Rights; the 1956 Supplementary Convention on the Abolition of Slavery, the Slave Trade, and Institutions and Practices Similar to Slavery; the 1948 American Declaration on the Rights and Duties of Man; the 1957 Abolition of Forced Labor Convention; the International Covenant on Civil and Political Rights; the Convention Against Torture and Other Cruel, Inhuman or Degrading Treatment or Punishment; United Nations General Assembly Resolutions 50/167, 51/66, and 52/98; the Final Report of the World Congress against Sexual Exploitation of Children (Stockholm, 1996); the Fourth World Conference on Women (Beijing, 1995); and the 1991 Moscow Document of the Organization for Security and Cooperation in Europe.

The Trafficking Victims Protection Act of 2000, Sec. 103, defines significant terms. Some of these definitions are included here.

In this division:

(2) COERCION.—The term "coercion" means—

(A) threats of serious harm to or physical restraint against any person;

(B) any scheme, plan, or pattern intended to cause a person to believe that failure to perform an act would result in serious harm to or physical restraint against any person; or

(C) the abuse or threatened abuse of the legal process.

(3) COMMERCIAL SEX ACT.—The term "commercial sex act" means any sex act on account of which anything of value is given to or received by any person.
(4) DEBT BONDAGE.—The term "debt bondage" means the status or condition of a debtor arising from a pledge by the debtor of his or her personal services or of those of a person under his or her control as a security for debt, if the value of those services as reasonably assessed is not applied toward the liquidation of the debt or the length and nature of those services are not respectively limited and defined.
(5) INVOLUNTARY SERVITUDE,—The term "involuntary servitude" includes a condition of servitude induced by means of—
(A) any scheme, plan, or pattern intended to cause a person to believe that, if the person did not enter into or continue in such condition, that person or another person would suffer serious harm or physical restraint; or
(B) the abuse or threatened abuse of the legal process.
(6) MINIMUM STANDARDS FOR THE ELIMINATION OF TRAFFICKING.—The term "minimum standards for the elimination of trafficking" means the standards set forth in section 108.[17]

The Office to Monitor and Combat Trafficking in Persons (2001)

Soon after the US Congress passed a federal statute, the Trafficking Victims Protection Act (TVPA), into law, the Office to Monitor and Combat Trafficking in Persons (OMCTP) was established in October 2001. The Trafficking Victims Protection Act has been subsequently renewed and reauthorized in 2003, 2006, 2008, and most recently in 2013 as an amendment to the Violence Against Women Act (VAWA). Currently, the Bureau of Justice Assistance (BJA) in coordination with the Office for Victims of Crime (OVC) and the Department of Health and Human Services (DHHS) is engaged in making concerted efforts to address human trafficking.

Human Trafficking Included as a Part 1 Crime in the Uniform Crime Reports

Following a mandate of the William Wilberforce Trafficking Victims Protection Reauthorization Act of 2008, human trafficking is now included as a Part 1 crime in the Uniform Crime Reports. The FBI's Uniform Crime Reporting (UCR) Program began collecting data regarding human trafficking on

January 1, 2013. Since January 1, 2013, UCR has two new categories of human trafficking: (i) commercial sex acts and (ii) involuntary servitude. The UCR defines these offenses as follows:

> **Human trafficking/commercial sex acts**—Inducing a person by force, fraud, or coercion to participate in commercial sex acts, or in which the person induced to perform such act(s) has not attained 18 years of age.
> **Human trafficking/involuntary servitude**—The obtaining of a person(s) through recruitment, harboring, transportation, or provision, and subjecting such persons by force, fraud, or coercion into involuntary servitude, peonage, debt bondage, or slavery (not to include commercial sex acts).

Law enforcement agencies can submit data about human trafficking and prostitution through either one of the UCR Program's two reporting systems: The National Incident-Based Reporting System (NIBRS) or the traditional Summary Reporting System (SRS), both of which define the offenses the same.

Human trafficking/commercial sex acts and human trafficking/involuntary servitude are Group A offenses in the NIBRS and Part I offenses in the SRS; agencies can submit both offense and arrest data for these offenses.

The crimes of assisting or promoting prostitution, purchasing prostitution, and prostitution are Group A offenses in the NIBRS, which captures offense and arrest data for Group A offenses, and Part II offenses in the SRS, which collects only arrest data for Part II crimes.[18]

Since 2004, BJA has funded a total of 42 Anti-Human Trafficking Task Forces. Those task forces have identified 3,336 persons as potential victims of human trafficking and have requested either continued presence or endorsed T-visa applications for 397 of those potential victims. The task forces have also trained 85,685 law enforcement officers and others in identifying the signs of human trafficking and its victims. Currently, BJA, in coordination with OVC, is funding 13 Anti-Human Trafficking Task Forces.[19]

Human Trafficking across Borders

Human Trafficking: Transnational Crime

As discussed earlier, the consideration of human trafficking as a significant national or intellectual concern is relatively new. It was not until the late

1990s that states began the task of differentiating trafficking from other practices with which it was commonly associated.[20] It was generally perceived that trafficking in persons is a transnational crime that transcends borders. It involves transportation of human beings across borders for exploitation, especially young women and girls for sex and men and young boys for labor. More recently, it is recognized that victims of trafficking do not necessarily need to be transported from foreign countries. In fact, human trafficking can occur within the same country, state, region, or even within the same city. It does not need to be transcending borders. This is evident from the findings reported by 106th Congress. For example, the first finding related that, "Trafficking in persons is a modern form of slavery, and it is the largest manifestation of slavery today. At least 700,000 persons annually, primarily women and children, are trafficked within or across international borders ..."[21] This is one of the findings that Public Law 106–386, 114 Stat. 1465, is based upon.

Origin and Destination Countries: Trafficking in Persons is Ubiquitous in Nature

According to the Global Report on Trafficking in Persons issued by the United Nations Office on Drugs and Crime (UNODC) in 2014, the crime of trafficking in persons affects virtually every country in every region of the world. Trafficking in persons is a global crime that transcends any boundaries and is ubiquitous in nature. The report stated that "between 2010 and 2012, victims with 152 different citizenships were identified in 124 countries across the globe".[22] There are cases in which trafficking flows connect the same origin country and destination country. UNODC has identified at least 510 flows. The UNODC reports that these figures may not be the true representation of the actual numbers. It predicts that the actual figures are perhaps much higher.[23] Most victims are trafficked close to home, within the region or even in their country of origin, and their exploiters are often fellow citizens. In some areas, trafficking for armed combat or petty crime, for example, are significant problems.

The 2014 Global Slavery Index (2015), reported that there are an estimated 35.8 million men, women, and children trapped in modern slavery. The world map is presented in Figure 1. This map demonstrates that all countries in the world are affected by human trafficking. Majority of the countries are both "origin" and "destination" countries.[24]

Figure 1: The 2013 Global Slavery Index

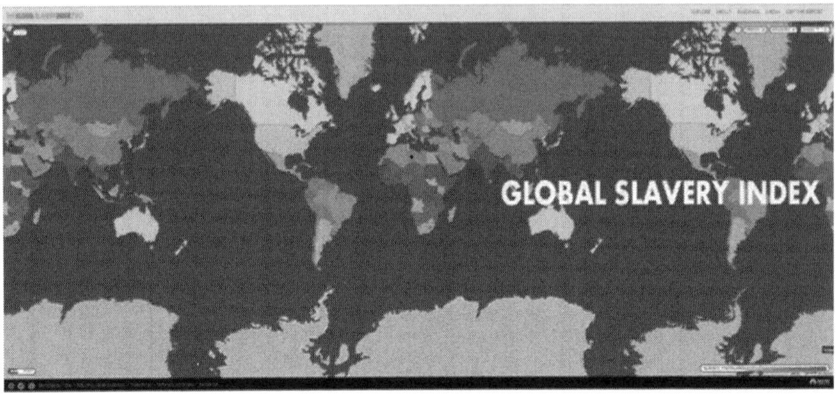

Source: http://www.globalslaveryindex.org/report/.

Human Trafficking Profits

Modern slavery is a big business and significantly contributes to the world economy. According to the 2014 Global Slavery Index (2015), slaves are used in production of at least 122 goods from 58 countries worldwide. The International Labor Organization (ILO) estimates the illicit profits of forced labor to be US$150 billion a year.[25]

According to the Global Report on Trafficking in Persons issued by the UNODC (2012), human trafficking is a crime that ruthlessly exploits women, children, and men for numerous purposes including forced labor and sex. This global crime generates billions of dollars in profits for the traffickers. The International Labor Organization estimates that 20.9 million people are victims of forced labor globally. This estimate also includes victims of human trafficking for labor and sexual exploitation.[26]

According to the ILO Report *Profits and Poverty: The Economics of Forced Labor*, (2014), the trafficked labor generated annual profits of US$150 billion. The report highlighted that two thirds of the estimated total of US$150 billion, or US$99 billion, came from commercial sexual exploitation, while another US$51 billion resulted from forced economic exploitation, including domestic work, agriculture, and other economic activities. The report indicated that more than 50 percent of the trafficked labor primarily in the areas of commercial sexual exploitation and domestic work is provided by women and girls. The other sectors such as agriculture, construction, and mining use men and boys. According to this report, trafficked labor brought a profit of US$34

Figure 2: Annual Profits of Forced Labor per Region

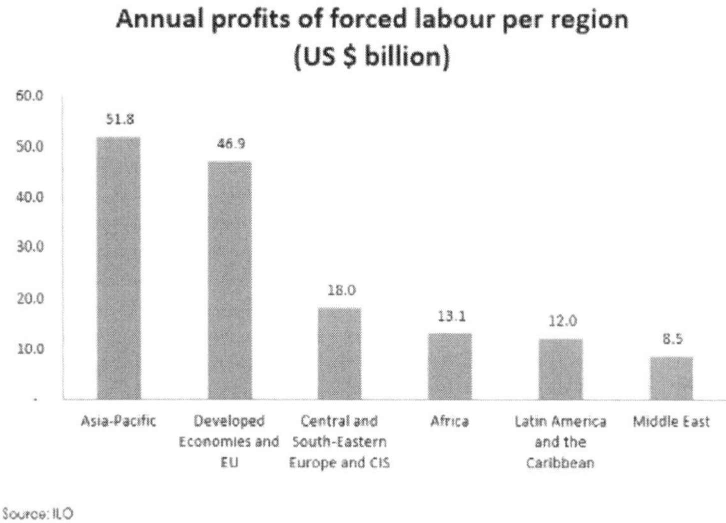

Source: ILO Report, *Profits and Poverty: The Economics of Forced Labor*, 2014.

billion to construction, manufacturing, mining, and utilities and US$9 billion to agriculture, including forestry and fishing. Private households saved US$8 billion by not paying or underpaying to the trafficked domestic workers.[27]

Figure 3: Annual Profit per Victim of Forced Labor per Region

Source: ILO Report, *Profits and Poverty: The Economics of Forced Labor*, 2014.

Figure 4: Annual Profits per Victim per Sector of Exploitation

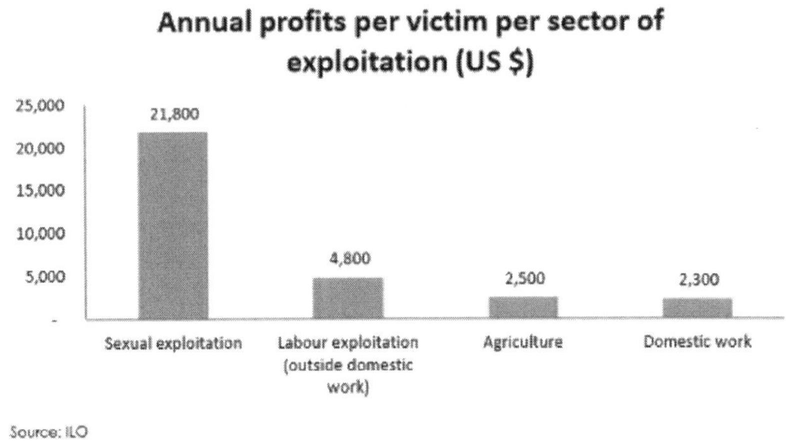

Source: ILO Report *Profits and Poverty: The Economics of Forced Labor*, 2014.

Poverty, Unemployment, Homelessness, and Human Trafficking

Poverty and unemployment are two of the most significant precursors of trafficking victimization. There is a great demand for cheap labor in the world. The global economic crisis and increase in population has left many people looking for jobs far from home. Desperate people looking for survival are easy targets for deception and fraud. They are often deceived and tricked into forced labor or sexual exploitation. Poverty and unemployment place the poor at a higher risk of being in debt. Poor and unemployed people leave their homes for urban and metropolitan areas to find employment. Traffickers exploit poor people's unemployment status and their inability to pay the debts and/or find employment, and their desire to have a better life for themselves and their families. The poor and unemployed drowning in debt become easy targets for fraud and manipulation. Although anyone, regardless of socioeconomic status, education, age, or gender, can be a victim of human trafficking, data shows that majority of the victims are often impoverished, illiterate, and living under very poor conditions.[28]

According to a report, "An Introduction to Human Trafficking: Vulnerability, Impact and Action," issued by the UNODC (2008), the poor,

Figure 5: Precursors of Trafficking Victimization

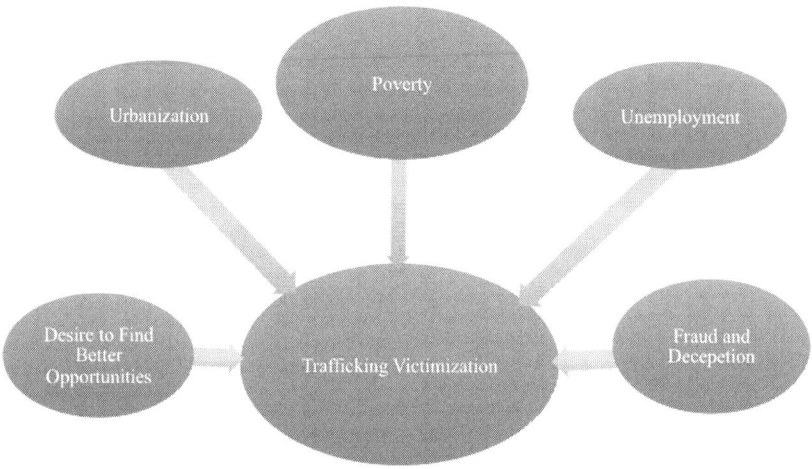

isolated and weak become easy targets for exploitation by traffickers. Figure 5 presents the causes of human trafficking.[29]

The global financial crisis, high unemployment, and poor economy lead to a rise in the supply of poor and unemployed workers willing to take poorly paid jobs. In 2009, an ILO global employment report titled *Cost of Coercion* estimated that migrant workers around the world lose more than $20 billion through the "cost of coercion."[30] During the times when employment rates are high, poverty and the cheap labor supply proliferate. Competition and scarcity of employment results in pressure on young workers, including women, to seek work away from home or abroad. This enhances the risks of exploitation and trafficking. The ILO report (2009) stated that the "traffickers and exploitative employers prey on an expanding pool of more vulnerable and unprotected workers ..."[31]

Human Trafficking: A Global Health Issue

According to ILO Report (2012), human trafficking poses a serious emerging global public health threat that involves a great number of victims worldwide each year. Figure 6 presents estimates of the number of victims of forced labor by region in the world.

According to this report, 18.7 million (90 percent) are exploited in the private economy, by individuals or enterprises. Of these, 4.5 million (22

Figure 6: Victims of Forced Labor by Region in the World

Source: ILO 2012 Global Report—Summary of the ILO 2012 Global Estimate of Forced Labor.

percent) are victims of forced sexual exploitation and 14.2 million (68 percent) are victims of forced labor exploitation in economic activities, such as agriculture, construction, domestic work, or manufacturing, and 2.2 million (10 percent) are in state-imposed forms of forced labor, for example in prisons, or in work imposed by the state military or by rebel armed forces.[32]

Trafficking victims are placed in horrifically risky situations. Belser (2005), Oram (2012), and Zimmerman et al. (2009) report that trafficking victims are recruited from vulnerable populations and geographic areas. Generally, people who fall prey to the tactics of traffickers are running from a variety of problems such as poverty, abuse (physical and/or sexual), homelessness, mental or physical illnesses, etc. They are easily enticed with the promises of economic prosperity, education, security, or love. However, rather than having employment, job security, and prosperity they are trapped in coercive situations as varied as forced prostitution, agricultural labor, factory labor, and domestic servitude. Often they are also in debt which they are unable to pay. Victims may be used for organs. They may be transported from other countries, or trafficked "domestically" within national and local borders. Despite their national origin and immigration status, they are vulnerable to a wide range of physical and psychological maladies as a result of coercion and horrendous experiences—leading to a wide variety of physical and mental maladies.[33]

The United States Government Accounting Office (2006) stated that human trafficking is a worldwide form of exploitation in which men, women, and children are bought, sold, and held against their will in involuntary servitude. In addition to the tremendous personal damage suffered by individual trafficking victims, this global crime has broad societal repercussions, such as fueling criminal networks and imposing public health costs.[34]

Human trafficking has severe adverse effects on the health, development, and overall well-being of vulnerable young people globally and in the United States. Victims are subjected to physical, sexual, and emotional violence. They are manipulated through violence, fraud, coercion, drugs, and other means that may work. Victims of human trafficking come from diverse backgrounds in terms of geography, income, race, ethnicity, religion, sex, and sexual orientation. They, perhaps, are among the "most marginalized and abused in our society.[35]" As trafficking victims, they are subjected to abuse, torture, exploitation, and other forms of maltreatment including physical, sexual, mental, and psychological abuse. For example, children and adolescents who have experienced sex trafficking include young people who have been sexually abused as well as youth who lack stable housing or live in dysfunctional families. They themselves may have been addicted to drugs and alcohol even prior to the recruitment. They may have experienced homelessness, foster care placement, or juvenile justice involvement.[36]

Literature indicates that effects of human trafficking are felt in all aspects of physical, mental, and sexual health. Trafficking victims may suffer from an array of physical and psychological health issues stemming from inhumane living conditions, poor sanitation, inadequate nutrition, poor personal hygiene, brutal physical and emotional attacks at the hands of their traffickers, dangerous workplace conditions, occupational hazards, and general lack of quality healthcare. They may suffer from sexually transmitted diseases, pregnancies, and abortions as a result of repeated rapes; chronic back, hearing, cardiovascular, or respiratory problems from endless days toiling in dangerous agriculture, sweatshop, or construction conditions; weak eyes and other eye problems from working in dimly lit sweatshops; malnourishment; and serious dental problems. Younger individuals often suffer from retarded growth and poorly formed or rotted teeth; infectious diseases like tuberculosis; undetected or untreated diseases, such as diabetes or cancer; bruises, scars, and other signs of physical abuse and torture; and substance abuse problems or addictions either from being coerced into drug use by their traffickers or by turning to substance abuse to help cope with or mentally escape their desperate situations.

Figure 7: Health Consequences of Trafficking in Persons Victimization

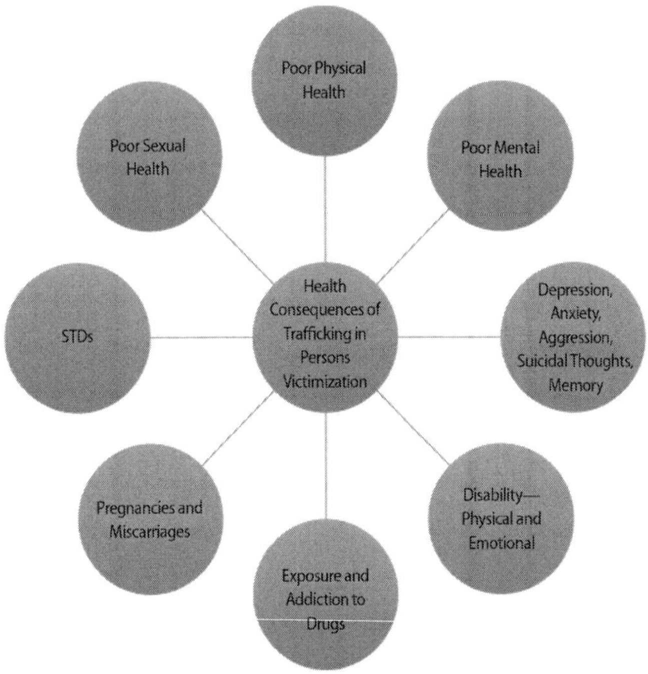

In terms of physical, mental, and psychological health, victims of trafficking experience high rates of depression and post-traumatic stress disorder. They suffer from anxiety, aggression, suicidal ideations, and other similar disorders. In terms of sexual health, victims often suffer from unwanted pregnancies, miscarriages, sexually transmitted infections, and a myriad of other sexual dysfunctions. Often high rates of posttraumatic stress disorder, anxiety disorder, substance abuse, depression, and panic attacks coexist in survivors of violence/trauma events. Figure 7 presents health consequences of human trafficking.

Trafficking victims often are subjected to beatings; burns, tattooing, or branding for identification; forced drug use; shame; and humiliation. Traffickers may confiscate all forms of identification, including passports, to prevent victims from fleeing. Some victims may begin to feel that they are in romantic relationships with their traffickers and may identify them as their intimate partners. With migration across state or country borders, victims may be disoriented or may not speak the local language, making it difficult for them to ask for help. The adverse effects of such prolonged mistreatment are felt in all three spheres of health, as discussed above.

Human Trafficking: Individual Enterprise or Organized Business?

"The global integration of economies, including labor markets, has brought many opportunities for workers and businesses. Despite the past years of economic crisis, it has generally spurred economic growth. However, the growth in the global economy has not been beneficial for all. Today, about 21 million men, women and children are in forced labor, trafficked, held in debt bondage or work in slave-like conditions."[37]

According to Human Rights First (2015), 150 years after the United States ratified the Thirteenth Amendment, officially abolishing slavery, human trafficking is the fastest growing criminal enterprise in the world, entrapping an estimated 21 million victims.[38] The Organization for Security and Co-operation in Europe (2010), reported that human trafficking is the second largest criminal enterprise in the world, earning exploiters more than US$150 billion each year. The human trafficking business promises high monetary rewards with very little cost and very low risk of punishment. It may involve transnational recruitment of victims who are then transported across borders into another country for labor and sex exploitation. It may occur domestically—where little or no transportation is involved in recruitment. However, in all cases, victims are exploited for labor and sex in the same manner without any consideration of whether victims are domestic in origin or international citizens.[39]

Victims of modern-day slavery can be found in virtually every state and city in America, working in construction, manufacturing, agriculture, as domestic workers, in brothels, and in many other industries. Victims are kept as prisoners in private homes and/or hotels run by corporate business men to be exploited for labor and sex. In the labor sector, victims are forced to work in agricultural farms, factories, and fishing boats for little or no pay. In the sex industry, women, girls, and boys are forced to work in brothels, on the streets, and traded from brothel to brothel in sex trafficking rings. The main motive—regardless of labor or sex—under all these forms of exploitation is greed. Human trafficking is a lucrative criminal enterprise, generating an enormous amount of profits at almost negligible cost.

Box 1 and Box 2 present two trafficking cases prosecuted in the United States.

Box 1: Essex County Man Admits Helping Run Human Trafficking Ring for Hair Salon

ESSEX COUNTY—A West African immigrant pleaded guilty today to helping run a human trafficking operation that investigators say forced women to braid hair for up to 14 hours a day at salons in Newark and East Orange. Speaking through a translator, Lassissi Afolabi, 46, told a federal judge in Newark that his ex-wife, Akouavi Kpade Afolabi, headed the ring that smuggled victims from villages in Ghana and Togo in a case prosecutors equated to modern-day slavery. She is scheduled to stand trial next month.

Prosecutors say the Afolabis, who are from Togo, manipulated a visa program to slip up to 20 women into the country, ranging in age from 10 to 19. Once here, they seized the victims' passports and visas and forced them to braid hair for up to 14 hours a day, seven days a week, authorities said. "And the girls were not allowed to keep any of the money they earned?" asked Shana W. Chen, an assistant U.S. attorney.

"No," said Afolabi, a burly man who sat shackled before U.S. District Judge Jose Linares, wearing a dark-green jail uniform. Attempts to reach Lassissi Afolabi's lawyer were unsuccessful last night. An attorney for his wife disputes the charges against her, saying the girls were treated well and paid generously. The lawyer, Olubukola O. Adetula, said the case stems in part from prosecutors misunderstanding West African culture. Tens of thousands of people fall victim to human trafficking each year and wind up in the United States, authorities said. They are often lured from impoverished nations with promises of employment, but then forced to work as prostitutes, house cleaners or in bars and restaurants for little or no pay.

Some of the Afolabi's alleged victims recalled living in ramshackle houses with dirt floors in the home villages. Once in the United States, they lived in East Orange with Afolabi and his ex-wife in a house where rules were harsh and punishments were worse, authorities said. They were forbidden to make friends, learn English or venture alone in public without permission, prosecutors said. Those who disobeyed were beaten, prosecutors said.

"These young women were forced to work for nothing to satisfy the greedy motives of the defendants," said Ralph J. Marra, acting U.S. attorney for New Jersey. "The dignity and basic human rights of the victims clearly meant nothing to this defendant or his co-conspirators."

During today's hearing, Afolabi admitted trying to have sex with one of the girls, who was under 18, during a trip to North Carolina, where he hoped to open a hair braiding salon.

"And she begged you not to do it—'You are old enough to be my father,'" Chen said, quoting the alleged victim. "Yes," Afolabi said.

He pleaded guilty today to forced labor, aggravated sexual abuse and traveling with intent to engage in illicit sexual conduct with a minor. He faces up to 12 years and six months in jail under the terms of his plea agreement, Chen said. Judges, however, are not bound by plea deals and have wide discretion when imposing sentence.

Afolabi is the second member of the alleged ring to admit guilt. He has been in custody since 2007, when he was arrested with his ex-wife and her son, Dereck Hounakey, who pleaded guilty in March. A third man, Geoffry Kouevi, was convicted earlier this month of visa fraud in connection to the case.

Peter T. Edge, head of the U.S. Immigration and Customs Enforcement office in Newark, said the agency "will not tolerate anyone who exploits or victimizes innocent people looking for a better life in the United States."

Source: http://www.nj.com/news/index.ssf/2009/08/east_orange_man_admits_human_t.html.

Box 2: The Case of the Florida Fruit-Pickers Slave Ring—Labor Boss Gets 15 Years for Heinous Crimes

Drive south from Orlando for about 100 miles along Rt. 27 and you'll come to the city of Lake Placid, positioned squarely between Sarasota on the Gulf of Mexico and Port Saint Lucie on the Atlantic. The steady Florida sunshine and the gentle breezes flowing from its 27 freshwater lakes makes Lake Placid ideal for growing citrus. Indeed, the region supplies much of the nation's crop of oranges and grapefruits.

To pick all this fruit every season, it takes a lot of hands. The Ramos brothers—Ramiro and Juan—were among those who helped furnish a stream of workers to local fruit growers. In the process, they made millions. The Ramos family owned three fruit harvesting businesses, a grocery, two clothing stores, and over 30 pieces of real estate.

One problem, though, and the reason for this story: their workers weren't workers in the traditional sense. They were more like slaves. And the Ramos brothers employed as many as 700 of them. They forced these individuals to pick fruit for ten hours a day, six days a week, with no time off. They threatened them at gunpoint, promising torture and death if they tried to escape. And they made them live in filthy, substandard, and overcrowded apartments.

How did they recruit these workers? From across the border. In this case, Mexican workers slipped into Arizona illegally with the help of a smuggler or "coyote." The Ramos brothers would ask the coyote to ship them illegal aliens. When the workers arrived, the brothers would charge them $1,000 for their transportation to Florida. Each week, the Ramoses would take most of the workers' meager paychecks to "repay" the debt and to cover the cost of food and rent. In reality, though, no one was ever set free.

How was the ring broken? The Ramos brothers got caught attacking (and knocking unconscious) the owner of a van service that transported migrant workers out of the area. Then, in April 2001, four Ramos workers escaped with the help of the Coalition for Immokalee Workers. In 2002, the Ramos brothers were tried and convicted. Earlier this month, Ramiro Ramos was re-sentenced to 15 years in prison. His brother Juan, originally sentenced to 12 years, will be re-sentenced in May. Both were also ordered to forfeit $3 million earned from their crimes.

Cooperation Makes the Case: Once again, partnerships were key. Special thanks to the U.S. Border Patrol and the Highland County Sheriff's Office. And thanks to all those who offered assistance to the victims, including the Mexican Consulate in Miami and the U.S. Department of Health and Human Services.

Source: FBI News Stories. March 9, 2004. https://www.fbi.gov/news/stories/2004/march/florida_030904.

It is a business, where the business owner makes a one-time small investment and keeps making inordinate amounts of profit through recycling the one-time small investment.

Trafficking as a business is run similarly to regular business enterprises. It can be run as a small business or a large complex corporate business. "Traffickers could range from small-time, solo operators to loose networks of criminals, to highly sophisticated criminal organizations that operate internationally." "Traffickers choose to trade in humans ... because there are low start-up costs, minimal risks, high profits and large demand. For organized crime groups, human beings have one added advantage over drugs: they can be sold repeatedly" (Shelley, 2010).[40] The most widely recognized form of human trafficking is sexual exploitation, but trafficking exploitation occurs in many different forms including "commercial sex, hospitality, construction, agriculture, manufacturing, janitorial services, construction, shipyards, restaurants, health and elder care etc."[41]

Profits and Human Trafficking

In addition to sex industry, almost all industries make profits off trafficked and smuggled labor. Factories, farms, hotels, restaurants, the domestic service economy—all benefit from a ready supply of cheap labor. All forms of forced labor involve appalling, insanitary living and working conditions. Victims are subjected to conditions resembling slavery, kept in virtual debt-bondage, and subjected to the control of armed guards and soldiers. This is evident in one of the cases listed below.

In the United States in 2004, the Ramos brothers were convicted of human trafficking. They employed 700 workers to pick fruit in Lake Placid, Florida.[42] This case is presented in Box 2.

The New Jersey and Florida cases listed above are two of the many cases that provide an overview of how human trafficking takes place. These cases portray techniques used by traffickers. Victims can be found in almost all industries. Victims are lured through fraud and false promises of high paying jobs. Regardless of the industry they are placed in, they are subjected to force and coercion. In the Florida case described above, the Ramos brothers hired smugglers to bring a group of victims to the US from Arizona to work on farms in Florida. When victims arrived, they were told they owed debts of $1,000 each for their transportation costs. The victims were housed in a facility infested with insects, and with undrinkable water and inadequate showers. Victims were forced to work more than 16 hours a day for six to seven days per week. This is a common state of trafficking victims.

A common perception is that victims of trafficking are poor, illiterate, unemployed, and unskilled workers who are easily enticed by the promise of paying jobs, money, security, romance and love, etc. That is true in a majority of cases but not always. Sometimes highly skilled individuals can be caught up too, particularly if they're on foreign soil. For example, a recent case presented by *Time*, Business Insider, BBC, and CNN narrates a story of how an

Indonesian woman, Shandra Woworuntu, who worked in finance in Indonesia, was taken away from New York's busy John F. Kennedy (JFK) airport with a gun to her head by an organized gang working in the heart of the world's economic superpower. She was traded from brothel to brothel in a sex trafficking ring in 2001 for several months and finally escaped by jumping from a second story window. This is a trafficking case in which a financial analyst from Indonesia became a victim of sex trafficking ring.[43]

Human trafficking is a complex business. The victims go through a number of different stages—recruitment, transportation, exploitation, and disposal across borders as well as within the borders. At every stage, victims are exploited through fraud and coercion, and deprived of basic rights such as liberty, safety, and security. They are denied access to adequate living conditions, healthcare or medical services, education, or contact with their families. They are not paid at all or underpaid and made to work 14–20 hours a day. They are stripped of their identity, passports, and sometimes even their name. They are branded and treated as property in literal sense.

Chapter Review

In this chapter, we have discussed human trafficking from historical and global perspectives. We learned about the fundamental causes of human trafficking such as poverty, homelessness, and unemployment that facilitate and perpetuate human trafficking. In essence, we discussed the following:

- Human Trafficking from Historical and Global Perspectives
- Origin and Destination Countries
- Human Trafficking and Profits
- Global Poverty, Homelessness, Unemployment, and Human Trafficking
- Human Trafficking: A Global Health Issue
- Human Trafficking: Individual Enterprise or Organized Business?

Discussion Questions

1) Identify at least three differences between slavery and human trafficking. Give examples.

2) Explain why trafficking is equated to slavery and why it is called "modern slavery."

3) List the precursors of trafficking victimization.

4) Discuss two reasons why the Trafficking Victims Protection Act was passed in 2000.

5) Discuss whether trafficking is an organized enterprise. Provide supporting arguments for your answer.

6) Discuss how the effects of trafficking victimization are manifested in the victims' health.

7) Discuss why the Mann Act is important. What was the main objective of this act?

8) Discuss functions of the Office to Monitor and Combat Trafficking in Persons (OMCTP).

References

Belser, Patrick. "Forced Labour and Human Trafficking: Estimating the Profits." International Labour Organization, 2005. SSRN 1838403.

Biddle, Jo, and Agence France Presse. "How a Financial Analyst from Indonesia Wound Up Being a Sex Slave in New York City." *Business Insider*. January 31, 2014. http://www.businessinsider.com/how-an-financial-analyst-wound-up-being-a-sex-slave-in-nyc-2014-1.

Human Rights First. "Bankrupt Slavery: Dismantling the Business of Human Trafficking." http://www.humanrightsfirst.org/campaigns/bankrupt-slavery.

International Labour Organization (ILO). Abolition of Forced Labor Convention (No. 105). Entry into force: 17 Jan 1959, Adoption: Geneva, 25 Jun 1957, Status: Up-to-date instrument (Fundamental Convention). http://www.ilo.org/dyn/normlex/en/f?p=1000:12100:0::NO::P12100_ILO_CODE:C105.

International Labour Organization (ILO). *Profits and Poverty: The Economics of Forced Labour*. 2014. http://www.ilo.org/global/publications/ilo-book store/order-online/books/WCMS_243391/lang—en/index.htm.

Kangaspunta, Kristiina, Michèle Clark, Judith Dixon, and Mike Dottridge. "An Introduction to Human Trafficking: Vulnerability, Impact, and Action." New York: UN Office on Drugs and Crime, 2008.

Kara, Siddharth. *Sex Trafficking: Inside the Business of Modern Slavery*. Columbia University Press, 2009.

Oram, Siân, Heidi Stöckl, Joanna Busza, Louise M. Howard, and Cathy Zimmerman. "Prevalence and Risk of Violence and the Physical, Mental, and Sexual Health Problems Associated with Human Trafficking: Systematic Review." *PLoS Med* 9, no. 5 (2012): e1001224. (Reprinted) JAMA Pediatrics. Published online September 8, 2015 1/2 Copyright 2015 American Medical Association. All rights reserved. http://archpedi.jamanetwork.com/.

Shelley, Louise. *Human Trafficking: A Global Perspective.* Cambridge University Press, 2010.

United Nations. The Universal Declaration of Human Rights. UN News Center. December 10, 1948. http://www.un.org/en/universal-declaration-human-rights/.

United Nations Human Rights Office of the High Commissioner. International Covenant on Civil and Political Rights. Entry into force 23 March 1976, in accordance with Article 49. http://www.ohchr.org/en/professionalinterest/pages/ccpr.aspx.

United Nations Human Rights Office of the High Commissioner. The 1956 Supplementary Convention on the Abolition of Slavery, the Slave Trade, and Institutions and Practices Similar to Slavery. Entry into force: 30 April 1957, in accordance with Article 13. http://www.ohchr.org/EN/ProfessionalInterest/Pages/SupplementaryConventionAbolitionOfSlavery.aspx.

United Nations Office on Drugs and Crime (UNODC). Protocol to Prevent, Suppress, and Punish Trafficking in Persons, Especially Women and Children. Supplement to United Nations Convention against Transnational Organized Crime. New York, NY: United Nations, 2004.

United Nations Office on Drugs and Crime (UNODC). *Global Report on Trafficking in Persons 2014.* United Nations Office on Drugs and Crime, November 2014. https://www.unodc.org/unodc/data-and-analysis/glotip.html.

United States Congress. Mann Act. 18 United States Code §§ 1581–1588.

United States Congress. Trafficking Victims Protection Act (TVPA). Pub. L. No. 106-386, 114 Stat. 1473. 2000.

United States Federal Bureau of Investigation. "Labor Boss Gets 15 Years for Heinous Crimes." 2004. https://archives.fbi.gov/archives/news/stories/2004/march/florida_030904.

United States Government Accounting Office. *Human Trafficking: Better Data, Strategy, and Reporting Needed to Enhance U.S. Anti-trafficking Efforts Abroad.* GAO-06-825. Published: Jul 18, 2006. Publicly Released: Aug 14, 2006. http://www.gao.gov/products/GAO-06-825.

Walk Free Foundation. *Global Slavery Index 2014.*

Further Suggested Readings

Aronowitz, Alexis, Gerda Theuermann, and Elena Tyuryukanova. "Analysing the Business Model of Trafficking in Human Beings to Better Prevent the Crime." Vienna: Organization for Security and Co-operation in Europe, 2010.

Buscher, Dale. "Displaced Women and Girls at Risk: Risk Factors, Protection Solutions and Resource Tools." New York: Women's Commission for Refugee Women and Children, 2006.

Cohen, C. Desmond, and Elizabeth Reid, "The Vulnerability of Women: Is This a Useful Construct for Policy and Programming?" Issues Paper No. 28, HIV and Development Programme. New York, United Nations Development Programme, 1996.

English, Abigail. "Human Trafficking of Children and Adolescents: A Global Phenomenon with Horrific Health Consequences." *JAMA Pediatrics* 169, no. 9 (2015): e152283-e152283.

International Labour Organization (ILO). *ILO Global Estimate of Forced Labour: Results and Methodology*. ILO Publications, 2012.

Kunz, Josef L. The Bogota Charter of the Organization of American States. *Am. J. Int'l L.* 42 (1948): 568.

Lee, Hyun Ju. "The Impact of US Foreign Aid on Human Rights Conditions in Post-Cold War Era." Ames, Iowa: Iowa State University, Graduate Theses and Dissertations. Paper 12068. 2011.

Miko, Francis T. "Trafficking in Women and Children: The US and International Response—Updated March 26, 2004." Cornell University ILR School, 2004.

Organization for Security and Co-operation in Europe. *Analyzing the Business Model of Trafficking in Human Beings to Better Prevent the Crime*. Vienna: Office of the Special Representative and Co-ordinator for Combating Trafficking in Human Beings, September 30, 2010, p. 21.

Organization for Security and Co-operation in Europe. "Concluding Meeting of the 24th OSCE Economic and Environmental Forum." http://www.osce.org/.

Roby, Jini L. "Women and Children in the Global Sex Trade." *International Social Work* 48, no. 2 (2005): 136–147.

Thomas, Ann Van Wynen, and Aaron Joshua Thomas. *The Organization of American States*. Southern Methodist University Press, 1963.

United Nations General Assembly. Convention for the Suppression of the Traffic in Persons and of the Exploitation of the Prostitution of Others. 1949.

United Nations General Assembly. Protocol to prevent, suppress and punish trafficking in persons, especially women and children, supplementing the United Nations convention against transnational organized crime. Resolution 55 (2000): 25.

United Nations Human Rights Office of the High Commissioner. Convention for the Suppression of the Traffic in Persons and of the Exploitation of the Prostitution of Others. Resolution 317 (IV). 2 December 1949. Entry into force: 25 July 1951, in accordance with Article 24.

United Nations Office on Drugs and Crime (UNODC). http://www.unodc.org/unodc/en/crime_cicp_signatures_trafficking.html.

United Nations Office on Drugs and Crime (UNODC). *Fact Sheet on Human Trafficking.* 2006.http://www.unodc.org/unodc/en/trafficking_victim_consents.html#how.

United Nations Office on Drugs and Crime (UNODC). "Global Report on Trafficking in Persons 2014." November 2014. https://www.unodc.org/unodc/data-and-analysis/glotip.html.

United Nations Office on Drugs and Crime (UNODC). *Trafficking in Human Beings.* 2006. http://www.unodc.org/unodc/en/trafficking_human_beings.html.

United States Congress. Trafficking Victims Protection Reauthorization Act (TVPRA). Pub. L. No. 108-193, 117 Stat. 2875. 2003.

United States Congress. Trafficking Victims Protection Reauthorization Act (TVPRA). Pub. L. No. 109-164. 2005.

United States Congress. Victims of Trafficking and Violence Protection Act of 2000. Public Law 106 (2000): 386.

United States Department of Justice (USDOJ). "Assessment of U.S. Government Efforts to Combat Trafficking in Persons in Fiscal Year 2006." 2007. http://www.usdoj.gov/ag/annualreports/tr2007/assessment-of-efforts-to-combat-tip0907.pdf.

United States Department of Justice (USDOJ). *Report on Activities to Combat Human Trafficking: Fiscal Years 2001–2005.* 2006. http://www.usdoj.gov/crt/crim/trafficking_report_2006.pdf.

United States Department of State, Office to Monitor and Combat Trafficking in Persons. *Trafficking in Persons Report.* 2004. http://www.state.gov/g/tip/rls/tiprpt/2004/34021.htm.

United States Department of State, Office to Monitor and Combat Trafficking in Persons. *Trafficking in Persons Report.* 2005. http://www.state.gov/g/tip/rls/tiprpt/2005/.

United States Department of State. Special State Department Briefing. *Federal News Service.* June 3, 2005. LexisNexis.

United States Government Accountability Office (USGAO). "Human Trafficking: Better Data, Strategy, and Reporting Needed to Enhance US Anti-trafficking Efforts Abroad." *Trends in Organized Crime* 10, no. 1 (2006).

Vital Voices Global Partnership. *Stateless and Vulnerable to Human Trafficking in Thailand.* Washington, DC, June 2007, p. 13. see www.vitalvoices.org.

Weitzer, Ronald. "Moral Crusade against Prostitution." *Society* 43, no. 3 (2006): 33–38.

Wilson, Deborah G., William F. Walsh, and Sherilyn Kleuber. "Trafficking in Human Beings: Training and Services among US Law Enforcement Agencies." *Police Practice and Research* 7, no. 2 (2006): 149–160.

Zimmerman, Cathy. "Trafficking in Women: The Health of Women in Post-trafficking Services in Europe Who Were Trafficked into Prostitution or Sexually Abused as Domestic Labourers." PhD diss., London School of Hygiene & Tropical Medicine, 2007.

Zimmerman, Cathy, Mazeda Hossain, Kate Yun, Brenda Roche, Linda Morison, and Charlotte Watts. "Stolen Smiles: A Summary Report on the Physical and Psychological Health Consequences of Women and Adolescents Trafficked in Europe." London School of Hygiene & Tropical Medicine, 2006.

Notes

1. Kara, S. (2009). *Sex trafficking: Inside the business of modern slavery.* New York: Columbia University Press.

2. Walk Free Foundation. *Global Slavery Index 2014.*

3. Walk Free Foundation. *Global Slavery Index 2014.*

4. Mann Act, 18 United States Code §§1581–1588. Ch. 395, 36 Stat. 825; codified as amended at 18 U.S.C. §§2421–2424.

5. Article 23, Covenant of the League of Nations, Treaty of Versailles, and Minority Rights Treaties.

6. United Nations General Assembly. (1948, December 10). The Universal Declaration of Human Rights. Paris.

7. International Labor Organization (ILO). (1957). Abolition of Forced Labor Convention (No. 105). Entry into force: 17 Jan 1959, Adoption: Geneva, 25 Jun 1957, Status: Up-to-date instrument (Fundamental Convention). http://www.ilo.org/dyn/normlex/en/f?p=1000:12100:0::NO::P12100_ILO_CODE:C105.

8. United Nations General Assembly. (1948, December 10). The Universal Declaration of Human Rights. UN News Center. http://www.un.org/en/universal-declaration-human-rights/.

9. International Labor Organization (ILO). (1957). Abolition of Forced Labor Convention, (No. 105). Entry into force: 17 Jan 1959, Adoption: Geneva, 25 Jun 1957, Status: Up-to-date instrument (Fundamental Convention). http://www.ilo.org/dyn/normlex/en/f?p=1000:12100:0::NO::P12100_ILO_CODE:C105.

10. Lee, M. (2011). *Trafficking and global crime control.* Sage Publications.

11. United Nations General Assembly. (1948, December 10). The Universal Declaration of Human Rights. UN News Center. http://www.un.org/en/universal-declaration-human-rights/.

12. United Nations Human Rights Office of the High Commissioner. (1956, April 30). The 1956 Supplementary Convention on the Abolition of Slavery, the Slave Trade, and Institutions and Practices Similar to Slavery. Entry into force: 30 April 1957, in accordance with Article 13. http://www.ohchr.org/EN/ProfessionalInterest/Pages/SupplementaryConvention AbolitionOfSlavery.aspx.

13. United Nations Human Rights Office of the High Commissioner. (1966, December 16). International Covenant on Civil and Political Rights. Entry into force 23 March 1976, in accordance with Article 49. http://www.ohchr.org/en/professionalinterest/pages/ccpr.aspx.

14. United Nations General Assembly. (2000). *Protocol to prevent, suppress and punish trafficking in persons, especially women and children.* Supplement to the United Nations Convention against Transnational Organized Crime. Resolution 55: 25.

15. United Nations Office on Drugs and Crime (UNODC). (2004). *Protocol to prevent, suppress, and punish trafficking in persons, especially women and children.* Supplement to United Nations Convention against Transnational Organized Crime. New York, NY: United Nations.

16. Trafficking Victims Protection Act (TVPA). (2000). Pub. L. No. 106-386, 114 Stat. 1473.

17. Trafficking Victims Protection Act (TVPA). (2000). Pub. L. No. 106-386, 114 Stat. 1473.

18. Federal Bureau of Investigation. (2015) Human Trafficking in the Uniform Crime Reporting (UCR) Program.

19. United States Department of Justice, Bureau of Justice Assistance. (2014). bja.gov.

20. United Nations High Commissioner for Refugees. (2014). Global Report. http://www.unhcr.org/gr14/index.xml.

21. This endnote has two references:

1) Commodity Futures Modernization Act. (2000). S. 2697, 106th Cong. (2000); HR 4541, 106th Cong. (2000); Appendix E, Pub. 114.

2) US Code. (2000). Victims of trafficking and violence protection act of 2000. Public Law 106-386.

22. United Nations Office on Drugs and Crime (UNODC). (2014, November). *Global report on trafficking in persons 2014.*

23. United Nations Office on Drugs and Crime (UNODC). (2014, November). *Global report on trafficking in persons 2014.*

24. Walk Free Foundation. *Global slavery index 2014.*

25. Walk Free Foundation. *Global slavery index 2014.*

26. United Nations Office on Drugs and Crime (UNODC). (2012). Global report on trafficking in persons.

27. International Labor Organization. (2014). *Profits and poverty: The economics of forced labour.*

28. Wheaton, E. M., E. J. Schauer, & T. V. Galli. (2010). Economics of human trafficking. *International Migration, 48*(4), 114–141.

29. Kangaspunta, K., M. Clark, J. Dixon, and M. Dottridge. (2008). *An introduction to human trafficking: Vulnerability, impact, and action.* New York: UN Office on Drugs and Crime.

30. International Labour Conference. (2009). *The cost of coercion.* Global Report under the follow-up to the ILO Declaration on Fundamental Principles and Rights at Work. 98th Session.

31. International Labour Conference. (2009). *The cost of coercion.* Global Report under the follow-up to the ILO Declaration on Fundamental Principles and Rights at Work. 98th Session.

32. ILO. (2012). *Global Report—Summary of the ILO 2012 Global Estimate of Forced Labor.*

33. This endnote has three references:

1) Belser, P. (2005, March 1). Forced labour and human trafficking: Estimating the profits. Geneva: ILO. *SSRN 1838403.*

2) Oram, S., H. Stöckl, J. Busza, L. M. Howard, & C. Zimmerman. (2012, May 29). Prevalence and risk of violence and the physical, mental, and sexual health problems associated with human trafficking: Systematic review. *PLOS Med*, *9*(5) : e1001224. (Reprinted) JAMA Pediatrics. Published online September 8, 2015 1/2 Copyright 2015 American Medical Association. All rights reserved. http://archpedi.jamanetwork.com/.

3) Zimmerman, C., S. Oram, R. Borland, & C. Watts. (2009). Meeting the health needs of trafficked persons. *BMJ* 339: b3326.

34. United States Government Accounting Office. (2006, July 18). *Human trafficking: Better data, strategy, and reporting needed to enhance U.S. anti-trafficking efforts abroad.* GAO-06-825. Publicly released: Aug 14, 2006. http://www.gao.gov/products/GAO-06-825

35. Box, H. Human Trafficking and Minorities: Vulnerability Compounded by Discrimination. *Topical Research Digest: Minority Rights (nd)*, 28–29.

36. English, A. (2015). Human trafficking of children and adolescents: A global phenomenon with horrific health consequences. *JAMA Pediatrics, 169*(9), e152283-e152283.

37. International Labor Organization. (2014). *Profits and poverty: The economics of forced labour.* http:// http://www.ilo.org/wcmsp5/groups/public/—ed_norm/—declaration/documents/publication/wcms_243391.pdf.

38. Human Rights First. *Bankrupt slavery: Dismantling the business of human trafficking.* http://www.humanrightsfirst.org/campaigns/bankrupt-slavery.

39. Organization for Security and Co-operation in Europe Ambassador Madina Jarbussynova. (2014, December 15). OSCE Special Representative and Co-ordinator for Combating Trafficking in Human Beings Presentation to the OSCE Permanent Council, SEC.GAL/204/14.

40. Shelley, L. (2010). *Human trafficking: A global perspective.* Cambridge University Press.

41. Shelley, L. (2010). *Human trafficking: A global perspective.* Cambridge University Press.

42. Federal Bureau of Investigation. (2004). Labor boss gets 15 years for heinous crimes. https://archives.fbi.gov/archives/news/stories/2004/march/florida_030904.

43. Biddle, J., and Agence France Presse. (2014, January 31). How a financial analyst from Indonesia wound up being a sex slave in New York City. *Business Insider.* http://www.businessinsider.com/how-an-financial-analyst-wound-up-being-a-sex-slave-in-nyc-2014-1.

Chapter 3

Domestic Human Trafficking: Local Perspectives

Chapter Objectives

This chapter provides a comprehensive understanding of the following:

- Human Trafficking: Local Perspectives
  - Domestic Human Trafficking
- Human Trafficking: Around Us
- Essentials of Human Trafficking Process
  - Nature and Extent of Domestic Human Trafficking
  - Lack of Systematic Data
  - Nature of Crime
  - Lack of Uniformity: Various Definitions
  - Source of Data
- Human Trafficking: A Routine Activity
- Human Trafficking and Economics
- U.S. Code and Protection for the Victims of Involuntary Servitude or Forced Labor
- Who Are the Victims of Domestic Trafficking?

Introduction: Human Trafficking: Local Perspectives

Domestic Human Trafficking

Human trafficking is also known as trafficking in persons. Forced exploitation, enslavement, or servitude of a person for profit or benefit[1] are some of the other names used for human trafficking. Regardless of what it is called, it is a crime that permeates all corners of the world—every country and every region. It is not discriminative in nature—rather it transcends all geographical and demographic boundaries. It has been associated with transnational criminal organizations, small criminal networks, and local gangs, as well as with violations of labor and immigration codes and government corruption.[2] It is a problem that affects countries around the world. As there is an increased awareness of this horrendous crime that affronts individual liberty, it is emerging as a significant concern in the United States. Different reports provide different statistics as to the nature and extent of human trafficking in the United States. By some estimates, approximately 20,000 foreign nationals are brought to the US every year as human trafficking victims and majority of these victims are young women and girls who are subjected to sexual exploitation.

Generally, it is assumed that trafficking happens in poor nations and to impoverished people. Another common misperception is that it involves illegals and/or transportation of foreign nationals into the country. In the Trafficking Victims Protection Act of 2000 (TVPA) Congress defines severe forms of trafficking in persons as:

a) Sex trafficking in which a commercial sex act is induced by force, fraud, or coercion, or in which the person induced to perform such act has not attained 18 years of age; or
b) The recruitment, harboring, transportation, provision or obtaining of a person for labor or services, through the use of force, fraud, or coercion for the purpose of subjection to involuntary servitude, peonage, debt bondage, or slavery (8 U.S.C. §1101).[3]

Trafficking of individuals within US borders is commonly referred to as domestic human trafficking. It occurs primarily for labor, most often in domestic service, agriculture, manufacturing, janitorial services, hotel services, construction, health and elder care, hair and nail salons, and strip clubs or dancing establishments.[4] Some research indicates that in the United States, vulnerable workers have been recruited from homeless shelters and transported

Box 1: Domestic Labor Trafficking Case

Labor camp owners recruited homeless African American addicts from shelters throughout the Southeast, including Tampa, Miami, Orlando, and New Orleans, to work at labor camps, promising food and shelter for only $50 a week. The camp owners picked up the prospective workers in vans and transported them to isolated labor camps in North Florida and North Carolina. Once on site, the workers were supplied with crack cocaine. The cost of the drug was deducted from their pay checks. Every evening camp owners gave workers the opportunity to buy crack, untaxed generic beer, and cigarettes from the company store. Most workers spiraled into debt. On average, workers were paid about 30 cents on the dollar after deductions. The case broke in 2005 after a federal raid on the North Florida camp. Advocates were stunned that the camps could so easily exploit American citizens.

Source: *Naples Daily News*, "Labor Camps Kept Workers in Servitude with Crack Cocaine," September 23, 2006.

to isolated labor camps where, hidden and far from the rest of the town, they are exploited and abused. According to some experts in the labor movement, the power differential between a farm worker and an employer can create a situation that may escalate into exploitation, regardless of the immigration status of the worker.[5] Below is an example of a domestic human trafficking case that came to the attention of the authorities and was prosecuted by federal law enforcement. Read this case in Box 1.

Although a majority of human trafficking victims may have been brought from overseas, there are also many domestic victims. Local men and women as well as children as young as 12 years old are also trafficked for labor and sex by traffickers across the country. Domestic trafficking occurs inter- and intra-state and is largely facilitated by organized criminal groups. Domestic victims are typically recruited from lower- to middle-class families by male peers, either through threats of violence to them or their families or through the promise of affection and job offers. Trafficking and recruitment of victims occurs in both large urban as well as rural areas. Victims are often moved inter- or intra-state for various reasons. These reasons may include a demand for "new faces," i.e., newer sexual prey for those who would abuse them; to isolate victims from their previous social networks; and to impede law enforcement efforts. Criminal networks and street gangs that actively traffick women and underage girls include violent groups that have been linked to gun violence and drug trafficking.

The Trafficking Victims Protection Reauthorization Act of 2005 (22 U.S.C §7103)[6] clarified and emphasized that it is the exploitation (force, fraud, or coercion) of the victim for labor, sex, or any other purpose that makes it a trafficking incident, not, necessarily, the transportation or physical movement of the victim.[7] It emphasized that trafficking can and does involve exploitation of US citizens and permanent residents, in particular minor victims of sex trafficking or the prostitution of minors, within US borders. It may or may not involve transportation but it definitely involves exploitation (force, fraud, or coercion) of the victim. All the subsequent reauthorizations of TVPA provide a standard legal definition of the crime of human trafficking and a framework for current and future US anti-trafficking efforts.[8]

The most recent legislation that addresses domestic human trafficking has been the Justice for Victims of Trafficking Act of 2015 passed by the 114th Congress (2015–2016) that became Public Law No. 114-22 on May 29, 2015.[9] The Justice for Victims of Trafficking Act provides vital services and protections to the survivors of child sex trafficking in the United States. Title III of this act is known as the Human Exploitation Rescue Operations Act of 2015 or the HERO Act of 2015.[10] This act provides express statutory authorization for the existing ICE Cyber Crimes Center ("C3").[11]

C3 is a powerful tool in the fight against sexual exploitation of children; the production, advertisement, and distribution of child pornography; and child sex tourism. It allows C3 to collaborate with the Department of Defense and the National Association to Protect Children for the purpose of recruiting, training, and hiring wounded and transitioning military veterans to serve as law enforcement officials engaged in the investigation of child exploitation cases. C3's Child Exploitation Section uses sophisticated investigative techniques to target violators who operate on the Internet, including through the use of websites, e-mail, chatrooms, and file-sharing applications.[12]

Human Trafficking: Around Us

Up until recently most Americans believed that human trafficking is a crime that occurs in other countries and to foreigners who should have known better. A study by Laczko & Gozdziak (2005) reported that estimates of human trafficking have focused almost exclusively on international trafficking victims. Despite a number of new laws, policies, and attempts at educating the public, many Americans still believe that it does not happen in the United States. It is also a commonly held belief that foreigners who claim to be victims of trafficking are responsible for their own predicament. It is believed that the victims bring it upon themselves.[13]

The truth is quite the contrary. Human trafficking is one of the world's fastest-growing crimes. It does not happen only in faraway places such as Philippines, Thailand, China, India, Bangladesh, Saudi Arabia, Cambodia, and Russia or some other poor country or region where people are desperately looking for a ticket out of poverty. It does not happen only to the poor, unemployed, uneducated, and helpless people, but it happens and can happen to anyone regardless of socioeconomic status, education, or employment and it can happen anywhere—even in the United States. It happens to the United States citizens in all states regardless of their immigration status, level of education, gender, race, religion, or ethnicity (contrary to many citizens' beliefs). This chapter presents recent examples of human trafficking cases demonstrating that not only does it happen in almost all states of the United States and to United States citizens, but it is also increasing at an alarming rate in all 50 states.

It may very well be true that foreigners who arrive in the United States illegally are more susceptible to human trafficking situations. However, US citizens and legal immigrants are equally vulnerable and fall prey to the greed of traffickers and are victimized at an alarming rate. Traffickers, motivated by greed, do not recognize the nationality or immigration status of victims as a deterrent. They describe victims not as human beings but in terms of commodities that have the potential of bringing an enormous amount of profits to them. They exploit those who are most vulnerable—the young, the desperate, and the easily manipulated—and to work on farms, in factories, in strip clubs, in the sex industry, or in other establishments where the traffickers believe they can make maximum profits.[14] When US citizens are exploited and manipulated through force, fraud, or coercion in the United States, US federal law recognizes them as victims of domestic human trafficking.

Typically, trafficking has been perceived in terms of sexual exploitation, such as the manipulation of poor and helpless women and children for prostitution or other immoral purposes.[15] However, recently trafficking has been defined to include other types of exploitations through force, fraud, or coercion beyond sexual exploitation. It has been further clarified that victims do not need to be transported across international or other boundaries for trafficking to exist. Today's traffickers believe the human trafficking business is totally democratic. In this business, everybody has an equal opportunity of owning and exploiting fellow human beings. The trafficking business provides criminals an equal opportunity of making profit through the sale of their fellow human beings and their services as well their organs.

The Essentials of the Human Trafficking Process

Running a trafficking business demands three main essentials. These essentials are—motivation, vulnerability, and a conducive environment. The main prerequisites for someone to be motivated in running a human trafficking business are greed, risk-taking ability or nature, and strong political, social, and economic connections. For a person to be motivated to engage in human trade, a person has to be so greedy that he/she is able to treat humans as commodities and overlook any ethical, moral, or social concerns and reactions. The person has to be able to take enormous risks and have strong political, social, and economic connections so as to avoid any possibility of being caught and or punished. Figure 1 demonstrates these essentials.

Although any one can become a trafficking victim, in general the victim often is highly motivated and has a strong desire to make lots of money. The victim has to have a trusting and risk-taking nature. The environment in which victims are recruited and convinced to comply with the traffickers' requests has to be conducive to such activities. Additionally, for the transactions to be carried out and be profit-producing, there has to be demand for the services victims can provide—regardless of their nature—sexual or labor.

Estes & Weiner (2001) estimated that approximately 300,000 "American youth were considered at risk for sexual exploitation, and an estimated 199,000 incidents of sexual exploitation of minors occur each year in the United States."[16] Hammer, Finkelhor, & Sedlak (2002) reported the results of the Second National Incidence Studies of Missing, Abducted, Runaway, and Throwaway Children and stated that the prevalence of minors trafficked or at risk of being trafficked domestically into the commercial sex industry is high among such populations. These estimates included only youth.[17] However, adults are equally at risk of being trafficked into the labor and sex industry. Although children and juveniles who are already at a disadvantage and in trouble, such as runaway/throwaway youth, youth exploited through prostitution, and abused and neglected children may be more likely to be manipulated and preyed upon by traffickers' tricks. Other children and adults are equally vulnerable to be defrauded, coerced, forced, and exploited for labor and sex. An International Labor Organization study (2002) indicated that girls are more likely to be trafficked for commercial sexual exploitation and domestic services, and boys tend to be trafficked for forced labor in commercial farming, petty crimes, and the drug trade.[18]

Family and Youth Services Bureau (FYSB) reported that in 2007 the Department of Health and Human Services (DHHS) provided services to runaway and homeless youth. The report speculated that majority of these children

Figure 1: Essentials for Human Trafficking

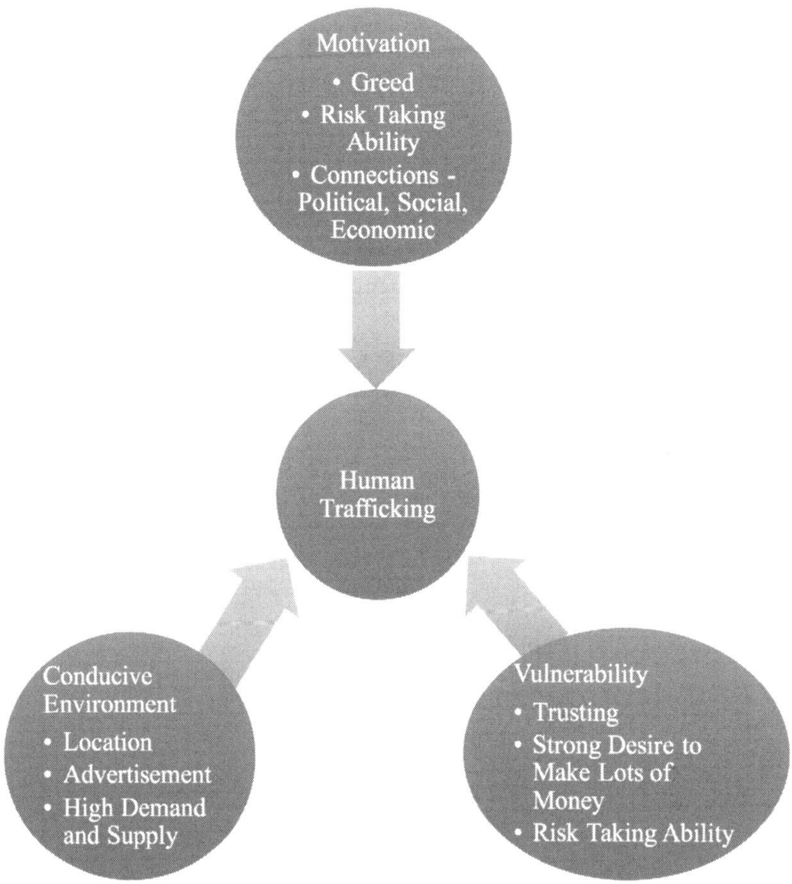

and youth were victims of exploitation. In addition to domestic sex trafficking, American minors and adults are also trafficked for forced labor.[19] Herzfeld (2002) stated that children are generally preferred to adults in the labor world as they are more easily controlled, cheaper, and less likely to challenge exploitation and/or demand better working conditions. However, there is not much empirical research documenting the extent and nature of domestic labor trafficking.[20]

Nature and Extent of Domestic Human Trafficking

The United States is known as a destination country for transnational trafficking. Transnational victims are primarily from Asia, Latin America, Eastern Europe, and Africa.[21] The victims of trafficking in persons, brought into the US for the purpose of both sexual and labor exploitation, are identified in a wide variety of settings.[22] People brought in for sexual exploitation are located within the commercial sex industry, including massage parlors, escort services, gentlemen's clubs, commercially fronted brothels, residential brothels, and strip clubs.[23]

Mostly domestic victims of trafficking are located in domestic work environments throughout the US, including private homes, small independently owned family businesses such as restaurants or nail salons, organized begging rings, and larger scale labor environments such as agricultural farms or large sweatshop-like factories. Victims—legal and illegal migrant workers—are found being exploited both in legitimate and underground industries.[24] Trafficking victims are often subjected to sexual exploitation in both labor and sex trafficking. Sexual and physical violence is used as a means to instill fear and maintain control over the victims.[25]

Existing research, Laczko & Gozdziak (2005), and reports present a convincing argument that human trafficking is a pernicious global problem threatening humanity in all parts of the world, including the United States. Although, in general, estimates of human trafficking have focused almost exclusively on international trafficking victims, some research provides an estimate of minors at risk for sexual exploitation as an estimate for US domestic trafficking.[26] In 2006, the Federal Bureau of Investigation (FBI) Uniform Crime Reports (2006), reported that law enforcement picked up across the United States and identified 36,402 boys and 47,472 girls younger than age 18 as runaways. Girls who run away from their homes, group homes, foster homes, or treatment centers are at greater risk of being targeted by a pimp (or trafficker) and becoming a victim. These estimates neither include adult US citizens trafficked into the sex industry nor provide any estimate on labor trafficking victims.[27]

Lack of Systematic Data

The United States is a source, transit point, and destination country for men, women, and children subjected to trafficking in persons. Human trafficking occurs in every state, and it victimizes both US citizens and noncitizens.[28] However, the controversy arises when an attempt is made to determine the extent of human trafficking incidence and prevalence. There are several reasons for such a state. The first and the most significant problem in determining the extent is that until recently no data were collected on human trafficking as a crime. Despite mandates in the TVPA, no federal, state, and local law enforcement agencies collected and maintained data on trafficking crimes or the number of victims.[29] There is also a significant disparity between estimates of "prevalence" or populations "at risk" and individuals actually identified as trafficking victims or enrolled in government programs.

Nature of the Crime

Human trafficking is termed as a crime "hidden in plain sight."[30] It happens right in the open yet generally goes undetected or documented. It happens so routinely that most of the time, a majority of the people go on with their daily lives, not only inadvertently condoning but actually perpetuating human trafficking. For example, most of the goods and produce consumed by the general public are in existence due to some cheap labor that was trafficked somewhere, may it be on farms, in factories, or other places. Such a covert nature of this criminal enterprise makes it difficult to estimate the number of trafficking victims in United States or anywhere in the world. Despite such a quandary, some estimates exist. According to the US Department of Health and Human Services (2009), there were between 14,500 and 17,500 victims trafficked into the United States each year.[31]

Lack of Uniformity: Various Definitions

The lack of a clear and accepted definition makes it harder to estimate the true nature and extent of trafficking in the United States. Despite the fact that the Trafficking Victims Protection Act (TVPA—2000,[32] 2003,[33] 2005,[34] 2008,[35] 2013[36]) has clearly defined what human trafficking is, different organizations and entities perceive, understand, and define it differently. Consequently, existing estimates on the nature and extent of human trafficking vary from one report to another and from one agency to another. They are collected from various perspectives and the extent varies depending upon what is accepted to be trafficking. Sometimes prostitution is equated to trafficking, other times smuggling is implied to be trafficking. Different entities consider different acts to be trafficking. Logan, Walker, & Hunt, (2009) indicated that any of the following sectors or employments could fall under trafficking: sex work, sex industry, pornography, entertainment (exotic dancing, stripping, etc.), personal service, domestic labor, agricultural/construction/mining labor, factory/

sweatshop labor, restaurant/bar labor, begging, panhandling, food service industry, etc.[37]

It is only recently (in 2013) that the Federal Bureau of Investigation (FBI) began collecting data on human trafficking and including these incidents in Uniform Crime Reports. Following a mandate of the William Wilberforce Trafficking Victims Protection Reauthorization Act of 2008, human trafficking is included as a Part 1 crime in Uniform Crime Reports.[38]

Since January 1, 2013, UCR has had two new categories of human trafficking: commercial sex acts and (ii) involuntary servitude.

According to the UCR, victims of commercial sex acts are forced to participate in commercial sex acts via the use of fraud or coercion except in the case when the person induced to perform such act(s) has not attained 18 years of age. Human trafficking/involuntary servitude refers to the obtaining of a person(s) through recruitment, harboring, transportation, or provision, and subjecting such persons by force, fraud, or coercion into involuntary servitude, peonage, debt bondage, or slavery (not to include commercial sex acts).

Source of Data

Another very important reason for such varying accounts of the nature and extent of human trafficking crimes is that the existing resources focus mainly on the description of human trafficking as reported by media, non-governmental agencies, service providers, survivors, and existing literature. Most data are generally based on the accounts narrated by survivors, victims, offenders, and/or crusaders. These generally are estimates based on anecdotal data without any external validation.

Human Trafficking: A Routine Activity

The fact that trafficking labor is consumed by all of us, even when majority of us may be unaware of our significant participation in perpetuating trafficking labor, makes it so much part of our daily routine lives that it goes undetected. Its covert nature and its routine existence facilitates its guise. It is a crime existing right in front of our eyes, yet not visible. It is "hidden in plain sight" as Hepburn & Simon (2010), and Newton, Mulcahy & Martin (2008) stated, making it difficult to differentiate between an employee and victim or an employer and a trafficker.[39] Logan, Walker, & Hunt, (2009) explained that a victim could be anyone providing services—for example, a person at a neighborhood nail salon, someone working at a restaurant, a live-in nanny of your neighbor, a janitor who cleans your office after hours, or a landscaper in your neighborhood—to name just a few routine service providers.[40] Along with drugs and weapons, it is now believed to be one of the leading sources of income for criminal organizations and gangs.[41] Additionally, as Clawson, Layne, & Small, (2006) state, trafficking victims are guarded closely by their captors and forced to stay silent. Victims are intimidated and silenced by varying degrees of force, coercion, or deception. Trafficked domestic servants remain "invisible" in private homes. Legitimate private businesses may also be used as a smokescreen for a back-end trafficking operation. In general, cases of forced labor and various forms of trafficking for forced labor are less likely to be detected and reported as compared to sex trafficking cases. It is difficult to "distinguish victims trafficked for forced labor from migrant laborers. These victims often work in hidden locations, such as agricultural fields in rural areas, mining camps, factories and the private houses in the case of domestic servitude."[42]

On the other hand, as Alvarez & Alessi, (2012) and Clawson, Dutch, Salomon, & Goldblatt-Grace, (2009) discuss, sex trafficking and child sex trafficking get a bigger share of news media and labor trafficking is overshadowed by sex trafficking, and worse, sometimes equated to illegal immigration.[43] Below are examples of trafficking cases reported by the Federal Bureau of Investigation (FBI). The first case describes sex trafficking of US children by US citizens in Boston, New York, Georgia, and Florida. Review the case of a Boston man trafficking a 16-year-old girl in Box 2.[44]

Box 3 presents a labor trafficking case prosecuted by the FBI in Ohio.

Here is another case of domestic trafficking, demonstrating that although most of the cases reported in the media focus on sex trafficking such as sex slavery, commercial sex exploitation, and other related work like pornography, etc., US citizens are also trafficked for labor.[45]

Both of these two cases demonstrate several elements of trafficking:

1) Victims and/or traffickers do not need to cross borders.
2) Victims can be US citizens.
3) Traffickers can be US citizens.
4) US citizens are trafficked for sex and labor exploitation.
5) Minors are used indiscriminately for sex and labor.
6) Traffickers can be two persons' operation or a larger organized enterprise.
7) Women and children are not only exploited for sex but also for labor along with men.
8) Victims are coerced into compliance using various tactics including narcotic drugs, violence, beatings, threats, sexual assaults, humiliation, and deprivation of sleep, food, and bathroom facilities.

Box 2: Case of Domestic Sex Trafficking

Boston Man Sentenced to Ten Years in Prison for Child Sex Trafficking

BOSTON—**A Boston man was sentenced today in U.S. District Court in Boston in connection with sex trafficking a 16-year-old girl.**

Jonathan White, 29, of Dorchester, was sentenced by U.S. District Court Judge Indira Talwani to 10 years in prison and five years of supervised release. In December 2014, White pleaded guilty in U.S. District Court for the Eastern District of New York to recruiting and transporting a minor to engage in prostitution. The matter was transferred to the District of Massachusetts for sentencing.

In June 2012, a 16-year-old girl from Georgia began chatting, over Tagged.com, a social networking site, with an individual who was working for White as a prostitute and recruited others to prostitute for White. White paid for the victim's bus ticket from Atlanta to Orlando, Fla. Once there, the victim engaged in commercial sex acts with clients solicited through Backpage.com ads, with White ultimately receiving the money that customers paid. White and the prostitute then drove the victim from Florida to Brooklyn, where she engaged in more commercial sex acts solicited over the Internet. A few weeks later, the victim became involved with another pimp. After that pimp was arrested, law enforcement discovered White's role in the victim's exploitation and he was charged.

United States Attorney Carmen M. Ortiz and Harold H. Shaw, Special Agent in Charge of the Federal Bureau of Investigation in Boston, made the announcement today. The case was prosecuted in Boston by Assistant U.S. Attorney Seth Kosto of Ortiz's Civil Rights Enforcement Team, and in Brooklyn by Assistant U.S. Attorney Soumya Dayanana.

Source: United States Attorney's Office, District of Massachusetts, May 17, 2016, https://www.justice.gov/usao-ma/pr/boston-man-sentenced-ten-years-prison-child-sex-trafficking.

9) Victims are constantly monitored to establish and continue a pattern of domination and control.
10) Victims are humiliated and deprived of their identity and dignity.
11) Traffickers do not spare anybody. The disabled—physically or cognitively—are equally vulnerable.

Human Trafficking and Economics

Human trafficking and economics are closely interwoven—as the very foundation of human trafficking involves profit and greed. "The trade in people is surely the most morally repugnant of all the illicit trades that flourish today. But it's deeply entrenched and interwoven with the world's ever more complex

Box 3: Case of Domestic Labor Trafficking

An Ashland, Ohio, man was sentenced to 30 years in prison for holding a woman with cognitive disabilities and her child against their will and forcing the woman to perform manual labor for them, said Steven M. Dettelbach, U.S. Attorney for the Northern District of Ohio, and Stephen D. Anthony, Special Agent in Charge of the FBI's Cleveland office. Jordie L. Callahan, 28, and Jessica L. Hunt, 33, were convicted in March following a three-week trial before U.S. District Judge Benita Y. Pearson of the Northern District of Ohio. Callahan and Hunt were both convicted on one count each of conspiracy to violate laws, forced labor, and acquiring a controlled substance by deception.

"Mr. Callahan, through his cruelty, sought to deprive the victims in this case of their dignity and their freedom," US Attorney Dettelbach said. "He failed in the former, and the victim's strength ended up trumping his. As for the freedom part—now it is the defendant whose freedom will be taken, for a long time." "Hopefully this well-deserved lengthy sentence will provide a sense of justice that will assist the victims in their ongoing healing process," Special Agent in Charge Anthony said. Hunt is scheduled to be sentenced by Judge Pearson on July 24.

Daniel J. Brown, 35, and Dezerah L. McGuire (formerly Silsby), 33, also of Ashland, both previously pleaded guilty to related crimes are serving sentences in federal prison. Brown was sentenced to five years in prison and McGuire was sentenced to nearly four years in prison. Callahan and Hunt used a combination of violence, threats, sexual assaults, humiliation, deprivation and monitoring to establish and continue a pattern of domination and control over their victims, identified only as S.E. and B.E., according to the court documents and trial testimony. Their tactics included beating S.E., threatening to beat to S.E. and B.E., taunting and threatening the victims with pit bulls and snakes, causing the victims to sleep in unsafe and unsanitary conditions, restricting B.E. and S.E.'s access to the bathroom, preventing them from eating regular and suitable meals and forcing S.E. to eat dog food and crawl on the floor while wearing a dog collar, according to the court documents and trial testimony.

According to court documents and trail testimony, Callahan pointed a firearm at S.E.'s head and threatened to kill her if she did not perform the labor and services he and other conspirators commanded. Callahan also forced S.E. on multiple occasions to engage in sex acts with him and threatened that he and Hunt would kill S.E. if she told anyone about the forced sexual acts. The conspiracy between Callahan, Hunt, McGuire and Brown took place between August 2010 and October 2012. The object of the conspiracy included holding S.E. in a condition of forced labor and involuntary servitude and intentionally causing painful injuries to S.E. so they could use the narcotic pain medications she was prescribed to satisfy their personal drug cravings. Callahan and Hunt recruited S.E. and B.E. to live with them in their two-bedroom apartment in Ashland, knowing that S.E. suffered a traumatic brain injury that left her with a cognitive disability and that S.E. and B.E. received monthly public assistance payments.

In August 2011, McGuire, at the direction of Callahan and Hunt, smashed S.E.'s hand with a rock with such force that S.E. needed to go to the hospital emergency room. Callahan, Hunt and McGuire then forced S.E. to give them the narcotic pain pills and prescription for narcotic pain pills she obtained after being treated at the emergency room. In December 2011, Callahan and Hunt injured S.E.'s back with such force that she needed medical treatment. Again, Callahan and Hunt forced S.E. to give them the narcotic pain pills and prescription for narcotic pain pills she obtained after being treated. In March 2012, Callahan kicked S.E. in the hip with such force that she needed medical treatment. Callahan and Hunt forced S.E. to give them the narcotic pain pills and prescription for narcotic pain pills she obtained after being treated. On multiple occasions between August 2010 and October 2012, Callahan and Hunt threatened S.E. and B.E. with serious physical harm, including death, if S.E. did not clean up the apartment, care for their numerous pit bull dogs, snakes and other reptiles, purchase items at the store and perform other labor and services ordered by the conspirators.

Callahan and Hunt used a video camera to monitor S.E. and B.E.'s activities and conversations in the apartment. They often forced S.E. to walk to the store to buy groceries, cigarettes, dog food and other items for Callahan, Hunt and Hunt's four sons and to pay for these purchases with her public assistance card. They allotted S.E. only a brief time period to complete the shopping and warned her she was not allowed to speak with anyone while she was out. They frequently required B.E. to remain with them at the apartment while S.E. was out and threatened physical harm to B.E. and S.E. if S.E. broke any of their rules.

Callahan and Hunt also threatened to contact Ashland County Job and Family Services and have B.E. taken away if S.E. purchased any items at the store other than those they ordered or if she told anyone about their unlawful conduct. In June 2011, after S.E. and B.E. had attempted to flee the apartment, Callahan and Hunt ordered Brown and McGuire to find S.E. and B.E. and bring them back to the apartment. Brown and McGuire lured S.E. and B.E. into their vehicle by promising to take them to Dairy Queen, only to deposit them afterwards back at the apartment. On multiple occasions, Callahan and Brown locked S.E. and B.E. in a room with a window that was nailed shut and a door that had been locked from the outside. In October 2011, Callahan and Hunt forced S.E. to hit her child while they recorded a video, and threatened to inflict much greater physical harm on both S.E. and B.E. if S.E. did not comply.

One month later, Callahan and Hunt again forced S.E. to strike B.E. while they captured a video recording of the staged incident on Callahan's cell phone. Callahan and Hunt repeatedly threatened have B.E. taken away by showing the videos to authorities in order to secure S.E.'s compliance to the conspirators' commands.

The case was prosecuted by Assistant U.S. Attorneys Chelsea Rice and Thomas E. Getz following an investigation by the FBI and Ashland Police Department, with assistance from the Ashland County Prosecutor's Office.

Source: FBI, "Ohio Man Sentenced to 30 Years in Prison for Labor Trafficking and Related Crimes," July 22, 2014, https://www.fbi.gov/cleveland/press-releases/2014/ohio-man-sentenced-to-30-years-in-prison-for-labor-trafficking-and-related-crimes.

migration flows."[46] Brewer (2008) provides an excellent example of how a normal, average advisement for any kind of service providing job could be used as a façade for recruiting trafficking victims. For example, a normal sounding advertisement could be used as a bait to recruit innocent applicants.[47]

Review an excerpt from a typical advertisement placed for soliciting applications for jobs in a cruise line business.

"International cruise line seeks attractive and adventuresome hostess to greet passengers. See the world, meet new people and earn a stable income!" (Brewer: 46).[48]

Brewer (2008) explains that a cursory examination of the excerpt of an advertisement presented above depicts it as a normal, regular advertisement soliciting applicants for a real job in the cruise line industry, until an unsuspecting applicant with seemingly nothing to lose applies, is recruited from her home, and arrives at her destination only to be forced into prostitution.[49] This example demonstrates that trafficking is "hidden in plain sight," and it is extremely difficult to distinguish a genuine employee from trafficking victim or an employer from a trafficker. According to the International Labor Organization (2008) at any given time, in the world, there were estimated to be 2.4 million people involved in forced labor and subjected to exploitation as a result of trafficking. Traffickers often deceive their victims through false promises of economic opportunities that await them in destinations away from home.[50]

U.S. Code and Protection for the Victims of Involuntary Servitude or Forced Labor

A number of provisions in the US Code target trafficking in persons, also known as involuntary servitude, slavery, or forced labor. These provisions are contained in Chapter 77 of Title 18 and are sometimes referred to generally as Chapter 77 offenses. The Trafficking Victims Protection Act (TVPA) of 2000 supplemented existing laws, primarily 18 U.S.C. § 1584 (Involuntary Servitude), and also provided new tools to combat trafficking. Key statutes are excerpted below.

Peonage

Summary: Section 1581 of Title 18 makes it unlawful to hold a person in "debt servitude," or peonage, which is closely related to involuntary servitude. Section 1581 prohibits using force, the threat of force, or the threat of legal coercion to compel a person to work against his/her will. In addition, the victim's involuntary servitude must be tied to the payment of a debt.

18 U.S.C. §1581
(a) Whoever holds or returns any person to a condition of peonage, or arrests any person with the intent of placing him in or returning him to a condition of peonage, shall be fined under this title or imprisoned not more than 20 years, or both. If death results from the violation of this section, or if the violation includes kidnapping or an attempt to kidnap, aggravated sexual abuse or an attempt to commit aggravated sexual abuse, or an attempt to kill, the defendant shall be fined under this title or imprisoned for any term of years or life, or both.
(b) Whoever obstructs, or attempts to obstruct, or in any way interferes with or prevents the enforcement of this section, shall be liable to the penalties prescribed in subsection (a).

Involuntary Servitude

Summary: Section 1584 of Title 18 makes it unlawful to hold a person in a condition of slavery, that is, a condition of compulsory service or labor against his/her will. A Section 1584 conviction requires that the victim be held against his/her will by actual force, threats of force, or threats of legal coercion. Section 1584 also prohibits compelling a person to work against his/her will by creating a "climate of fear" through the use of force, the threat of force, or the threat of legal coercion [i.e., "If you don't work, I'll call the immigration officials."] which is sufficient to compel service against a person's will.

18 U.S.C. §1584
Whoever knowingly and willfully holds to involuntary servitude or sells into any condition of involuntary servitude, any other person for any term, or brings within the United States any person so held, shall be fined under this title or imprisoned not more than 20 years, or both. If death results from the violation of this section, or if the violation includes kidnapping or an attempt to kidnap, aggravated sexual abuse or the attempt to commit aggravated sexual abuse, or an attempt to kill, the defendant shall be fined under this title or imprisoned for any term of years or life, or both.

Forced Labor

Summary: Section 1589 of Title 18, which was passed as part of the TVPA, makes it unlawful to provide or obtain the labor or services of a person through one of three prohibited means. Congress enacted §1589 in response to the Supreme Court's decision in *United States v. Kozminski*, 487 U.S. 931 (1988), which interpreted §1584 to require the use or threatened use of physical or legal coercion. Section 1589 broadens the definition of the kinds of coercion that might result in forced labor.

18 U.S.C. §1589
Whoever knowingly provides or obtains the labor or services of a person—
(1) by threats of serious harm to, or physical restraint against, that person or another person;
(2) by means of any scheme, plan, or pattern intended to cause the person to believe that, if the person did not perform such labor or services, that person or another person would suffer serious harm or physical restraint; or
(3) by means of the abuse or threatened abuse of law or the legal process,
shall be fined under this title or imprisoned not more than 20 years, or both. If death results from the violation of this section, or if the violation includes kidnapping or an attempt to kidnap, aggravated sexual abuse or the attempt to commit aggravated sexual abuse, or an attempt to kill, the defendant shall be fined under this title or imprisoned for any term of years or life, or both.

Trafficking with Respect to Peonage, Slavery, Involuntary Servitude, or Forced Labor

Summary: Section 1590 makes it unlawful to recruit, harbor, transport, or broker persons for labor or services under conditions which violate any of the offenses contained in Chapter 77 of Title 18.

18 U.S.C. §1590
Whoever knowingly recruits, harbors, transports, provides, or obtains by any means, any person for labor or services in violation of this chapter shall be fined under this title or imprisoned not more than 20 years, or both. If death results from the violation of this section, or if the violation includes kidnapping or an attempt to kidnap, aggravated sexual abuse, or the attempt to commit aggravated sexual abuse, or an attempt to kill, the defendant shall be fined under this title or imprisoned for any term of years or life, or both.

Sex Trafficking of Children by Force, Fraud, or Coercion

Summary: Section 1591 criminalizes sex trafficking, which is defined as causing a person to engage in a commercial sex act under certain statutorily enumerated conditions. A commercial sex act means any sex act, on account of which anything of value is given to or received by any person. The specific conditions are the use of force, fraud, or coercion, or conduct involving persons under the age of 18. The punishment for conduct that either involves a victim who is under the age of 14 or involves force, fraud, or coercion is any term of years or life. The punishment for conduct that involves a victim between the ages of 14 and 18 is 40 years.

> 18 U.S.C. § 1591
> Whoever knowingly—
> (1) in or affecting interstate or foreign commerce, or within the special maritime and territorial jurisdiction of the United States, recruits, entices, harbors, transports, provides, or obtains by any means a person; or
> (2) benefits, financially or by receiving anything of value, from participation in a venture which has engaged in an act described in violation of paragraph (1), knowing that force, fraud, or coercion described in subsection (c)(2) will be used to cause the person to engage in a commercial sex act, or that the person has not attained the age of 18 years and will be caused to engage in a commercial sex act, shall be punished as provided in subsection (b).

Unlawful Conduct with Respect to Documents in Furtherance of Trafficking, Peonage, Slavery, Involuntary Servitude, or Forced Labor

Summary: Section 1592 makes it illegal to seize documents in order to force others to work. By expanding its coverage to false documents as well as official documents, § 1592 recognizes that victims are often immobilized by the withholding of whatever documents they possess, even if the documents are forged or fraudulent. Section 1592 expands the scope of federal trafficking statutes to reach those who prey on the vulnerabilities of immigrant victims by controlling their papers.

18 U.S.C. §1592
(a) Whoever knowingly destroys, conceals, removes, confiscates, or possesses any actual or purported passport or other immigration document, or any other actual or purported government identification document, of another person—
(1) in the course of a violation of section 1581, 1583, 1584, 1589, 1590, 1591, or 1594(a);
(2) with intent to violate section 1581, 1583, 1584, 1589, 1590, or 1591; or
(3) to prevent or restrict or to attempt to prevent or restrict, without lawful authority, the person's liberty to move or travel, in order to maintain the labor or services of that person, when the person is or has been a victim of a severe form of trafficking in persons, as defined in section 103 of the Trafficking Victims Protection Act of 2000, **shall be fined under this title or imprisoned for not more than 5 years, or both.**
(b) **Subsection (a) does not apply to the conduct of a person who is or has been a victim of a severe form of trafficking in persons, as defined in section 103 of the Trafficking Victims Protection Act of 2000, if that conduct is caused by, or incident to, that trafficking.**[51]

Additional provisions of the TVPA provide for mandatory restitution (18 U.S.C. §1593) and forfeiture (18 U.S.C. §1594(b)), criminalize attempt (18 U.S.C. §1594(a)), and give victims an avenue for civil lawsuits (18 U.S.C. §1595).

As discussed earlier, children and adults holding United States citizenship also fall prey to the tactics of traffickers and are victimized. An International Labor Organization (2002) study indicated that men, women, boys, and girls are all vulnerable to the traffickers' tricks and can be victimized. In the United States, exploitation of children for labor falls in specific labor categories.[52] Data from the National Longitudinal Survey of Youth 1997 (NLSY97) demonstrated a substantial work activity among 14- and 15-year-old children.[53] A more recent report by the US Department of State, (2012) stated that according to the International Labor Organization's second global estimate of forced labor, there are 20.9 million individuals trapped in modern slavery around the world at any given time. According to International Labor Office, (2012) approximately 5.5 million children are victims of labor exploitation. Child victims in the United States may be either documented or undocumented foreigners.[54] The Child Labor Coalition (CLC, 2001) estimated that approximately 5.5 million youth between the ages of 12 and 17 were employed across the United States.[55]

The CLC (2007) reported that 500,000 US children were also working in various agricultural settings, with most being members of minority groups.[56]

Clawson (2009) reported that according to the CLC (2007) estimates, about 50,000 children are involved in street peddling, including peddling magazines, candy, and other consumer goods. Many teens become involved, believing peddling is a good way to make money, and do not realize the dangers associated with these activities. The same study also suggested that the majority of the 14- and 15-year-olds were employed in a small number of industries, with restaurants and supermarkets as well as babysitting and yard work being common sectors.[57] This is also confirmed by the US Department of State (2012).

According to the Polaris Project Fact Sheet, (2012):

> Labor trafficking of children occurs in diverse contexts in the U.S., including domestic service—where children work in employers' homes 10–16 hours per day with very low or little wages; agriculture—where children work alongside their parents in brutal, unsanitary, and dangerous conditions; and other service industries, such as restaurants—where children are often given low or no wages, and may sometimes be required to engage in commercial sex.
>
> One little-recognized form of child trafficking is peddling of candy, magazines, and other consumer products and traveling sales crews. Street peddlers often "work long hours with little pay, in extreme temperatures, and with no access to bathrooms, water, or food; work for activities or prizes they never receive; and work alone in strange neighborhoods or cities.[58]

Traffickers take advantage of the most vulnerable people, such as children, and those who are poor, unemployed, greedy, anxious, and willing to take risks in order to make lots of money. They prey on those who have a few economic opportunities and those who are struggling to meet basic needs. Traffickers take advantage of the unequal status of women and girls in disadvantaged countries and communities, and capitalize on the demand for cheap, unprotected labor and the promotion of sex tourism in some countries.[59]

Who Are the Victims of Domestic Trafficking?

Victims of trafficking are found in all types of human trafficking including labor and sex, although they are more easily detected and reported in sex trafficking as compared to labor trafficking. For example, it is difficult to distinguish between an exploited farm worker and a migrant laborer. Victims often work in agricultural fields in rural areas, mining camps, factories and private houses (in the case of domestic servitude) and thus remain hidden. As a consequence, the trafficking victims of forced labor are less likely to be identified and reported as compared to the victims of sex trafficking.

Traffickers use a variety of tactics to entice and entrap potential victims. These tactics may include a promise of a good job with attractive salary and benefits, a false marriage proposal, or being sold by parents, husbands, or boyfriends, etc. Generally, victims know their recruiters, whom the victims tend to believe or trust, such as neighbors, friends, friends of a friend, boyfriends, acquaintances, and family friends. Most often, victims are recruited through personal contacts and also through job advertisements on television, billboards, newspapers, and the Internet. Some victims enter the country legally on work visas while others enter illegally. The most common industries where trafficked people work are agriculture, mining, logging, construction, fishery, sweatshop factory (e.g., garments, packaging, and food processing), domestic servitude, begging, drug dealing, janitorial, and food services. By some estimates, approximately 30 to 50 percent of all trafficking victims are children and youth below the age of 18. It could be because younger people are easy to manipulate and exploit in the sex industry as well as in other industries such as fishing, agriculture, and clothing manufacturing. It is easier for the traffickers to dupe children and/or their parents into leaving home with the promise of a better life, and sometimes parents, themselves, may sell their children to a trafficker. Sometimes children are trafficked to work as soldiers in war zones. The Coalition to Stop the Use of Child Soldiers estimates that there are tens of thousands of children who are used as combatants and/or sexually exploited in armed forces.

Victims of human trafficking, both international and domestic, share some other specific characteristics as well that place them at a higher risk for being trafficked. These include poverty, young age, limited education, lack of work opportunities, lack of family support (e.g., they are orphaned, runaway/throwaway, or homeless, or family members collaborated with traffickers), history of previous sexual abuse, health or mental health challenges, and living in vulnerable areas e.g., areas with police corruption and high crime.[60] According to some experts in the labor movement, the power differential between a farm worker and an employer can create a situation that may escalate into exploitation, regardless of the immigration status of the worker.[61]

Figure 2 presents the common characteristics of the victims of human trafficking.

The most common attributes of human trafficking victims are poverty and marginalized status. Generally, victims are poor and unemployed. They are looking for opportunities to find employment and to have a better life that

Figure 2: Characteristics of the Victims of Domestic Human Trafficking

they believe they deserve but are unable to attain. Some of these potential victims are looking for a quick way out of poverty and traffickers offer that venue, where they will have a job to fulfil their dream of making their lives better. Younger victims are often victims of abuse, neglect, and molestation. Some of these are running away from abusive and exploitative situations and are homeless. In other cases, they may be addicted to drugs or other substances, and others may have been sold by their families or friends. According to the reports by the ILO and UNICEF, although poverty is one of the main risk factors that pushes people into accepting exploitation via trafficking, it is not the only factor. Poverty supplemented with other risk factors such as family environment, drugs, and homelessness facilitates victimization. Variables at the individual level as well as at the household, community, regional, institutional, and systematic levels often push victims into trafficking.

Although immigration status is another risk factor that enhances the chances of illegal migrants for exploitation and abuse, citizens and legal migrants are also subjected to such exploitation.[62] In the United States, vulnerable workers have been recruited from homeless shelters and streets, transported to isolated labor camps, and ultimately exploited and abused.[63]

Young adults—immigrants or American children—are equally vulnerable to abuse and exploitation. Many of the trafficking victims (including United States citizens and legal immigrants) are deceived, manipulated, forced, or coerced into prostitution every day. For example, service providers in New York City report that the average age that girls enter prostitution has dropped from 14 to 13 or 12 years of age in recent years. The average age that boys and transgender youth begin prostitution is even younger: 11–13 years old.[64] All adolescents regardless of their race or ethnicity are at risk for exploitation. Some research results report that African American girls and women are arrested in prostitution at a far higher rate than girls and women of other races. Poverty is also a risk factor that enhances chances of exploitation.

A troubled childhood—such as history of abuse and neglect—is also known as a risk factor increasing the probability of trafficking victimization. One common characteristic or risk factor for prostituted girls is a history of childhood sexual abuse. In twenty recent studies of adult women who were sexually exploited through prostitution, the percentage of those who had been abused as children ranged from 33 percent to 84 percent.

Conclusion and Chapter Review

In this chapter, we have discussed what is domestic human trafficking. We learned various aspects of domestic human trafficking to develop an understanding of the nature and extent of domestic human trafficking around us. The discussions, cases, and data presented in this chapter dispel several misperceptions about trafficking in persons. It has demonstrated that trafficking in persons is as much a domestic problem as it is international, involving United States citizens—both as victims and perpetrators—as much as it involves foreigners. In essence, we discussed the following:

- Human Trafficking: Local Perspectives
  - Domestic Human Trafficking
  - Human Trafficking: Around Us
  - Essentials of the Human Trafficking Process
  - Nature and Extent of Domestic Human Trafficking
    - Lack of Systematic Data
    - Nature of Crime
    - Lack of Uniformity: Various Definitions

        - Source of Data
    - Human Trafficking: A Routine Activity
    - U.S. Code and Protection for the Victims of Involuntary Servitude or Forced Labor
    - Who Are the Victims of Domestic Trafficking?

Discussion Questions

1) Discuss two classifications of trafficking in persons: a) transnational crime b) domestic crime.
2) What is the HERO Act of 2015?
3) How does C3 assist in prosecuting traffickers? In what type of trafficking does this provide the most assistance?
4) What are the three main essentials of the human trafficking process?
5) Describe human trafficking as an economic crime. Review your local newspaper, find a trafficking case, and discuss it in economic terms.
6) Discuss at least two tactics traffickers use to entice and entrap potential victims. Demonstrate with examples.
7) Discuss two main types of trafficking. Illustrate using examples.

References

Alvarez, Maria Beatriz, and Edward J. Alessi. "Human Trafficking Is More Than Sex Trafficking and Prostitution: Implications for Social Work." *Affilia* 27, no. 2 (2012): 142–152.

Aronowitz, Alexis A. "Smuggling and Trafficking in Human Beings: The Phenomenon, the Markets That Drive It and the Organisations That Promote It." *European Journal on Criminal Policy and Research* 9, no. 2 (2001): 163–195.

Brewer, Devin. "Globalization and Human Trafficking." *Tropical Research Digest: Human Rights and Human Welfare* (2008): 46–56.

Clawson, Heather J., Mary Layne, and Kevonne Small. "Estimating Human Trafficking into the United States: Development of a Methodology." Document no. 215475. Fairfax, Virginia: Caliber, an IFC International Company, 2006.

Estes, Richard J., and Neil Alan Weiner. *The Commercial Sexual Exploitation of Children in the US, Canada and Mexico*. University of Pennsylvania, School of Social Work, Center for the Study of Youth Policy, 2001.

Finklea, Kristin, Adrienne L. Fernandes-Alcantara, and Alison Siskin. *Domestic Human Trafficking Legislation in the 114th Congress.* Washington, DC: Congressional Research Service, 2015.

Hepburn, Stephanie, and Rita J. Simon. "Hidden in Plain Sight: Human Trafficking in the United States." *Gender Issues* 27, no. 1–2 (2010): 1–26.

Herzfeld, Beth. "Slavery and Gender: Women's Double Exploitation." *Gender & Development* 10, no. 1 (2002): 50–55.

Laczko, Frank, and Elzbieta M. Gozdziak, eds. *Data and Research on Human Trafficking: A Global Survey. International Migration* 43, no. 1–2. Geneva: International Organization for Migration, 2005.

Logan, T. K., Robert Walker, and Gretchen Hunt. "Understanding Human Trafficking in the United States." *Trauma, Violence, & Abuse* 10, no. 1 (2009): 3–30.

Miko, Francis T. "Trafficking in Women and Children: The US and International Response—Updated March 26, 2004." Cornell University ILR School, 2004.

Moisés, Naim. *Illicit: How Smugglers, Traffickers, and Copycats Are Hacking the Global Economy*. New York: Doubleday, 2005.

Newton, Phyllis J., Timothy M. Mulcahy, and Susan E. Martin. *Finding Victims of Human Trafficking.* University of Chicago, National Opinion Research Center, 2008.

Sigmon, Jane Nady. "Combating Modern-Day Slavery: Issues in Identifying and Assisting Victims of Human Trafficking Worldwide." *Victims and Offenders* 3, no. 2–3 (2008): 245–257.

Siskin, Alison, and Kristen. A Finklea. *Sex Trafficking of Children in the United States: Overview and Issues for Congress.* Washington, DC: Congressional Research Service, 2015.

Siskin, Alison, and Liana Sun Wyler. *Trafficking in Persons: US Policy and Issues for Congress.* Washington, DC: Congressional Research Service, 2012.

United States Attorney's Office District of Massachusetts. "Boston Man Sentenced to Ten Years in Prison for Child Sex Trafficking." May 17, 2016. https://www.justice.gov/usao-ma/pr/boston-man-sentenced-ten-years-prison-child-sex-trafficking.

United States Congress. Trafficking Victims Protection Act (TVPA). 2000. Pub. L. No. 106-386, 114 Stat. 1473.

United States Congress. Trafficking Victims Protection Reauthorization Act (TVPRA). 2003. Pub. L. No. 108-193, 117 Stat. 2875.

United States Congress. Trafficking Victims Protection Reauthorization Act (TVPRA). 2005. Pub. L. No. 109-164.

United States Department of State. *Trafficking in Persons Report 2010*. 2010. http://www.state.gov/j/tip/rls/tiprpt/2010/

United States Department of State. *Trafficking in Persons Report 2014*. June 2014. http://www.state.gov/j/tip/rls/tiprpt/2014/.

United States Federal Bureau of Investigation. "Crime in the United States 2006." 2010. https://ucr.fbi.gov/crime-in-the-u.s/2006.

United States Federal Bureau of Investigation. "Ohio Man Sentenced to 30 Years in Prison for Labor Trafficking and Related Crimes." July 22, 2014. https://www.fbi.gov/contact-us/field-offices/cleveland/news/press-releases/ohio-man-sentenced-to-30-years-in-prison-for-labor-trafficking-and-related-crimes.

Further Suggested Readings

Desmond Cohen and Elizabeth Reid, "The Vulnerability of Women: Is This a Useful Construct for Policy and Programming?" Issues Paper No. 28, HIV and Development Programme. New York, United Nations Development Programme, 1996.

Gozdziak, Elzbieta M., and Elizabeth A. Collett. "Research on Human Trafficking in North America: A Review of Literature." *International Migration* 43, no. 1 2 (2005): 99–128.

Hammer, Heather, David Finkelhor, and Andrea J. Sedlak. "Runaway/Thrownaway Children: National Estimates and Characteristics." *National Incidence Studies of Missing, Abducted, Runaway, and Thrownaway Children*. US Department of Justice, Office of Juvenile Justice and Delinquency Prevention, 2002.

Ho, Christine G. T., and James Loucky. *Humane Migration: Establishing Legitimacy and Rights for Displaced People*. Kumarian Press, 2012.

International Labor Organization (ILO). Abolition of Forced Labor Convention. Convention concerning the Abolition of Forced Labor. No. 105. Adoption: 25 Jun 1957. Entry into force: 17 Jan 1959. http://www.ilo.org/dyn/normlex/en/f?p=1000:12100:0::NO::P12100_ILO_CODE:C105.

International Labor Organization (ILO), Special Action Programme to Combat Forced Labour (SAP-FL). *Profits and Poverty: The Economics of Forced Labour*. Fundamental Principles and Rights at Work Branch (FPRW). 2014. http:// http://www.ilo.org/wcmsp5/groups/public/—ed_norm/—declaration/documents/publication/wcms_243391.pdf.

Roby, Jini L. "Women and Children in the Global Sex Trade." *International Social Work* 48, no. 2 (2005): 136–147.

United Nations Human Rights Office of the High Commissioner. International Covenant on Civil and Political Rights. Resolution 2200A (XXI). 16 December 1966. Entry into force: 23 March 1976, in accordance with Article 49. http://www.ohchr.org/en/professionalinterest/pages/ccpr.aspx.

United Nations Human Rights Office of the High Commissioner. The 1956 Supplementary Convention on the Abolition of Slavery, the Slave Trade, and Institutions and Practices Similar to Slavery. Resolution 608(XXI). 30 April 1956. Entry into force: 30 April 1957, in accordance with Article 13. http://www.ohchr.org/EN/ProfessionalInterest/Pages/SupplementaryConvention AbolitionOfSlavery.aspx.

United Nations Office on Drugs and Crime (UNODC). http://www.unodc.org/unodc/en/crime_cicp_signatures_trafficking.html.

United Nations Office on Drugs and Crime (UNODC). *Fact Sheet on Human Trafficking.* 2006. http://www.unodc.org/unodc/en/trafficking_victim_consents.html#how.

United Nations Office on Drugs and Crime (UNODC). *Global Report on Trafficking in Persons—Executive Summary.* 2014. http://www.unodc.org/documents/data-and-analysis/glotip/GLOTIP14 ExSum_english.pdf.

United Nations Office on Drugs and Crime (UNODC). *Trafficking in Human Beings.* 2006. http://www.unodc.org/unodc/en/trafficking_human_beings.html.

United States Congress. Mann Act, 18 United States Code §§ 1581–1588.

United States Department of Health and Human Services, Administration for Children and Families. "About Rescue and Restore." http://www.acf.hhs.gov/trafficking/rescue_restore/index.html.

United States Department of Health and Human Services. *The Campaign to Rescue and Restore Victims of Human Trafficking: About Human Trafficking* from http://www.acf.hhs.gov/trafficking/about/index.html#wwd.

United States Department of Justice (USDOJ). "Assessment of U.S. Government Efforts to Combat Trafficking in Persons in Fiscal Year 2006." 2007. http://www.usdoj.gov/ag/annualreports/tr2007/assessment-of-efforts-to-combat-tip0907.pdf.

United States Department of Justice (USDOJ). *Report on Activities to Combat Human Trafficking: Fiscal Years 2001–2005.* http://www.usdoj.gov/crt/crim/trafficking_report_2006.pdf.

United States Department of Justice, Department of Health and Human Services, Department of State, Department of Labor, Department of

Homeland Security, and Agency of International Development. *Assessment of US Government Efforts to Combat Trafficking in Persons*. June 2004, p. 4.

United States Department of State. *Domestic Human Trafficking: An Internal Issue*, Washington, DC: Human Smuggling and Trafficking Center, December 2008, p. 2.

United States Department of State. Special State Department Briefing. *Federal News Service*. June 3, 2005. LexisNexis.

United States Department of State, Office to Monitor and Combat Trafficking in Persons. *Trafficking in Persons Report*. 2004. http://www.state.gov/g/tip/rls/tiprpt/2004/34021.htm.

United States Department of State, Office to Monitor and Combat Trafficking in Persons. *Trafficking in Persons Report*. 2005. http://www.state.gov/g/tip/rls/tiprpt/2005/.

United States Government Accounting Office (USGAO). *Human Trafficking: Better Data, Strategy, and Reporting Needed to Enhance U.S. Anti-trafficking Efforts Abroad*. GAO-06-825. Published: Jul 18, 2006. Publicly Released: Aug 14, 2006. http://www.gao.gov/products/GAO-06-825.

Vital Voices Global Partnership. *Stateless and Vulnerable to Human Trafficking in Thailand*. Washington, DC, June 2007, p. 13. www.vitalvoices.org.

Weitzer, Ronald. "Moral Crusade against Prostitution." *Society* 43, no. 3 (2006): 33–38.

Wilson, Deborah G., William F. Walsh, and Sherilyn Kleuber. "Trafficking in Human Beings: Training and Services among US Law Enforcement Agencies." *Police Practice and Research* 7, no. 2 (2006): 149–160.

Women's Commission for Refugee Women and Children. *Displaced Women and Girls at Risk: Risk Factors, Protection Solutions and Resource Tools*. February 2006. https://www.womensrefugeecommission.org/images/stories/WomRisk.pdf.

Notes

1. Sigmon, J. N. (2008). Combating modern-day slavery: Issues in identifying and assisting victims of human trafficking worldwide. *Victims and Offenders*, 3(2–3), 245–257.

2. This endnotes has four references:

1) Europol. *Annual report 2005*. Europa.eu.

2) Miko, F. T. (2004). Trafficking in women and children: The US and international response—Updated March 26, 2004. Cornell University ILR School.

3) US Government Accountability Office. *Human trafficking: Better data, strategy, and reporting*. GAO-06-825. www.gao.gov/new.items/d06825.pdf.

4) Trafficking Victims Protection Act (TVPA). (2000). Pub. L. No. 106-386, 114 Stat. 1473.

3. Trafficking Victims Protection Act (TVPA). (2000). Pub. L. No. 106-386, 114 Stat. 1473.

4. Bales, K. (2012). *Disposable people: New slavery in the global economy*. University of California Press.

5. Bales, K. (2004). *Disposable people: New slavery in the global economy.* University of California Press; Bales, K. (2012). *Disposable people: New slavery in the global economy*. University of California Press.

6. Trafficking Victims Protection Act (TVPA). (2000). Pub. L. No. 106-386, 114 Stat. 1473.

7. Clawson, H. J., N. Dutch, A. Solomon, & L. Goldblatt Grace. (2009). *Human trafficking into and within the United States: A review of the literature*. Washington, DC: Office of the Assistant Secretary for Planning and Evaluation, US Department of Human and Health Services.

8. US Government Accountability Office. (2006, July 18). *Human trafficking: Better data, strategy, and reporting*. GAO-06-825. www.gao.gov/new.items/d06825.pdf.

9. This endnote has two references.

1) S.178—Justice for Victims of Trafficking Act of 2015, 114th Congress (2015–2016).

2) Finklea, K., A. L. Fernandes-Alcantara, & A. Siskin. (2015, April 16). *Domestic human trafficking legislation in the 114th Congress*. Washington, DC: Congressional Research Service.

10. Finklea, K., A. L. Fernandes-Alcantara, & A. Siskin. (2015, January 28). *Sex trafficking of children in the United States: Overview and issues for Congress*. Washington, DC: Congressional Research Service.

11. S.178—Justice for Victims of Trafficking Act of 2015, 114th Congress (2015–2016).

12. Finklea, K., A. L. Fernandes-Alcantara, & A. Siskin. (2015, April 16). *Domestic human trafficking legislation in the 114th Congress*. Washington, DC: Congressional Research Service.

13. Laczko, F., & E. M. Gozdziak, eds. (2005). *Data and research on human trafficking: A global survey. International Migration, 43*(1–2). SAGE Publications.

14. Clawson, H. J., N. Dutch, A. Solomon, & L. Goldblatt Grace. (2009). *Human trafficking into and within the United States: A review of the literature*. Washington, DC: Office of the Assistant Secretary for Planning and Evaluation, US Department of Human and Health Services.

15. Europol. *Annual Report 2005*. Europa.eu.

16. Estes, R. J., & N. A. Weiner. (2001). *The commercial sexual exploitation of children in the US, Canada and Mexico*. University of Pennsylvania, School of Social Work, Center for the Study of Youth Policy.

17. Hammer, H., D. Finkelhor, & A. J. Sedlak. (2002, October). Runaway/throwaway children: National estimates and characteristics. *National Incidence Studies of Missing, Abducted, Runaway, and Throwaway Children*. Washington, DC: US Department of Justice, Office of Juvenile Justice and Delinquency Prevention.

18. Humblet, M., et al. (2002). *International labour standards: A global approach*. Geneva: International Labour Office.

19. US Department of Health and Human Services. *Report to congress on the runaway and homeless youth programs of the family and youth services bureau for fiscal years 2008 and*

2009. Washington, DC: US Department of Health and Human Services, Family and Youth Services Bureau.

20. Herzfeld, B. (2002). Slavery and gender: Women's double exploitation. *Gender & Development*, *10*(1), 50–55.

21. Polaris Project. (2010). Human trafficking. https://polarisproject.org/human-trafficking.

22. National Sexual Violence Resource Center (NSVRC). (2004). *Global perspectives on sexual violence: Findings from the world report on violence and health*. Enola, PA: National Sexual Violence Resource Center.

23. World Health Organization. (2014). *Global status report on violence prevention 2014*. Geneva: World Health Organization.

24. World Health Organization. (2014). *Global status report on violence prevention 2014*. Geneva: World Health Organization.

25. United Nations Office on Drugs and Crime. (2009). World Drug Report. https://www.unodc.org/documents/wdr/WDR_2009/WDR2009_eng_web.pdf.

26. This endnote has two references:

1) Laczko, F., & E. M. Gozdziak, eds. (2005). *Data and research on human trafficking: A global survey. International Migration*, *43*(1–2). SAGE Publications.

2) Estes, R. J., & N. A. Weiner. (2001). *The commercial sexual exploitation of children in the US, Canada and Mexico*. University of Pennsylvania, School of Social Work, Center for the Study of Youth Policy.

27. Federal Bureau of Investigation. (2010). Crime in the United States, 2006. https://ucr.fbi.gov/crime-in-the-u.s/2006.

28. US Department of State. (2014, June). *Trafficking in persons report 2014*. http://www.state.gov/j/tip/rls/tiprpt/2014/.

29. US Department of State. (2010). *Trafficking in persons report 2010*. p. 340. http://www.state.gov/j/tip/rls/tiprpt/2010/.

30. This endnote has two references:

1) Hepburn, S., & R. J. Simon. (2001). Hidden in plain sight: Human trafficking in the United States. *Gender Issues*, *27*(1–2), 1–26.

2) Newton, P. J., T. M. Mulcahy, & S. E. Martin. (2008). *Finding victims of human trafficking*. University of Chicago, National Opinion Research Center.

31. US Department of Health and Human Services. (2009). The campaign to rescue and restore victims of human trafficking: About human trafficking. http://www.acf.hhs.gov/trafficking/about/index.html#wwd.

32. Trafficking Victims Protection Act (TVPA). (2000). Pub. L. No. 106-386, 114 Stat. 1473.

33. Trafficking Victims Protection Reauthorization Act (TVPRA). (2003). Pub. L. No. 108-193, 117 Stat. 2875.

34. Trafficking Victims Protection Reauthorization Act (TVPRA). (2005). Pub. L. No. 109-164.

35. William Wilberforce Trafficking Victims Protection Reauthorization Act of 2008. (2008, December 23). Public Law 110–457.

36. H.R.898—Trafficking Victims Protection Reauthorization Act of 2013, 113th Congress (2013–2014).

37. Logan, T. K., R. Walker, & G. Hunt. (2009). Understanding human trafficking in the United States. *Trauma, Violence, & Abuse*, *10*(1), 3–30.

38. William Wilberforce Trafficking Victims Protection Reauthorization Act of 2008. (2008, December 23). Public Law 110–457.

39. This endnote has two references:

1) Newton, P. J., T. M. Mulcahy, & S. E. Martin. (2008). *Finding victims of human trafficking*. University of Chicago, National Opinion Research Center.

2) Hepburn, S., & R. J. Simon. Hidden in plain sight: Human trafficking in the United States. *Gender Issues, 27*(1–2), 1–26.

40. Logan, T. K., R. Walker, & G. Hunt. Understanding human trafficking in the United States. *Trauma, Violence, & Abuse, 10*(1), 3–30.

41. Siskin, A., & L. Sun Wyler. (2013, February 19). *Trafficking in persons: US policy and issues for congress*. Washington, DC: Congressional Research Service.

42. Clawson, H. J., M. Layne, & K. Small. (2006). *Estimating human trafficking into the United States: Development of a methodology*. Document no. 215475. US Department of Justice. Unpublished.

43. This endnote has two references:

1) Alvarez, M. B., & E. J. Alessi. (2012). Human trafficking is more than sex trafficking and prostitution: Implications for social work. *Affilia, 27*(2), 142–152.

2) Clawson, H. J., N. Dutch, A. Solomon, & L. Goldblatt Grace. (2009). *Human trafficking into and within the United States: A review of the literature*. Washington, DC: Office of the Assistant Secretary for Planning and Evaluation, US Department of Human and Health Services.

44. US Attorney's Office District of Massachusetts. (2016, May 17). Boston man sentenced to ten years in prison for child sex trafficking. https://www.justice.gov/usao-ma/pr/boston-man-sentenced-ten-years-prison child-sex-trafficking.

45. Federal Bureau of Investigation. (2014, July 22). Ohio man sentenced to 30 years in prison for labor trafficking and related crimes. https://www.fbi.gov/contact-us/field-offices/cleveland/news/press-releases/ohio-man-sentenced-to-30-years-in-prison-for-labor-trafficking-and-related-crimes.

46. Moisés, N. (2005). *Illicit: How smugglers, traffickers, and copycat are hacking the global economy*. New York: Doubleday.

47. Brewer, D. (2008). Globalization and human trafficking. *Tropical Research Digest: Human Rights and Human Welfare*, 46–56.

48. Brewer, D. (2008). Globalization and human trafficking. *Tropical Research Digest: Human Rights and Human Welfare*, 46.

49. Brewer, D. (2008). Globalization and human trafficking. *Tropical Research Digest: Human Rights and Human Welfare*, 46–56.

50. Plant, R. (2008). Forced labor: Critical issues for U.S. business leaders. Paper prepared for the conference on "Engaging business: Addressing forced labor," Atlanta, Georgia. International Labor Organization.

51. Trafficking Victims Protection Act (TVPA). (2000). Pub. L. No. 106-386, 114 Stat. 1473.

52. International Labor Organization. (2002). *Every child counts: New global estimates on child labor*. Geneva, Switzerland: International Labor Office.

53. Bureau of Labor Statistics. (2001). *Youth employment in the United States*. http://www.bls.gov/opub/mlr/2001/08/art2exc.htm.

54. ILO. (2012). *ILO global estimate of forced labor: Results and methodology*. ILO Publications.

55. U.S. Department of Labor's Bureau of International Labor Affairs (2011) U.S. Department of Labor's 2011 Findings on the Worst Forms of Child Labor. Child Labor Coalition announces Top 10 Child Labor Stories of 2011. https://www.dol.gov/ilab/reports/pdf/2011tda.pdf.

56. Child Labor Coalition. (2007). http://www.nclnet.org/child_labor_coalition_content.

57. Clawson, H. J., N. Dutch, A. Solomon, & L. Goldblatt Grace. (2009). *Human trafficking into and within the United States: A review of the literature.* Washington, DC: Office of the Assistant Secretary for Planning and Evaluation, US Department of Human and Health Services.

58. Polaris Project Fact Sheet. (2012). https://polarisproject.org/resources/human-trafficking-trends-2007-2012.

59. Aronowitz, A. A. (2001). Smuggling and trafficking in human beings: The phenomenon, the markets that drive it, and the organisations that promote it. *European Journal on Criminal Policy and Research,* 9(2), 163–195.

60. Clawson, H. J., N. Dutch, A. Solomon, & L. Goldblatt Grace. (2009). *Human trafficking into and within the United States: A review of the literature.* Washington, DC: Office of the Assistant Secretary for Planning and Evaluation, US Department of Human and Health Services.

61. Bales, K. (2012). *Disposable people: New slavery in the global economy.* University of California Press.

62. ILO. (2012). *ILO global estimate of forced labor: Results and methodology.* ILO Publications.

63. Clawson, H. J., Dutch, N., Solomon, A., & Grace, L. G. (2009). Human trafficking into and within the United States: A review of the literature. *Washington, DC: Office of the Assistant Secretary for Planning and Evaluation, US Department of Human and Heath Services.*

64. Estes, R. J., & N. A. Weiner. (2001). *The commercial sexual exploitation of children in the US, Canada and Mexico.* University of Pennsylvania, School of Social Work, Center for the Study of Youth Policy.

Chapter 4

Conceptual Frameworks to Explain and Understand Trafficking in Persons

Chapter Objectives

This chapter provides a comprehensive understanding of the following theories to explain human trafficking:

- Introduction: Trafficking in Persons: Theories
- Trafficking in Persons: A Multidimensional Crime and Multiple Explanations
- The Need for a Conceptual Framework
- Trafficking in Persons and Globalization
  - Push and Pull Factors
  - Trafficking in Persons and Capitalism Theory: Globalization
  - Trafficking in Persons and Economic Theory of Value
  - Trafficking in Persons and Capitalism Theory
  - Trafficking in Persons and Industrial Capitalism
  - Trafficking in Persons and Migration
- Trafficking in Persons: Process
- Trafficking in Persons and Theories of Victimization
  - Trafficking in Persons and Victim Precipitation Theory
  - Trafficking in Persons and Lifestyle Theory
  - Trafficking in Persons and Deviant Place Theory
  - Trafficking in Persons and Rational Choice Theory
  - Trafficking in Persons and Anomie Theory

- Trafficking in Persons and Conflict Theory
- Trafficking in Persons and General Strain Theory
- Trafficking in Persons and Trauma Theory

Introduction: Trafficking in Persons: Theories

Although the study of human trafficking as a part of higher education curriculum is an emerging field, it has been the subject of discussion for quite some time among higher education curriculum developers. It began with the inclusion of human trafficking in the form of one- or two-week lectures into existing courses. However, it did not take long for this one-to-two-week lecture inclusion to flourish into a subject area on its own. Presently, this heightened interest in human trafficking as an area of study has been incorporated into school, college, and university curricula. An interest in studying trafficking in persons as an academic discipline has increased since the early 1990s. In 1994, the International Organization for Migration (IOM) defined human trafficking as "the facilitation for money of largely voluntary illegal migration," a definition that today would adequately describe the term "human smuggling."[1] Since the UN Palermo Protocol clarified what trafficking in persons entails and how it is different from human smuggling, it has come to mean a coercive and exploitative "forced" crossing of international borders.

Burgeoning interest in the subject and its inclusion in academic curricula has resulted in a significant amount of literature in the form of written reports, books, movies, monographs, documentaries, and articles. These are excellent resources—the majority are descriptive explanations of human trafficking based on the observations made by the authors or based on the stories told by survivors, victims, offenders, and/or crusaders. These accounts, in some cases, may be supplemented with news media in form of news, documentaries, reports, movies, and videos, etc. However, this expanding literature has not translated into development of an effective conceptual framework for understanding human trafficking. Apart from the description of processes, practices, routes, and the exploitation and torture that victims suffer at the hands of the traffickers, there has not been any recognized conceptual framework for understanding human trafficking.[2] Such a lack of theoretical framework impedes comprehension of critical concepts and rudimentary features of the environment that lead to the inception, existence, proliferation, and perpetuation of trafficking in persons, despite national and international endeavors to control and prevent it. There have not been any established conceptual frameworks explaining what causes human trafficking, what induces these slave-like conditions, or why it persists.

Trafficking in Persons: A Multidimensional Crime and Multiple Explanations

Trafficking in persons is a multidimensional crime occurring both between and within nations.[3] Human trafficking as a crime is ubiquitous in nature—it affects virtually every country in every region of the world. It is a global crime that transcends all geographical and demographic boundaries. It engenders conditions of modern-day slavery and severe human rights violations where victims are exploited for economic gain. In many situations, victims are trapped into abusive and exploitative predicaments due to their economic, emotional, geographical, and other situational vulnerabilities. They are unable to free themselves from these tortuous conditions. It is an enterprise that violates basic human rights and deprives a significant proportion of the world's population of their rights to life and liberty in order to make profits. The majority of the people who fall prey to the fraudulent, cruel, and innovative ploys of the traffickers are socially, economically, and politically vulnerable and come from marginalized segments of the society. Its pervasive and multidimensional disposition presents challenges in ascertaining the roots of its inception and the factors that allow it to perpetuate. It appears in myriad forms and silently penetrates the society. It happens right in front of us and yet most of us do not recognize it. It is illegal everywhere but it happens everywhere. The complicated nature of this crime makes its identification and apprehension difficult.

A general assumption is that economic, social, and legal factors contribute to the facilitation of trafficking in persons. These factors contribute in making it easy for the traffickers to entice and entrap unsuspecting individuals who may be looking for an opportunity to better themselves. Traffickers buy and trade people and collect financial profits. They carefully target those who have dysfunctional family histories, have no or little education, are homeless, and live in poverty-stricken developing countries with limited knowledge or access to the basic resources necessary for life. They also target those who have already been victims of sexual, mental, and or physical abuse.

By some accounts, trafficking in persons is a global crisis that is inextricably linked to the current move of globalization. Greed coupled with maximum profit and minimum investment is the driving force that perpetuates trafficking enterprises—be it labor, sex, or body parts and organs. Social and economic vulnerabilities impel people to consent to working in less than ideal environments, and sometimes to sell themselves and/or their family members in labor and sex bondage. Victims are exploited in a myriad of enterprises, including labor, sex, body parts, and organs—to name a few.

The Need for a Conceptual Framework

A conceptual/theoretical framework is an essential element for understanding human trafficking and developing effective strategies for reducing it and preventing it from perpetuating. A framework should be able to examine the crime of human trafficking as a process as well as an act. It should be able to integrate a complex array of factors considered necessary to better understand these crimes. Human trafficking is a complex issue and difficult to conceptualize. It is difficult to separate the act from the process and the offense from the offender. Since trafficking in persons is an emerging area of research, there are no specific theories that have been used to explain trafficking in persons and its aftermath. In this chapter, we use the existing theories to explain human trafficking as an event as well as a process. Here we discuss theories of crime that help us understand trafficking as a crime as well as the nature of trafficker. We begin with the theories that are associated with economic and political developments such as globalization, capitalism, and industrialization. Then we move into the theories that explain crime using social and personal variables such as culture, poverty, victimization, education level, and other related aspects of society and people.

Trafficking in Persons and Globalization

Push and Pull Factors

The existing literature on trafficking in persons provides enough information to speculate what factors in a social, cultural, and economic environment propel and which ones curtail vulnerability to trafficking. These are known as mitigating and aggravating factors and classified as push and pull factors in literature.[4] Push factors describe the supply side—potential victims awaiting opportunities to offer their services. Their desperation and eagerness to move out of poverty propels them towards traffickers. Social and economic vulnerabilities intensify their susceptibility. Disadvantaged or marginalized social groups are highly vulnerable to being entrapped by traffickers. These factors include poverty, marginalized social and economic status, traditional and cultural practices, lack of education, lack of employment opportunities, political and economic instability—in form of political and ethnic wars, discrimination based policies, and natural disasters displacing people and forcing them to migrate to safer places—among many others. These factors propel people towards traffickers readily and eagerly waiting to receive and exploit them. The pull factors, on the other hand, represent the "demand" side of trafficking—such as the need for cheap, submissive labor; commercialization and the sex industry; low-risk, high-profile trade; easy and fast means of travel and/or transportation; poor enforcement of international treaties and policies on legal rights and protection for trafficked victims; and victims' perceptions of a better life away from their homes.[5]

Trafficking in Persons and Capitalism Theory: Globalization

Capitalism theory in the context of globalization seems to demonstrate the normalcy of exploitation of labor—thus, in a sense, justifying the inception, existence, perpetuation, and proliferation of trafficking in persons as an act as well as a process. An understanding of the main principles of globalization abridges this conceptual justification. Globalization expands economic markets, leading to a rise in demand for cheap labor. It also shrinks the world—bringing the diverse and distant parts of the world together—leading to the expanded market with an ever-expanding supply of labor. Such a high and insatiable demand for cheap labor and ready and often surplus supply of such labor breeds and perpetuates trafficking in persons. In a globalized world market, trafficking in persons takes the form of any trade where fundamental services—in the form of labor, sex, or coerced donation or removal of body parts—are exchanged for some type of compensation. The existence of a relationship between supply and demand indicates that trafficking in persons for labor and sex exploitation or other purposes can most directly be addressed from an economic standpoint. An economic system that promotes human greed and labels money and power as most important aspects of one's success and status in society leads people to exploit those who are in vulnerable positions. People in harsh economic settings are more vulnerable to the deceptive tactics of traffickers and from these harsh economic backdrops originate most victims.

Trafficking in Persons and Economic Theory of Value

According to economic theory of value, profit is the driver behind capitalist production. This theory purports that a capitalist buys individual labor with an understanding that the capitalist has the right to make use of the bought labor for a particular period of time in order for the capitalist to keep making profits and ensuring that the workers receive wages. The capitalist is able to exploit the worker in order to pay the worker and gain profits, which in the form of surplus value, is also known as unpaid labor,[6] so as to continue paying the worker, expanding capital gains, and replacing and/or hiring workers to continue the business. Thus, according to this theory, trafficking of persons for exploitation in labor, sex, or other operations emerges as an integral part of globalization and economics.[7] For globalization to yield its promised outcomes in form of economic prosperity, the use of infinite cheap and surplus labor to satiate the ever-growing need and demand for such labor is normal. It is also within the normed expectations of globalization as a system in order to maintain the anticipated prosperity in the globalized shrunken world—where trafficking is not only normal but in fact a necessity. Thus, it facilitates and stimulates its inception, existence, perpetuation, and proliferation. Some of the byproducts of globalization, including quintessential expeditious human migration, international trade, rapid movements of capital, and integration of financial markets, also assist in fostering interdependence between states for commerce and facilitating the transfer of commodities for maximized production at the lowest cost. Globalization inadvertently leads to the objectification and exploitation of humans for economic ends and the result is human trafficking. Since the main objective is profit and profits are based on supply and demand, a high demand for cheap labor by multinational corporations in developed countries automatically translates into trafficking and exploitation of desperate workers who, in turn, are subjected to a lifetime of slave-like conditions.

Trafficking in Persons and Capitalism Theory

Capitalism theory demonstrates that labor exploitation—or what we may call trafficking in persons for labor—is an integral element of capitalism theory. Its very existence is contingent upon surplus value which is a byproduct of labor exploitation. Capitalism theory in the context of globalization can be used to explain human trafficking. Technology has shrunk distances and condensed the world into a global community ruled by profit. In this condensed, globalized community, relocation of people, both voluntary and coerced, has become more prevalent than ever before—almost commonplace. The world is integrated into "one capitalist political economy operating under a neo-liberal free market ideology" marked by "disintegration, deregulation, denationalization, disinvestment and digitalization."[8] Whereas globalization has disseminated practices, values, technology, and other human products throughout the globe[9] and created a borderless global economy reinforced by free trade, free flow of capital, and tapping of cheaper foreign labor markets, it has also been an instrumental force in facilitating and perpetuating trafficking in persons and intensified impoverishment, social disparities, insecurity, fragmentation of society, and violation of human rights and human dignity. In a globalized world and industrial capitalism, trafficking in persons translates into the commodification of human beings and the objective is profit—in simple terms, providing compensation for services which both parties have consented to exchange. Administration of such an agreement ensures trafficking of persons for profit by any means and for any purpose—including labor, sex, organs, and body parts. The structure of capitalist society propagates trafficking in persons as a crime committed by organizations due to the increased need for profit in a competitive economic environment[10] where there is an immense supply of cheap (surplus) labor.

Trafficking in Persons and Industrial Capitalism

Industrial capitalism is an economic system that allows breeding and proliferation of maximized profits with the minimized investment. It flourishes on the economic concept of high demand and surplus supply to attain maximum output with minimum input. Trafficking in persons thrives on an economic system that promotes industrial capitalism. Its emerging trend of commodification of human beings fuels the growth of human trafficking market. The capitalistic roots of trafficking in persons stem from an apparent existence of a ready supply of surplus labor in the globalized market to satiate the ever-increasing desire, of buyers as well as sellers, to make more and more profits. On the part of capitalists, it translates into exploitation of the available people who are ready to provide that labor, and on part of the suppliers of labor (potential victims), it translates into compliance with the demands of the capitalists (traffickers) to maintain jobs in an environment where jobs are scarce. Easy and fast travel as well as increased immigration rates and the offers of incredibly irresistible opportunities for better life and better money by the traffickers to vulnerable populations have contributed to the growth of market for profit in human trafficking.

In capitalism, consent and coercion, and freedom and force go hand in hand and alternate their places—each one is necessary for trafficking to continue. For example, in this system, workers are made to believe that the wealth, accumulated in the hands of the capitalists (a minority) will sooner or later be redistributed among all the workers. Thus, the workers are motivated to comply and work intensively without asking questions—even under horrendous conditions—in order to enable the employers to accumulate wealth, with the hope that sooner or later workers will be rewarded for their work and dedication.[11] However, that never happens. According to the capitalist theory, the ultimate goal of capitalism is not the redistribution of wealth but its accumulation and concentration.

According to the liberal capitalist theory, one's property represents a sacrosanct extension of oneself, to be disposed of according to personal predilection, and protected as if part of one's person. John Locke, in his famous phrase "everyone has right to 'life, liberty and estate,'" implying that an individual is free to sell one's "estate," or indeed to buy from someone else, so long as both parties exchange consensually and without their liberty being infringed upon by force or coercion,[12] may have very well predicted the inception, perpetuation, and proliferation of trafficking in persons. Under capitalism, labor/work is a property-like commodity to be bought and sold like any other inanimate object. From this perspective—provided the worker can freely consent to the sale of his labor-power, without being subjected by the capitalist to force or coercion—nothing untoward is said to have taken place, and the labor-capital exchange can be formalized in contract, precisely as one does, for instance, with the sale of a house.[13] According to the capitalism theory, globalization as well as the dynamics of particular industries engender an environment where people's dependence on money and markets for subsistence creates a ready supply of eager and desperate workers vulnerable to serious exploitation. Simultaneously, it creates intensified demand for cheap labor and facilitates recruitment and transfer of such labor—leading to the potential victims accepting offers made by traffickers.

Globalization has expanded the economic market. Both employers and employees have access to advertising, buying, and selling of their services and products anywhere in the world. This encourages capitalists to look for labor and services where they are in surplus supply and cheap to acquire. On the other hand, people looking for jobs want to try their luck in those countries where there is a high demand for their labor and better pay. However, legal avenues for migration and work permits are restrictive. In some cases, people (potential victims) looking for employment are eager to offer their services where there is a demand but cannot get there fast and are afraid to be left behind. They get restless and desperate. These desperate people, eager to provide their services for money, start searching for brokers, recruitment, travel, and other service providing agencies. During their search, they may stumble upon advertisements, and actual traffickers or their agents, that inform them of places and persons who can help them get those jobs. Their eagerness and desperation, most often, lands them right in the trap of the traffickers.

Other times, private recruitment agencies, intermediaries and employers may take advantage of this situation and lure potential migrants into exploitative employment.[14] Often, traffickers pose as recruiters for large nationally and internationally reputable companies. They advertise false job opportunities as waitresses, models, nannies, dishwashers, and maids; false marriage proposals; and false educational opportunities, among other forms of deception.[15] Literature suggests that although lack of education is one of the significant variables that increases probability for a person to fall prey to the traffickers' tactics, people with a diverse range of educational levels, including some with graduate degrees, have also succumbed to the deceptive and enticing offers made by the conniving traffickers.

People at the margins of the global economy, regardless of their level of education, often choose to adventure and apply for such advertised opportunities. In some cases, applicants knowingly submit themselves to such exploitation as the least-worst option among their very limited set of alternatives. This includes many of those identified as victims of trafficking, slavery, and forced labor, who had initially consented and submitted their services willingly to their traffickers and exploiters, rather than being tricked or kidnapped—making traffickers' job easy. Review the following case in Box 1.

Box 1: Case of a Sri-Lankan Woman

Karin, a young mother of two, was looking for a job in Sri Lanka when a man befriended her and convinced her that she could land a better job in Singapore as a waitress. He arranged and paid for her travel. A Sri Lankan woman met Karin upon arrival in Singapore, confiscated her passport, and took her to a hotel. The woman made it clear that Karin had to submit to prostitution to pay back the money it cost her to be flown into Singapore. Three months after her arrival, [she] was arrested by the Singaporean police during a raid on the brothel. She was deported to Sri Lanka.

Source: US Department of State, Victim Stories: Singapore, 2005. https://2001-2009.state.gov/g/tip/c16482.htm.

Sometimes, traffickers (recruiters) advertise and are not subtle about their expectations. One of the advertisements in a Kyiv (Ukraine) newspaper read:

> Girls: Must be single and very pretty. Young and tall. We invite you to work as models, secretaries, dancers, choreographers, gymnasts. Housing is supplied. Foreign posts available. Must apply in person.[16]

Howard Neil (2015) postulates that international policymakers and global civil society are realizing that "human trafficking, slavery and forced labor are not anomalies perpetuated by a few 'bad apple' employers. Rather, such severe labor exploitation is an endemic feature of the contemporary global economy." Howard states, "... from slavery and trafficking in the production of shrimp in Thailand to artisanal cheese and clothing made by US prison labor, forced labor plays a significant role in commodity production, as well as care, domestic, and sex work." According to him, "poverty and globalization are indeed fundamental for the rise and proliferation of seriously exploitative labor." He discusses some examples of such transactions where consent and coercion become blurred and difficult to separate. Some of his examples are discussed here.

For example, consider a situation in which a mother feels an obligation to feed and take care of her children but has no means of so doing. Out of desperation, "she has to accept the proposal of a 'trafficker' who promises to feed her children only if she'll commit to a period of sexual servitude. She accepts the offer and is able to feed and take care of her children. In this case, did she consent or was she coerced? If she was coerced, then who is guilty of coercion here? And where is the line between freedom and force?" Is the woman who willingly "accepted the offer and sold herself in sexual servitude" a victim of trafficking or an employee who willingly accepted the offer, knowing very well that she is expected to be exploited and serve as a sex slave? Or in another example, "... a farmer, who is so indebted, as a result of trying to keep his family afloat, ... agrees to sell himself into slavery-like debt-bondage in order to pay off what he owes? Is his contract illegitimate simply because we find it morally unpleasant, and even though he has offered his consent?"[17]

Many a time, marginalized classes (as discussed above) have limited or no opportunities within their reach. For survival, they actually seek brokers, agents, or others who may promise to assist them to get a job that will pay them even if it means exploitation. They opt for such opportunities and accept these knowing very well of the forthcoming exploitation, as they know the alternative is not having any opportunity. They believe "exploitation" to be a better option than "starvation." They consent and accept manipulative treatment in exchange for an opportunity to take care of themselves and/or family. Thus, in globalized world, consent, contract, coercion, and exploitation become muddled terms, making it harder to understand, address, determine, and distinguish employment from exploitation.

Trafficking in Persons and Migration

According to Salt and Stein (1997) human trafficking, especially international trafficking involving movement across borders, can be explained as a profit-maximizing endeavor in the context of migration. They contend that trafficking serves as an intermediary of the global migration business. It facilitates movement of people and goods between origin and destination countries with relative ease. The model is divided into three stages: the recruitment and transportation of new recruits/applicants; their movement en route; and their insertion and integration into labor markets and host societies of destination countries.[18]

Trafficking in Persons: Process

In order to understand the explanation of trafficking, it is imperative to understand the process of trafficking in persons. This process involves several steps. Trafficking begins with recruitment and transportation. In this phase, traffickers gather information on sites where potential victims congregate and reside, their social and economic vulnerabilities, stakeholders of the communities they reside in, and laws regarding movement and transportation of people and goods. Next, they devise recruitment strategies—such as advertisements, intermediary friends and businesses, identification of potential victims willing to comply, and organizing travel visas and other documents. Traffickers have a vested interest in convincing potential victims of the benefits of the job offer. Their advertisements and sale promotion techniques provide a façade of authenticity and legitimacy. They have brochures and pamphlets describing the process and breakdown of costs and benefits. Recruiters use a variety of techniques to manipulate and entrap potential victims. Some traffickers openly advertise about their hiring needs and others use some euphemistic advertisements. For example, some traffickers use local newspapers to advertise information about opportunities in foreign countries for "dancers," "waitresses," or "call girls." Applicants are given a contact or website to provide their profile to match them with the available job opportunities. Other times, prospective job seekers (potential victims) on their own seek services of intermediaries—who often are traffickers—to assist them in the process of finding jobs and travel.

Traffickers use a variety of means of transportation and equipment to transport potential victims. They may use transportation means—in the form of trucks, pickups, buses, ships, speed boats, and airplanes. They collaborate with different travel agencies to arrange for transportation of the recruits. Traffickers also need the assistance of document forgers to arrange for adequate documentation and for the enforcement of procedures. They collaborate with forgers to provide falsified passports and entry visas, fake marriage certificates, false work contracts with multinational firms and shipping companies, or false documents relating to studies at universities and colleges, requests for family reunions, or visits for medical treatment. Traffickers make sure that the potential job seekers understand that they are responsible for their travel, living, and other necessary expenses. So, they either pay in advance in cash or mortgage their assets in form of a signed contract or verbal agreement. The potential job seekers understand that there is no guarantee of success and there is "no return" policy on their passports, identity cards, and other documents which they must forfeit to the traffickers on arrival at the destination. They also sign a document certifying that they will pay all the costs, will not talk or complain to any authorities, and will accept jobs in sectors selected by the network with no right to complain (for example, prostitution for girls, manual labor for men). The potential victims also understand that any of the broken promises will generate police arrest and deportation, and in fact may also result in death by accident.

Transporting would-be workers and victims involves a careful and coordinated preparation. It involves a clear set of organizational roles for the management of migrants while travelling to their destinations. Immigration policies of the origin and destination countries; the distance between the origin and destination; the political, legal, and social environment of the destination; and border and port security in the origin and destination countries are some of the significant factors that determine the routes and plans of transportation. It is an organized venture managed by collaboration of many actors from several agencies and entities. The traffickers establish contacts with corrupt officials, border patrol officers, law enforcement agencies, and other pertinent agencies and try to smuggle the potential workers through bribing. Some reach their final destination in days while others may take months and years, depending upon the distance, route taken, and the availability of corrupt law enforcement authorities.

The final stage involves their insertion and integration into labor markets of the destination country. Once the victims reach their destinations, traffickers strip them of their identifying documents, isolate them, and take them to the places where they can start working and making profits for the traffickers.

Trafficking in Persons and Theories of Victimization

Frances and Zhilina (2010) propose that the victimization theory of domestic violence may be applied to explain human trafficking at least partially—especially where the victims are females and they are sexually exploited. They suggest that given the fact that the victims of trafficking are significantly similar to the victims of domestic violence, it is worthwhile to use victimization theory to explain trafficking in persons' victimization. They propose to employ the victimization theory of domestic violence to comprehend why sex trafficking victims may stay in abusive and life-threatening situations and explain how and why criminal justice agencies may find it difficult to "identify victims who may have initially agreed to leave their homes upon false promises of legitimate jobs and education and why victims may be very reticent to assist with any law enforcement efforts on their behalf." Consistent with victimization theory, victims of trafficking may suffer in silence and be unwilling to report or seek help as they may have convinced themselves that they have to live/suffer the consequences of their actions since they believe that their situation is what they "agreed to" or what they "deserve." They suggest that if "enforcement barriers to anti-trafficking laws are to be overcome, then victim risk assessment, vulnerability assessment, gender inequality, immigration fears, and fears of criminal justice system personnel need to be understood in the context of how existing legislation may help legal and social service agencies work together to combat trafficking." In order to effectively address trafficking in persons, assist victims, and prosecute perpetrators, it is essential that the social and political conditions of the areas where victims reside are identified and the reasons that dissuade them from coming forward and cooperating with the authorities are understood so as to develop a local as well as globalized coordinated response.[19]

Trafficking in Persons and Victim Precipitation Theory

The victim precipitation theory can be applied to explain the inception, existence, perpetuation, and proliferation of trafficking in persons as a crime. According to victim precipitation theory, often victims are responsible for their victimization, at least partially if not wholly. This theory suggests the victim him/herself initiates a contact and agrees to participate in the activity that may eventually lead to victimization. In trafficking situations, literature suggests, people are desperately searching for opportunities to improve their standard of living, to get away from the place that has limited employment or advancement opportunities, or to get away from a place where they believe they are unhappy, politically and personally repressed, or victimized in some other aspect. They are on the lookout for opportunities, places, or persons that can facilitate their search and assist them in accomplishing their goals. When they are unable to find legal means of accomplishing their goals, they seek assistance from brokers, recruitment and travel service providing agencies, or the like.[20] In most cases, they find traffickers awaiting such eagerness and desperation. They are not only willing to assist them but they convince them that with their help, their dreams and anticipated lifestyle are within their easy reach. They convince them that they will help them accomplish their goals. The potential victims

Box 2: Case of Victimization Initiated by the Victim's Family

At the age of 15, Nasreen's family sent her to live with her uncle in New York after experiencing severe financial troubles at home in Central Asia. Before she arrived, her uncle promised her that he would register her for school and she would work for him part-time in his corner store. But when she arrived she was put straight to work. Nasreen was forced to do domestic work in her uncle's home all day, and he made her work as the cashier in his store until late every night. He never offered to pay her for her work and he insisted that she was selfish to want to continue her education.

Nasreen lived like this for two years, working long hours and experiencing constant verbal abuse from her uncle. Whenever Nasreen asked when she would be allowed to go to school, her uncle punished her by preventing her from speaking with her family back in her home country.

Source: "Examples of Human Trafficking." http://www.nyc.gov/html/endht/html/trafficking/studies.shtml.

willingly and happily begin their doomed journey into becoming victims of trafficking.

This theory suggests that, in most cases, the potential victims themselves initiate contact and agree to participate in the activities that may eventually lead to victimization. Precipitation on part of the victim can either be active or passive. Active precipitation exists when the victim knowingly accepts the offer and passive participation is when the victim participates in activities without being fully cognizant of the cost. In any case, the initial contact with the perpetrator is voluntarily made by the potential victim who was fully aware of what he/she is looking for and the subsequent activities and actions were also voluntarily accepted or in some cases even proposed by the victim. For example, review the following two cases. The case in Box 2 describes a case where family approached an uncle in New York and sought his assistance in educating their daughter and finding a job for her, as they were experiencing severe financial troubles at home in Central Asia. The uncle graciously and eagerly obliged and offered to help. He promised that he would register her for school and in her free time, she could work part-time for him in his corner store to gain experience. However, when the niece arrived, he changed his mind and she was put straight to work and exploited. She was never registered in any school.

Box 3 describes a case where a 15-year-old girl, "Alex," living in a group home and frustrated with her life there, was seeking an avenue to get out of the situation, which she believed was repressive. She assumed she had found means to get out of this wretched situation when she met a 31-year-old man—

Box 3: Case of Victimization Initiated by the Victim Herself

Alex was 15 years old and living in a group home in Queens when she met her boyfriend. She was frustrated with her life in the group home and felt that the workers only noticed her when she was doing something wrong. In contrast, David, her new 31-year-old boyfriend, showered her with love and attention. When he offered that she could move in with him, Alex didn't think twice. At first Alex loved living with David but soon their relationship grew violent and he began pressuring her to contribute financially. Alex knew David was struggling to support her and she wanted to help out but she didn't feel comfortable with his suggestion that she sleep with men for money. He argued that plenty of women do this and it would be a sign of her love for him. He said they needed the money in order to continue to be able to stay together in his apartment. If they lost the apartment she would have to go back to foster care, and he told her that they would place her in a locked facility because she had previously run away. Alex agreed to enter into prostitution and eventually wound up working on a well-known prostitution stroll. Sometimes outreach workers would come by and give the women who were working packs of condoms, while offering to talk with them about available services. Alex often thought about running away from David, especially after he beat her up. But where would she go? She didn't want to go back to foster care because she feared they would lock her up. She couldn't return to her old neighborhood in Queens, because David often told her what he would do to her if she ever left him, and he would know to find her there. Alex could not think of a safe place to run, and so she stayed.

Source: "Examples of Human Trafficking." http://www.nyc.gov/html/endht/html/trafficking/studies.shtml.

David was kind, gentle, and showed respect and affection towards her. She believed she was in love with him and he was her boyfriend. She was convinced that her ticket out of the group home was David, her new 31-year-old boyfriend, who showered her with love and attention. She approached him and he eagerly offered that she could move in with him. Alex immediately agreed. Soon after she moved in with Alex, David grew violent and began pressuring her to contribute financially and pay for her stay. He suggested that if she could not find any other paying job, then she should offer to sleep with other men to make money. When Alex did not like this idea, David convinced Alex that doing so would show her commitment to the relationship, and besides, many other girls of her age in similar situations engage in sex for money to maintain their lifestyles. He scared her with the real possibility of losing the relationship, apartment, and freedom, if she did not comply. He convinced her that her options were limited, as she could not go back anywhere, he was her only savior, and accepting his offer was the only way out. Alex was convinced that

David loved her and in order to maintain the relationship, she voluntarily agreed to be pimped out.

Both of these cases demonstrate that victims themselves initiated the actions that landed them into trafficking victimization situations. Although the victims were duped into agreeing to accept the conditions and to be readily available to provide services on demand by the traffickers and in both cases the victims were later coerced and forced into victimization—making them eligible to be certified as victims of trafficking in persons' crime—the theory of victim precipitation will purport that nobody else but the victims themselves are responsible for their situations and victimization. According to the TVPA and the United States they may be victims and eligible for services, but according to the victim precipitation theory, they brought it upon themselves.

Trafficking in Persons and Lifestyle Theory

Another theory that can be used to understand and explain trafficking in persons' inception, existence, perpetuation, and proliferation is lifestyle theory. This theory purports that victimization is a function of one's lifestyle—victimization probability varies by lifestyle, absence of capable guardians, the environment with which the potential victim interacts and the routine activities of the potential victim.[21] It states that crime is a function of an individual's chosen lifestyle and it is not random. According to this theory, certain lifestyles have a higher probability of exposing and tempting the potential victims to engage in activities that are more likely to increase the probability of victimization. Behaviors such as soliciting the services of intermediaries to assist in finding jobs, going into the professions of modeling or acting, going on websites to look for relationships, associating with certain type of individuals, and moving in with strangers—so-called "boyfriends"—or similar activities increase the probability of victimization.

According to this theory, people who choose high-risk lifestyles such as taking drugs, drinking, running away, or participating in similar deviant and/or criminal activities have a higher probability of becoming victims of trafficking. Runaways and abused and molested youth have a higher probability of being convinced by the traffickers' offer of a stable, safe, and loving environment and becoming entrapped in the web of trafficking. Young people, college students who want to maintain their glamorous lifestyle, and people in similar situations are more likely to be convinced by the traffickers' offers of high paying jobs and making easy money. Such people are easily duped into signing contracts

Box 4: Case of a Dancer and Stripper

Alena P. was a dancer and performer in Russia. She came to the United States on a visa for cultural performances to work in a theater troupe. When she arrived, she was taken to an apartment in New Jersey and told that she was to work as a stripper to pay off the debt that she accrued from coming to the United States. She was physically threatened and her passport was confiscated.

She worked for almost a year, only receiving about $50 a week that she had to use to pay for meals. Every day, her traffickers picked her up from an apartment, which she shared with other young women who also worked at the strip club, and brought her directly to work. She was not told how long she had to work there to pay off her debt. The total amount that she owed was not clear either because her traffickers deducted rent, transportation, and costume fees from her income.

Source: "Examples of Human Trafficking." http://www.nyc.gov/html/endht/html/trafficking/studies.shtml.

and moving in, and sometimes even leaving homes/hometowns/countries, with the traffickers.

Trafficking in Persons and Deviant Place Theory

Another theory that can be used to explain and understand victimization of trafficking in persons is the deviant place theory. This theory suggests that victims may not actively engage or solicit the help of perpetrators that may increase their chances of becoming trafficking victims. Rather, their probability of becoming a victim is enhanced because they live in areas that are disorganized and contain high crime rates. According to this theory, people living in such areas—which are termed "deviant places"—have the highest risk of coming into contact with traffickers. The extant literature on human trafficking, in form of reports and other research, points out that majority of the victims are from marginalized populations, residing in marginalized areas of the communities. Thus, using deviant place theory, it can be demonstrated that recruiters mostly go to the areas where they believe they will find potential victims—who are poor, frustrated, helpless, and entrapped in poverty—to recruit, awaiting their arrival and welcoming their offers and sometimes actually even paying them and rewarding them for their offers of assistance. The mere location of their residence makes them more vulnerable to victimization. Both cases presented in Boxes 4 and 5 demonstrate that sometimes the location where a person is, may influence and lead to enhanced probabilities for victimization. In the case of a dancer (presented in Box 4), she came to the United

Box 5: Case of a Runaway and Drug Addiction

John was 16 years old when he ran away from his home in Nebraska, hoping to see the country. He arrived in New York City and was quickly stranded once he ran out of money. He was sleeping on the streets and fell in with a group of older homeless youth who introduced him to injecting heroin. Within a few months, they also introduced him to some older men who would pay him for sexual favors so that he could afford the heroin that he now needed in order to get through the day.

Source: "Examples of Human Trafficking." http://www.nyc.gov/html/endht/html/trafficking/studies.shtml.

States with an expectation that she will be able to perform at better places for better pay and be part of the theater troupe, but the fact that she was a dancer and performed in bars and clubs in Russia increased her probability of being exploited and trafficked. She ended up being a stripper and working almost without any remuneration—the $50 she received barely paid for her stay, meals, and transportation. In most cases, potential victims may borrow money to finance their travel. Money advanced to the potential victims is from organized crime syndicates[22] entrapping victims in debt bondage as well.

In the case of a runaway youth, his desperation and drug addiction enhanced his likelihood of becoming a victim and exploited. He was pimped out to older men for sex. The fact that he was a runaway and homeless, sleeping on the streets, increased his vulnerability and made it easy for the traffickers to exploit him and pimp him out. His addiction to drugs and lack of self-esteem also contributed to his victimization.

Trafficking in Persons and Rational Choice Theory

According to the rational choice theory, criminals are rational beings whose decisions to commit crime are generally based on their rationalization of anticipated minimum costs and maximum benefits involved in the process of crime perpetration. According to this theory, the criminal decision making process is a function of free will requiring careful evaluation of the risks involved and the probability of successful commission of the planned crime.[23] This theory posits that victimization is not random; rather, criminals carefully evaluate who to victimize[24] so as to realize successful commission of the crime with minimum effort and to gain maximum benefits. This theory can be used to explain the rationale of the traffickers as well as the victims.

Traffickers carefully select potential victims. Knowing from their experiences and their associates, they target those who have dysfunctional family histories, lack education, and are homeless or live in poverty-stricken areas of the local or international communities, with limited knowledge of resources to begin living a normal life. They also identify people who are desperate and eager to snatch any offer of employment that will provide a way out of their miserable lives and communities. They may also target victims who have already been victims of physical, sexual, psychological, or other forms of abuse and who also don't have any sure means of escaping the torture. They cash in on potential victims with such mental, social, and economic situations and conditions. In all cases, victims' and traffickers' rationalizations are based on their understanding of a successful commission of the act which will bring them maximum benefits,

On the other hand, potential victims also evaluate and make decisions to participate after a careful evaluation of risks and benefits involved. To desperate people who believe they are trapped in situations where they perceive no opportunities to get out of their social and economic adversity, traffickers' offers may present some attractive alternatives to their marginalized lives. They may rationalize that even if they were to be working in situations that may be below their anticipated standards and actually involve exploitation, they will still make a lot of money. They believe traffickers' offers to be the only few options they may ever have to help themselves. So, after careful deliberation, they willingly consent to the offers. According to the rational choice theory, both traffickers and the would-be victims carefully evaluate, rationalize, and make decisions to participate in the act—implying that would-be victims knowingly and, in fact, after a careful deliberation make a decision to risk victimization—in very much the same fashion as criminals (traffickers) evaluate, rationalize, and make a decision to take a risk of apprehension if they were caught in the act of committing a crime.

Trafficking in Persons and Anomie Theory

Anomie theory posits that the common individualistic goal of "monetary success at all costs" encourages and facilitates an environment conducive to developing and using innovative ways of making profit. Often this innovation manifests in the form of criminal enterprises—such as trafficking. Limited opportunities to make fast money and the need for profit create an enormous amount of "strain." This "strain," coupled with cultural beliefs, politics, and external contingencies, thrusts individuals into such a psychological state that they view unethical behaviors as "normal way of life" and begin to believe it as a necessary step to reach the individualistic goal of "monetary success." The strong emphasis on economic prosperity, the materialistic focus of society and the need for monetary success at all costs overwhelm and overshadow individual and societal ethics. The four main tenets of the "American Dream"—achievement, individualism, universalism, and materialism—steer individuals into developing strategies for monetary success by any means necessary and regardless of the available opportunities.[25]

Trafficking in Persons and Conflict Theory

To some extent, conflict theories may be used to explain human trafficking as a crime of both types—labor and sex. The main explanatory variables in conflict theories are power and control. According to conflict theories, social, political, or material inequality among different groups allows the powerful to control activities and movements of those without any, or with little, power in their communities. Conflict theories premise that social inequality is created by the rich and powerful in order to maintain their own power and wealth. They create social structures that are geared towards maintaining the unequal distribution of power and wealth and blocking all possibilities of exit or upward mobility for poor classes. The people without power and money depend on the powerful to survive. The powerful have the authority to exploit and control the existing resources including human beings.[26]

Conflict theory can be applied to understand the thinking processes of traffickers and potential victims. For example, it purports that crime is a function of economic and social drives within a society. The potential victims feel marginalized in their current situations and are looking for ways and means of getting out of their situations. So, they start looking outside their close circles and seek the assistance of the people they believe will help them with their goal of moving out and moving up. There is a constant conflict between potential victims searching for ways of getting out of helpless and powerless situations and the traffickers making sure that does not happen. The traffickers have power and resources while the potential victims—who have no resources and no power—are dependent upon traffickers for survival. Thus, traffickers use their power to exploit groups with less power than themselves. Victims accept the offers given by traffickers hoping they will be helped. Unequal distribution of power relations in a community fuels control and exploitation, leading to the inception of trafficking in persons.

Traffickers are empowered further by the victims' acceptance of the offers. These offers give traffickers power to further strip the victims of any little power they have in the form of their identities tied to their families, traditions, and connections to their communities. So, now the traffickers have power, money, the victims' identity documents in the form of passports or other documentation, and have separated them from their families, traditions, and communities. Victims have no power or money to escape the situation they are trapped in. They willingly gave up the little power they may have had. Their only option is to work their way out. On the other hand, the traffickers have the power and means to make rules and control the victims and their families. They make every effort and manipulate to ensure that there is no exit or movement of the victims from a "without power" position to a "with power" position.

Trafficking in Persons and General Strain Theory

General strain theory may offer some help in understanding the dynamics of trafficking in persons and the attitude of the victims who may willing accept situations where they will be exploited and manipulated. According to Agnew (2007) "people engage in crime because they experience strains or stressors."[27] This concept of experiencing stress or stressors can be applied to understand victims' state of mind and their thinking process in accepting traffickers' offers of jobs or other opportunities happily and willingly (in some cases, even when they are fully aware of what is expected of them and the possibilities of exploitation). For example, when people feel trapped in poverty and desperate situations and believe that in their local communities, they do not have any chance of ever getting out of poverty, they may experience a range of negative emotions, including desperation, which leads them to traffickers. Most of the cases—both in labor and sex—demonstrate that people (potential victims) willingly accept traffickers' offers out of desperation and stay in those exploitative situations even when they are given opportunity to leave. They perceive traffickers' offers, even though exploitative, as better than the alternative of no offers. Thus, in order to relieve themselves of their stress, desperation, and other negative emotions, they accept job offers that may involve exploitation and manipulation on the part of the traffickers.

Trafficking in Persons and Trauma Theory

Trauma theory can also provide some help in understanding trafficking in persons as a crime as well as the state of mind and decision making process of the victims. Terr (1990) purports that "psychic trauma occurs when a sudden, unexpected, overwhelming intense emotional blow or a series of blows assault the person from outside. Traumatic events are external, but they quickly become incorporated into the mind."[28] Van der Kolk (1989, 2012) stated that "Traumatization occurs when both internal and external resources are inadequate to cope with external threat."[29] These definitions and statements imply that it is not the trauma in itself but rather it is the victim's reaction to the traumatic event that determines their response. In manipulating and maintaining power and control over the victims, traffickers use betrayal of their trust, pain, and punishment as instruments to inflict pain, fear, and trauma on the potential victims. As the trauma theory suggests, trauma victims "keep repeating the same destructive interpersonal behaviors without even recognizing the pattern of repetition and without acquiring the knowledge to manage the high emotions surrounding the change."[30] Victims and survivors of trauma experience flashbacks, body memories, post-traumatic nightmares, and behavioral reenactments. This is evident in victims of trafficking. The extant research shows that the victims are unwilling to ask for help or make efforts in escaping from trafficking situations, as they do not "recognize the pattern" and they do not acquire the knowledge to manage the situation. So, they keep staying in the situation. Just like victims of trauma, trafficking victims who survive and are rescued are also not able to forget about their experiences; they re-experience this trauma and the crime over and over, most often for the rest of their lives. Like trauma victims, trafficking victims also experience flashbacks, body memories, post-traumatic nightmares, and behavioral reenactments. Trauma theory can also be used to explain traffickers' tactics in maintaining control over victims through infliction of fear and trauma as well as victims' state of mind and decision making process. Such control hampers victims' ability to ask for help or accept any assistance. They stay in the situations.

Conclusion and Chapter Review

We have discussed the use of various existing theories to explain and understand trafficking both from traffickers' and victims' perspective. Based on the theories we used to explain trafficking in persons, it is fair to assume that social, cultural, and economic environment; a poor home environment; and the desire for a better life but lack of opportunities for such a desire to be fulfilled, coupled with traffickers' convincing arguments and offers to help, push people to willingly and knowingly move towards situations and accept to engage in activities that may lead to victimization. Figure 1 presents this relationship.

Figure 1: Social, Cultural, and Economic Environment and Trafficking in Persons Victimization

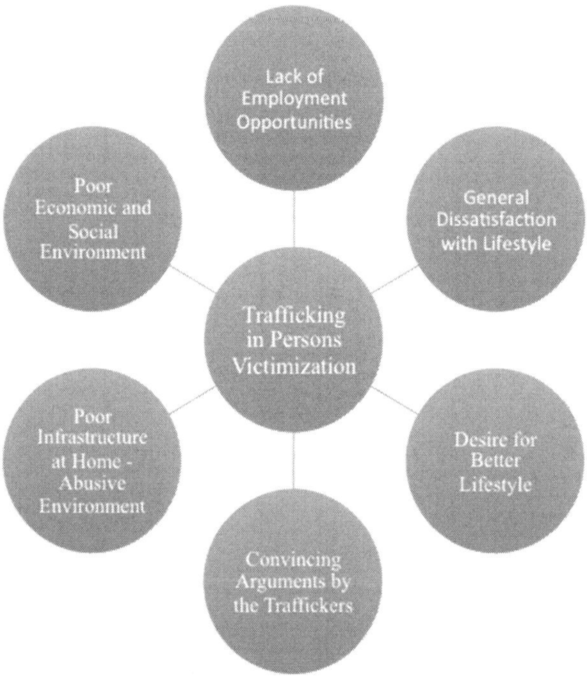

So, in essence, we discussed the following:

- Trafficking in Persons—A Multidimensional Crime and Multiple Explanations
- The Need for a Conceptual Framework
- Trafficking in Persons and Globalization
    - Push and Pull Factors
        - Trafficking in Persons and Capitalism Theory: Globalization
        - Trafficking in Persons and Economic Theory of Value
        - Trafficking in Persons and Capitalism Theory
        - Trafficking in Persons and Industrial Capitalism
        - Trafficking in Persons and Migration
        - Trafficking in Persons: Process
        - Trafficking in Persons and Theories of Victimization
        - Trafficking in Persons and Victim Precipitation Theory
        - Trafficking in Persons and Lifestyle Theory

- Trafficking in Persons and Deviant Place Theory
- Trafficking in Persons and Rational Choice Theory
- Trafficking in Persons and Anomie Theory
- Trafficking in Persons and Conflict Theory
- Trafficking in Persons and General Strain Theory
- Trafficking in Persons and Trauma Theory

Discussion Questions

1) Identify the theories that explain trafficking as a byproduct of globalization.

2) Discuss the role of victims in their victimization. Identify the theory that holds victims themselves are responsible for their victimization.

3) What are three pull and three push factors that propel trafficking victimization? Give examples.

4) How are fear and trauma used as mechanisms to control victims of trafficking?

5) Describe the similarities between the victims of trafficking and victims of domestic violence.

6) How does rational choice theory explain victims' response to trafficking? Discuss.

7) Find a trafficking in persons case as reported in one of the newspapers and discuss it.

References

Agnew, Robert. *Pressured into Crime: An Overview of General Strain Theory.* Oxford University Press, 2007.

Bales, Kevin. *Understanding Global Slavery: A Reader.* University of California Press, 2005.

Barnett, Randy E. "Review Essay/Public Decisions and Private Rights." *Criminal Justice Ethics* 3, no. 2 (1984): 50–62.

Barry, Kathleen. *Female Sexual Slavery.* NYU Press, 1984.

Bernat, Frances P., and Tatyana Zhilina. "Human Trafficking: The Local Becomes Global." *Women & Criminal Justice* 20, no. 1–2 (2010): 2–9.

Bloom, S. L. *Creating Sanctuary: Toward the Evolution of Sane Communities.* Routledge, 1997.

Bowe, John. *Nobodies: Modern American Slave Labor and the Dark Side of the New Global Economy.* Random House Incorporated, 2008.

Brown, Stephen Eugene, Finn-Aage Esbensen, and Gilbert Geis. *Criminology: Explaining Crime and Its Context.* Cincinnati: Anderson, 1998.

Bruckert, Chris, Colette Parent, and Royal Canadian Mounted Police. *Trafficking in Human Beings and Organized Crime: A Literature Review.* Research and Evaluation Branch, Community, Contract and Aboriginal Policing Services Directorate, Royal Canadian Mounted Police, 2002.

Howard, Neil. "On Capitalism and Coercion: Are Trafficking, Slavery and Forced Labour Actually Necessary for Maintaining Liberal Capitalism?" AlJazeera. April 18, 2014. http://www.aljazeera.com/indepth/opinion/2014/04/capitalism-coercion-2014417133923106962.html.

Howard, Neil. "Trafficking,' 'Slavery,' and 'Forced Labour'—Liberal Capitalism's (Un)Holy Trinity?" The GRaSe Blog. April 24, 2014. https://blogs.eui.eu/grase/trafficking-slavery-and-forced-labour-liberal-capitalisms-unholy-trinity.html.

Hughes, Donna M. "The Role of 'Marriage Agencies' in the Sexual Exploitation and Trafficking of Women from the Former Soviet Union." *International Review of Victimology* 11, no. 1 (2004): 49–71.

James, C. and Atler, S. *Highly Affected, Rarely Considered: The International Youth Parliament Commission's Report on the Impacts of Globalization on Young People.* Sydney: International Youth Parliament (lYP) Oxfam Community Aid Abroad, 2003.

Laczko, Frank. "Data and Research on Human Trafficking." *International Migration* 43, no. 1 2 (2005): 5–16.

Lanier, Mark M., Stuart Henry, and Desiré J. M. Anastasia. *Essential Criminology.* Perseus Books Group, 2014.

Lapon, Gary. "What Do We Mean by Exploitation?" SocialistWorker.org. September 19, 2016. https://socialistworker.org/2011/09/28/what-do-we-mean-exploitation.

Lebaron, Genevieve and Neil, Howard. "Introducing Beyond Slavery's Month on Forced Labour in the Global Political Economy." Open Democracy. February 16, 2015. https://www.opendemocracy.net/beyondslavery/genevieve-lebaron-neil-howard/introducing-beyond-slavery%E2%80%99s-month-on-forced-labour-in-g.

Lewis, W. Arthur. "Economic Development with Unlimited Supplies of Labour." *The Manchester School* 22, no. 2 (1954): 139–191.

Malarek, Victor. *The Natashas: Inside the New Global Sex Trade.* New York: Arcade Publishing, 2003.

Malarek, Victor. *The Natashas: The Horrific Inside Story of Slavery, Rape, and Murder in the Global Sex Trade.* Skyhorse Publishing Inc., 2011.

Messner, Steven F., and Richard Rosenfeld. *Crime and the American Dream.* Cengage Learning, 2012.

Messner, Steven F., and Richard Rosenfeld. "Political Restraint of the Market and Levels of Criminal Homicide: A Cross-National Application of Institutional-Anomie Theory." *Social Forces* 75, no. 4 (1997): 1393–1416.

Salt, John, and Jeremy Stein. "Migration as a Business: The Case of Trafficking." *International Migration* 35, no. 4 (1997): 467–494.

Skeldon, Ronald. "East Asian Migration and the Changing World Order." In *Population Migration and the Changing World Order.* 173. Chichester: John Wiley & Sons, 1994.

Terr, Lenore. *Too Sacred to Cry: Psychic Trauma in Childhood.* HarperCollins Publishers, 1990.

United Nations Global Initiative to Fight Human Trafficking. http://www.ungift.org/.

United States Agency for International Development. "Trafficking in Persons: USAID's Response." 2006.

Van der Hoven, A., and Alice Maree. "Victimisation Risk Factors, Repeat Victimisation and Victim Profiling." *Victimology in South Africa* (2005): 65.

Van der Kolk, Bessel A. "The Compulsion to Repeat the Trauma." *Psychiatric Clinics of North America* 12, no. 2 (1989): 389–411.

Van der Kolk, Bessel A., and Alexander C. McFarlane, eds. *Traumatic Stress: The Effects of Overwhelming Experience on Mind, Body, and Society.* Guilford Press, 2012.

Further Suggested Readings

Adepoju, Aderanti. "Review of Research and Data on Human Trafficking in Sub Saharan Africa." *International Migration* 43, no. 1 2 (2005): 75–98.

Akers, Timothy A., and Mark M. Lanier. "'Epidemiological Criminology': Coming Full Circle." *American Journal of Public Health* 99, no. 3 (2009): 397–402.

Andrews, Sara K. "US Domestic Prosecution of the American International Sex Tourist: Efforts to Protect Children from Sexual Exploitation." *The Journal of Criminal Law and Criminology* 94, no. 2 (2004): 415–454.

Bales, Kevin. *Disposable People: New Slavery in the Global Economy*. Berkeley: University of California Press, 1999.

Bales, Kevin. Presentation at the University of Central Florida. January 15, 2009.

Bales, Kevin, and Steven Lize. "Trafficking in Persons in the United States." Croft Institute for International Studies, University of Mississippi. 2005.

Bales, Kevin, and Zoe Trodd, eds. *To Plead Our Own Cause: Personal Stories by Today's Slaves*. Cornell University Press, 2013.

Barry, Kathleen. *The Prostitution of Sexuality*. NYU Press, 1996.

Belser, Patrick. "Forced Labour and Human Trafficking: Estimating the Profits." Cornell University ILR School. 2005. http://digitalcommons.ilr.cornell.edu/cgi/viewcontent.cgi?article=1016&context=forcedlabor.

Bhabha, Jacqueline. "Trafficking, Smuggling, and Human Rights." *Migration Information Source*. 2005. http://www.migrationinformation.org/article/trafficking-smuggling-and-human-rights.

Bruckert, Chris, Colette Parent, and Royal Canadian Mounted Police. *Trafficking in Human Beings and Organized Crime: A Literature Review*. Research and Evaluation Branch, Community, Contract and Aboriginal Policing Services Directorate, Royal Canadian Mounted Police, 2002.

Carpenter, Michael. "The Modern Slave Trade in Post-Communist Europe." *Center for Slavic and East European Studies Newsletter* 20, (2003): 5–8. http://iseees.berkeley.edu/sites/default/files/u4/iseees/publications_/2003_20-01.pdf.

Chisolm-Straker, Makini. "Human Trafficking: Information and Resources for Emergency Healthcare Providers." 2009. www.humantraffickinged.com.

Coy, Maddy, Miranda Horvath, Liz Kelly, and A. Horvath. *"It's Just Like Going to the Supermarket": Men Buying Sex in East London*. Report for Safe Exit at Toynbee Hall. London: London Metropolitan University, Child and Woman Abuse Studies Unit, 2007.

Dessy, Sylvain E., and Stéphane Pallage. "A Theory of the Worst Forms of Child Labour." *The Economic Journal* 115, no. 500 (2005): 68–87.

Dryden Witte, Ann, and Robert Witt. "What We Spend and What We Get: Public and Private Provision of Crime Prevention and Criminal Justice." *Fiscal Studies* 22, no. 1 (2001): 1–40.

Eagle, Joshua G., and David R. Betters. "The Endangered Species Act and Economic Values: A Comparison of Fines and Contingent Valuation Studies." *Ecological Economics* 26, no. 2 (1998): 165–171.

Farrell, Amy, Jack McDevitt, and Stephanie Fahy. *Understanding and Improving Law Enforcement Responses to Human Trafficking*. The Institute on Race and Justice at Northeastern University. Washington, DC: National Institute of Justice, 2007.

Federal Bureau of Investigation, Atlanta Division, "Pair Indicted, Appear in Court for Sex Trafficking of a Minor." April 16, 2009. http://www.fbi.gov/atlanta/press-releases/2009/at041609.htm.

Federal Bureau of Investigation, Atlanta Division, "Pimp Who Claimed to Be a Modeling Agent Sentenced to Prison." June 4, 2009. http://www.fbi.gov/atlanta/press-releases/2009/atl060409.htm.

Federal Bureau of Investigation, Jacksonville Division, "Jury Finds New York Man Guilty of Sex Trafficking Women by Force, Threats of Force, and Fraud." February 17, 2011. http://www.fbi.gov/jacksonville/press-releases/2011/ja021711.htm.

Federal Bureau of Investigation, Los Angeles Division, "Man Pleads Guilty and Is Sentenced to 17? Years in Federal Prison for Sex Trafficking of Minors." June 10, 2010. http://www.fbi.gov/losangeles/press-releases/2010/la061010.htm.

Federal Bureau of Investigation, New York Field Office. "Last of 14 Gambino Crime Family Members and Associates Plead Guilty to Racketeering, Murder Conspiracy, Extortion, Sex Trafficking, and Other Crimes." January 10, 2011. http://www.fbi.gov/newyork/press-releases/2011/last-of-14-gambino-crime-family-members-and-associates-plead-guilty-to-racketeering-murder-conspiracy-extortion-sex-trafficking-and-other-crimes/.

Federal Bureau of Investigation, New York Field Office. "Nine Gambino Crime Family Members Sentenced in Manhattan Federal Court for Racketeering, Murder Conspiracy, Extortion, Sex Trafficking, and Other Crimes." May 12, 2011. http://www.fbi.gov/newyork/press-releases/2011/nine-gambino-crime-family-members-sentenced-in-manhattan-federal-court-for-racketeering-murder-conspiracy-extortion-sex-trafficking-and-other-crime.

Federal Bureau of Investigation, Seattle Field Office. "Army Sergeant Sentenced to 11 Years in Prison for Sex Trafficking Juveniles." US Department of Justice. October 26, 2010. http://seattle.fbi.gov/dojpressrel/pressrel10/se102610a.htm.

Federal Bureau of Investigation, Seattle Field Office. "Tacoma Felon Sentenced to 13 Years in Prison for Sex Trafficking Offenses." Department of Justice. May 11, 2010. http://www.fbi.gov/seattle/press-releases/2010/se051110.htm.

Fick, Nicolé. *Coping with Stigma, Discrimination and Violence: Sex Workers Talk about Their Experiences*. Cape Town: SWEAT, 2005.

Gould, Chandré, and Nicolé Fick. "Report to the South African Law Reform Commission: Preliminary Research Findings of Relevance to the Draft Legislation to Combat Trafficking in Persons and Legislation Pertaining to Adult Prostitution." Institute for Security Studies, SWEAT, 2007.

Groom, T. M., and R. Nandwani. "Characteristics of Men Who Pay for Sex: A UK Sexual Health Clinic Survey." *Sexually Transmitted Infections* 82, no. 5 (2006): 364–367.

Henry, Stuart, and Dragan Milovanovic. "Constitutive Criminology. Beyond Postmodernism und Alison Young: Imagining Crime. (Ludwig-Meyerhofer)." *Kriminologisches Journal* 30, no. 3 (1998): 223–227.

Hughes, Donna M. "Best Practices to Address the Demand Side of Sex Trafficking." University of Rhode Island. 2004.

Jordan, Ann D. "Human Rights or Wrongs? The Struggle for a Rights-Based Response to Trafficking in Human Beings." *Gender & Development* 10, no. 1 (2002): 28–37.

Joubert, S. "Contemporary Theoretical Explanations for Youth Misbehaviour." In *Child and Youth Misbehaviour in South Africa: A Holistic Approach*, edited by C. Bezuidenhout and S. Joubert, 108–122. Pretoria: Van Schaik Publishers, 2008.

Kantola, Johanna and Judith Squires. "Discourses Surrounding Prostitution Policies in the UK." *European Journal of Women Studies* 11, (2004): 77–101.

Kimathi Lewis, "Arrests Made in Child Sex Crimes as Agencies Join Forces." *Examiner.com.* August 6, 2010. http://www.examiner.com/crime-in-atlanta/arrests-made-child-sex-crimes-as-agencies-join-forces.

King, Lindsey. "International Law and Human Trafficking." *Topic Research Digest: Human Rights and Human Trafficking.* 2015. http://www.du.edu/korbel/hrhw/researchdigest/trafficking/InternationalLaw.pdf.

Kinnu, Gunjan. *From Bondage to Freedom: An Analysis of International Legal Regime on Human Trafficking.* New Delhi: National Human Rights Commission, 2006.

Kyckelhahn, Tracey, Allen J. Beck, and Thomas H. Cohen. *Characteristics of Suspected Human Trafficking Incidents, 2007–08.* Washington, DC: US Department of Justice, Bureau of Justice Statistics, January 2009.

Lanier, Mark M. "Epidemiological Criminology (EpiCrim): Definition and Application." *Journal of Theoretical and Philosophical Criminology* 2, no. 1 (2010): 63–103.

Lanier, Mark M. "Epidemiological Criminology: A Critical Cross-Cultural Analysis of the Advent of HIV/AIDS." *Acta Criminologica* 22, no. 2 (2009): 60–73.

Lanier, Mark M., Stuart Henry, and Desire J. M. Anastasia. *Essential Criminology*. Perseus Books Group, 2014.

Lutya, Thozama Mandisa. "An Integrated Theoretical Framework to Describe Human Trafficking of Young Women and Girls for Involuntary Prostitution." In *Public Health—Social and Behavioral Health*, edited by Jay Maddock. InTech: 2012.

Macleod, Jan, Melissa Farley, Lynn Anderson, and Jacqueline Golding. "Challenging Men's Demand for Prostitution in Scotland: A Research Report Based on Interviews with 110 Men Who Bought Women in Prostitution." Women's Support Project, 2008.

Månsson, Sven-Axel. "Men's Demand for Prostitutes." *Sexologies* 15, no. 2 (2006): 87–92.

McCray, J. "Dynamics and the Economic Theory of Crime." Criminology and Economics Summer Workshop. University of Michigan, June 5, 2006.

Persson, Mats, and Claes Henric Siven. "The Becker Paradox and Type I versus Type II Errors in the Economics of Crime." *International Economic Review* 48, no. 1 (2007): 211–233.

Phinney, Alison. *Trafficking of Women and Children for Sexual Exploitation in the Americas.* Women, Health and Development Program, Pan-American Health Organization, 2001.

Pratt, Travis C. "Rational Choice Theory, Crime Control Policy, and Criminological Relevance." *Criminology & Public Policy* 7, no. 1 (2008): 43–52.

Rao, Smriti, and Christina Presenti. "Understanding Human Trafficking Origin: A Cross-Country Empirical Analysis." *Feminist Economics* 18, no. 2 (2012): 231–263.

Rosenfeld, Richard, and Steven F. Messner. "Crime and the American Dream: An Institutional Analysis." In *The Legacy of Anomie Theory*, vol. 6 (1995): 159–181.

Simić, Olivera. *Victims of Trafficking for Forced Prostitution: Protection Mechanisms and the Right to Remain in the Destination Countries.* Global Commission on International Migration, 2004.

Snyman, Rika. "Overview of and Concepts in Victimology." In *Victimology in South Africa*, edited by Linda Davis and Rika Snyman, 3–14. Pretoria: Van Schaik Publishers, 2005.

South African Law Reform Commission (SALRC). Discussion Paper 0001/2009, Project 107: Sexual Offences Adult Prostitution. Pretoria: SALRC, 2009.

South Africa Parliament. The Children's Act (Act No. 38 of 2005). *Government Gazette*, 28944. Pretoria: Government Printer, 2005.

South Africa Parliament. Criminal (Sexual Offences and Related Matters) Amendment Act (Act No. 32 of 2007). *Government Gazette*. Pretoria: Government Printer, 2007.

South Africa Parliament. Immigration Act (Act No. 13 of 2002). *Government Gazette*, 26901. Pretoria: Government Printer, 2002.

South Africa Parliament. Social and Behavioral Health Prevention of Organized Crime Act (Act No. 121 of 1998). *Government Gazette*, 19553. Pretoria: Government Printer, 1998.

State of Connecticut. An Act Providing a Safe Harbor for Exploited Children. Conn. Pub. Act 10-115.

State of New York. Safe Harbor for Exploited Children. N.Y. Soc. Serv. Law §447-a (McKinney 2008).

Texas Association Against Sexual Assault. *Human Trafficking Report*. 2009.

Truong, Thanh-Dam. *Poverty, Gender and Human Trafficking in Sub-Saharan Africa: Rethinking Best Practices in Migration Management*. UNESCO Project to Fight Human Trafficking in Africa. 2006.

United Nations. Protocol to Prevent, Suppress and Punish Trafficking in Persons, Especially Women and Children, Supplementing the United Nations Convention against Transnational Organized Crime. 2000. http://www.un.org.za.

United States Attorney General. "Attorney General's Annual Report to Congress on US Government Activities to Combat Trafficking in Persons: Fiscal Year 2005." US Department of Justice. 2006. http://www.justice.gov/archive/ag/annualreports/tr2005/agreporthumantrafficing2005.pdf.

United States Congress. Domestic Minor Sex Trafficking: Hearings on H.R. 5575, Before the Subcommittee on Crime, Terrorism, and Homeland Security. 111th Cong. 154. 2010.

United States Congress. Victims of Trafficking and Violence Protection Act of 2000. 18 U.S.C. §1591(a)(1). October 28, 2000.

United States Department of Justice, US Attorney's Office for the Western District of Missouri. "Human Trafficking Rescue Project." http://www.justice.gov/usao/mow/programs/humantrafficking.html.

United States Department of State. *Assessment of U.S. Government Activities to Combat Trafficking in Persons: Fiscal Year 2006*. Washington, DC: US Department of Justice.

United States Department of State. *Trafficking in Persons Report*. 2009. http://www.state.gov/g/tip/rls/tiprpt/2009/.

United States Department of State. *Trafficking in Persons Report*. June 2011, 372.

United States Equal Employment Opportunity Commission. "Employment Discrimination Laws 'New Frontier' in War Against Human Labor." January 19, 2011. http://www.eeoc.gov/eeoc/newsroom/release/1-19-11.cfm.

United States Equal Employment Opportunity Commission. "EEOC Resolves Slavery and Human Trafficking Suit against Trans Bay Steel for an Estimated $1 Million." December 8, 2006. http://www.eeoc.gov/eeoc/newsroom/release/archive/12-8-06.html.

United States Equal Employment Opportunity Commission Meeting. "Human Trafficking and Forced Labor." Written testimony of Anna Park, EEOC regional attorney. January 19, 2011. http://www.eeoc.gov/eeoc/meetings/1-19-11/park.cfm.

United States Immigration and Customs Enforcement. "Kansas Man Gets 15 Years in Prison for Attempted Sex Trafficking of a Child." December 1, 2009. https://www.ice.gov/news/releases/0912/091201kansascity.htm.

United States Immigration and Customs Enforcement. "Maryland Man Pleads Guilty in Sex Trafficking Conspiracy Involving 3 Minor Girls." July 16, 2009. http://www.ice.gov/news/releases/0907/090716baltimore.htm.

United States v. Myers, 2011 WL 2391306 (11th Cir., June 15, 2011), at *6.

Van Impe, Kristof. "People for Sale: The Need for a Multidisciplinary Approach Towards Human Trafficking." *International Migration* 38, no. 3 (2000): 113–191.

Witte, A.D., & Witt, R. Crime Causation: Economic Theories. In *Encyclopaedia of Crime and Justice* 1, (2002): 302–308. New York: Macmillan, 2002.

Zimmerman, Cathy, Mazeda Hossain, Kate Yun, Brenda Roche, Linda Morison, and Charlotte Watts. *Stolen Smiles: A Summary Report on the Physical and Psychological Health Consequences of Women and Adolescents Trafficked in Europe*. London: London School of Hygiene & Tropical Medicine, 2006.

Notes

1. Laczko, F. (2005). Data and research on human trafficking. *International Migration*, 43(1 2), 5–16.

2. Bruckert, C., C. Parent, & Royal Canadian Mounted Police. (2002). *Trafficking in human beings and organized crime: A literature review*. Research and Evaluation Branch, Community, Contract and Aboriginal Policing Services Directorate, Royal Canadian Mounted Police.

3. Barry, K. (1984). *Female sexual slavery*. NYU Press.

4. Hughes, D. M. (2004). The role of "marriage agencies" in the sexual exploitation and trafficking of women from the former Soviet Union. *International Review of Victimology*, *11*(1), 49–71.

5. This endnote has two references:

1) James, C. & Atler, S. (2003). *Highly affected, rarely considered: The International Youth Parliament Commission's report on the impacts of globalization on young people*. Sydney: International Youth Parliament (IYP) Oxfam Community Aid Abroad.

2) US Agency for International Development. (2006, March). *Trafficking in persons: USAID's response*. Washington, DC: US Agency for International Development, Office of Women in Development.

6. Lapon, G. (2016, September 19). What do we mean by exploitation? SocialistWorker.org. https://socialistworker.org/2011/09/28/what-do-we-mean-exploitation.

7. Brewer, D. (2008). Globalization and human trafficking. *Tropical Research Digest: Human Rights and Human Welfare*, 46–56.

8. Shift, G. (2011). Mapping the Changing Contours of the World Economy. *New York: Guilford.*

9. Bales, K. (2005). *Understanding global slavery: A reader*. University of California Press.

10. Barnett, Randy E. (1984). Review essay/public decisions and private rights. *Criminal Justice Ethics*, *3*(2), 50–62.

11. Lewis, W. A. (1954, May). Economic development with unlimited supplies of labour. *The Manchester School*, *22*(2), 139–191.

12. This endnote has two references:

1) Bowe, J. (2008). *Nobodies: Modern American slave labor and the dark side of the new global economy*. Random House Incorporated.

2) Howard, N. (2014, April 24). 'Trafficking', 'Slavery' and 'Forced Labour'—Liberal Capitalism's (Un)Holy Trinity? The GRaSe Blog. https://blogs.eui.eu/grase/trafficking-slavery and-forced-labour-liberal-capitalisms-unholy-trinity.html.

13. Lebaron, G., & N. Howard. (2015, February 15). Introducing Beyond Slavery's month on forced labour in the global political economy. Open Democracy. https://www.opendemocracy.net/beyondslavery/genevieve-lebaron-neil-howard/introducing-beyond-slavery%E2%80%99s-month-on-forced-labour-in-g.

14. United Nations Global Initiative to Fight Human Trafficking (UN.GIFT), 2014. http://www.ungift.org/.

15. Malarek, V. (2011). The natashas: The horrific inside story of slavery, rape, and murder in the global sex trade. Skyhorse Publishing Inc.

16. Malarek, V. (2003). *The natashas: Inside the new global sex trade*. New York: Arcade Publishing.

17. Howard, N. (2014, April 18). On capitalism and coercion: Are trafficking, slavery and forced labour actually necessary for maintaining liberal capitalism? AlJazeera. http://www.aljazeera.com/indepth/opinion/2014/04/capitalism-coercion-2014417133923106962.html.

18. Salt, J., & J. Stein. (1997). Migration as a business: The case of trafficking. *International Migration*, *35*(4), 467–494.

19. Bernat, F. P., & T. Zhilina. (2010). Human trafficking: The local becomes global. *Women & Criminal Justice*, *20*(1–2), 2–9.

20. United Nations Global Initiative to Fight Human Trafficking (UN.GIFT), 2014. http://www.ungift.org/.

21. Van der Hoven, A., & A. Maree. (2005). Victimisation risk factors, repeat victimisation and victim profiling. *Victimology in South Africa*, 65.

22. Skeldon, R. (1994). East Asian migration and the changing world order. *Population*

Migration and the Changing World Order. Chichester, UK: John Wiley & Sons, 173.

23. Lanier, M. M., S. Henry, & D. J. M. Anastasia. (2014). *Essential criminology*. Perseus Books Group.

24. Brown, S. E., F.-A. Esbensen, & G. Geis. (1998). *Criminology: Explaining crime and its context*. Cincinnati: Anderson.

25. This endnote has two references:

1) Messner, S. F., & Rosenfeld, R. (1997). Political restraint of the market and levels of criminal homicide: A cross-national application of institutional-anomie theory. *Social Forces*, 1393–1416.

2) Messner, S. F., & R. Rosenfeld. (2012). *Crime and the American dream*. Cengage Learning.

26. Box, H. Human Trafficking and Minorities: Vulnerability Compounded by Discrimination. Topical Research Digest: Minority Rights (nd), 28–29.

27. Agnew, R. (2007). *Pressured into crime: An overview of general strain theory*. Oxford University Press.

28. Terr, L. (1990). *Too sacred to cry: Psychic trauma in childhood*. HarperCollins Publishers.

29. This endnote has two references:

1) Van der Kolk, B. A. (1989). The compulsion to repeat the trauma. *Psychiatric Clinics of North America, 12*(2), 389–411.

2) Van der Kolk, B. A., & A. C. McFarlane, eds. (2012). *Traumatic stress: The effects of overwhelming experience on mind, body, and society*. Guilford Press.

30. Bloom, S. L. (1997). *Creating sanctuary: Toward the evolution of sane communities*. Routledge.

Chapter 5

Trafficking in Persons: Human Trade

Chapter Objectives

This chapter provides a comprehensive understanding of the following:

- Commercializing Humans for Organ Removal
- Trafficking in Persons and Organ Trade: An Overview
    - Organ Transplantation: A Medical Wonder? Or Designer of a New Branch of Trafficking?
    - Who Are the Main Actors Involved in Organ Trafficking?
    - Organ Trafficking: An Organized Crime?
    - Who Are the Donors: Victims?
    - Process: How Are the Donors/Victims Recruited?
- Trafficking in Persons Protocol and Organ Trafficking
- The United Network for Organ Sharing (UNOS) and Organ Transplant Tourism
- Organ Trafficking: History
- Laws Prohibiting Organ Trafficking
    - The Trafficking in Persons Protocol and Removal of Organs
    - The Optional Protocol to the Convention on the Rights of the Child
    - Council of Europe (CoE) Convention: The Oviedo Convention
    - The Charter of Fundamental Rights of the European Union, (2000/C 364/01) Article 1
    - The Declaration of Istanbul on Organ Trafficking and Transplant Tourism (2008)

- Issue of Consent or Coercion?
- Trafficking in Persons for Organ Removal and Organ Trafficking: Same or Different?
- International Guidelines for Human Cell, Tissue and Organ Transplant
- Strategies for the Prevention and Control of Organ Trafficking and Trafficking in Persons for Removal of Organs
  - Address the Root Causes
  - Reduce the Demand for Irregularly Procured Organs
  - Raise Awareness
  - Local and International Laws Coordination
- Conclusion
  - Challenges: Detection, Investigation, and Prosecution of Organ Trafficking Crime
  - Indicators of Trafficking of Persons for Organ Removal
  - Assistance to the Victims

Introduction: Trafficking in Persons: The Organ Trade

Trafficking in persons for the purposes of organ removal is believed to be an industry bringing in profits worth billions of dollars. In the most recent times, it has become a human import/export industry—more ruthless and sophisticated than ever before, employing a growing array of opportunists who trap, exploit, rape, and rob victims not only of their dignity and identity but also of body parts. Carrying out these transactions involves not just traffickers, organized crime syndicates, greedy corporations, and businesses but also unscrupulous health professionals, hospital staff, adoption agencies, and other entrepreneurs. This import and export industry knows no moral, social, or geographic boundaries. This is an industry where hopelessness and greed create a "sinister and sometimes lethal combination."[1] The drive for money without any ethical standards directs businesses, creating a climate where people are seen only as means to an end. Greed transforms human beings into commodities for sale and/or to be exploited for profits. Trafficking causes a corruption of spirit and turns involved people into robotic machines devoid of any humane regard for the physical and emotional well-being of their victims or others.

Although organ trafficking and trafficking in persons for the purpose of organ removal are considered significant transnational crimes, neither international criminal law nor individual states' domestic criminal laws provide adequate guidelines as to how to address these crimes. It has thus functioned in practice largely as what might be judged a "stateless" offense, out of the purview of both international and national courts. Thus, these forms of organ trafficking remain widespread—and devastating to those who are its victims.[2]

Trafficking; smuggling; exploitation for sex and labor; the stealing, buying, and selling of babies with its accompanying exploitation of pregnant teenage girls; and organ removal are some of the latest schemes that bring enormous amounts of money to feed the greed of traffickers. It has become one of the most lucrative and the most lethal trades in the world. The "ferocious violence and anarchy in the business has kept the scales of profits and misery hidden,"[3] often under the pretense of helping poverty stricken people with jobs, giving them an opportunity to lead normal lives, and saving lives through organ donations.

Human trafficking is a depraved crime against humanity wreaking havoc upon the social fabric of each community, city, state, region, and nation. No country is immune to this crime, with all serving in one or the other capacity—as origin, transit, or destination for victims. It takes place in the poorest slums of the least-developed countries just as it does in the major cities of one of the most prosperous nations on earth—the United States. Most human trafficking is facilitated by transnational criminal organizations, which have integrated networks, connections, and resources that allow for their activities to go under the radar.[4] In a true sense, trafficking in humans is "a manifestation of a continued theme that, at root level, is still a by-product of the class war and prejudices of old. It is driven by greed and a lack of value for oneself and, ultimately one's neighbor."[5]

This chapter discusses the economics of human trade in terms of organ trafficking and other exploitations for profit. It provides an overview of trafficking in persons for the purpose of organ removal, organ trafficking, and trafficking of organs—distinct forms of trafficking that require special knowledge and skills to be understood and addressed. This chapter examines the phenomenon and the context in which trafficking in persons for organ removal takes place, the relevant legislative framework that provides information on what it is, and how to address this issue. The chapter also provides an overview of international legislation and guidance, as well as the main actors involved and the process used to carry out this sinister crime.

Commercializing Humans for Organ Removal

Trafficking in Persons and the Organ Trade: An Overview

Trafficking of human beings for organ removal, also referred to as illicit organ trafficking and the unlawful sale of human organs, is a multimillion-dollar black market industry.[6] This illegal trade has been banned in all World Health Organization (WHO) member states with the exception of Iran. The Global Observatory and Database on Donation and Transplantation—the product of a collaboration between WHO and the Spanish National Transplant Organization—reported that 118,127 solid organ transplantations (kidney, liver, heart, lung, pancreas, or small bowel) were performed in 2013. A majority (79,000), were kidney transplants, followed by 25,000 liver transplants.[7] According to the Global Observatory on Donation and Transplantation Report, in 2013 there was about 2.98 percent increase in the number of organ transplantations in the globe compared to 2012. The same report also stated that this reflects only 10 percent or less of the global transplantation needs being met. In a section of Europe—known as the Euro Transplant Region—more than 10,000 patients were registered on the waiting list for an organ in 2012.[8] In the United States, as of January 6, 2014, there are more than 120,999 candidates waiting for organs (77,073 of whom are active waiting list candidates), but only 10,587 donors registered in the US as of March that year.[9]

According to WHO Report (2010) over 119,000 people are on the transplant list in the United States alone as of 2015. Around 6,000 heart transplants and 21,000 liver transplants take place yearly, whereas there are close to 65,000 kidney transplants yearly. However, the number of organ transplants worldwide is meeting less than 10 percent of the demand for necessary transplants needed. The demand for organs significantly outweighs the supply of organs. The cost of healthcare and technical capacity of countries along with stringent laws in certain countries have led to the growth of the illegal organ trading market.[10]

Organs Transplantation: A Medical Wonder? Or Designer of a New Branch of Trafficking?

Organ transplantation is one of the most remarkable medical inventions. Since the first kidney transplant in 1954, it has evolved from experimental procedure to common therapy for many serious conditions—saving and prolonging the lives of thousands of patients worldwide. Advancement in medicine and technology has made transplantation of organs, cells, and tissues viable and effective therapies across a wide range of both fatal and non-fatal diseases. The high success and survival rates of transplantation of organs and cells, such as the kidney, liver, and heart or hematopoietic stem cells in immunosuppressed patients, have led to high levels of demand globally. The success rates for transplantation of certain cells or tissues which do not require immunosuppression have also ensured that such procedures are frequently the treatment of choice in the respective therapeutic areas.[11]

Owing to the continuous improvements in medical technology, particularly in relation to organ and tissue rejection, the transplantation of human organs, tissues, and cells has become a worldwide practice which has extended, and greatly enhanced, the quality of life for hundreds of thousands of patients. Simultaneously, such advancements have also led to an increase in demand for organs and tissues, which has always exceeded supply despite a substantial expansion in deceased organ donation as well as greater reliance on donation from living persons in recent years.[12] Consequently, more and more transplantations are performed and more and more patients are certified to be fit to receive the transplant. Since the number of patients needing the transplant exceeds the available organs, they are placed on the waiting list for transplantation. This sets a stage for innovative ways of getting organs.

While organ transplants have been carried out for a long time, the issue of organ trafficking has only recently emerged as a problem considered to be of such a magnitude that it requires international concern. In the 1980s, advancement in anti-rejection drugs—drugs that facilitate body's acceptance of foreign objects—provided doctors a way to perform transplants with high success rates. The living donor procedures of the kidney, liver, cornea, and lung transplants are supported by medicine. Medical regulations regarding live human transplantation of organs were relaxed a few years later, allowing for organs to be potentially traded.[13]

According to the US Department of Health & Human Services, on the national level in 2015, there were a total of 120,977 people in need of organ transplantation and approximately 15,000 organ donations were made. On average, in the United States, one person is added every ten minutes to the national organ waiting list and about 22 people waiting for organs for transplantation are dying each day.[14] Tragically, the advancements that prolonged and enhanced quality of life years for many, have also led to an increase in the demand for organs and tissues in the black market. When the demand cannot be met by legally obtained donations from the deceased or living persons' organ donations, the alternate black market surfaces. Critical demand for organs and such a severe shortage of supply serve as motivation for traffickers to buy and sell organs for profit. Desperate patients, especially the ones who can afford it, may seek strategies to obtain organs illegally, outside legal transplantation frameworks. Medical and scientific advances have brought an opportunity for survival and a chance at second life for people who can afford it. However, the same advances have also led to the increased demand for organs, resulting in the exploitation of poor, ignorant, and helpless people. In order to give a chance of life to some, traffickers employ tactics to snatch life out of others.

Who Are the Main Actors Involved in Organ Trafficking?

The successful transplantations have created a long list of patients waiting for transplantation, which in turn have created an avenue ready for exploitation by national as well as international organ trafficking syndicates. Simultaneously, it has provided temptations to the poor and desperate masses who see selling organs as a means of survival and providing for their families. Such desperate situations facilitate traffickers' sinister tactics. The transnational organized crime syndicates are involved in trafficking people for the purpose of organ removal and the organs themselves. Traffickers exploit the desperation of both parties—donors and recipients. They exploit potential donors (victims) who have healthy organs, have seen advertisements, and have heard convincing arguments that some organs can be donated (sold) without any harm to their health. They perceive their organs as means to improve the economic situation of themselves and their families. On the other hand, the traffickers exploit the desperation of recipients who may have the money but only a few options to improve or prolong their lives. The victims of this crime—like the victims of other forms of trafficking—may be impoverished and from otherwise marginalized populations, however, this crime involves a high order of sophisticated technical skills on the part of the traffickers. Organ trafficking requires more actors than the usual trafficking enterprise in which traffickers solicit and recruit victims and then supply them to others for exploitation. In the case of organ trafficking, in addition to the solicitors and recruiters as in other trafficking ventures, there have to be hospitals, donors, highly trained technical staff, nurses, medical personnel handling the organs when they are in transit, and doctors. Thus, the traffickers in this crime may not be common criminals. Rather in most cases, they are: recruiters (also called brokers, organizers, connectors, coordinators, middlemen, or kidney hunters); medical professionals (including specialist doctors such as surgeons and nephrologists—medical doctors who specialize in kidney care and treating diseases of the kidneys—as well as nursing staff and other medical staff); and other private and public sector facilitators (such as hospitals, transplant centers, laboratories and other medical facilities, as well as their staff, insurance companies, travel agencies, airlines and their staff, guards, drivers, service providers, law enforcement officials, and translators). Although organ recipients ("patients," "buyers") have largely not been found to be perpetrators of trafficking in persons for organ removal, they may have been knowingly or unknowingly involved as recipients of organs that come from trafficking victims. Victims of trafficking in persons for organ removal (also called "donors," "victim-donors," "sellers," or "organ suppliers") may not have actively engaged in the trafficking schemes. They may, however, take on active roles, e.g., by approaching brokers and offering their kidney for sale.[15] In many cases, reputed hospitals may operate as brokers, while also providing accommodation for both recipients and suppliers. Potential organ suppliers (traffickers) may directly approach medical facilities, especially those that are presumed to be involved in the illegal transplantation business. Generally, a number of tests are performed before the donor is accepted. Thus, laboratories and laboratory technicians also become part of the team of traffickers working to bypass legal and ethical standards. These facilities and the technicians may be part of the brokers' teams, engaged in matching a vulnerable, inadequately informed, or totally uninformed donor to a recipient. Laboratories may also take on "brokering" functions, by spreading the word of the benefits of organ sales among possible organ suppliers and recipients and establishing contacts with organ brokers.

Other actors in trafficking for organ removal may include travel agencies specialized in medical tourism, translators, and corrupt law enforcement officers. The Organization for Security and Cooperation in Europe (OSCE) reported that drivers, minders (persons who accompany organ suppliers and recipients, who are from countries that are different from the country in which the removal and transplantation take place, during their travel to and from the transplant operations), and others who would have mere supporting roles in networks, functions that would be relatively minor but necessary to a network's undertaking, are also part of the trafficking team. Translators are needed in situations where medical personnel, brokers, suppliers, and recipients originate from different countries. They may also be part of the group/team engaged in victimizing ill-informed victims/donors.[16]

According to the UNODC (2015), trafficking syndicates may also include corrupt law enforcement officers. For example, immigration and customs officials might receive payoffs for not reporting forged travel documents or to "secure" a border crossing.[17] In some cases, local politicians and police and their family members and friends function as brokers—receiving kickbacks from hospitals, doctors, and other agencies "in exchange for recommending them to handle various aspects or phases of kidney transplantation."[18] Some medical professionals and hospitals involved in illegal organ transactions have been found to have close links with law enforcement officers assisting the trafficking venture by overlooking rules governing transplantations.[19] Others may include bankers, lawyers, pharmaceutical companies, religious organizations and charitable trusts, patient organizations, embassy staff, and advertisers for online and print advertisements. Such an expansion of the prospective pool of traffickers and change in the typology of the traffickers (perpetrators) makes their detection and apprehension even more difficult and challenging.

Organ Trafficking: An Organized Crime?

As discussed above, for the successful existence and operation of organ trafficking, solid collaboration among various actors and entities is imperative. In many cases, these actors and entities may be spread over the globe. All these variables point towards it being a form of organized crime. According to Article 2(a) of the UN Organized Crime Convention, an "organized criminal group shall mean a structured group of three or more persons, existing for a period of time and acting in concert with the aim of committing one or more serious crimes or offenses established in accordance with this Convention, in order to obtain, directly or indirectly, a financial or other material benefit."[20] According to UNODC's 2014 Global Report on Trafficking in Persons, criminals who commit trafficking in persons' crimes can act alone, with a partner, or in different types of groups and networks. The more complex and more transnational trafficking operations are, the more likely they require concerted actions of several actors, that is, some degree of organization.[21]

According to UNODC (2015), in case of organ trafficking, some brokers, doctors, former kidney suppliers, and government officials may work as a team or operate individually. In other cases, "the groups may be well-organized, to some extent hierarchical networks, but also have some improvised elements, with some actors coming in rather spontaneously—such as low-level, local recruiters, who might be quite easy to replace."[22] Since a strong collaboration among various actors in the organ trafficking enterprise is almost a requisite, and the enterprise often involves locals as well people across borders, it may be easier for the criminal justice practitioners to classify cases of trafficking in persons for the purpose of organ removal as cases of organized crime and/or transnational organized crime. This classification may provide additional funding, better investigative techniques, and means of international cooperation.

Who Are the Donors: Victims?

The extant literature suggests that donors come from all over the world, so their nationalities vary. However, the most common characteristic of all donors—regardless of their nationality—is that they seem to be poor and predominantly from countries with a large proportion of the population living below the poverty line. The majority also come from countries where the laws and regulations are weak and authorities are unable or unwilling to effectively prohibit and prosecute trafficking in human beings for the purpose of organ removal. In general, victims of trafficking in persons vary from case to case and include men, women, and children; the well educated, the illiterate; and being from very poor countries, as well as from developed countries. The same is true in cases of the victims of trafficking in persons for organ removal. Because kidneys from young suppliers are the most marketable, the majority of the donors are young men—with an average age of 30 years old.

Process: How Are the Donors/Victims Recruited?

Traffickers—sometimes known as recruiters or brokers—use different tactics to entice donors into an illicit or illegal transplant scheme. The potential donors are identified generally form poverty stricken and marginalized sections of communities and approached by a third party, such as recruiters, brokers, etc. The most common deceptive tactics and convincing influences used by brokers or recruiters include convincing the donor that the "operation is painless and risk-free," "a second kidney is not needed," and "the removed kidney grows back." Other times donors are promised a legal permit to travel abroad and find a job there. They are also promised a hefty amount of money. However, the existing literature suggests none of these promises is kept and the donors/victims receive nothing or very minimal post-operative care (if at all) and are without the financial means to access local health institutions.[23] In some cases, the literature suggests that the donors who sell their organs may have been "recruited, transported, transferred, harbored and/or received by persons—recruiters, brokers, recipients, doctors etc.—who may have an enormous amount of power to influence the would be donors' decisions."[24] They may abuse their position of vulnerability, frequently deceive them, and on occasion coerce them into parting with one of their organs and convince them that this is/was their best option.[25]

Trafficking in Persons Protocol and Organ Trafficking

The trafficking in Persons Protocol supplementing the Transnational Organized Crime Convention includes trafficking in *persons* for the purpose of organ removal. The United Nations Trafficking in Persons Protocol defines "Organ Trafficking." According to UNODC, organ trafficking entails "the recruitment, transportation, transfer, harboring or receipt of persons, by means of the threat or use of force or other forms of coercion, of abduction, of fraud, of deception, of the abuse of power or of a position of vulnerability or of the giving or receiving of payments or benefits to achieve the consent of a person having control over another person, for the purpose of exploitation" by the removal of organs, tissues, or cells for transplantation.[26]

This definition of organ trafficking captures various exploitative measures used in the processes of soliciting a donor in a commercial transplant. Exploitation is the threat or use of force or other forms of coercion, abduction, fraud, deception, and abuse of power or position of vulnerability. The commercial transaction is a central aspect of organ trafficking—the organ becomes a commodity and financial considerations become the priority for the involved parties instead of the health and well-being of the donors and recipients. Transplant tourism has come to connote organ trafficking.[27]

The United Network for Organ Sharing (UNOS) and Organ Transplant Tourism

Despite immense focus on prevention of disease, the global needs of patients for transplantation are not being met. The demand has outstripped the supply of organs, cells, and tissues from both deceased donors and from the altruistic living relatives of patients in need of transplantation. Organs from deceased donors are meeting the needs of transplantation of only a very small percentage of the patients needing transplantation in few countries, if any. Potential donors are reluctant to commit to donate after death and their families may refuse permission when approached after death.[28] The use of executed prisoners as organ donors in some countries causes great concern that these donations are perceived to be coerced and devoid of free consent. Member states employ different models of consent including: presumed consent or "opt out"; required requesting; "opt-in"; and mixtures of these three models.[29] Thus, the post-mortem donation is affected by how the volunteers were identified and the consent obtained. Over the past ten years, increased use of living donation of non-regenerative organs has extended from kidneys to livers and even to the lung and pancreas in some instances, despite the hope that reliance on living donors could be reduced.

There remains great concern that a market in body parts (especially the kidneys) has flourished over the past few years with vulnerable persons being tricked or coerced into donating and some recipients travelling with their surgeons to countries where "donated organs may be purchased legally or illegally."[30] Human cells, human tissues, and human organs provide different concerns. Tissues are processed and traded in many member states by both for-profit and not-for-profit organizations. The extant literature does not provide enough information on the extent to which donors or their families are aware of the profit that is created through this trade. Human cells, in particular hematopoietic stem cells, on the other hand, are widely and increasingly exchanged globally between donors and patients through arrangements made by not-for-profit organizations which isolate and protect the anonymity of both patient and donor.[31]

This has caused a significant concern at the national and international level. During the sixty-third World Health Assembly in May 2010, in Resolution WHA63.22, the World Health Organization (2010) asserted that:

> The shortage of available organs has not only prompted many countries to develop procedures and systems to increase supply but has also stimulated commercial traffic in human organs, particularly from living donors who are unrelated to recipients. The evidence of such commerce, along with the related traffic in human beings, has become clearer in recent decades. Moreover, the growing ease of international communication and travel has led many patients to travel abroad to medical centers that advertise their ability to perform transplants and to supply donor organs for a single, inclusive charge.[32]

Purchase and sale of organs comes in myriad variations—from human trafficking for organ removal, to selling the body parts of deceased persons,[33] the sale of kidneys by the poor,[34] the purchase of organs by patients on the black market,[35] and advertising the sale of organs online.[36] Other forms involve financial or material benefit between willing donors and recipients. The cross-border variety involves recipients travelling to "supply" countries to receive a new organ, a phenomenon known as "transplant tourism."[37]

The United Network for Organ Sharing (UNOS), recently defined transplant tourism as "the purchase of a transplant organ abroad that includes access to an organ while bypassing laws, rules, or processes of any or all countries involved."[38] However, not all medical tourism that entails the travel of transplant recipients or donors across national borders is organ trafficking. Transplant tourism may be legal and appropriate. Examples include, when travel of a related donor and recipient pair is from countries without transplant services to countries where organ transplantation is performed or if an individual travels across borders to donate or receive a transplant via a relative. Any officially regulated bilateral or multi-lateral organ sharing program is not considered organ trafficking, if it is based on a reciprocated organ sharing program among jurisdictions.

Since kidney transplantation is the most frequently carried out transplantation around the world, there is a high demand for kidneys. A normal process would be that transplant organs are donated by blood relatives—however, the demand for donated organs exceeds the supply. Normal donations leading to transplantation fulfill only a small percentage of the total need. Many developed nations, including the United States, have a significant shortage of donor organs. The supply of transplantable organs from donors (live or deceased) fails to meet the demand—giving rise to long waiting periods and the uncertainty about availability. These variables—high demand, low supply—coupled with long wait and uncertainty have given rise to an illegal trade in human organs. They are sold, "harvested," stolen, or otherwise obtained from poor and marginalized people in developing countries and trafficked to developed nations—where recipients pay large amounts of money for the donated/bought organs. "In other cases, recipients travel to countries where organs are more readily available and where the illegal trade is rife."[39]

Organ transplant can only be carried out if the human organs are available from one of two sources—deceased or living donors. This means that any action in the field of organ transplantation must be carried out in accordance with the highest ethical and professional standards. All of these advances have brought an opportunity for survival and a chance at a second life for people who can afford to pay for the transplant. However, the same advances also work to snatch life out of people—those who do not have money and are willing to part with their organs to make money—and bring misery to them and their families. Just as the successful transplantations have created a long list of patients waiting for organs, it has also created a new business venue for the traffickers and a new source of income for the desperate, marginalized, and poor people, who can be easily duped into selling their organs. The alternative treatments and medical support for patients with end-stage organ failure, especially renal dialysis, are expensive and limited in many countries. Since such medical transplantation requires highly sophisticated skills, there is also a lack of clinical expertise and funds to carry out transplant surgeries in some regions and countries of the world. Thus, in all member states, one or more influences prevent the sufficient supply of transplantation therapies and lead to pressure for non-altruistic living donations—meaning the purchase and sale of organs.

Organ Trafficking: History

Trafficking in persons for the purpose of organ removal is not a new phenomenon. It has been in practice for a long time. Some of the first known accounts of organ purchases and sales surfaced in the late 1980s and not much attention was paid to this issue. However, interest in the trafficking of humans for organ removal has been refueled by the advancement in medicine and technology. These advances in medicine and technology, especially in organ transplantation, have been touted as saving many lives and restoring essential functions for many otherwise untreatable patients both in developing and developed countries. The increased awareness of organ donation and transplantation has led to the international trade in human organs being on the increase, fueled by growing demand as well as the unscrupulous nature and attitude of traffickers. The rising trend has prompted a serious reappraisal of current legislation, while the WHO has called for more protection for the most vulnerable people, who might be tempted to sell a kidney for as little as US$1,000.

The first case of 1980s reported that the transplant doctors in the Gulf States were confronted with patients with needs for medical follow-up who had received transplants of purchased kidneys in India.[40] Around the same time, Scheper-Hughes (1990) reported "body snatching rumors" that she claimed to have observed during her ethnographic research in Brazil.[41] Such incidents and reports in the 1990s did not receive much response from media or any national or international entities during those years. However, over the years, this form of trafficking has received significant attention from the media, NGOs, and academia as well as from international and regional entities, such as the Special Rapporteur on trafficking in persons, especially in women and children,[42] the Organization for Security and Co-operation in Europe, and the Office of the Special Representative and Co-ordinator for Combating Trafficking in Human Beings, 2013.[43] This crime of trafficking in persons for organ removal also prompted discussions in 2013 at the UN Economic and Social Council (UNESCO) and the General Assembly—leading to the adoption of resolutions that inter alia request UNODC to collect and analyze information on trafficking in persons for organ removal and encourage member states to provide to the UNODC evidence-based data on patterns, forms, and flows of trafficking in persons, including the purpose of the removal of organs.[44]

Despite the fact that the business of organ trafficking has caused such a stir, prompting UNESCO and the General Assembly meetings and adoption of resolutions, this crime still remains a hidden and an underground activity that is greatly underreported. The 2014 UNODC Global Report on Trafficking in Persons states that despite legislative progress made concerning the crime of trafficking in persons, globally, there are still very few convictions for trafficking in persons.[45] Although trafficking of all forms are "hidden in plain view," identifying and addressing the problem of trafficking in persons for organ removal is even harder due to the very technical nature of the processes and the involvement of professionals from the medical sector as well as highly technically sophisticated sectors and super specialists. According to the 2014 UNODC Global Report on Trafficking in Persons, surgeons who perform illegal organ transplantations that involve financial gain over organ purchases, remain free, since it is difficult to differentiate between their regular job and the jobs they perform as organ traffickers. They rarely get indicted or extradited following requests by prosecution authorities. Such a low number of convictions reflects the difficulties of the criminal justice systems to effectively respond to trafficking in persons for organ removal—especially when the traffickers are among medical professionals and respected hospitals and centers. It is an intricate and multifaceted challenge for law enforcement and criminal justice to initiate investigations against members of a highly regarded medical profession.[46]

Laws Prohibiting Organ Trafficking

The Trafficking in Persons Protocol and Removal of Organs

Terms like "organ trafficking," "illegal organ trade," "transplant tourism," "organ purchase," and others are often used interchangeably with trafficking in persons for the purpose of organ removal.[47] The Trafficking in Persons Protocol (2000) lists removal of organs as one of the listed forms of exploitation. According to Article 3(a) of the Trafficking in Persons Protocol:

> "Trafficking in persons" shall mean the recruitment, transportation, transfer, harboring or receipt of persons, by means of the threat or use of force or other forms of coercion, of abduction, of fraud, of deception, of the abuse of power or of a position of vulnerability or of the giving or receiving of payments or benefits to achieve the consent of a person having control over another person, for the purpose of exploitation. Exploitation shall include, at a minimum, the exploitation of the prostitution of others or other forms of sexual exploitation, forced labor or services, slavery or practices similar to slavery, servitude or the removal of organs.

The Optional Protocol to the Convention on the Rights of the Child

Trafficking in persons for organ removal is also defined and prohibited in other international/regional instruments, such as the Optional Protocol to the Convention on the Rights of the Child on the Sale of Children, Child Prostitution and Child Pornography[48] and the Council of Europe Convention on Action against Trafficking in Human Beings.[49, 50] The convention applies the definition of trafficking in persons presented in the UN Trafficking in Persons Protocol and seeks to strengthen the protection afforded by the protocol and other international instruments. Another law prohibiting trafficking in persons for organ removal is the Directive 2011/36/EU of the European Parliament and of the council on preventing and combating trafficking in human beings and protecting its victims.

Council of Europe (CoE) Convention: The Oviedo Convention

The Council of Europe Convention on Human Rights and Biomedicine (known as the Oviedo Convention) also prohibits sale and purchase of organs.[51] The Article 21 of the convention states that "the human body and its parts shall not, as such, give rise to financial gain." The Council of Europe Additional Protocol to the Convention on Human Rights and Biomedicine Concerning Transplantation of Organs and Tissues of Human Origin (Strasbourg, 24.I.2002), declares very similarly, in Article 21, that "the human body and its parts shall not, as such, give rise to a financial gain or comparable advantage."[52] Article 21(2) of the Additional Protocol prohibits "advertising the need for, or availability of, organs or tissues, with a view to offering or seeking financial gain or comparable advantage." Article 22 of the Additional Protocol prohibits illicit trafficking in organs of human origin because such practices exploit vulnerable people and may undermine people's faith in the transplant system. The preamble to the Additional Protocol to the Convention on Human Rights and Biomedicine acknowledges the risks posed to vulnerable persons and mandates "protecting the rights and freedoms of donors, potential donors, and recipients of organs and tissues." It requires institutions to ensure that individual rights and freedoms are protected, and the commercialization of parts of the human body involved in organ and tissue procurement, exchange, and allocation activities is prohibited.

The Charter of Fundamental Rights of the European Union, (2000/C 364/01) in **Article 1** on human dignity and **Article 3** on the right to the integrity of the person, refer to the prohibition on making the human body and its parts as such a source of financial gain.[53]

The Declaration of Istanbul on Organ Trafficking and Transplant Tourism (2008), urges member states "to take measures to protect the poorest and vulnerable groups from 'transplant tourism' and the sale of tissues and organs, including attention to the wider problem of international trafficking in human tissues and organs." The Istanbul Declaration defines organ trafficking as "the recruitment, transport, transfer, harboring or receipt of living or deceased persons or their organs by means of the threat or use of force or other forms of coercion, of abduction, of fraud, of deception, of the abuse of power or of a position of vulnerability, or of the giving to, or the receiving by, a third party of payments or benefits to achieve the transfer of control over the potential donor, for the purpose of exploitation by the removal of organs for transplantation." It defines transplant commercialism as a "policy or practice in which an organ is treated as a commodity, including by being bought or sold or used for material gain." It defines travel for transplantation as "the movement of organs, donors, recipients or transplant professionals across jurisdictional borders for transplantation purposes." It clarifies that "travel for transplantation becomes transplant tourism if it involves organ trafficking and/or transplant commercialism or if the resources (organs, professionals and transplant centers) devoted to providing transplants to patients from outside a country undermine the country's ability to provide transplant services for its own population."[54]

Issue of Consent or Coercion?

Like all medical interventions, the issue of organ removal should also require consent and the ethical guidelines for such consent should be followed. The WHO "Guiding Principles on Human Cell, Tissue and Organ Transplantation," suggest that "live donations are acceptable when the donor's informed and voluntary consent is obtained" and that "live donors should be informed of the probable risks, benefits and consequences of donation in a complete and understandable fashion; they should be legally competent and capable of weighing the information; and they should be acting willingly, free of any undue influence or coercion." The principle emphasizes the need for a real and well-informed choice, "which requires full, objective, and locally relevant information and excludes vulnerable persons who are incapable of fulfilling the requirements for voluntary and knowledgeable consent."[55] Other international guidance documents advise that in cases of organ removal from a living donor, the necessary consent must have been given expressly and specifically in written form or before an official body.

Trafficking in Persons for Organ Removal and Organ Trafficking: Same or Different?

Often terms such as "trafficking in persons for the purpose of organ removal" and "organ trafficking" or "trafficking in organs" are used interchangeably. "Trafficking in persons for organ removal," however, is specifically defined in the Trafficking in Persons Protocol, and does not encompass the term "trafficking in organs" or "organ trafficking." In 2008, the Council of Europe and the United Nations agreed to prepare a "Joint Study on trafficking in organs, tissues and cells and trafficking in human beings for the purpose of the removal of organs."[56] The results of the Joint Study (2009) identified a number of issues related to the trafficking in human organs, tissues, and cells which deserved further consideration. The study reported that "trafficking in organs and trafficking in persons for organ removal are different crimes, though frequently confused in public debate and among the legal and scientific communities. In the case of trafficking in organs, the object of the crime is the organ, whereas in the case of human trafficking for organ removal, the object of the crime is the person. Trafficking in organs may have its origin in cases of human trafficking for organ removal, but organ trafficking will also frequently occur with no link to a case of human trafficking. The mixing up of these two phenomena can potentially obstruct efforts to combat both phenomena and provide comprehensive victim protection and assistance."[57]

The report stated that both the Trafficking in Persons Protocol and the Council of Europe Convention on Action against Trafficking in Human Beings provide a consistent and unanimous definition of trafficking in persons and effectively address the issue of human trafficking, including for the purposes of organ removal, and there was no need for an additional international legal instrument dealing specifically with human trafficking for organ removal. Consequently, there is no single definition of trafficking in organs. None of the existing international legal instruments addressed the consensual removal of organs for financial gain or comparable advantage and/or outside of the approved domestic systems. The report identified a "need to develop a dedicated international legal tool, which builds on an agreed upon definition of trafficking in organs, includes provisions for the criminalization of this practice, along with provisions targeted to its prevention, and to victim protection and assistance."

Following the results of this study, the Committee of Ministers of the Council of Europe (CoE) established an ad-hoc Committee of Experts on Trafficking in Human Organs, Tissues and Cells.

According to the Convention, trafficking in human organs entails intentional commission of any activities such as:

> the illicit removal of organs: removal without the free, informed and specific consent of the living donor, or, in the case of the deceased donor, without the removal being authorized under its domestic law, OR where in exchange for the removal of organs, the living donor, or a third party, has been offered or has received a financial gain or com-

> parable advantage, OR where in exchange for the removal of organs from a deceased donor, a third party has been offered or has received a financial gain or comparable advantage.

It could also be

> the use of illicitly removed organs; the illicit solicitation or recruitment (of organ donors or recipients), or the offering and requesting of undue advantages; the preparation, preservation, storage, transportation, transfer, receipt, import and export of illicitly removed human organs; aiding or abetting and attempt.
>
> Parties to the Convention shall take the necessary legislative and other measures to establish as a criminal offense under its domestic law the practices mentioned above. Parties shall also consider taking the necessary legislative or other measures to establish as a criminal offense under its domestic law, when committed intentionally, the removal or the implantation of human organs from living or deceased donors where performed outside of the framework of its domestic transplantation system, or in breach of essential principles of national transplantation laws or rules. The Convention also requires States parties to take the necessary legislative or other measures to: ensure corporate liability if certain conditions are met (i.e., the offense is committed by a person in a leading position); punish the offenses described in the Convention through sanctions which are effective, proportionate and dissuasive. A set of circumstances will be aggravating if the offense caused the death of, or serious damage to the physical or mental health of the victim; the offense was committed by persons abusing their position; the offence was committed in the framework of a criminal organization; the perpetrator has previously been convicted of offenses established in accordance with this Convention; the offense was committed against a child or any other particularly vulnerable person.[58]

International Guidelines for Human Cell, Tissue, and Organ Transplant

The World Health Organization (WHO) issued "Guiding Principles on Human Cell, Tissue and Organ Transplantation," which the 63rd World Health Assembly endorsed in May 2010 through resolution WHA63.22. These principles govern the removal of organs from both deceased and living donors for the purpose of transplantation. They provide key international standards. According to these standards, in the case of deceased donor donation, the international guidelines (Guiding Principle 1) requires that the cells, tissues or organs may be removed from a deceased person if the person had expressly consented to such removal during his or her lifetime; depending upon domestic law, such consent may be made orally or recorded on a donor card, driver's license or identity card or in the medical record or a donor registry. When the deceased has neither consented nor clearly expressed opposition to organ removal, permission should be obtained from a legally specified surrogate, usually a family member.[59]

The guidelines also require "development of the deceased donor programs." In case of living donor donation, the guidelines mandate that living donors should be, in general, genetically related to their recipients (unless such related persons and recipients do not match well immunologically). Living donors are required to give informed and voluntary consent and act willingly—free of any undue influence or coercion. The living donors are required to be informed of the probable risks, benefits, and consequences of the donation in a complete and understandable fashion. The hospital and the physicians are responsible for ensuring professional care of donors and well-organized follow-up. The guidelines mandate that the ethical standards need to be strictly adhered to and the criteria for donor selection and to allocate organs must be based on clinical criteria and ethical norms, not financial considerations. The guidelines prohibit removal of organs from minor (and legally incompetent) donors, except when such is not allowed under national law for narrowly defined cases. The organ donation should be done freely, without any monetary payment or other reward of monetary value (except for the reimbursement of reasonable and verifiable expenses incurred by the donor, such as loss of income.[60]

According to the **International Guidelines for Human Cell, Tissue and Organ Transplant**, purchase or sale of organs is banned. Physicians and other health professionals are prohibited from engaging in transplantation procedures where it is suspected that organs are obtained through coercion. The Seventh Principle of the Guiding Principles of the World Health Organization suggest that "Physicians and other health professionals should not engage in transplantation procedures, and health insurers and other payers should not cover such procedures, if the cells, tissues or organs concerned have been obtained through exploitation or coercion of, or payment to, the donor or the next of kin of a deceased donor."[61]

Health insurance companies are advised not to cover such procedures if the organs have been obtained through exploitation or coercion of, or payment to, the donor. Advertising the need for or availability of organs, with a view to offering or seeking payment to individuals for their organs, should be prohibited.

The guidelines prohibit any payment to the donors in consideration for their donation of organs except the legitimate promotion of altruistic donation of organs by means of advertisement or public appeal in line with domestic regulation. All healthcare facilities and professionals involved in cell, tissue, or organ procurement and transplantation procedures are prohibited from receiving any payment exceeding the justifiable fee for the services rendered. The guidelines also require maintaining transparency for all donation and transplantation activities. All personnel and facilities involved are required to maintain confidentiality and privacy of the donors and recipients.[62]

The Consensus Statement of the Amsterdam Forum on the Care of the Living Donor and the Declaration of Istanbul on Organ Trafficking and Transplant Tourism offer international professional guidelines, recommendations, and principles to develop universal standards concerning organ donations from both living and deceased donation.[63]

Strategies for the Prevention and Control of Organ Trafficking and Trafficking in Persons for Removal of Organs

Address the Root Causes

The first and foremost effective preventive strategy in addressing the crime of organ trafficking and/or the trafficking of persons for the removal of organs will entail addressing the root causes to reduce people's vulnerability to falling victim to the traffickers' tactics. States should take measures to alleviate the factors that make people vulnerable to trafficking, such as poverty, underdevelopment, and lack of equal opportunity. Since poverty is determined to be one of the most prevalent features in trafficking in persons for the purpose of organ removal, the states need to develop sustainable and empowering poverty-alleviation programs targeted at communities which are vulnerable to being recruited as donors.

Reduce the Demand for Irregularly Procured Organs

In order to reduce the demand for transplantations caused by organ failure, the states need to promote healthy lifestyles. States need to optimize both deceased and living donations through providing comprehensive information to potential donors and to family members of deceased (potential) donors, as well to the potential organ recipients.

Raise Awareness

States need to institute awareness raising programs to inform potential donors and recipients of the risks and benefits of live organ donation. The donors should be fully informed and educated about the risks of trafficking in persons for the purpose of organ removal. They should also be informed that the sale and purchase of organs is a crime. Governments, hospitals and other facilities used as transplant centers, civil society, nongovernmental organizations, and international organizations should institute programs to educate and inform persons who are vulnerable to exploitation by traffickers as potential donors.

Hospitals and/or transplant clinics should be responsible for informing and educating the patients—potential recipients—about the medical, ethical, and legal risks in purchasing organs. They should distribute the brochures of the Declaration of Istanbul Custodian Group, "Thinking of Buying a Kidney? Stop. What You Need to Know" etc. Such materials can be placed in buildings and institutions that potential sellers and buyers are more likely to visit, such as immigration offices and airports. People intending to travel abroad to buy or sell a kidney, medical and health professionals, and others who may come into contact with trafficking in persons for organ removal must be educated about the great risks they will be taking when engaging in this enterprise.

"Target audiences"—the potential buyers and sellers as well as brokers, hospitals medical personnel, and others must be made aware of the ethical and social issues relating to trafficking in persons for organ removal, as well as laws pertaining to organ donation and transplantation. In general, all staff at the agencies that potentially play some role in facilitating organ trafficking must be educated and made aware of their responsibility in reporting such activities. The potential whistle-blowers in medical institutions, or in other organizations, should be able to report anonymously and confidentially, with legal protection from employer reprisal/retaliation, as well as easy reporting access. They should be made aware of protections in place for them, in the event they report suspicions and/or otherwise assist criminal justice authorities. Engagement of media in raising awareness can also play a significant role in preventing organ-related crimes by ensuring that reporting about trafficking in persons for the purpose of organ removal and related conduct is accurate and evidence-based. Social media could be used for training and awareness raising. Law enforcement officers, commercial airline employees, journalists, reporters, and others should be trained to detect and address the crime of trafficking in persons for organ removal.

Local and International Laws Coordination

Each member state should strengthen their laws to regulate organ donation and transplantation. They should develop a legal framework in coordination with international instruments and standards. Individual state laws should clearly establish that trafficking in persons for the purpose of organ removal is a serious offense and define punitive measures related to the violation of such laws. Laws should not have any ambiguities or loopholes for exploitation and corruption.[64]

Medical and ethical standards should be established to guide and define informed consent. All interested parties and stakeholders should be educated about the laws pertaining to the consent to the organ removal. All potential donors must receive complete medical and psychological counselling and evaluation prior to being accepted as donors. In accordance with international regulations, all donors should be provided complete information regarding the process and the risks involved, as well as post-operative healthcare needs. The hospitals and the medical personnel should be held responsible for ensuring that the potential donors are able to give free and fully informed consent. Hospitals should be required to maintain clear records of consent forms signed by donors. Laws should be implemented to hold hospitals and medical personnel accountable for their involvement in trafficking in persons for organ removal.[65]

Advertising—electronically and print—pertaining to the selling, buying, or brokering of organs should be prohibited. The states should create rules, regulations, and laws mandating transparency in all organ transplantation activities. The state, the medical sector, nongovernmental organizations, and international organizations should ensure transparency and accountability in all activities, regulations, and practices concerning organ transplantation. Efforts should be made to improve the safety and efficacy of donation and transplantation by applying and promoting international best practices. They should promote public discussions, research, and monitoring organ donation and transplantation programs as well as educational campaigns on organ-related crimes of trafficking in persons for the purpose of organ removal. The states should take responsibility for ensuring that organs are not procured through financial transactions.

Conclusion

Challenges: Detection, Investigation, and Prosecution of Organ Trafficking Crime

Some of the greatest challenges in addressing the crime of organ trafficking or trafficking in persons for organ removal include detection, investigation, and prosecution of this crime. First of all, this is a crime of a transnational nature requiring a transnational criminal justice response. It involves actors from various parts of the globe—donors coming from one country, recipients from another, and maybe brokers from yet another one, and the transplantation taking place in a country different from all these countries, thus involving doctors and other medical staff from different countries. Thus, to effectively address such a crime, there is a need for a collaborative transnational criminal justice response. Secondly, the crime takes place in hospitals or transplantation centers—generally perceived and accepted to be legitimate sectors. These places must be required to keep systematic records and make all transactions transparent and subject to scrutiny. Thirdly, like victims of any crime, in general, victims of this crime are also often reluctant to contact authorities out of fear for the safety of themselves and retaliation against their families. Victims who are aware that the sale of organs is a crime may not report to the authorities for the fear of prosecution for their own role in the process and involvement in this crime.

Law enforcement officers and customs, immigration, and border officials are the frontline gatekeepers of borders. They are the first ones to encounter both trafficking victims and traffickers. In order to identify and prosecute the traffickers, frontline gatekeepers should be provided with training that equips them to identify potential and actual victims as well as perpetrators of trafficking in persons for the purpose of organ removal. They should be trained to have the skills to identify and manage crime scenes that may exist in otherwise legitimate locations, such as hospitals and transplantation centers.

Indicators of Trafficking of Persons for Organ Removal

Law enforcement and other personnel should be able to differentiate between legal and illegal organ transplant. If the hospital, doctor, or the other personnel or facility does not have any documentation of donor consent; consent forms signed by organ donor for any given organ donation; or social, medical, and psychological evaluation reports on the donor, then these are clear indicators of suspicious activity worth investigation. If immigration authorities are getting a higher than usual number of people migrating to and receiving invitation letters from a particular hospital; find someone with a fresh (48 hours old or more recent) nephrectomy (kidney removal) going on an airplane; notice many people arriving at the same time and being put at an airport hotel; discover a person arriving at the airport with huge amounts of cash strapped around their body; or find persons arriving at the airport claiming to be coming for medical consultations, but unable to provide any documents, these are all indicators of potential organ trafficking activities.

Assistance to the Victims

In general, victims may refuse to cooperate with the authorities because of the fear of retaliation against them and their families. They may also be afraid of police because of their own role in the process. In order to get victims' cooperation, their fears should be allayed and they should be provided adequate protection and support. Medical and healthcare practitioners who suspect a victim of trafficking in persons for the purpose of organ removal should refer that person to providers of protection and assistance services. Specific protection and assistance services should be made available to victims of trafficking for the purpose of organ removal that cater to their individual and specific needs. The law enforcement agencies should be empowered in investigating, gathering more information, and sharing intelligence about possible cases of trafficking in organs or trafficking in persons for the purpose of organ removal. They should be trained and be able to recognize the means and methods used by organized criminal groups for the purpose of trafficking in persons for organ removal.

Chapter Review

In this chapter, we have discussed the human trade for organs. We have discussed in detail the process of commercializing humans for organ removal. We learned various aspects of trafficking in persons for the purpose of organ removal to develop an understanding of human trafficking in our contemporary world. In essence, we discussed the following:

- Commercializing Humans for Organ Removal
  - Trafficking in Persons and the Organ Trade: An Overview
    - Organ Transplantation: A Medical Wonder? Or Designer of a New Branch of Trafficking?
    - Who Are the Main Actors Involved in Organ Trafficking?

        - Organ Trafficking: An Organized Crime?
        - Who Are the Donors: Victims?
        - Process: How Are the Donors/Victims Recruited?
    - Trafficking in Persons Protocol and Organ Trafficking
    - The United Network for Organ Sharing (UNOS) and Organ Transplant Tourism
    - Organ Trafficking: History
    - Laws Prohibiting Organ Trafficking
        - The Trafficking in Persons Protocol and Removal of Organs
        - The Optional Protocol to the Convention on the Rights of the Child
        - Council of Europe (CoE) Convention: The Oviedo Convention
        - The Charter of Fundamental Rights of the European Union, Article 1
        - The Declaration of Istanbul on Organ Trafficking and Transplant Tourism (2008)
    - Issue of Consent or Coercion?
    - Trafficking in Persons Organ Removal and Organ Trafficking: Same or Different?
    - International Guidelines for Human Cell, Tissue and Organ Transplant
    - Strategies for the Prevention and Control of Organ Trafficking and Trafficking in Persons for Removal of Organs
        - Address the Root Causes
        - Reduce the Demand for Irregularly Procured Organs
        - Raise Awareness
        - Local and International Laws Coordination
    - Conclusion
        - Challenges: Detection, Investigation, and Prosecution of Organ Trafficking Crime
        - Indicators of Trafficking of Persons for Organ Removal
        - Assistance to the Victims

Discussion Questions

1) Identify differences and similarities between trafficking in persons for organ removal and organ trafficking. Give examples.

2) Discuss how advancement in transplant science has helped some people and how it has created more health problems for some.

3) Who are the perpetrators in the case of organ trafficking? Who are the victims? Provide examples.

4) Find an organ trafficking case reported in one of the newspapers and determine whether the case is domestic or international.

5) What are the cues that can indicate that a hospital or doctors are involved in organ trafficking?

6) List at least three strategies that can be used to prevent and control organ trafficking.

7) Identify at least two international laws/documents/protocols that prohibit organ trafficking.

8) Check your state's laws and identify if there are any laws or statutes that prohibit organ trafficking and provide guidance on how to address the crime of organ trafficking.

References

Ambagtsheer, J. A. E., Assya Pascalev, Jessica de Jong, Susanne Lundin, Ninoslav Ivanovski, Natalia Codreanu, Martin Gunnarson, et al. "Trafficking in Human Beings for the Purpose of Organ Removal: A Comprehensive Literature Review." *Transplant Immunology* 4, no. 31 (2014): 254.

Assaya, Pascalev, De Jong, Jessica, Ambagtsheer, Frederike, Susanne Lundin, Ivanovski Ninoslav, Codreanu, Natalia, Martin Gunnarson, et al. "Trafficking in Human Beings for the Purpose of Organ Removal: A Comprehensive Literature Review." Hott Project. 2013. http://hottproject.com/userfiles/HOTTProject-TraffickinginHumanBeingsforthePurposeofOrganRemoval-AComprehensiveLiteratureReview-OnlinePublication.pdf.

Berglund, S., and Lundin, S. "'I Had to Leave': Making Sense of Buying a Kidney Abroad." In *The Body as a Gift, Resource, and Commodity: Exchanging Organs, Tissues and Cells in the 21st Century*, edited by Gunnarson M. and F. Svenaeus, 321–42. Huddinge: Södertörn Studies in Practical Knowledge, 2012.

Betancourt, Antonio. "The Face of Human Trafficking in America." Washington, DC Forum. Washington, DC: UPF International, 2012.

Budiani Saberi, Debra A., and Amr Mostafa. "Care for Commercial Living Donors: The Experience of an NGO's Outreach in Egypt." *Transplant International* 24, no. 4 (2011): 317–323.

Budiani Saberi, Debra A., and Francis L. Delmonico. "Organ Trafficking and Transplant Tourism: A Commentary on the Global Realities." *American Journal of Transplantation* 8, no. 5 (2008): 925–929.

Caplan, Arthur, Beatriz Dominguez-Gil, Rafael Matesanz, and Carmen Prior. "Trafficking in Organs, Tissues and Cells and Trafficking in Human Beings for the Purpose of the Removal of Organs, Joint Council of Europe/United Nations Study." Strasbourg: Council of Europe/United Nations, 2009.

Council of Europe. Additional Protocol to the Convention on Human Rights and Biomedicine Concerning Transplantation of Organs and Tissues of Human Origin. Strasbourg, January 24, 2002.

Council of Europe. Convention on Human Rights and Biomedicine. CETS 165. April 4, 1997.

Council of Europe on Action against Trafficking in Human Beings. CETS No.197. Warsaw, May 16, 2005.

Dalal, Aparna R. "Philosophy of Organ Donation: Review of Ethical Facets." *World Journal of Transplantation* 5, no. 2 (2015): 44.

Danovitch, Gabriel M., ed. *Handbook of Kidney Transplantation*. Lippincott Williams & Wilkins, 2009.

Dennis, Michael J. "Newly Adopted Protocols to the Convention on the Rights of the Child." *The American Journal of International Law* 94, no. 4 (2000): 789–796.

Francis, Leslie P., and John G. Francis. "Stateless Crimes, Legitimacy, and International Criminal Law: The Case of Organ Trafficking." *Criminal Law and Philosophy* 4, no. 3 (2010): 283–295.

Gunnarson, Martin, and Susanne Lundin. "The Complexities of Victimhood: Insights from the Organ Trade." *Somatechnics* 5, no. 1 (2015): 32–51.

Matas, David, and David Kilgour. *Report into Allegations of Organ Harvesting of Falun Gong Practitioners in China*. 2006.

Mendoza, Roger Lee. "Price Deflation and the Underground Organ Economy in the Philippines." *Journal of Public Health* 33, no. 1 (2011): 101–107.

Office of the Special Representative and Co-ordinator for Combating Trafficking in Human Beings. "Trafficking in Human Beings for the Purpose of Organ Removal in the Osce Region: Analysis and Findings." Vienna: Organization for Security and Cooperation in Europe, 2013.

Rahmel, A. "Eurotransplant Annual Report 2012." Eurotransplant International Foundation. Leiden: Eurotransplant Foundation, 2012.

Salahudeen, Abdulla K., H. F. Woods, A. Pingle, M. Nur-El-Huda Suleyman, K. Shakuntala, M. Nandakumar, T. M. Yahya, and A. S. Daar. "High Mortality among Recipients of Bought Living-Unrelated Donor Kidneys." *The Lancet* 336, no. 8717 (1990): 725–728.

Scheper-Hughes, Nancy. "Theft of Life." *Society* 27, no. 6 (1990): 57–62.

Schloenhardt, Andreas, and Samantha Garbutt. "Trafficking in Persons for the Purpose of Organ Removal: International Law and Australian Practice." *Criminal Law Journal* 36, no. 3 (2012): 145–158.

Sembacher, Anke. "The Council of Europe Convention on Action against Trafficking in Human Beings." *Tul. J. Int'l & Comp. L.* 14 (2005): 435.

Shimazono, Y. "Mapping 'Transplant Tourism.'" Presentation at the World Health Organization's Second Global Consultation on Human Transplantation. 2007.

Sixty-Third World Health Assembly. "WHO Guiding Principles on Human Cell, Tissue and Organ Transplantation." *Cell and Tissue Banking* 11, no. 4 (2010): 413.

Tong, Allison, Jeremy R. Chapman, Germaine Wong, Nicholas B. Cross, Pikli Batabyal, and Jonathan C. Craig. "The Experiences of Commercial Kidney Donors: Thematic Synthesis of Qualitative Research." *Transplant International* 25, no. 11 (2012): 1138–1149.

United Nations General Assembly. Protocol to Prevent, Suppress and Punish Trafficking in Persons, Especially Women and Children, Supplementing the United Nations Convention against Transnational Organized Crime. Resolution 55 (2000): 25.

United Nations General Assembly. Trafficking in Persons, Especially Women and Children. Note by the Secretary Secretary-General, Report of the Special Rapporteur on Trafficking in Persons, Especially Women and Children. A/68/256. 68th Session. August 2, 2013.

United Nations Office on Drugs and Crime (UNODC). *Global Report on Trafficking in Persons: Executive Summary*. 2014. http://www.unodc.org/documents/data-and-analysis/glotip/GLOTIP14_ExSum_english.pdf.

United Nations Office on Drugs and Crime (UNODC). Trafficking in Persons for the Purpose of Organ Removal. 2015.

United States Department of Health and Human Services. "Organ Procurement and Transplantation Network." Health Resources and Services Administration. 2014.

World Health Organization. "Organ Trafficking and Transplantation Pose New Challenges." *Bulletin of the World Health Organization* (2004): 82–89.

Further Suggested Readings

Capron, Alexander Morgan, Elmi Muller, Gilad Erlich, Manoj John, Ric Esther Bienstock, Mark McCarren, Robin Palmer, Nancy Scheper-Hughes, Dina

Siegel, and Jordan Yankov. "Stimulating and Enhancing Partnerships between Transplant Professionals and Law Enforcement: Recommendations." *Transplantation Direct* 2, no. 2 (2016): e57.

Clawson, Heather J., Nicole Dutch, Amy Solomon, and L. Goldblatt Grace. "Human Trafficking into and within the United States: A Review of the Literature." Washington, DC: Office of the Assistant Secretary for Planning and Evaluation, US Department of Health and Human Services, 2009.

Cohen, Desmond, and Elizabeth Reid. "The Vulnerability of Women: Is This a Useful Construct for Policy and Programming?" Issues paper No. 28, HIV and Development Programme. New York: United Nations Development Programme, 1996.

Council of Europe. *Explanatory Report to the Additional Protocol to the Convention on Human Rights and Biomedicine concerning Transplantation of Organs and Tissues of Human Origin*. European Treaty Series No. 186. Strasbourg: 2002.

Human Trafficking Center. "Domestic Human Trafficking—An Internal Issue." United Nations. Optional protocols to the Convention on the Rights of the Child (A/54/L.84). Geneva: United Nations, 2000.

International Labor Organization (ILO). Abolition of Forced Labor Convention. (No. 105). Convention Concerning the Abolition of Forced Labor. Adoption: 25 Jun 1957. Entry into force: 17 Jan 1959. http://www.ilo.org/dyn/normlex/en/f?p=1000:12100:0::NO::P12100_ILO_CODE:C105.

International Labor Organization (ILO). *Profits and Poverty: The Economics of Forced Labour.* http:// http://www.ilo.org/wcmsp5/groups/public/—ed_norm/—declaration/documents/publication/wcms_243391.pdf.

Miko, Francis T. "Trafficking in Women and Children: The US and International Response—Updated March 26, 2004." Graduate Theses and Dissertations. Paper 12068. Cornell University ILR School, 2004.

Roby, Jini L. "Women and Children in the Global Sex Trade." *International Social Work* 48, no. 2 (2005): 136–147.

Roby, Jini L., Jennifer Turley, and JoAnna Garrick Cloward. "US Response to Human Trafficking: Is It Enough?" *Journal of Immigrant & Refugee Studies* 6, no. 4 (2008): 508–525.

United Nations Human Rights Office of the High Commissioner. International Covenant on Civil and Political Rights. Resolution 2200A (XXI) of 16 December 1966. Entry into force: 23 March 1976, in accordance with Article 49. http://www.ohchr.org/en/professionalinterest/pages/ccpr.aspx.

United Nations Human Rights Office of the High Commissioner. The 1956 Supplementary Convention on the Abolition of Slavery, the Slave Trade, and Institutions and Practices Similar to Slavery. Resolution 608(XXI) of

30 April 1956. Entry into force: 30 April 1957, in accordance with Article 13. http://www.ohchr.org/EN/ProfessionalInterest/Pages/SupplementaryConventionAbolitionOfSlavery.aspx.

United Nations Office on Drugs and Crime (UNODC). *Fact Sheet on Human Trafficking.* 2006. http://www.unodc.org/unodc/en/trafficking_victim_consents.html#how.

United Nations Office on Drugs and Crime (UNODC). *Trafficking in Human Beings* 2006. http://www.unodc.org/unodc/en/trafficking_human_beings.html.

United States Congress. Mann Act, 18 United States Code §§. 1581–1588.

United States Congress. Trafficking Victims Protection Act (TVPA). Pub. L. No. 106-386, 114 Stat. 1473. 2000.

United States Congress. Trafficking Victims Protection Reauthorization Act (TVPRA). Pub. L. No. 108-193, 117 Stat. 2875. 2003.

United States Congress. Trafficking Victims Protection Reauthorization Act (TVPRA). Pub. L. No. 109-164. 2005.

United States Department of Justice (USDOJ). *Assessment of U.S. Government Efforts to Combat Trafficking in Persons in Fiscal Year 2006.* 2007. http://www.usdoj.gov/ag/annualreports/tr2007/assessment-of-efforts-to-combat-tip0907.pdf.

United States Department of Justice (USDOJ). *Report on Activities to Combat Human Trafficking: Fiscal Years 2001–2005.* 2006. http://www.usdoj.gov/crt/crim/trafficking_report_2006.pdf.

United States Department of State, Office to Monitor and Combat Trafficking in Persons. *Trafficking in Persons Report.* 2004. http://www.state.gov/g/tip/rls/tiprpt/2004/34021.htm.

United States Department of State, Office to Monitor and Combat Trafficking in Persons. *Trafficking in Persons Report.* 2005. http://www.state.gov/g/tip/rls/tiprpt/2005/.

Vital Voices Global Partnership. *Stateless and Vulnerable to Human Trafficking in Thailand.* Washington, DC, June 2007, p. 13. www.vitalvoices.org.

Weitzer, R. "Moral Crusade against Prostitution." *Society* March/April 2006: 33–38.

Wilson, D., Walsh, W. and Kleuber, S. Trafficking in Human Beings: Training and Services among US Law Enforcement Agencies. *Police Practice and Research* 7 no. 2 (2006): 149–160. Taylor & Francis Online.

Notes

1. Human Trafficking: Crime Inc.—The Underground Economy ©2011 http://www.films.com/dealerpreview/47318.

2. Francis, L. P., & J. G. Francis. (2010). Stateless crimes, legitimacy, and international criminal law: The case of organ trafficking. *Criminal Law and Philosophy*, *4*(3), 283–295.

3. Sengupta, K. (2006). Human Trafficking: Greed and the Trail of Death. The Independent. https://www.crin.org/en/library/news-archive/human-trafficking-greed-and-trail-death.

4. Betancourt, A. (2012, October 3). Washington, DC Forum: The face of human trafficking in America. Roundtable meeting of UPF's Office for Peace and Security Affairs. Washington, DC.

5. Washington DC Peace & Security Forum: The Face of Human Trafficking (2012). UPF Office of Peace and Security Affairs, Washington, DC, USA.

6. World Health Organization. (2010). WHO guiding principles on human cell, tissue and organ transplantation. *Transplantation*, *90*(3), 229.

7. Global Observatory on Donation and Transplantation Data. (2013). http://www.transplant-observatory.org/.

8. Rahmel, A., ed. (2012). *Eurotransplant annual report 2012.* Published annually by Eurotransplant International Foundation. Leiden: Eurotransplant Foundation.

9. US Department of Health and Human Services. (2014). Organ Procurement and Transplantation Network. Health Resources and Services Administration.

10. World Health Organization. (2010). WHO guiding principles on human cell, tissue and organ transplantation. *Transplantation*, *90*(3), 229.

11. World Health Organization. (2004). Organ trafficking and transplantation pose new challenges. *Bulletin of the World Health Organization*, 82–89.

12. World Health Organization. (2010). WHO guiding principles on human cell, tissue and organ transplantation. *Transplantation*, *90*(3), 229.

13. World Health Organization. (2010). "WHO guiding principles on human cell, tissue and organ transplantation." *Transplantation*, *90*(3), 229.

14. US Department of Health & Human Services. (2015). https://www.organdonor.gov/statistics-stories/statistics.html.

15. US Department of Health and Human Services. (2014). Organ Procurement and Transplantation Network. Health Resources and Services Administration. United Nations Office on Drugs and Crime. (2015). Trafficking in persons for the purpose of organ removal.

16. Office of the Special Representative and Co-ordinator for Combating Trafficking in Human Beings. (2013). Trafficking in human beings for the purpose of organ removal in the OSCE region: Analysis and findings. Vienna: Organization for Security and Cooperation in Europe.

17. US Department of Health and Human Services. (2014). Organ Procurement and Transplantation Network. Health Resources and Services Administration. United Nations Office on Drugs and Crime. (2015). Trafficking in Persons for the Purpose of Organ Removal.

18. Mendoza, R. L. (2011). Price deflation and the underground organ economy in the Philippines. *Journal of Public Health*, *33*(1), 101–107.

19. Danovitch, G. M., ed. (2009). *Handbook of kidney transplantation.* Lippincott Williams & Wilkins.

20. United Nations Secretariat. (2005). United Nations Convention Against Transnational Organized Crime and the Protocols Thereto.

21. United Nations Office on Drugs and Crime (UNODC). (2014). *Global report on trafficking in persons: Executive summary.* http://www.unodc.org/documents/data-and-analysis/glotip/GLOTIP14_ExSum_english.pdf.

22. US Department of Health and Human Services. (2014). Organ Procurement and Transplantation Network. Health Resources and Services Administration. United Nations and United Nations Office on Drugs and Crime. (2015). Trafficking in Persons for the Purpose of Organ Removal.

23. Gunnarson, M., & S. Lundin. (2015). The complexities of victimhood: Insights from the organ trade. *Somatechnics*, *5*(1), 32–51.

24. McCaghy, C. H., T. A. Capron, J. D. Jamieson, & S. H. Carey. (2016). *Deviant behavior: Crime, conflict, and interest groups.* Routledge.

25. Tong, A., J. R. Chapman, G. Wong, N. B. Cross, P. Batabyal, & J. C. Craig. (2012). The experiences of commercial kidney donors: Thematic synthesis of qualitative research. *Transplant International*, *25*(11), 1138–1149.

26. UN General Assembly. (2000). Protocol to prevent, suppress and punish trafficking in persons, especially women and children. Supplement to the United Nations convention against transnational organized crime. Resolution 55, 25.

27. US Department of Health and Human Services. (2014). Organ Procurement and Transplantation Network. Health Resources and Services Administration. United Nations and United Nations Office on Drugs and Crime. (2015). Trafficking in Persons for the Purpose of Organ Removal.

28. World Health Organization. (2004). Organ trafficking and transplantation pose new challenges. *Bulletin of the World Health Organization*, 82–89.

29. Dalal, A. R. Philosophy of organ donation: Review of ethical facets. *World Journal of Transplantation*, *5*(2), 44.

30. Scutti, S. (2015). "Organ Trafficking: An International Crime Infrequently Punished," Medical Daily, Jul 9, 2013.

31. World Health Organization. (2004). Organ trafficking and transplantation pose new challenges. *Bulletin of the World Health Organization*, 82–89.

32. World Health Organization. (2010). WHO guiding principles on human cell, tissue and organ transplantation. *Transplantation*, *90*(3), 229.

33. Matas, D., & D. Kilgour. (2006, July 6). Report into allegations of organ harvesting of Falun Gong practitioners in China.

34. Budiani Saberi, D. A., & F. L. Delmonico. (2008). Organ trafficking and transplant tourism: A commentary on the global realities. *American Journal of Transplantation*, *8*(5), 925–929.

35. Berglund, S., & Lundin, S. (2012). 'I had to leave': Making sense of buying a kidney abroad. In Gunnarson, M., & F. Svenaeus (eds.), *The body as a gift, resource, and commodity: Exchanging organs, tissues and cells in the 21st century*, (pp. 321–42). Huddinge: Södertörn Studies in Practical Knowledge.

36. Budiani Saberi, D., & A. Mostafa. (2011). Care for commercial living donors: The experience of an NGO's outreach in Egypt. *Transplant International*, *24*(4), 317–323.

37. Shimazono, Y. (2007). Mapping "transplant tourism." Presentation at the World Health Organization's Second Global Consultation on Human Transplantation.

38. World Health Organization. (2010). WHO guiding principles on human cell, tissue and organ transplantation. *Transplantation*, *90*(3), 229.

39. Schloenhardt, A., & S. Garbutt. (2012). Trafficking in persons for the purpose of organ removal: International law and Australian practice. *Criminal Law Journal*, *36*(3), 145–158.

40. Salahudeen, A. K., H. F. Woods, A. Pingle, M. Nur-El-Huda Suleyman, K. Shakuntala, M. Nandakumar, T. M. Yahya, & A. S. Daar. (1990). High mortality among recipients of bought living-unrelated donor kidneys. *The Lancet*, *336*(8717), 725–728.

41. Scheper-Hughes, N. (1990). Theft of life. *Society*, 27(6), 57–62.

42. United Nations General Assembly. (2013, August 2). Trafficking in persons, especially women and children. Note by the Secretary Secretary-General, Report of the Special Rapporteur on Trafficking in Persons, Especially Women and Children, at P. 6/24. A/68/256. 68th Session.

43. Office of the Special Representative and Co-ordinator for Combating Trafficking in Human Beings. (2013). Trafficking in human beings for the purpose of organ removal in the Osce Region: Analysis and findings. Vienna: Organization for Security and Cooperation in Europe.

44. United Nations General Assembly. (2013, August 2). Trafficking in persons, especially women and children. Note by the Secretary Secretary-General, Report of the Special Rapporteur on Trafficking in Persons, Especially Women and Children, at P. 6/24. A/68/256. 68th Session.

45. United Nations Office on Drugs and Crime (UNODC). (2014). Global report on trafficking in persons: Executive summary. http://www.unodc.org/documents/data-and-analysis/glotip/GLOTIP14_ExSum_english.pdf.

46. United Nations Office on Drugs and Crime (UNODC). (2014). Global report on trafficking in persons: Executive summary. http://www.unodc.org/documents/data-and-analysis/glotip/GLOTIP14_ExSum_english.pdf.

47. UN General Assembly. (2000). Protocol to prevent, suppress and punish trafficking in persons, especially women and children. Supplement to the United Nations convention against transnational organized crime. Resolution 55, 25.

48. Dennis, M. J. (2000). Newly adopted protocols to the Convention on the Rights of the Child. *The American Journal of International Law*, *94*(4), 789–796.

49. The Council of Europe. (2005, May 16). Convention on Action against Trafficking in Human Beings. (CoE, CETS No.197). Warsaw.

50. Sembacher, A. (2005). Council of Europe Convention on Action against Trafficking in Human Beings, The. *Tul. J. Int'l & Comp. L.*, *14*, 435.

51. Council of Europe. (1997, April 4). Convention on Human Rights and Biomedicine. Oviedo; Council of Europe. (2002, January 24). Additional protocol to the Convention on Human Rights and Biomedicine Concerning Transplantation of Organs and Tissues of Human Origin. Strasbourg.

52. Council of Europe. (1997, April 4). Convention on Human Rights and Biomedicine. Oviedo; Council of Europe. (2002, January 24). Additional Protocol to the Convention on Human Rights and Biomedicine Concerning Transplantation of Organs and Tissues of Human Origin. Strasbourg.

53. The Charter of Fundamental Rights of the European Union. (2000/C 364/01).

54. The Declaration of Istanbul on Organ Trafficking and Transplant Tourism. (2008).

55. Sixty-Third World Health Assembly. (2010). WHO guiding principles on human

cell, tissue and organ transplantation. *Cell and Tissue Banking, 11*(4), 413.

56. Permanent Mission of Slovenia to the UN co-sponsored the launching event of the Joint Council of Europe and UN study on trafficking in organs, tissues and cells and trafficking in human being for the purpose of the removal of organs (2009). http://www.newyork.predstavnistvo.si/index.php?id=824&L=1&tx_ttnews%5Btt_news%5D=2849&cHash=4c24a19bc35c43844bec14f3d0228e65.

57. Caplan, A., B. Dominguez-Gil, R. Matesanz, & C. Prior. (2009). Trafficking in organs, tissues and cells and trafficking in human beings for the purpose of the removal of organs. Joint Council of Europe/United Nations Study. Strasbourg: Council of Europe/United Nations.

58. United Nations Office of Drugs and Crime (2015). Assessment Toolkit—Trafficking in Persons for the Organ Removal.

59. Sixty-Third, W. H. A. (2010). WHO Guiding Principles on Human Cell, Tissue and Organ Transplantation. *Cell and tissue banking, 11*(4), 413. http://www.eatb.org/media/uploads/Guiding_PrinciplesTransplantation_WHA63%2022en.pdf.

60. Sixty-Third World Health Assembly. WHO guiding principles on human cell, tissue and organ transplantation. *Cell and Tissue Banking, 11*(4), 413.

61. Sixty-Third, W. H. A. (2010). WHO Guiding Principles on Human Cell, Tissue and Organ Transplantation. *Cell and tissue banking, 11*(4), 413. http://www.eatb.org/media/uploads/Guiding_PrinciplesTransplantation_WHA63%2022en.pdf.

62. Council of Europe. (2002). Additional protocol to the Convention on Human Rights and Biomedicine Concerning Transplantation of Organs and Tissues of Human Origin." Strasbourg.

63. Committee of the Transplantation Society. (2004). The consensus statement of the Amsterdam Forum on the care of the live kidney donor. *Transplantation, 78*(4).

64. Zazula, C. P. (2012). Liver transplantation: The illusion of choice. *Virtual Mentor, 14*(3), 269.

65. Lantos, J. D., & B. A. Warady. (2012). "Should a nonadherent adolescent receive a second kidney?" *Virtual Mentor, 14*(3), 190.

Chapter 6

Trafficking in Persons: Global Response to Human Trafficking

Chapter Objectives

This chapter provides a comprehensive understanding of the following:

- Human Trafficking
  - The Global Response to Trafficking in Persons
  - International Treaties, Conventions, and Protocols
    - United Nations Conventions and Protocols
    - Article 9 of the Trafficking in Persons (TIP) Protocol
    - Article 31 of the Organized Crime Convention
    - International Labor Organization (ILO) Conventions
    - The Council of Europe (COE) Convention on Action against Trafficking in Human Beings
    - Global Initiatives
  - United States' Response to Human Trafficking
    - Trafficking Victims Protection Act
    - The Tier System
    - Office to Monitor and Combat Trafficking in Persons
    - Overview of Campaigns, Initiatives, and Programs Funded by the United States

Introduction: Human Trafficking

The Global Response to Trafficking in Persons

Trafficking in persons, also known as human trafficking, is a horrifying crime. It is an extreme form of exploitative enterprise in which men, women, and children are bought, sold, and held against their will in involuntary servitude for sex and labor. In addition to the tremendous personal damage suffered by individual trafficking victims, this global crime has broad societal repercussions, such as fueling criminal networks and imposing public health costs.[1] Although it is difficult to ascertain its absolute economic and social impact, it is estimated that millions of victims are trapped in the web of human trafficking and that it brings billions of dollars annually to the traffickers. It is also speculated to be the second most profitable criminal enterprise, trailing behind the illegal drug trade and tied with the illegal arms and weaponry trade. It is defined as the recruitment, transportation, harboring, or receipt of persons by means of force, fraud, or coercion.[2]

Globalization that has brought technological and economic advances to the world has also been listed as a significant contributor in facilitating and fueling this crime by several studies. A recent report from the International Labor Organization (ILO) denoted that, "The global integration of economies, including labor markets, has brought many opportunities for workers and businesses. Despite the past years of economic crisis, it has generally spurred economic growth. However, the growth in the global economy has come with a large cost to many and it has not been beneficial to all. Today, about 21 million men, women and children are in forced labor, trafficked, held in debt bondage or work in slave-like conditions."[3] Rising incidents of human trafficking have prompted a need for a comprehensive and coordinated global response to this crime. Consequently, enhanced global efforts have been launched to combat it through heightened awareness and educational campaigns, and a great number of international and state laws have been passed, outlawing its practices.

The accounts of incidence and prevalence of the trafficking victimization vary by the reporting agency. Some estimates assert that long after the Thirteenth Amendment to the U.S. Constitution and Article 4 of the UN's Universal Declaration of Human Rights were passed to eradicate slavery, there are more slaves today than at any other time in human history—the estimated number is 27 million.[4] Others claim that there are more slaves today than homicides in the United States. However, the most recent estimate is that 800,000 persons or more are trafficked annually within or across international borders.[5] The estimates also reveal that half of the trafficked persons are children. According to the State Department's 2010 Trafficking in Persons (TIP) report, 12.3 million adults and children are currently held in modern-day slavery, including forced labor and prostitution. Millions more are trafficked within their own national borders for a variety of purposes, including forced labor, bonded labor, sexual servitude, and involuntary servitude. The more recent updated estimate is provided by the Global Report on Trafficking in Persons, issued by the United Nations Office on Drugs and Crime in 2014. According to this report, "between 2010 and 2012, human trafficking victims with 152 different citizenships were identified in 124 countries across the globe."[6]

Given the magnitude of the problem and its aftermath, it is imperative that there is a comprehensive, coordinated, global approach to address human trafficking. The approach should incorporate prevention and control efforts with protection of the victims and survivors. This chapter provides information and discussions on global and United States' response to the crime of trafficking in persons. It discusses the laws passed and the progress made by the global community as well as the United States to address the scourge of human trafficking to date and identifies the areas in which global and U.S. efforts to prevent trafficking, protect victims, and prosecute traffickers have been successfully made and where more efforts are needed.

Global Response

Global efforts should focus on four main areas in responding to the crime of trafficking in persons. Trafficking in persons for labor and sex proliferates because there is a high demand for cheap and free services and at the same time rapidly growing surplus services in all parts of the globe—which are easy to order and bring at the disposal of anyone who can pay—through globalization. It also thrives due to the lax international and individual state laws in the investigation and apprehension, as well as the prosecution and punishment, of traffickers. Another factor that allows it to flourish is that there is no protection for the victims—rather they are treated as offenders for their role in complying with the traffickers' demands. Victims' role in the crime many times turns them into offenders as well. Thus, global approach should be four pronged: (1) outlaw trafficking in persons; (2) raise awareness and educate people; (3) enhance punishments for the prosecuted offenders; and (4) provide protection for the victims. To this effect, a number of international campaigns, treaties, conventions, and protocols have been launched and a variety of laws have been passed.

International Campaigns

Several international organizations have launched several successful campaigns to end human trafficking. These include the UN Office on Drugs and Crime (UNODC), the UN Children's Fund (UNICEF), the International Labor Organization (ILO), Amnesty International UK, End Child Prostitution and Trafficking (ECPAT), and Anti-Slavery International. Additionally, several campaigns, by different names, exist in different nations of the globe.

International Treaties, Conventions, and Protocols

United Nations Conventions and Protocols

The Trafficking in Persons Protocol (2000) was passed as the first united international response to trafficking crime. This protocol defines trafficking in persons and lists the activities that can be categorized as trafficking, it defines the process through which trafficking in persons is carried out, and it provides guidance as to how to respond to the crime of human trafficking in a comprehensive manner. It reflects the reality of trafficking, provides an update on antiquated laws against slaves, and promotes a more accurate, contemporary understanding of this crime. It has served as a "universal instrument that addresses all aspects of trafficking in persons." It mandates a holistic approach to human trafficking and provides an opportunity for states to develop and implement new policies with a focus on promoting rights and human dignity.[7]

Article 9 of the Trafficking in Persons (TIP) Protocol emphasizes the need for states to address trafficking in persons. Following is an excerpt from the TIP Protocol, Article 9.

> 1. States Parties shall establish comprehensive policies, programs and other measures:
>
> (a) To prevent and combat trafficking in persons; and
>
> (b) To protect victims of trafficking in persons, especially women and children, from re-victimization.
>
> 2. States Parties shall endeavor to undertake measures such as research, information and mass media campaigns and social and economic initiatives to prevent and combat trafficking in persons.
>
> 3. Policies, programs and other measures established in accordance with this article shall, as appropriate, include cooperation with non-governmental organizations, other relevant organizations and other elements of civil society.

> 4. States Parties shall take or strengthen measures, including through bilateral or multilateral cooperation, to alleviate the factors that make persons, especially women and children, vulnerable to trafficking, such as poverty, underdevelopment and lack of equal opportunity.
>
> 5. States Parties shall adopt or strengthen legislative or other measures, such as educational, social or cultural measures, including through bilateral and multilateral cooperation, to discourage the demand that fosters all forms of exploitation of persons, especially women and children, that leads to trafficking.
>
> The Trafficking in Persons Protocol also provides guidance on how to address the multifaceted problems of human trafficking. It:
>
> • requires states to endeavor to undertake measures such as social and economic initiatives, research, and media campaigns targeting potential victims. Policies, programs, and other measures taken should include cooperation with non-governmental and other relevant organizations.
>
> • reaffirms that effective action to prevent and combat trafficking in persons requires a comprehensive international approach, including measures to prevent such trafficking, protect victims of such trafficking, and prosecute traffickers.
>
> • indicates that states should take or strengthen these measures, including through bilateral and multilateral cooperation, to alleviate the factors—lack of equal opportunity and poverty—that make persons, especially women and children, vulnerable to trafficking.

The TIP Protocol requires states to allocate resources to develop and implement anti-trafficking strategies flexible enough to adapt to changing trafficking patterns and to address the root causes of trafficking in countries of origin and destination. It requires prevention efforts to confront the underlying fundamental causes that allow trafficking in persons to perpetuate. It mandates addressing gender, poverty, age, and other demographic and social variables that contribute to trafficking.

The TIP Protocol, in conjunction with Article 31 of the Organized Crime Convention, requires states parties to adopt a comprehensive prevention strategy. It requires social prevention measures to address the adverse underlying social and economic conditions that may be contributing factors and accelerating this crime. People living in marginalized social and economic communities desire to migrate because they are convinced that such a migration is a ticket out of wretched and miserable lives that they live at home and an entry ticket to the rich and comfortable lives waiting for them on the other side. Hence, they are highly vulnerable to the traffickers' fraudulent tactics. It requires states to adopt prevention strategies that educate the vulnerable populations and raise awareness about the perils of migration. It requires states to inform their citizens that illegal migration is a crime and criminals do not have rich and comfortable lives. It is states' responsibility to educate citizens about legal and illegal migration and challenges encountered by the migrants.

Article 31 of the Organized Crime Convention and Article 9 of the TIP Protocol require states to incorporate campaign strategies to raise awareness of the problem, to mobilize support for measures against it, and to focus on targeted and marginalized groups, believed to be at high risk of victimization. TIP Protocol also requires that efforts should focus on recognizing that trafficking could be dealt with from both the demand and supply sides. Article 9 includes measures intended to discourage the demand for services that fosters the exploitive element of trafficking and its major source of illicit revenue.[8] The protocol also requires that states consider and address the aftermath of trafficking victimization. The states need to provide for after care and protection of the victims against re-victimization, especially if the victims are repatriated to places where trafficking is common. In addition to the basic requirements to protect victims from intimidation or retaliation by offenders, Article 9 also calls for measures to protect victims from being trafficked again and from other forms of re-victimization. The protocol also requires states to make it more difficult for traffickers to use conventional means of transport and entry into states. It requires states to ensure that border controls are effective and make efforts to prevent the misuse of passports and other travel or identification documents.[9]

International Labor Organization (ILO) Conventions. Trafficking in persons for purposes of labor exploitation, in particular forced and compulsory labor and other slavery-like practices, is covered by a number of International Labor Organization conventions: the Forced Labor Convention, 1930 (No. 29), the Abolition of Forced Labor Convention, 1957 (No. 105), the Migration for Employment Convention (Revised), 1949 (No. 97), the Migrant Workers (Supplementary Provisions) Convention, 1975 (No. 143), the Private Employment Agencies Convention, 1997 (No. 181), the Discrimination (Employment and Occupation) Convention, 1958 (No. 111), the Minimum Age Convention, 1973 (No. 138), and the Worst Forms of Child Labor Convention, 1999 (No. 182), adopted in June 1999.

The Council of Europe (COE) Convention on Action against Trafficking in Human Beings, (CETS no. 197, Warsaw, 2005) was adopted in 2005. It is a comprehensive treaty focusing on the protection of victims of trafficking and the safeguarding of their rights. The convention applies to all forms of trafficking, whether national or transnational, whether or not related to organized crime. It applies to all victims: women, men, or children, and whatever the form of exploitation: sexual exploitation, forced labor or services, etc. The convention provides for the setting up of an independent monitoring mechanism guaranteeing parties' compliance with its provisions. It expands the scope of the UN definition of trafficking (set out in the Palermo Protocol) to include internal trafficking within the borders of one state and trafficking not necessarily involving organized criminal groups.[10] It provides a framework for the enhanced protection of the human rights of trafficked persons. It requires the parties to the convention to prevent trafficking and prosecute traffickers and adopt procedures to identify trafficked persons. It also requires that people who are reasonably believed to have been trafficked are not involuntarily removed until the identification process has been completed and at a minimum they are provided safe and secure housing; psychological and emergency medical assistance, interpretation and translation services; and information about their rights—including compensation—and such assistance may not be on the condition that they act as a witness in any proceedings against their traffickers. The COE also requires that the trafficked people are allowed to stay at least thirty days in the state in which they are found to recover, escape the influence of their trafficker(s), and to make informed decisions about their future, and in certain situations and if needed grant them renewable residence permits. The repatriation of the trafficking victims should be carried out with due regard to their rights, safety, and dignity. The COE requires parties ensure that the trafficked persons have access to redress and receive compensation for the abuses of their human rights.[11]

Global Initiatives

Based on the principles of Article 9 of the TIP Protocol, Article 31 of the Organized Crime Convention, International Labor Organization (ILO) conventions, the Trafficking Victims Protection Act (TVPA), and the Council of Europe (COE) Convention on Action against Trafficking in Human Beings, several efforts have been launched in form of campaigns, initiatives, policies, and programs.

Global response to human trafficking is a multilateral response that addresses social weaknesses that make victims of human trafficking vulnerable to exploitation, such as gender inequalities, underemployment, and family conflicts. It is designed to take into account accelerators of crime, such as the illicit economy, sex tourism, and gangs. The program and service providers work with governments, the private sector, and civil society to advocate for victims and effectively respond to human trafficking.

All multilateral organizations, including the UN, the OECD, ASEAN, the AU, and the OAS, have been working together and have developed global and regional strategies to degrade and disrupt transnational trafficking networks. The most recent example of global response to human trafficking is GLO.ACT.[12] With the collaboration and coordination of efforts by the European Union (EU) and the United Nations Office on Drugs and Crime (UNODC), GLO.ACT developed a joint initiative—The Global Action to Prevent and Address Trafficking in Persons and the Smuggling of Migrants in partnership with the International Organization for Migration (IOM) and the United Nations Children's Fund (UNICEF). It is part of a joint response to trafficking in persons and the smuggling of migrants. Its focus is on the implementation and delivery in up to 15 strategically selected countries across Africa, Asia, Eastern Europe, and Latin America with the main objective of assisting governmental authorities, civil society organizations, victims of trafficking, and smuggled migrants. It implements comprehensive national counter-trafficking and counter-smuggling responses and strengthens states' capacities to efficiently address human trafficking crimes and the inter-linkages between them. Its multidisciplinary implementation strategy places trafficking in persons and the smuggling of migrants under the scope of different relevant sectors such as criminal law, migration, labor, and social policies, thus, enhancing the prosecution of offenders.[13]

From 2012 to 2015, the United Nations Office on Drugs and Crime (UNODC) has trained more than 2,000 criminal justice practitioners and government officials from more than 70 countries to investigate and prosecute the trafficking in persons and smuggling crimes. UNODC has also trained criminal justice practitioners and government officials to determine and provide appropriate support to trafficking victims and smuggled migrants. Such a strategy enhances prosecution and protection efforts.[14]

Another international effort is the involvement of INTERPOL in addressing the crime of trafficking in persons. INTERPOL—the world's largest international police organization, with 190 member countries today—was officially created in 1923 as the International Criminal Police Commission.[15] The organization became known as INTERPOL in 1956. Its main function is to facilitate international police cooperation even where diplomatic relations do not exist between particular countries. Action is taken within the limits of existing laws in different countries and in the spirit of the Universal Declaration of Human Rights. The General Secretariat is located in Lyon, France, and operates 24 hours a day, 365 days a year. INTERPOL also has seven regional offices across the world and a representative office at the United Nations in New York and at the European Union in Brussels. Each of the 190 member countries maintains a National Central Bureau staffed by its own highly trained law enforcement officials.

INTERPOL coordinates and collaborates with various agencies such as the Economic Community of West African States, Eurojust, Europol, Frontex, the International Centre for Migration Policy Development, the International Labor Organization, the International Organization for Migration, the Organization of American States, the Organization for Security and Co-operation in Europe, the Southeast European Law Enforcement Center, the UK Missing Persons Bureau, and the United Nations Office on Drugs and Crime.

INTERPOL has several programs to support national police in tactical deployments in the field, aimed at breaking up the criminal networks behind trafficking in human beings and people smuggling. These operations are preceded by training workshops to ensure that officers on the ground are trained in a range of skills, including specialist interview techniques and the use of specialized equipment. Deployments effectively combine police action with input from a number of different sectors, such as customs and environmental officers, non-governmental organizations, officials from the Ministries of Health and Social Affairs, and prosecutors.

Its most recent success is rescuing of over 2,700 human trafficking victims in an INTERPOL-coordinated operation on July 28, 2016.[16]

International efforts, the TIP Protocol, and regional instruments provide an invaluable structure for governments' national legislative responses to human trafficking. The United States' efforts to address human trafficking have been influenced by the United Nations (UN), the European Union (EU)[17] conventions and directives, and the "Palermo Protocol."[18]

United States' Response to Human Trafficking

For international conventions and protocols to be successfully and effectively implemented, it is imperative that similar state-level efforts are also made. Addressing a complex and multifaceted crime such as human trafficking mandates a comprehensive, coordinated, and multidisciplinary effort at an international as well as state level.[19] It requires participation and coordination of various agencies—criminal enforcement, labor enforcement, victim outreach and services, public awareness, education, trade policy, international development and programs, immigration, intelligence, and diplomacy. Coordinated efforts are essential for an integrated, effective, and successful response to human trafficking. Such a response should have the ability to leverage resources and amplify results.[20] Although to coordinate such a massive effort is challenging, it is a critical and worthwhile endeavor that can yield anticipated success and progress. Given the enormity and complexity of this crime, the United States engages in robust interagency coordination and advocates that other state governments undertake interagency coordination efforts as well (United States Department of State, 2016). This sentiment is reflected in the recent presidential speech:

> Founded on the principles of justice and fairness, the United States continues to be a leader in the global movement to end modern-day slavery. We are working to combat human trafficking, prosecute the perpetrators, and help victims recover and rebuild their lives …[21]

Trafficking Victims Protection Act

Soon after the United Nations General Assembly adopted the Protocol to Prevent, Suppress and Punish Trafficking in Persons, especially Women and Children, in 2000, the U.S. Congress passed a federal statute, the Trafficking Victims Protection Act (TVPA) (Public Law 106–386—Oct. 28, 2000, 114 Stat. 1465) to combat trafficking in persons, especially into the sex trade, slavery, and involuntary servitude.[22] The TVPA reauthorized certain federal programs to prevent violence against women and for other purposes. Under this public law, the Trafficking Victims Protection Act of 2000 was established to combat trafficking in persons, to ensure just and effective punishment of traffickers, and to protect their victims. The Trafficking Victims Protection Act (TVPA) of 2000 has been subsequently renewed in 2003,[23] 2006,[24] and 2008. In 2008, it was renamed the William Wilberforce Trafficking Victims Protection Reauthorization Act of 2008.[25] In 2011, the law lapsed, and in 2013, the Trafficking Victims Protection Act, in its entirety, was attached as an amendment to the Violence Against Women Act and passed.[26]

According to the amended TVPA, human trafficking may include but does not require movement, transportation, or crossing the borders. Under this amended TVPA, people may be considered trafficking victims regardless of whether they were transported to the exploitative situation, previously consented to work for a trafficker, or participated in a crime as a direct result of being trafficked. The main element of the act that makes it a crime of trafficking is the traffickers' intent to exploit and enslave their victims using a variety of coercive and deceptive practices. The United States' law, TVPA, recognizes that trafficking is an opportunistic crime and traffickers non-discriminately target all types of people—adults and children, women, men, and transgender individuals, citizens and noncitizens alike.[27] No socioeconomic group is immune; new immigrants, Native Americans, runaways, the homeless, and lesbian, gay, bisexual, and transgender youth are particularly vulnerable (Department of State, 2016). The common variable that facilitates victimization and makes entrapping humans in this web easy is the victims' vulnerability. Most of the victims come from the poorest and most isolated communities, whether overseas or in the United States. Others who do not fall in these categories get ensnared because of their aspirations for a better life and the lack of options in their home communities to fulfill them.

The Tier System

As mandated by the TVPA, an evaluation system was created. This is called the Tier System and is divided into three tiers. The department evaluates each country's efforts towards controlling and preventing trafficking in persons and places each country onto one of the tiers, as mandated by the TVPA. This placement is based more on the extent of government action to combat trafficking than on the size of the country's problem. The analyses are based on the extent of governments' efforts to reach compliance with the TVPA's minimum standards for the elimination of human trafficking—consistent with the Palermo Protocol.

Tier 1 placements mean the countries' governments fully comply with the Trafficking Victims Protection Act's (TVPA) minimum standards. Tier 2 placement means that countries' governments do not fully comply with the TVPA's minimum standards, but are making significant efforts to bring themselves into compliance with those standards.

The Tier 2 Watch List refers to countries whose governments do not fully comply with the TVPA's minimum standards, but are making significant efforts to bring themselves into compliance with those standards and (a) the absolute number of victims of severe forms of trafficking is very significant or is significantly increasing; (b) there is a failure to provide evidence of increasing efforts to combat severe forms of trafficking in persons from the previous year; or (c) the determination that a country is making significant efforts to bring itself into compliance with minimum standards was based on commitments by the country to take additional future steps over the next year. Tier 3 placement means that countries' governments do not fully comply with the minimum standards and are not making significant efforts to do so.

Tier 1 is the highest ranking and Tier 1 placement means that the countries' governments fully comply with the Trafficking Victims Protection Act's (TVPA) minimum standards. However, it does not mean that a country has no human trafficking problem or that it is doing enough to address the problem. Rather, a Tier 1 ranking indicates that a government has acknowledged the existence of human trafficking, has made efforts to address the problem, and meets the TVPA's minimum standards. Each year, governments need to demonstrate appreciable progress in combating trafficking to maintain a Tier 1 ranking.[28]

Office to Monitor and Combat Trafficking in Persons

With the authority under the Trafficking Victims Protection Act (TVPA), the Office to Monitor and Combat Trafficking in Persons (OMCTIP) was established in October 2001 by the U.S. Department of State. The OMCTIP leads the United States' global engagement in combating human trafficking and supporting the coordination of anti-trafficking efforts across the U.S. government. This office partners with foreign governments, international organizations, civil societies, and the private sector to develop and implement effective strategies for confronting human trafficking. The OMCTIP is responsible for bilateral and multilateral diplomacy, targeted foreign assistance, and public engagement on trafficking in persons.[29]

In accordance with the United Nations Palermo Protocol to Prevent, Suppress and Punish Trafficking in Persons,[30] the OMCTIP pursues policies, partnerships, and practices that uphold the 3P paradigm of prosecuting traffickers, protecting victims, and preventing trafficking and pursues that. The OMCTIP is organized into four sections: Reports and Political Affairs, International Programs, Public Engagement, and Resource Management and Planning. The primary role of the Reports and Political Affairs (RPA) section is to engage foreign governments regarding human trafficking issues and to prepare the annual *Trafficking in Persons (TIP) Report*—the U.S. government's principal diplomatic and diagnostic tool to guide relations with foreign governments on human trafficking. The TIP Report is the world's most comprehensive resource of governmental anti-trafficking efforts and reflects the U.S. government's commitment to global leadership on this key human rights and law enforcement issue.

The OMCTIP's International Programs (IP) section develops annual regional programming strategies, oversees a competitive grant process, monitors current projects, and provides technical assistance to grantees, which include international organizations and non-governmental organizations. This section collaborates with the Department of State and other interagency counterparts and builds partnerships with other bilateral and private donors to enhance coordination. Since its inception, it has supported more than 880 anti-trafficking projects worldwide in accordance with the trends and recommendations identified in the TIP Report and in alignment with the 3Ps. Since 2002, most governments around the world have ratified and implemented elements of the Palermo

Protocol using the 3P framework—protection, prosecution, and prevention—to fight human trafficking and have passed laws that criminalize all forms of human trafficking. Over the last two decades, promising practices have emerged in victim identification, law enforcement, and victim care, such as incorporating survivor voices in all aspects of anti-trafficking policy development and implementation.

The OMCTIP's Public Engagement (PE) section serves as a liaison to Capitol Hill, ensuring that members of Congress and their staff are aware of the Department of State's actions to combat trafficking. The section is entrusted with working and building partnerships with Congress, the media, NGOs, other U.S. government agencies, multilateral organizations, corporations, academia, research institutes, and civil society to raise awareness about human trafficking and the U.S. government's anti-trafficking efforts. The other agencies or divisions within agencies that have duties regarding combatting trafficking are the Department of Defense, Department of Education, Government Accountability Office, Department of Health and Human Services, Department of Homeland Security, Department of Justice, Department of Labor, and Department of State.[31]

This PE section provides support to the President's Interagency Task Force to Monitor and Combat Trafficking in Persons (PITF), a cabinet-level entity created by the TVPA to coordinate U.S. government-wide efforts to combat trafficking in persons. The PITF functions to strengthen federal efforts to combat human trafficking by coordinating efforts from the government leaders, the private sector, advocates and survivors, faith leaders, law enforcement, and academia.

The PE section also formulates and supports the U.S. Advisory Council on Human Trafficking. This council is comprised of survivors of human trafficking and charged with making recommendations to the PITF on federal anti-trafficking policies. The Multilateral Affairs team of the PE section serves as the OMCTIP's focal point on all matters related to the United Nations, the International Labor Organization, the Organization for Security and Cooperation in Europe, the Organization of American States, the Regional Conference on Migration, and other multilateral bodies. The team works with other member states to ensure that new resolutions and initiatives, including the Palermo Protocol, have been universally ratified and fully implemented. It also endeavors to promote a victim-centered approach to preventing and combating all forms of human trafficking in multilateral venues.

The 4th section of the OMCTIP—Resource Management and Planning (RMP)—is responsible for providing management support, such as strategic planning, performance management, evaluation oversight, budget formulation, and execution for foreign assistance. It provides management support to state operations resources, human resource liaison services, general services, travel assistance, and contract support.

Owing to such concentrated and exhaustive endeavors of the United States government through the OMCTIP and other entities, most countries around the globe now have laws criminalizing all forms of human trafficking. Since the inception of TVPA and the OMCTIP, several promising practices, including incorporation of survivor voices in all aspects of anti-trafficking policy development and implementation, have emerged in victim identification, law enforcement, and victim care. However, there are still millions of victims trapped in human trafficking. The 2016 Trafficking in Persons Report encourages governments to work with local communities, law enforcement, and civil society to help identify those who may be especially vulnerable to human trafficking, and take preventive action. It identifies five critical areas and proposes that the governments and local communities collaborate and coordinate to prevent human trafficking.[32]

For prevention efforts to be effective, it is essential to overcome the difficulties and unreliability in data collection at local, regional, and global level. To this effect, the federal and state agencies should endeavor to increase data collection and research to get reasonably accurate estimates of the victims and perpetrators, understand the anatomy of this crime, and develop strategies to control and prevent it. Given the complex and subtle nature of this crime and in order to understand the causes, characteristics, trends, and consequences of all forms of trafficking in persons,, it is essential that governments and civil society encourage and fund research that provides baseline data. Another focus of the human trafficking research should be on understanding underlying vulnerabilities that facilitate human trafficking in communities, regions, countries, and other places.

Secondly, all major entities, such as governments, civil society, and the private sector, should collaborate to develop awareness and prevention campaigns. Next, governments, the private sector, and all other stakeholders should collaborate to develop policies and programs to prevent trafficking and keep at-risk individuals safe. They should monitor recruitment agencies and train labor inspectors to end fraudulent recruitment practices. All workers should have the freedom to form and join trade unions. The recruiters should have honest and regulated policies and the violators should be held civilly and criminally liable. The governments and civil society should integrate anti-trafficking elements into other programs, including those that focus on health or economic development. The governments should also make efforts and laws to reduce the demand for forced labor and commercial sex.[33]

Fourthly, all stakeholders—governments, civil society, academia, the private sector, and survivors—should enhance multilateral collaboration to exchange information on experiences, challenges, best practices, and emerging issues related to human trafficking. Governments should engage at the multilateral level and enforce international obligations related to human trafficking. Finally, governments should endeavor to encourage all stakeholders to collaborate and create partnerships among trafficking survivors, NGOs, faith groups, donors, academics, and businesses.

Overview of Campaigns, Initiatives, and Programs Funded by the United States

Based on the principles of Palermo Protocol and the TVPA, several campaigns, initiatives, and programs have been launched. A few of these are discussed here.

The **National Human Trafficking Resource Center** (NHTRC) is one of the important entities engaged in combating human trafficking. It is a nonprofit, non-governmental organization working exclusively on the issue of human trafficking. The NHTRC, a Department of Health and Human Services (HHS) funded program is operated and implemented by Polaris Project for the purpose of providing a national, 24-hour, toll-free hotline number for the human trafficking field in the U.S. The center also provides referrals, resources, general information, and training and technical assistance. It takes tips about potential situations of human trafficking and facilitates reporting to specialized human trafficking task forces, federal authorities, local law enforcement, and service providers throughout the country.[34]

It is a national anti-trafficking hotline and resource center serving victims and survivors of human trafficking and the anti-trafficking community in the United States. The toll-free hotline is available to answer calls from anywhere in the country, 24 hours a day, 7 days a week, every day of the year in more than 200 languages. Its mission is to provide human trafficking victims and survivors with access to critical support and services to get help and stay safe, and to equip the anti-trafficking community with the tools to effectively combat all forms of human trafficking. This service offers around-the-clock access to a safe space to report tips, seek services, and ask for help. It provides innovative anti-trafficking training, technical assistance, and capacity building support. The NHTRC has been operated since December 7, 2007, by Polaris. The center maintains one of the most extensive data sets on the issue of human trafficking in the United States. So far, as of June 30, 2016, there have been 13,454 calls received and 3,646 human trafficking cases reported to NHTRC.[35]

Polaris—a nonprofit, non-governmental organization—was founded in 2002. It has become a leader in the global fight to eradicate modern slavery and is one of the largest anti-trafficking organizations in the U.S., with programs operating at local and national levels through their offices in Washington, DC, and Newark, New Jersey. It is not a government entity, law enforcement agency, or immigration bureau. The United States' Department of Health and Human Services (HHS), private donors, and other supporters provide funding. Its approach includes conducting direct outreach and victim identification and providing social services and transitional housing to victims. Since 2007, it has also been operating the National Human Trafficking Resource Center (NHTRC), serving as the central national hotline on human trafficking. It also advocates for stronger state and federal anti-trafficking legislation, and engages community members in local and national grassroots efforts.

Since 2013, it has been providing training and technical assistance locally and internationally. It also provides technical assistance on new hotline projects, conducts hotline skills trainings, and provides technical assistance on hotline operations and data management. The organization also works with non-governmental organizations (NGOs), law enforcement, and government-run hotlines in various countries around the globe. It is one of the organizations that addresses all forms of trafficking and all aspects of trafficking, including supporting survivors who are male, female, transgender people, and children; U.S. citizens and foreign nationals; and survivors of both labor and sex trafficking. In April 2013, Polaris Project launched a Global Human Trafficking Hotline Network with Google's grant to connect with international anti-trafficking organizations running hotlines and coordinating efforts. Polaris Project used Salesforce to help improve tactics and increase their social impact. In early 2013, Polaris Project, along with Thorn, Salesforce, and Twilio, launched a new hotline for texting. By simply texting "BeFree" (233733), victims and captives could quickly and directly send out a message. This method of communication gives Polaris Project the ability to gather information and use it to coordinate with law enforcement to help victims of human trafficking.

Polaris follows a three-part model that systemically disrupts human trafficking. This model including responding to the victims of human trafficking effectively and immediately, equipping key stakeholders and communities to address and prevent human trafficking, and disrupting the business of human trafficking through targeted campaigns. Its main programs are discussed here. It operates national hotlines, such as the National Human Trafficking Resource Center hotline and BeFree Textline, to connect survivors to critical support systems to get help and stay safe, and equip communities with tools to combat human trafficking. Its global hotlines encourage multinational collaboration—with a focus on North America—among hotlines, service providers, governments, and law enforcement entities to share data, strategies, and resources to eradicate flows of trafficking that cross borders. It provides direct services in Washington, DC, including crisis intervention, case management, and counseling, to ease the effects of trauma. It establishes a relationship with the government to connect victims with the appropriate departments. As a premiere source of human trafficking policy expertise, it builds government support to eradicate all forms of modern slavery and protect victims of this crime.

Polaris also offers advisory services. It provides customized solutions and consultation to support individuals and institutions in the public and private sectors working to combat human trafficking. Other services provided by Polaris include data collection and data analysis. It uses data to find out where and how traffickers operate in order to understand the scope, size, and systems of modern slavery. Another program includes strategic interventions. These include disrupting human trafficking networks in illicit massage businesses and residential brothels by strengthening the safety net for victims in these venues and calling for strategic action that stops traffickers from harming more people.

Based on the 3P paradigm, the United States funds a number of initiatives, NGOs, and programs. Below is a description of some of these initiatives. This list is not exhaustive. It does not list all the initiatives. There are many more initiatives operating in North America as well as other regions of the globe.

The 8th Day Center for Justice is a Roman Catholic nonprofit organization based in Chicago, Illinois. It was founded in 1974 by six congregations of religious men and women. Currently the center is advocacy-centered (primarily around Catholic social teaching) and is associated with over 40 religious communities, allowing the congregations to pool their resources for the work.[36]

The A21 Campaign is a 501(c)(3) nonprofit, non-governmental organization that focuses on fighting human trafficking of all kinds—including sexual exploitation and forced slave labor. The campaign was founded by Christine Caine, an international motivational speaker, in 2008. The A21 Campaign focuses on combatting slavery around the world through educational awareness and prevention, the protection of victims (by providing services such as medical and psychological treatment, as well as legal and vocational assistance to the victims of human trafficking in their crisis centers, shelters, and transitional homes), the prosecution of traffickers, and various partnerships (including with official bodies, community members, other non-governmental organizations, and corporations). The A21 Campaign has teams on the ground in Ukraine, Greece, Bulgaria, the United Kingdom, Norway, the United States, South Africa, Thailand, the Netherlands, and Australia. The A21 Campaign is a nonprofit, non-governmental organization. The organization is funded through donations from individuals, faith-based organizations, businesses, and other partnerships. Its objective is to "abolish injustice in the 21st century."[37]

The Arizona League to End Regional Trafficking (ALERT) is a coalition representing partnerships with law enforcement, faith-based communities, nonprofit organizations, social service agencies, attorneys, and concerned citizens. ALERT helps the victims of human trafficking by providing food and shelter, medical care, mental health counseling, immigration assistance, legal assistance, language interpretation, case management, and other culturally appropriate services throughout the state of Arizona. Its main objective is to end the suffering and dehumanization of the victims of human trafficking through education, outreach, and a variety of other innovative programs and services.[38]

Bishop Outreach is another nonprofit, non-governmental organization that offers services in rescuing those enslaved in human trafficking. The organization promotes the awareness of and education about different aspects associated with human trafficking along with working with local, state, and federal law enforcement (FBI, DHS, and DOJ) to expose, arrest, and prosecute traffickers, while providing the necessary support systems that aid in the healing of physical and mental damages that the victim has endured.[39]

California Against Slavery (CAS), is a human rights organization that is engaged in strengthening California state laws to protect victims of sex trafficking and to increase law enforcement efforts. Its most recent efforts include a vote on a ballot question (Proposition 35) that would (1) make stiffer criminal penalties, (2) aid district attorneys in prosecuting human trafficking offenses, (3) increase protection for human trafficking victims, (4) mandate two-hour human trafficking training for law enforcement officers, and (5) increase allocation of certain seized assets and fines to organizations that serve human trafficking victims.[40]

The Centre to End All Sexual Exploitation is another nonprofit organization that helps human trafficking victims, sex workers, and the homeless by providing them with resources.

The Coalition to Abolish Slavery and Trafficking (CAST) is a Los Angeles-based anti-human trafficking organization. It is a nonprofit organization that helps human trafficking victims by providing social services, legal services, and outreach and training. It helps rehabilitate survivors of human trafficking, raises awareness, and affects legislation and public policy surrounding human trafficking.

CAST was founded in 1998 as a response to the landmark El Monte Thai Garment Slavery Case of 1995, in which 72 Thai immigrants were forced to work in slave-like conditions for 18-hours a day, while locked up in the Los Angeles suburb of El Monte. The victims were paid about 69 cents an hour, and charged exorbitant amounts for basic necessities, ensuring they would never be able to pay off their original debt to their traffickers and remain under their control. The case garnered national press coverage, and brought the issue of modern slavery and human trafficking into the mainstream media.[41]

Free the Slaves is an international non-governmental organization and lobby group, established to campaign against the modern practice of slavery around the world.

Global Alliance Against Trafficking Women (GAATW) is a network of more than 100 non-governmental organizations from all regions of the world, who share a deep concern for the women, children, and men whose human rights have been violated by the criminal practice of trafficking in persons. GAATW is committed to work for changes in the political, economic, social, and legal systems and structures which contribute to the persistence of trafficking in persons and other human rights violations in the context of migratory movements for diverse purposes, including security of labor and livelihood. It was founded in 1994 by several feminist activists.[42]

Love146 was founded in 2004. It is a U.S.-based 501(c)(3) nonprofit international human rights organization that works toward the abolition of child trafficking and exploitation through survivor care, prevention education, professional training, grassroots empowerment, and contribution to a growing body of research.

Not for Sale was founded in 2001. It is an international 501(c)(3) nonprofit organization based out of San Francisco, California, that works to protect people and communities around the world from human trafficking and modern-day slavery. The organization equips and empowers survivors of human trafficking and those at risk of exploitation by providing shelter, healthcare, and legal services and education, job skills, and life-skills training and partners with leading companies and organizations to create long-term employment opportunities for survivors and at-risk communities.[43]

Physicians for Human Rights (PHR) was established in 1986 to use the unique skills and credibility of health professionals to advocate for persecuted health workers, prevent torture, document mass atrocities, and hold those who violate human rights accountable. It is a U.S.-based not-for-profit human rights NGO that uses medicine and science to document and advocate against mass atrocities and severe human rights violations around the world. PHR headquarters are in New York City, with offices in Boston and Washington, DC.[44]

The Redlight Children Campaign is a nonprofit organization created by New York lawyer and president of Priority Films Guy Jacobson and Israeli actress Adi Ezroni in 2002, to combat worldwide child sexual exploitation and human trafficking. Its mission is to decrease the demand side of the international sex trade through legislation and enforcement while raising awareness utilizing mass media and grassroots outreach. Through its partnership with Priority Films, Redlight Children has recently launched the K11 Project—three films which attempt to expose real life experiences of the underage sex trade. K11 consists of two documentaries and a feature-length narrative film, *Holly*, which were all filmed on location in Cambodia.[45]

Shared Hope International (SHI) is a nonprofit, non-governmental organization that exists to prevent sex trafficking and restore and bring justice to women and children who have been victimized through sex trafficking. Its focus is to prevent and eradicate sex trafficking and slavery. SHI operates programs in the United States, India, Nepal, and Jamaica. It leads awareness and training, prevention strategies, restorative care, research, and policy initiatives to mobilize a national network of protection for victims. SHI was founded in 1998 by former Congresswoman Linda Smith. Shared Hope's early efforts were focused on international sex trafficking. With a grant from the U.S. Department of State, Shared Hope spent three years facilitating meetings between government, law enforcement, and the private sector in six countries to encourage protection, prosecution, and prevention.[46]

Slavery Footprint is a survey that asks and responds to the question, "How Many Slaves Work for You?" The survey allows users to input select data about their consumer spending habits, which then outputs a graphical "footprint" of the user's participation in modern-day slavery (as quantified by their consumption of items created by forced labor and child labor.) Made in a Free World, the creators of Slavery Footprint, researched the supply chains of 400 consumer products to determine the likely number of slaves it takes to make each of those products. They put the information into an online survey where you can determine the number of slaves that are needed to maintain your personal lifestyle. After the survey, the user has the option to share the results or take action. The purpose of this project is to increase awareness of forced labor and child labor and engage the public in taking steps toward addressing the use of forced labor, by encouraging users to advocate with strategic actions in the marketplace.

With the support of the U.S. Department of State, Justin Dillon, founder and CEO of Made in a Free World, founded Slavery Footprint. The website launched on September 22, 2011, at the Clinton Global Initiative. This date marks the 149th anniversary of the signing of the Emancipation Proclamation.[47]

Stop Child Trafficking Now (also called SCTNow), an international organization, was founded in 2011. This nonprofit organization engages in advocacy work in an attempt to bring an end to the trafficking of children. SCTNow targets the demand for human trafficking, focusing on pedophiles, child abductions, and child pornography. The group seeks to have those who sexually abuse children prosecuted and convicted. SCTNow organizes a walk each year to raise awareness on the issue.

SW Florida Regional Human Trafficking Coalition, a nonprofit organization covering Collier, Lee, Charlotte, Hendry, and Glades Counties of southwest Florida, provides, in conjunction with its partners, comprehensive services to rescue and restore victims of human trafficking.[48]

Truckers Against Trafficking (TAT) was established in Oklahoma in 2009. It is a nonprofit organization that trains truck drivers to recognize and report instances of human trafficking. It teaches truck drivers about the results of human trafficking. TAT produces anti-trafficking materials which are commonly seen throughout the trucking industry. The organization teams up with law enforcement agencies and trucking companies to provide training on identifying sex trafficking, and asking transportation companies to require their drivers to go through it. Through their efforts, they have freed hundreds of human trafficking victims. According to the National Human Trafficking Resource Center, the majority of truck drivers who report tips learned about them through TAT. Since 2011, it has formed a partnership with Pilot Flying J in 2011 and in 2013 it also partnered with the Truckload Carriers Association. In 2012, the Ottawa, Ontario, Canada-based Persons Against the Crime of Trafficking in Humans was inspired by TAT to initiate TruckSTOP, a campaign that teaches truck drivers how to identify human trafficking victims. TAT was promoted in "Killer Truckers," a 2013 television special by Investigation Discovery.[49] The most recent success story involves a truck driver who, after suspecting human trafficking in a particular situation, called 911. His phone call precipitated the arrest and subsequent conviction of 31 traffickers, the release of 9 people from the sex industry, and the fall of an organized crime ring that had been active in 13 U.S. states.[50]

Vital Voices Global Partnership was established in 1999 following the United Nations Fourth World Conference on Women in Beijing to promote the advancement of women as a U.S. foreign policy goal. The organization is headquartered in Washington, DC. It is an American international, nonprofit, non-governmental organization that works with women leaders in the areas of economic empowerment, women's political participation, and human rights.[51]

A list of additional organizations with a primary, or significant, commitment to ending human trafficking is attached in Appendix 1.

Conclusion and Chapter Review

In this chapter, we have discussed the global and United States' response to the crime of human trafficking. We learned about the global as well as the United States response to this crime. This chapter provided a broader understanding of the United States' and global efforts to respond to human trafficking in a coordinated and collaborated manner. In essence, we learned about the following:

- The Global Response to Trafficking in Persons
- International Treaties, Conventions, and Protocols
    - United Nations Conventions and Protocols
    - Article 9 of the Trafficking in Persons (TIP) Protocol
    - Article 31 of the Organized Crime Convention
    - International Labor Organization (ILO) Conventions
    - The Council of Europe (COE) Convention on Action against Trafficking in Human Beings
    - Global Initiatives
- United States' Response to Human Trafficking
    - Trafficking Victims Protection Act
    - The Tier System
    - Office to Monitor and Combat Trafficking in Persons
    - Overview of Campaigns, Initiatives, and Programs Funded by the United States

Discussion Questions

1) What is the Tier System? What is the purpose of this Tier System?

2) Describe the role of the Office to Monitor and Combat Trafficking in Persons (OMCTIP).

3) Discuss the 3P framework and define what the 3 Ps mean in terms of protection, prosecution, and prevention.

4) Discuss three-part model used by Polaris. What is the main purpose of this model?

5) Review your state's laws and discuss what resources your state has to address trafficking in persons.

6) Discuss the Trafficking in Persons Protocol.

7) Discuss the Trafficking Victims Protection Act.

8) Identify the role of the National Human Trafficking Resource Center (NHTRC) in combating trafficking in persons.

9) List at least three organizations in your state that help trafficking in persons' victims.

References

8th Day Center for Justice. www.8thdaycenter.org/.

The A21 Campaign. www.a21.org/.

Arizona League to End Regional Trafficking (ALERT). traffickingaz.org.

Bishop Outreach. Human Trafficking Rescue Team. bishopoutreach.org/.

Bureau of Democracy, Human Rights and Labor. Country Reports on Human Rights Practices for 2014. U.S. Department of State, 2014.

California Against Slavery. californiaagainstslavery.org.

Coalition to Abolish Slavery & Trafficking (CAST). http://www.castla.org/homepage.

Council of Europe on Action against Trafficking in Human Beings, CETS No.197. Warsaw, May 16, 2005.

International Labour Office (ILO). *Profits and Poverty: The Economics of Forced Labor.* Special Action Programme to Combat Forced Labour (SAP-FL) Fundamental Principles and Rights at Work Branch (FPRW). 2014.

International Labour Organization. (ILO). Abolition of Forced Labor Convention. No. 105. Adopted: 25 June 1957. Entry into force: 17 January 1959, in accordance with Article 4. http://www.ilo.org/dyn/normlex/en/f?p=NORMLEXPUB:12100:0::NO::P12100_ILO_CODE:C105.

International Labour Organization (ILO). Convention Concerning Migration for Employment (Revised 1949). No. 97. Adoption: 1 Jul 1949. Entry into force: 22 Jan 1952. http://www.ilo.org/dyn/normlex/en/f?p=NORMLEXPUB:12100:0::NO::P12100_INSTRUMENT_ID:312242.

International Labour Organization (ILO). Discrimination (Employment and Occupation) Convention. Convention Concerning Discrimination in Respect of Employment and Occupation. No. 111. Adoption: 25 Jun 1958. Entry into force: 15 Jun 1960. http://www.ilo.org/dyn/normlex/en/f?p=NORMLEXPUB:12100:0::NO::P12100_ILO_CODE:C111.

International Labour Organization (ILO). Forced Labor Convention. Convention concerning Forced or Compulsory Labour. No. 29. Adoption: 28 Jun 1930.

Entry into force: 1 May 1932. http://www.ilo.org/dyn/normlex/en/f?p=NORMLEXPUB:12100:0::NO::P12100_ILO_CODE:C029.

International Labour Organization (ILO). Migrant Workers (Supplementary Provisions) Convention. Convention Concerning Migrations in Abusive Conditions and the Promotion of Equality of Opportunity and Treatment of Migrant Workers. No. 143. Adoption: 24 Jun 1975. Entry into force: 9 Dec 1978. http://www.ilo.org/dyn/normlex/en/f?p=NORMLEXPUB:12100:0::NO::P12100_ILO_CODE:C143.

International Labour Organization (ILO). Minimum Age Convention. Convention Concerning Minimum Age for Admission to Employment. No. 138. Adoption: 26 Jun 1973. Entry into force: 19 Jun 1976. http://www.ilo.org/dyn/normlex/en/f?p=1000:12100:0::NO::P12100_ILO_CODE:C138.

International Labour Organization (ILO). Private Employment Agencies Convention. Convention concerning Private Employment Agencies. No. 181. Adoption: 19 Jun 1997. Entry into force: 10 May 2000. http://www.ilo.org/dyn/normlex/en/f?p=NORMLEXPUB:12100:0::NO::P12100_INSTRUMENT_ID:312326.

International Labour Organization (ILO). Worst Forms of Child Labor Convention. Convention concerning the Prohibition and Immediate Action for the Elimination of the Worst Forms of Child Labor. No. 182. Adoption: 17 Jun 1999. Entry into force: 19 Nov 2000. http://www.ilo.org/dyn/normlex/en/f?p=NORMLEXPUB:12100:0::NO::P12100_ILO_CODE:C182.

Miko, Francis T. "Trafficking in Women and Children: The U.S. and International Response—Updated March 26, 2004." Graduate Theses and Dissertations. Paper 12068. Cornell University ILR School, 2004.

National Human Trafficking Resource Center. https://traffickingresourcecenter.org/.

Obama, Barack. Presidential Proclamation—National Slavery and Human Trafficking Prevention Month. Washington, DC: The White House, Office of the Press Secretary, 2015.

Physicians for Human Rights. physiciansforhumanrights.org/.

Red Light Campaign. www.redlightcampaign.org/.

Roby, Jini L. "Women and Children in the Global Sex Trade." *International Social Work* 48, no. 2 (2005): 136–147.

Sembacher, Anke. "The Council of Europe Convention on Action against Trafficking in Human Beings." *Tul. J. Int'l & Comp. L.* 14 (2005): 435.

Shared Hope International. sharedhope.org/.

Skinner, E. Benjamin. *A Crime So Monstrous: Face-to-Face with Modern-Day Slavery*. Simon and Schuster, 2008.

Slavery Footprint. Made in a Free World. slaveryfootprint.org/.
SW Florida Regional Human Trafficking Coalition. swfl-humantrafficking.org/.
Truckers Against Trafficking. www.truckersagainsttrafficking.org/.
United Nations General Assembly. Protocol to Prevent, Suppress and Punish Trafficking in Persons Especially Women and Children, supplementing the United Nations Convention against Transnational Organized Crime. Resolution 55/25. November 15, 2000.
United Nations Human Rights Office of the High Commissioner. International Covenant on Civil and Political Rights. Resolution 2200A (XXI). Entry into force: 23 March 1976, in accordance with Article 49. http://www.ohchr.org/en/professionalinterest/pages/ccpr.aspx.
United Nations Human Rights Office of the High Commissioner. The 1956 Supplementary Convention on the Abolition of Slavery, the Slave Trade, and Institutions and Practices Similar to Slavery. Resolution 608(XXI). Entry into force: 30 April 1957, in accordance with Article 13. http://www.ohchr.org/EN/ProfessionalInterest/Pages/SupplementaryConventionAbolitionOfSlavery.aspx.
United Nations Office on Drugs and Crime (UNODC). http://www.unodc.org/unodc/en/crime_cicp_signatures_trafficking.html.
United Nations Office on Drugs and Crime (UNODC). *World Drug Report 2010*. United Nations Publications, 2010.
United Nations Office on Drugs and Crime (UNODC). *Trafficking in Human Beings*. 2006. http://www.unodc.org/unodc/en/trafficking_human_beings.html.
United Nations Office on Drugs and Crime (UNODC). *Fact Sheet on Human Trafficking*. 2006. http://www.unodc.org/unodc/en/trafficking_victim_consents.html#how.
United Nations Office on Drugs and Crime (UNODC). *The Global Report on Trafficking in Persons: Executive Summary*. 2014. http://www.unodc.org/documents/data-and-analysis/glotip/GLOTIP14_ExSum_english.pdf.
United States Congress. Mann Act, 18 United States Code §§. 1581–1588.
United States Congress. Trafficking Victims Protection Act (TVPA). Pub. L. No. 106-386, 114 Stat. 1473. 2000.
United States Congress. Trafficking Victims Protection Reauthorization Act (TVPRA). Pub. L. No. 108-193, 117 Stat. 2875. 2003.
United States Congress. Trafficking Victims Protection Reauthorization Act (TVPRA). Pub. L. No. 109-164. 2005.
United States Department of Justice (U.S.DOJ). "Assessment of U.S. Government Efforts to Combat Trafficking in Persons in Fiscal Year 2006." 2007. http://

www.usdoj.gov/ag/annualreports/tr2007/assessment-of-efforts-to-combat-tip0907.pdf.

United States Department of Justice (U.S.DOJ). *Report on Activities to Combat Human Trafficking: Fiscal Years 2001–2005.* 2006. http://www.usdoj.gov/crt/crim/trafficking_report_2006.pdf.

United States Department of State. *Progress in Combating Trafficking in Persons: The U.S. Government Response to Modern Slavery 150 Years After the Emancipation Proclamation.* Office to Monitor and Combat Trafficking in Persons. April 9, 2013.

United States Department of State. Review of the 2016 Trafficking in Persons Report. State Department Testimony of Ambassador Susan Coppedge for the Senate Foreign Relations Committee. July 12, 2016.

United States Department of State. "Special State Department Briefing." *Federal News Service*, June 3, 2005. LexisNexis.

United States Department of State. *Trafficking in Persons Interim Assessment.* Office to Monitor and Combat Trafficking in Persons. March 6, 2015. http://www.state.gov/j/tip/.

United States Department of State. *Trafficking in Persons Report.* Office to Monitor and Combat Trafficking in Persons. 2004. http://www.state.gov/g/tip/rls/tiprpt/2004/34021.htm.

United States Department of State. *Trafficking in Persons Report.* Office to Monitor and Combat Trafficking in Persons. 2005. http://www.state.gov/g/tip/rls/tiprpt/2005/.

United States Department of State. *Trafficking in Persons Report.* Office to Monitor and Combat Trafficking in Persons. 2016. http://www.state.gov/j/tip/rls/tiprpt/2016/.

United States Department of State. *Trafficking in Persons Report 2016.* Office to Monitor and Combat Trafficking in Persons. 2016. https://www.state.gov/j/tip/rls/tiprpt/2016/.

United States Government Accounting Office (U.S.GAO). *Human Trafficking: Better Data, Strategy, and Reporting Needed to Enhance U.S. Anti-Trafficking Efforts Abroad.* GAO-06-825. Published: Jul 18, 2006. Publicly Released: Aug 14, 2006. http://www.gao.gov/products/GAO-06-825.

Vital Voices Global Partnership. *Stateless and Vulnerable to Human Trafficking in Thailand.* p. 13. Washington, DC, June 2007. www.vitalvoices.org.

Weitzer, Ronald. "Moral Crusade against Prostitution." *Society* 43, no. 3 (2006): 33–38.

Wilson, Deborah G., William F. Walsh, and Sherilyn Kleuber. "Trafficking in Human Beings: Training and Services among U.S. Law Enforcement Agencies." *Police Practice and Research* 7, no. 02 (2006): 149–160.

Women's Commission for Refugee Women and Children. *Displaced Women and Girls*. 2016.

Further Suggested Readings

Aradau, C. (2004). The perverse politics of four-letter words: risk and pity in the securitisation of human trafficking. *Millennium-Journal of International Studies, 33*(2), 251–277.

Aronowitz, A. A. (2009). *Human trafficking, human misery: The global trade in human beings*. Greenwood Publishing Group.

Bernat, F. P., & Zhilina, T. (2010). Human trafficking: The local becomes global. *Women & Criminal Justice, 20*(1–2), 2–9.

Bruch, E. M. (2004). Models wanted: The search for an effective response to human trafficking. *Stan. J. Int'l L., 40*, 1.

Brysk, A., & Choi-Fitzpatrick, A. (Eds.). (2012). *From human trafficking to human rights: Reframing contemporary slavery*. University of Pennsylvania Press.

Capous Desyllas, M. (2007). Critique of the Global Trafficking Discourse and U.S. Policy, A. *J. Soc. & Soc. Welfare, 34*, 57.

Chuang, J. (2006). Beyond a snapshot: Preventing human trafficking in the global economy. *Indiana journal of global legal studies, 13*(1), 137–163.

Chuang, J. A. (2006). The United States as global sheriff: Using unilateral sanctions to combat human trafficking. *Michigan Journal of International Law, 27*(2).

Clark, M. A. (2003). Trafficking in persons: An issue of human security. *Journal of Human Development, 4*(2), 247–263.

Coontz, P., & Griebel, C. (2004). International approaches to human trafficking: The call for a gender-sensitive perspective in international law. *Women's Health Journal, 4*(4), 47–59.

Dillon, S. A. (2008). What human rights law obscures: Global sex trafficking and the demand for children. *UCLA Women's Law Journal, 17*, 121.

Farrell, A., McDevitt, J., & Fahy, S. (2008). Understanding and improving law enforcement responses to human trafficking, final report, 2008, June. *Human Trafficking Data Collection and Reporting Center Research and Technical Reports*, 1.

Farrell, A., & Fahy, S. (2009). The problem of human trafficking in the U.S.: Public frames and policy responses. *Journal of Criminal Justice, 37*(6), 617–626.

Gallagher, A., & Holmes, P. (2008). Developing an effective criminal justice response to human trafficking lessons from the front line. *International criminal justice review, 18*(3), 318–343.

Gallagher, A. T. (2011). Improving the effectiveness of the international law of human trafficking: A vision for the future of the U.S. Trafficking in Persons reports. *Human Rights Review, 12*(3), 381–400.

Goodey, J. (2008). Human trafficking Sketchy data and policy responses. *Criminology and Criminal Justice, 8*(4), 421–442.

Hathaway, J. C. (2008). Human Rights Quagmire of Human Trafficking, The. *Va. J. Int'l L., 49*, 1.

Kandathil, R. (2005). Global sex trafficking and the Trafficking Victims Protection Act of 2000: Legislative responses to the problem of modern slavery. Mich. J. Gender & L., 12, 87.

Kyle, D., & Koslowski, R. (2011). *Global human smuggling: Comparative perspectives*. JHU Press.

Kneebone, S., & Debeljak, J. (2012). *Transnational crime and human rights: Responses to human trafficking in the Greater Mekong Subregion*. Routledge.

Konrad, H. (2002). Trafficking in human beings—the ugly face of Europe. *Helsinki Monitor, 13*(3), 260–271.

Laczko, F. (2002). Human trafficking: the need for better data. *Migration Information Source, 1*.

Lee, M. (2011). *Trafficking and global crime control*. Sage publications.

Logan, T. K., Walker, R., & Hunt, G. (2009). Understanding human trafficking in the United States. *Trauma, Violence, & Abuse, 10*(1), 3–30.

Nagle, L. E. (2008). Selling souls: the effect of globalization on human trafficking and forced servitude. *Wisconsin International Law Journal, 26*(1).

Okech, D., Morreau, W., & Benson, K. (2012). Human trafficking: Improving victim identification and service provision. *International Social Work, 55*(4), 488–503.

Roby, J. L., Turley, J., & Cloward, J. G. (2008). U.S. response to human trafficking: Is it enough?. *Journal of Immigrant & Refugee Studies, 6*(4), 508–525.

Sadruddin, H., Walter, N., & Hidalgo, J. (2005). Human trafficking in the United States: expanding victim protection beyond prosecution witnesses. *Stan. L. & Pol'y Rev., 16*, 379.

Segrave, M. (2009, August). Order at the border: The repatriation of victims of trafficking. In *Women's studies international forum* (Vol. 32, No. 4, pp. 251–260). Pergamon.

Smith, L., & Mattar, M. (2004). Creating International Consensus on Combating Trafficking in Persons: U.S. Policy the Role of the UN, and Global Responses and Challenges. Fletcher F. World Aff., 28, 155.

Srikantiah, J. (2007). Perfect victims and real survivors: The iconic victim in domestic human trafficking law. *Immigr. & Nat'lity L. Rev., 28*, 741.

Todres, J. (2011). Widening our lens: Incorporating essential perspectives in the fight against human trafficking. *Michigan Journal of International Law, 33*, 53–76.

United Nations Office on Drugs and Crime (UNODC) 2011. Legal and Policy Review—Responses to Human Trafficking in Bangladesh, India, Nepal and Sri Lanka. https://www.unodc.org/unodc/en/human-trafficking/2011/legal-and-policy-review—responses-to-human-trafficking-in-bangladesh-india-nepal-and-sri-lanka.html.

Wilson, D. G., Walsh, W. F., & Kleuber, S. (2006). Trafficking in human beings: Training and services among U.S. law enforcement agencies. *Police Practice and Research, 7*(02), 149–160.

Vital Voices Global Partnership, Stateless and Vulnerable to Human Trafficking in Thailand, (Washington, D.C., June 2007), p. 13 (see www.vitalvoices.org). 8th Day Center for Justice Www.8thdaycenter.org.

Worst Forms of Child Labor Convention, 1999 (No. 182). Convention concerning the Prohibition and Immediate Action for the Elimination of the Worst Forms of Child Labor (Entry into force: 19 Nov 2000). Adoption: Geneva, 87th ILC session (17 Jun 1999)—Status: Up-to-date instrument (Fundamental Convention).

Notes

1. U.S. Government Accountability Office. (2006). Human trafficking: Better data, strategy, and reporting needed to enhance U.S. anti-trafficking efforts abroad. *Trends in Organized Crime, 10*(1).

2. International Labor Organization. (2014). Profits and poverty: The economics of forced labour. http://http://www.ilo.org/wcmsp5/groups/public/—ed_norm/—declaration/documents/publication/wcms_243391.pdf.

3. International Labor Organization. (2014). Profits and poverty: The economics of forced labour. http:// http://www.ilo.org/wcmsp5/groups/public/—ed_norm/—declaration/documents/publication/wcms_243391.pdf.

4. Skinner, E. B. (2008). *A crime so monstrous: Face-to-face with modern-day slavery.*

Simon and Schuster.

5. U.S. Department of State. (2007). *Trafficking in persons report 2007.*

6. United Nations Office on Drugs and Crime (UNODC). (2014). *Global report on trafficking in persons: Executive summary.* http://www.unodc.org/documents/data-and-analysis/glotip/GLOTIP14_ExSum_english.pdf.

7. UN General Assembly. (2000). Protocol to prevent, suppress and punish trafficking in persons, especially women and children. Supplement to the United Nations convention against transnational organized crime. Resolution 55, 25.

8. United Nations Secretariat. (2005). United Nations Convention Against Transnational Organized Crime and the Protocols Thereto.

9. United Nations Office on Drugs and Crime (UNODC). (2010). *World drug report 2010.* United Nations Publications.

10. Council of Europe. (2005, May 16). Council of Europe Convention on Action against Trafficking in Human Beings. Treaty Series No. 197. Warsaw.

11. Sembacher, A. (2005). Council of Europe Convention on Action against Trafficking in Human Beings. *Tul. J. Int'l & Comp. L., 14,* 435.

12. "The Global Action to Prevent and Address Trafficking in Persons and the Smuggling of Migrants is a four-year (2015–2019) joint initiative by the European Union (EU) and the United Nations Office on Drugs and Crime (UNODC) being implemented in partnership with the International Organization for Migration (IOM) and the United Nations Children's Fund (UNICEF)." http://www.unodc.org/unodc/en/human-trafficking/glo-act/index.html.

13. "The Human Trafficking Knowledge Portal is an initiative to facilitate the dissemination of information regarding the implementation of the UN Convention against Transnational Organized Crime and specifically the Protocol to Prevent, Suppress and Punish Trafficking in Persons, Especially Women and Children. The Human Trafficking Knowledge Portal hosts a Case Law Database on officially documented instances of trafficking in persons crime." https://www.unodc.org/cld/en/v3/htms/index.html.

14. "The UNODC Global Report 2014 is the second of its kind mandated by the General Assembly. It covers 128 countries and provides an overview of patterns and flows of trafficking in persons at global, regional and national levels, based on trafficking cases detected between 2010 and 2012 (or more recent). The Global Report 2014 highlights the role of organized crime in trafficking in persons, and includes an analytical chapter on how traffickers operate. The worldwide response to trafficking in persons is also a focus of this edition of the Global Report." https://un.org.au/2015/07/31/global-report-on-trafficking-in-persons/.

15. "INTERPOL is the world's largest international police organization, with 190 member countries. [Its] role is to enable police around the world to work together to make the world a safer place. [Its] high-tech infrastructure of technical and operational support helps meet the growing challenges of fighting crime in the 21st century. [Its] aim [is] to facilitate international police cooperation even where diplomatic relations do not exist between particular countries. Action is taken within the limits of existing laws in different countries and in the spirit of the Universal Declaration of Human Rights. [Its] Constitution prohibits 'any intervention or activities of a political, military, religious or racial character.'" https://www.interpol.int/About-INTERPOL/Overview.

16. Interpol. (2016, July 28). More than 2,700 human trafficking victims rescued in INTERPOL-coordinated operation: Results mark INTERPOL support for World Day against Trafficking in Persons. http://www.interpol.int/News-and-media/News/2016/N2016-098.

17. "The EU is a unique political structure, currently composed of twenty-seven nations,

a complex supranational organization that has federal aspects analogous to the U.S. The countries that make up the EU ("Member States") remain independent sovereign nations, but they have ceded a part of their sovereignty in order to achieve a common market and other goals, as well as a global influence that none of them could have on their own (e.g., within the World Trade Organization)." http://filj.lawreviewnetwork.com/files/2011/10/EU_Citation_Manual_2010-2011_for_Website.pdf.

18. UN General Assembly. (2000, November 15). Protocol to Prevent, Suppress and Punish Trafficking in Persons Especially Women and Children. Supplement to the United Nations Convention against Transnational Organized Crime. Resolution 55/25.

19. U.S. Department of State. (2016, July 12). Review of the 2016 Trafficking in Persons Report. State Department Testimony of Ambassador Susan Coppedge for the Senate Foreign Relations Committee.

20. President's Interagency Task Force to Monitor and Combat Trafficking in Persons. (2013, April 9). Progress in Combating Trafficking in Persons: The U.S. Government Response to Modern Slavery. Washington, DC: U.S. Department of State. Office to Monitor and Combat Trafficking in Persons.

21. Obama, B. (2015, December 31). Presidential Proclamation—National Slavery and Human Trafficking Prevention Month. Washington, DC: The White House, Office of the Press Secretary.

22. U.S. Code. (2000). Victims of trafficking and violence protection act of 2000. Public Law 106, 386.

23. House Report 108-264. Trafficking Victims Protection Reauthorization Act of 2003 (Parts 1–2).

24. U.S. Congress. (2005). Trafficking Victims Protection Reauthorization Act of 2005. In the 109th Congress. 1st Session, vol. 4.

25. U.S. Congress. (2008). William Wilberforce Trafficking Victims Protection Reauthorization Act of 2008. Public Law 110, 457.

26. U.S. Congress. (2013). Trafficking Victims Protection Reauthorization Act of 2013 (Title XII of the Violence Against Women Reauthorization Act of 2013).

27. U.S. Department of State. (2016). *Trafficking in persons report 2016.*

28. U.S. Department of State. (2015, March 6). Trafficking in Persons Interim Assessment. U.S. Department of State. Office to Monitor and Combat Trafficking in Persons. http://www.state.gov/j/tip/rls/reports/2015/245641.htm.

29. U.S. Department of State. Office to Monitor and Combat Trafficking in Persons. http://www.state.gov/j/tip/.

30. UN General Assembly. (2000). Protocol to prevent, suppress and punish trafficking in persons, especially women and children. Supplement to the United Nations convention against transnational organized crime. Resolution 55, 25.

31. Bureau of Democracy, Human Rights and Labor. (2014). Country reports on human rights practices for 2014. U.S. Department of State.

32. U.S. Department of State. (2016). *2016 Trafficking in persons report.*

33. U.S. Department of State. (2016, July 12). Review of the 2016 Trafficking in Persons Report. State Department Testimony of Ambassador Susan Coppedge for the Senate Foreign Relations Committee.

34. National Human Trafficking Resource Center. https://traffickingresourcecenter.org/.

35. National Human Trafficking Resource Center. https://traffickingresourcecenter.org/.

36. 8th Day Center for Justice. www.8thdaycenter.org/.

37. The A21 Campaign. www.a21.org/.
38. Arizona League to End Regional Trafficking (ALERT). traffickingaz.org
39. Bishop Outreach. bishopoutreach.org/.
40. California Against Slavery. californiaagainstslavery.org.
41. CAST: Coalition to Abolish Slavery & Trafficking. www.castla.org/.
42. The Global Alliance Against Traffic in Women (GAATW). www.gaatw.org/.
43. Not For Sale. https://www.notforsalecampaign.org/.
44. Physicians for Human Rights. physiciansforhumanrights.org/.
45. Red Light Campaign. www.redlightcampaign.org/.
46. Shared Hope International. sharedhope.org/.
47. Slavery Footprint. Made in a free world. slaveryfootprint.org/.
48. SW Florida Regional Human Trafficking Coalition. swfl-humantrafficking.org/.
49. Truckers Against Trafficking. www.truckersagainsttrafficking.org/.
50. *Truck News*. http://www.trucknews.com/.
51. Vital Voices Global Partnership. https://www.vitalvoices.org/.

Chapter 7

Trafficking in Persons: The Criminal Justice Response to Trafficking

Chapter Objectives

This chapter provides a comprehensive understanding of the following:

- The Criminal Justice Response to Trafficking in Persons
  - The United States and Human Trafficking Legislation
  - Challenges in Identification of Trafficking Victims
  - Trainings/Strategies for Identification of Victims and Offenders
  - Awareness and Educational Campaigns
  - Task Forces
  - Warning Signs of Trafficking and Plans
  - Arrest and Prosecution of the Traffickers

Introduction: The Criminal Justice Response to Trafficking in Persons

Although history is replete with examples of physical and sexual exploitation of humans for labor and pleasure, the discussion of human trafficking in the context of exploitation has begun fairly recently. It has only recently gained the attention of law enforcement, human rights advocates, and policymakers. During the last few decades, there has been a heightened interest in understanding the nature and extent of human trafficking as well as its effects and consequences on victims and others. This heightened interest has translated into an increased awareness of human trafficking locally, nationally, and internationally. It is now widely understood that human trafficking exists and it exists everywhere. It affects virtually every person and every country in every region of the world. It is a global crime that transcends all geographical and demographic boundaries. It engenders conditions where economic gain becomes the guiding principle and human beings are treated as commodities and units of production.

This increased awareness and interest has triggered the international community to take action and pass legislation to address human trafficking. Consequently, Resolution 55/25—the Convention against Transnational Organized Crime—and its supplemental protocol, the Protocol to Prevent, Suppress and Punish Trafficking in Persons, especially Women and Children, was adopted by the United Nations General Assembly in 2000. This protocol is also known as Palermo Protocol.[1] Since the introduction and passing of the Resolution 55/25 and adoption of Palermo Protocol, there have been a number of other legislations passed, adopted, and implemented in many countries of the globe. This chapter focuses on examination of legal issues related to human trafficking and the criminal justice response to trafficking. It reviews trafficking in persons legislation and discusses the United States' legal response in confronting the crime of trafficking in persons. Then, the chapter reviews the development of strategies including trainings provided to law enforcement officers, educational and awareness trainings, and campaigns for the identification of victims and offenders. The chapter discusses warning signs of trafficking and criminal justice endeavors to control and prevent trafficking. It also presents information on the recommended processes for the arrest, prosecution, and punishment of the traffickers.

Cases like from that of a family-run sex-trafficking organization based in South Florida in the 1990s,[2] and the *Golden Venture* smuggling ship from China in 1993,[3] to the most recent one in 2015 where nine traffickers were charged in interstate human trafficking conspiracy[4]—have taken center stage in the news and media. Numerous news stories like the ones mentioned above have made the general public aware of the varied manifestations of the crime of human trafficking domestically and around the globe. These stories present the process and consequences of trafficking in human terms and in all its painful details.[5] Although trafficking cases involving sexual exploitation receive the most coverage and incite public outrage, labor trafficking cases account for more than 75 percent of all human trafficking cases globally.[6] Human trafficking has also been referred to as "modern-day slavery"[7] and has also been described as the second most profitable organized criminal activity in the world.

Consequently, there is an increased national and global interest in developing strategies and solutions to address this horrendous problem affecting humanity. The increased general awareness of the issue and public response has resulted in many new legislations being passed and old ones being modified. In preparation for an adequate and effective response to this heinous crime, the law enforcement, courts, and other legal personnel are also offered trainings.

In this chapter, we discuss the complex history and current status of criminal justice responses to "trafficking in persons" and anti-trafficking legislation in United States as well as in other parts of the world. This chapter builds on the discussions in Chapter 2, where we discussed historical and global perspectives on trafficking in persons—a history of the events leading up to the creation of the Trafficking Victims Protection Act of 2000, the federal law that first addressed the phenomenon of trafficking in persons and the discussions in Chapter 6 that provided insight on the global response to human trafficking.

The United States and Human Trafficking Legislation

Soon after November 15, 2000, when the United Nations General Assembly passed Resolution 55/25 adopting the Convention against Transnational Organized Crime and its supplemental protocols, the Protocol to Prevent, Suppress and Punish Trafficking in Persons, especially Women and Children—a protocol against Transnational Organized Crime was adopted by the United Nations General Assembly. This protocol—also known as Palermo Protocol—was entered into force on December 25, 2003.[8] As of 2015, it has been ratified by 167 parties.

Since the adoption of the Protocol to Prevent, Suppress and Punish Trafficking in Persons by the United Nations Assembly in 2000, the United States has been at the forefront of developing strategies to address the origin, process, and aftermath of human trafficking. The United States has been one of the most influential states in urging other states to develop an adequate response to human trafficking. It has been a pioneer in passing national and international legislation to combat human trafficking. It has taken the lead in efforts to prevent and control human trafficking. Owing to the United States' efforts, several new international, federal, and state legislations have been passed and the existing ones revised.

The U.S. Congress passed a federal statute, the Trafficking Victims Protection Act (TVPA), into law, offering protections for persons who may be in the country and victims of human trafficking, in 2000:

1) to combat trafficking in persons, especially into the sex trade, slavery, and involuntary servitude,
2) to reauthorize certain Federal programs to prevent violence against women, and for other purposes.[9]

Since the passing of Trafficking Victims Protection Act (2000), many new bills have been introduced and passed. Here is a list and description of major human trafficking legislation in the U.S. House and U.S. Senate 114th Congress (the legislation passed or submitted to Congress from January 2015 to January 2016).

S 178: The Justice for Victims of Trafficking Act of 2015 was passed by the U.S. Senate with a vote of 99–0 on April 22, 2015. This section expands the definition of "child abuse" under the Victims of Child Abuse Act of 1990 to include human trafficking and the production of child pornography and "provides a process by which an individual who is a human trafficking survivor can move to vacate any arrest or conviction records for prostitution or any other non-violent offense committed as a direct result of human trafficking." It "establishes a rebuttable presumption that any arrest or conviction of an individual for an offense associated with human trafficking is a result of being trafficked, if the individual—(I) is a person granted nonimmigrant status pursuant to section 101(a)(15)(T)(i) of the Immigration and Nationality Act (8 U.S.C. 1101(a)(15)(T)(i)); (II) is the subject of a certification by the Secretary of Health and Human Services under section 107(b)(1)(E) of the Trafficking Victims Protection Act of 2000 (22 U.S.C. 7105(b)(1)(E)); or (III) has other similar documentation of trafficking, which has been issued by a federal agency."[10]

This legislation also imposes a special assessment (to support the Domestic Trafficking Victims Fund) in the amount of $5,000 on individuals convicted of peonage, slavery, trafficking, sexual abuse, sexual exploitation, and other abuses of children, transportation for illegal sexual activity, and human smuggling. The Attorney General is authorized to award block grants to an eligible entity to develop, improve, or expand domestic child human trafficking deterrence programs. The Attorney General, in consultation with the Secretary of Health and Human Services, is authorized to award not more than $7,000,000 of the funds available in the Domestic Trafficking Victims' Fund, established under section 3014 of title 18, United States Code, for each of fiscal years 2016 through 2020. In the first fiscal year, the Inspector General will conduct audits of recipients of a covered grant to prevent waste, fraud, and abuse of funds by grantees.[11]

HR 460: The Human Trafficking Detection Act of 2015 was submitted to the Committee on Homeland Security and Governmental Affairs on March 4,

2015. This legislation directs the Secretary of Homeland Security (DHS) to implement a program that includes methods for identifying suspected victims and perpetrators of human trafficking, methods for approaching a suspected victim in a manner that is sensitive to the victim, training that is most appropriate for a particular location or environment, and a post-training evaluation of trainees. It authorizes the secretary, upon request, to provide training curricula to assist any state, local, or tribal government or private organization in establishing its program.[12]

S 166: The Stop Exploitation Through Trafficking Act of 2015 was placed on the Senate Legislative Calendar under General Orders on March 4, 2015. This legislation amends Part Q of Title I of the Omnibus Crime Control and Safe Streets Act of 1968 (42 U.S.C. 3796dd et seq.) to allow hiring of additional career law enforcement officers so as to delegate the new hires to the National Human Trafficking Hotline beginning in FY 2017. The Attorney General is expected to implement and maintain a National Strategy for Combating Human Trafficking.[13]

HR 500: The Survivors of Human Trafficking Empowerment Act was referred to the House Subcommittee on Crime, Terrorism, Homeland Security, and Investigations on February 19, 2015, to establish the United States Advisory Council on Human Trafficking, which shall provide advice and recommendations to the Senior Policy Operating Group and the President's Task Force to Monitor and Combat Trafficking in Persons. This legislation directs the council to meet at least annually to review federal government policy and programs intended to combat human trafficking, formulate assessments and recommendations to ensure that U.S. policy and programming efforts conform to the best practices in the field of human trafficking prevention, and meet with the group at least annually to present the council's findings and recommendations.[14]

HR 345: This bill "to make persons who conspire to commit, commit, or benefit from an act of human trafficking ineligible for admission to the United States of America" was referred to the Subcommittee on Immigration and Border Security on February 5, 2015. This legislation amends the Immigration and Nationality Act to make an alien who commits or conspires to commit a single human trafficking offense, or assists a trafficker, ineligible for U.S. admission. This bill makes the spouse, son, or daughter of such an inadmissible alien also permanently inadmissible if he or she has obtained a financial or other benefit from that alien's illicit activity, regardless of when the benefit was obtained, and knew that the benefit was the product of such illicit activity. This bill is intended to use the fear of ineligibility to enter the United States as deterrence.[15]

HR 159: The Stop Exploitation Through Trafficking Act of 2015 was passed in the House and referred to the Senate Committee on the Judiciary on February 4, 2015. HR 159 amends the Omnibus Crime Control and Safe Streets Act of 1968 to authorize the Attorney General to give preferential consideration in awarding Community Oriented Police Services grants. It amends the Victims of Trafficking and Violence Protection Act of 2000 (VTVPA) to require the Attorney General's annual report on federal agencies. It also amends the VTVPA to require the Secretary of Health and Human Services, annually beginning in FY2017, to make grants for a national communication system. It amends the Workforce Investment Act of 1998 to include victims of a severe form of trafficking in persons among those eligible for the Job Corps.[16]

HR 181: The Justice for Victims of Trafficking Act of 2015 was referred to the Senate Committee on the Judiciary on February 7, 2015. This amends the Trafficking Victims Protection Reauthorization Act of 2005 to authorize the Attorney General to make grants to eligible entities. It also amends the Victims of Child Abuse Act of 1990 to include human trafficking and the production of child pornography. It restricts the use of grant funds for conferences or lobbying. It amends the Trafficking Victims Protection Act of 2000 to provide that U.S. citizens or lawful permanent residents who are victims of severe forms of trafficking shall not be required to obtain an official certification from the Secretary of Health and Human Services in order to access any of the specialized services or any other federal benefits and protections.[17]

HR 515: The International Megan's Law to Prevent Demand for Child Sex Trafficking was referred to the Senate Committee on Foreign Relations on February 5, 2015. This directs the Secretary of Homeland Security to establish "the Angel Watch Center" within the Child Exploitation Investigations Unit of U.S. Immigration and Customs Enforcement. It authorizes the center to notify a destination country (including its visa-issuing agents in the United States) of impending or current international travel of a child-sex offender. It also encourages the president to use authorities under the Foreign Assistance Act of 1961 to assist foreign countries in identifying sex offenders and providing and receiving notification of child sex offender international travel. It also amends the TVPA of 2000 to include a mandate for a country's cooperation with other governments in the investigation and prosecution of such trafficking cases.[18]

HR 246: This bill "to improve the response to victims of child sex trafficking" was referred to the Senate Committee on the Judiciary on January 28, 2015. This amends the Missing Children's Assistance Act to include among the required uses of the Office of Juvenile Justice and Delinquency Prevention's annual grant to the National Center for Missing and Exploited Children operation of a cyber tip line to provide online users and electronic service providers an effective means of reporting Internet-related child sexual exploitation in the area of child sex trafficking, including child prostitution.[19]

HR 350: The Human Trafficking Prevention, Intervention, and Recovery Act of 2015 has been passed in the House and referred to the Senate Committee on the Judiciary on January 28, 2015. This legislation requires the Interagency Task Force to Monitor and Combat Trafficking to conduct a review of all cases as well as the grant recipient agencies' efforts in combating human trafficking. It also requires the Government Accountability Office (GAO) to report to Congress regarding federal and state law enforcement efforts to combat human trafficking in the United States and information on each relevant federal grant program. It also amends the Trafficking Victims Protection Act of 2000 to authorize grants for programs that provide housing assistance to the victims of trafficking.[20]

HR 398: The Trafficking Awareness Training for Health Care Act of 2015 was passed in the House and referred to the Senate Committee on Health, Education, Labor, and Pensions on January 28, 2015, to provide for the development and dissemination of evidence-based best practices for healthcare professionals to recognize victims of a severe form of trafficking and respond to such individuals appropriately. Under this legislation, The Secretary of Health and Human Services, acting through the director for the Agency of Healthcare Research and Quality, will be in charge of identifying such practices and keeping the appropriate congressional committees informed regarding all progress.[21]

HR 469: The Strengthening Child Welfare Response to Trafficking Act of 2015 was passed in the House and referred to the Senate Committee on Health, Education, Labor, and Pensions on January 28, 2015. This amends the Child Abuse Prevention and Treatment Act to condition eligibility to receive a state grant for child abuse or neglect prevention and treatment programs. This legislation has provisions to identify and assess reports of child human trafficking victims, train representatives of the state, and identify services and procedures for appropriate referral to address the needs of such children. It directs the Secretary of Health and Human Services to report to Congress on the specific type and prevalence of severe forms of trafficking in persons, the practices and protocols utilized by states, and any barriers in federal laws or regulations.[22]

HR 468: The Enhancing Services for Runaway and Homeless Victims of Youth Trafficking Act of 2015 was passed in the House. This act was read twice and referred to the Senate Committee on the Judiciary on January 27, 2015. This legislation amends the Runaway and Homeless Youth Act with respect to grants to states, localities, and private entities to carry out research, evaluation, demonstration, and service projects regarding activities designed to increase knowledge concerning human trafficking and the perils of running away from home and to improve services for runaway youth and homeless youth. It extends the secretary's authority to make grants to nonprofit private agencies and street-based services for the purpose of providing street-based services to runaway youth and homeless and street youth, who have been subjected to, or are at risk of being subjected to, sexual abuse, prostitution, or sexual exploitation.[23]

HR 514: The Human Trafficking Prioritization Act was passed in the House and referred to the Senate Committee on Foreign Relations on January 27, 2015. Under this legislation, the Office to Monitor and Combat Trafficking of the Department of State will be more effective in carrying out duties mandated by Congress in the Trafficking Victims Protection Act of 2000, and can do so without an increase in either personnel or budget; in doing so, the status of the Office will be changed to that of a Bureau. Efficiency will be delegated through an Assistant Secretary that will remain in direct contact with the Secretary of State.[24]

HR 61: The Securing the Assistance of Victims of Exploitation Act of 2015 (SAVE Act) was referred to the House Subcommittee on Nutrition on January 26, 2015. Under this legislation, human trafficking has no place in a civil society; all found engaging in human trafficking will "be prosecuted to the fullest extent of the law." Under this act, state and local law enforcement should acquire the tools and resources necessary to "identify, apprehend, and prosecute the criminals" who engage in human trafficking. "Notwithstanding any other provision of law, none of the funds made available to carry out the Food and Nutrition Act of 2008 (7 U.S.C. 2011 et seq.) may be used in contravention of section 107(b) of Division A of the Victims of Trafficking and Violence Protection Act of 2000 (114 Stat. 1482; 22 U.S.C. 7105(b))."[25]

S 205: The Trafficking Awareness Training for Health Care Act of 2015 was referred to the Senate Committee on Health, Education, Labor, and Pensions on January 21, 2015. The purpose of this act is to develop and provide awareness trainings in schools to facilitate identification of human trafficking cases and prevent victimization.[26]

HR 63: The CATCH Traffickers Act of 2015 was referred to the House Subcommittee on Crime, Terrorism, Homeland Security, and Investigations on January 12, 2015. This directs the Secretary of Homeland Security to establish and maintain a database to serve as a central location for information from law enforcement agency investigations relating to human trafficking. This act requires the head of a law enforcement agency to ensure that information the secretary determines to be appropriate is entered into the database. It authorizes the Attorney General to reduce by 20 percent the amount of a grant, under the Edward Byrne Memorial Justice Assistance Grant Program, received by a state or local government the law enforcement agency of which does not substantially comply with such requirement. It permits law enforcement agencies to access the database only in connection with an investigation related to human trafficking.[27]

S 140: The Combat Human Trafficking Act of 2015 was referred to the Senate Committee on the Judiciary on January 8, 2015. Under this act, the Director of the Bureau of Justice Statistics is required to prepare an annual report on rates of arrest, prosecution, and conviction. The report will be sent to the Committee on the Judiciary of the House of Representatives; the Committee on the Judiciary of the Senate; the Task Force; the Senior Policy Operating Group established under section 105(g) of the Trafficking Victims Protection Act of 2000 (22 U.S.C. 7103(g)); and the Attorney General. The right to be informed in a timely manner has been added to Section 3771(a) of title 18, United States Code.[28]

S 44: A bill to provide for the expedited processing of unaccompanied alien children illegally entering the United States, and for other purposes was referred to the Senate Committee on the Judiciary on January 7, 2015. This bill amends the William Wilberforce Trafficking Victims Protection Reauthorization Act of 2008 to declare that any unaccompanied alien child who has not been a victim of a severe form of trafficking in persons or does not have a credible fear of persecution on returning to his or her country of nationality shall be placed in removal proceedings, eligible for voluntary departure, and provided with access to counsel. This requires mandatory Department of Homeland Security detention of a UAC apprehended by U.S. Border Patrol or U.S. Immigration and Customs Enforcement. It also requires judges to make a decision within 72 hours.[29]

HR 4383: The DHS Human Trafficking Prevention Act of 2016 was introduced to the Senate on January 13, 2016. The act requires the Secretary of Homeland Security to enhance Department of Homeland Security coordination on how to identify and record information on individuals suspected or convicted of human trafficking, and for other purposes.[30]

In the section above, we have discussed some of the most recent legislation (January 2015–January 2016) passed or processed for passing. Although this list of legislation is not exhaustive, it demonstrates the United States' commitment and dedication in responding to the crime of human trafficking. The legislation presented above discusses the process for addressing trafficking in persons and provides guidance on resources and legal recourse for law enforcement, society, and the victims. There were a total of 111 bills introduced in 2015–2016 in the U.S. Congress related to the subject human trafficking. A list of these bills is presented at the end of the book in Appendix 1.

The next section reviews the challenges in identification of trafficking victims given the nature and definition of human trafficking as well as lack of awareness and general perceptions held by the public and service providers. This section deliberates difficulties in distinguishing normal activity from trafficking incidents and ascertaining the veracity of the incident so as to respond adequately.

Challenges in Identification of Trafficking Victims

Human trafficking is a complex crime, in the sense that victims are part of the general public and are subjected to labor and sexual exploitation, servitude, debt bondage, and child-soldiering worldwide. They are typically in plain sight while performing jobs in the assigned areas. Since victims become part of the economic and environmental landscape of the location they are exploited in, detection and identification become extremely difficult—if not impossible. It is diverse, complex, and so much a part of the routine activities of the general public, that it becomes difficult to detect and ascertain whether the individual is an employee or victim. Almost all of us, albeit inadvertently, participate in allowing it to perpetuate. Sometimes the victims may be kept behind locked doors, but often they are right in front of us performing their assigned jobs and providing services—however, they remain hidden, as we fail to recognize them because of our ignorance. For example, construction sites, restaurants, elder care centers, nail salons, agricultural fields, and hotels—just to name a few places—are full of such people, where we see and meet these victims but do not recognize them as such.

Victims of trafficking rarely come forward to seek help on their own, because of the fear of being caught and punished by the trafficker, or punished by the authorities, or deported, or sent home, and in some cases because of a language barrier.[31] Traffickers use force, fraud, or coercion to lure their victims and force them into labor or commercial sexual exploitation. They look for people who are susceptible for a variety of reasons, including psychological or emotional vulnerability, economic hardship, lack of a social safety net, natural disasters, or political instability. Trauma caused by traffickers can be so great that many may not identify themselves as victims or ask for help, even in highly public settings.[32] Traffickers' use of coercion—such as threats of deportation and harm to the victim or their family members—is so powerful that even when service providers offer help to rescue the victims, they are often too fearful to accept any help.[33] Some research demonstrates that victims may wish to remain in the country to which they have been trafficked and be exploited rather than return to their previous existence, in the absence of a viable economic alternative.[34] Illegal immigrants who are victims of trafficking may be reluctant to contact the authorities because of their lack of legal status, and when offered help may not accept support or accommodation when this requires involvement with any authorities. They may not trust police because of previous experiences.[35] Some studies report that the law enforcement and service providers who have worked with trafficking victims relate that traffickers often tell victims that they are to blame for their lifestyle and the choices they made. They are made to believe that they are criminals who violated state laws and that they will be arrested and deported (in the case of immigrants) or sent home (in case of domestic victims) if caught. They are also told that their safety and well-being is dependent on their compliance with traffickers' demands and the traffickers are their only saviors. Many victims, due to their past and current experiences, believe stories told by the traffickers and are convinced that the traffickers are the only people who care for them and are able to help them—making it harder to approach and help them.

In some cases, victims are isolated, however, even when they are not isolated, their movements, actions, and interactions are monitored and controlled. They are denied any and all contact with the outside world. Traffickers control and monitor who they can talk and associate with. Generally, in the case of labor trafficking, their points of contact are the traffickers and other victims, and in the case of sex trafficking, the johns. Victims become dependent on the trafficker and start accepting their life as the normal way of life and survival. They may not even consider themselves to be victims—making it more difficult to approach them, identify them, and offer help.[36] They are made to believe that law enforcement officers are out there looking for them to prosecute them and return them to their homes. They are also told that service providers and law enforcement cannot be trusted as they are in cahoots and working together to identify and prosecute them.[37] The traffickers use victims' fear as a mechanism to control and manipulate them. Coupled with this psychological control are the threats from traffickers to harm the victims and their families if they try to divulge their situations to anyone.[38] They are also made to feel ashamed of themselves and the dishonor and shame they have brought to the family for their involvement is shameful activities—such as running away or engaging in sex, prostitution, and other deviant activities.[39]

In addition to the subtle nature of the crime, the lack of awareness of the crime of human trafficking and misperceptions about who the victims are and where it happens compound the problem. Consequently, even when the victims are visible, the general public does not recognize them. The misperception that human trafficking does not exist in the United States and definitely not in their communities further hinders public understanding of the problem and recognizing its existence.[40] The misperception that people are not forced but rather they freely choose to work in certain professions and therefore are not victims but employees creates further confusion in differentiating between an unhappy, discontented employee and a trafficking victim.[41]

Not only the general public, but, in many instances, law enforcement and service providers are also affected by similar misperceptions and stereotypes. Many still believe victims are young women and children brought illegally into the United States to work as prostitutes. The idea that human trafficking can occur domestically and to a United States citizens and not only in the sex industry, but in all types of industries, still seems implausible to the general public as well as to many service providers or law enforcement officers. The fact that the prostitution of U.S. minors likely constitutes human trafficking is a difficult concept to understand for not only the general public but also for many service providers or even law enforcement officers. When accosted, victims are often seen and treated as criminals, not victims.

Selective reporting of human trafficking crimes in the news media causes confusion and is responsible, to some extent, for the confusion and lack of a comprehensive understanding of the crime of human trafficking and its victims. Specifically, the lack of reporting on domestic victims (e.g., U.S. citizens or legal permanent residents), male victims, and labor trafficking (especially single victim domestic servitude cases) contributes significantly to the misconceptions surrounding this crime.

There are some other reasons why victims who come in contact with law enforcement, shelter providers, and others who may be able to help them often go unidentified. The first and foremost reason for such a state is that in many cases, victims do not see themselves as victims. Many victims—both international and domestic—do not believe that they are being victimized, rather they see their treatment as a way of life.[42] In some cases, lack of education and understanding of human trafficking and their lack of awareness of their rights as a victim may create such an impression and in other cases, it may be the culture and environment that makes them accept their lifestyle as a way of life and not exploitation—despite education and understanding level.[43]

In some cases, victims do not report or believe that they are victims, or are unwilling to leave the situation because they have come to depend on their traffickers and view traffickers as their protectors or in some cases, boyfriends. Service providers equate this to Stockholm Syndrome experienced by prisoners of war. Graham & Wish, (1994) reported that victims of human trafficking, specifically young girls, may display symptoms of Stockholm Syndrome more often.[44] Other researchers reported that the victim begins to identify with the victimizer as a means of emotional and physical survival.[45] In such cases, the victims do not believe that they are victims. They actually start bonding with the traffickers and feel a connection with their traffickers and any interactions with service providers, law enforcement, or others trying to convince them that they are victims and need to be rescued are not only ineffective but can also backfire. This is more so in the case of domestic minor victims of sex trafficking.[46]

Another challenge in identifying and rescuing victims is the fact that many a time victims are perceived and treated as offenders. For example, often victims of sexual exploitation are arrested as prostitutes and charged with solicitation and placed in jail or detention. Others, including domestic and undocumented, or illegal, immigrants being exploited for labor, are treated as criminals and subjected to deportation. Such a treatment by the authorities further deteriorates the victims' confidence in the authorities and service providers—reinforcing the fear that traffickers instill in the minds of the victims—"that they will be treated as criminals if they come to the attention of authorities." Such perceptions and treatment also convince the victims that they are responsible for their actions and the only well-wishers are the traffickers—boosting the power and control of traffickers over their victims.[47]

Trainings/Strategies for Identification of Victims and Offenders

Despite the covert nature of the crime and deceitful and cunning strategies used by the traffickers to keep the crime hidden, it is inevitable that communities will encounter victims when they are working in different industries. The fact that the victims are exploited to provide services for sex and labor, means that they are generally visible in all routine places carrying out routine activities. For example, people being exploited in the sex industry run a high risk of injuries similar to the victims of domestic violence and rape. They frequently contract sexually transmitted infections or become pregnant. Victims of labor trafficking experience injuries on the job, physical abuse by their traffickers, and experience health issues caused by poor nutrition and hygiene (e.g., dental problems, diabetes, etc.). Thus, indisputably, law enforcement, people working at domestic violence shelters, runaway home shelters and similar institutions, and health service providers will encounter these victims, though may not realize it or recognize them. Thus, the challenge is not discovering where these victims are hidden but having the ability and awareness to recognize and identify them.

So, the first strategy should be to provide trainings to the people who may encounter them at the first point of entry into the system. By virtue of their jobs and the services they provide, immigration and airport personnel, bus and railway staff, law enforcement officers, health service providers—nurses and physicians and other support staff, health/dental clinic workers and emergency room personnel—are more likely to come in contact with the potential victims.

These personnel should be educated and provided training in picking up the cues and identifying the victims. They can serve as sources of victim referrals. Individuals providing services at the domestic violence and sexual assault shelters, crisis hotlines, social workers, community- and faith-based organizations, religious/community leaders, Good Samaritans/citizens, school personnel (e.g., vice principals, guidance counselors, teachers), business owners (e.g., of markets, beauty salons), postal workers, and inspectors (e.g., wage and hourly, housing, liquor license)—all have the potential of coming into contact with victims at some point during their routine work day. These service providers without training interact with the victims without having any suspicion that the person they just served was a victim of trafficking. Thus, a great opportunity of intervention is lost. The first step should be to educate and train those service providers and individuals who have the potential of being the first point of contact with the victim. The training should be customized to prepare the staff of each agency to identify and refer the victims to the relevant service providers and authorities who can rescue the victims and apprehend the traffickers.

Victims of trafficking in persons may simultaneously be victims of other crimes such as kidnapping, prostitution, assault, domestic violence, and even murder. So, sometimes law enforcement officers may come across victims of trafficking while they are processing another one of the crimes listed. Trainings should educate and enable law enforcement officers to recognize the concomitant crimes. Trained officers will be able to determine and distinguish one from the other. Currently task forces, such as Innocence Lost, Internet Crimes Against Children, and Anti-Trafficking Task Forces, assist and facilitate officers to identify cases. Special units should be trained so that they can focus on trafficking within police departments to assist in the identification and referral of cases and victims.

Awareness and Educational Campaigns

The awareness and educational campaigns raise awareness and educate about the incidence and prevalence of human trafficking in communities. Raising awareness and educating law enforcement and service providers is not the same as training them to identify, rescue, and refer them to appropriate agencies. Such campaigns are very different from trainings. Trainings are intense process related workshops that prepare, guide, and provide the officers with sufficient tools to identify and rescue the victims. Trainings should be customized to the level of skills needed by varied individuals in their customized roles.[48]

Task Forces

In addition to educating and preparing the general public to be on the lookout, spot, and identify victims and/or suspicious activity, multidisciplinary teams, task forces, and/or coalitions have been established. By 2006, the Federal Bureau of Investigation (FBI) had established 14 task forces in cities with the most reports of prostituted youth. Currently there are task forces in many cities. These task forces play a significant role in raising general awareness and preparing service providers to identify and train to eradicate human trafficking from their communities.

Task forces can serve as central resources for those engaged in community organizations and can serve as means of facilitating communication, coordination, and information sharing across agencies working on a case. Task forces assist in putting policies, procedures, and protocols in place to overcome some of the system barriers inherent in working across agencies and jurisdictions. These task forces are effective means of couching human trafficking issues in community context and presenting them as a priority to be addressed.[49] The Bureau of Justice Assistance has funded 42 Human Trafficking Task Forces to synchronize federal, state, and local law enforcement authorities, government agencies, and nongovernmental victim-service providers in a multidisciplinary approach. The objective of these task forces is to identify human trafficking crimes, assist human trafficking victims, and prosecute human trafficking cases.[50]

Warning Signs of Trafficking and Plans

Traffickers employ sleek tactics to avoid raising suspicion about their crime and to keep victims enslaved. Notwithstanding the sinister and surreptitious nature of trafficking, victims inevitably come in the public view, although it may be difficult to recognize and identify them. The very nature of trafficking forces victims to be part of the working people. Victims are found in a variety of sectors and industries, including domestic servitude, agriculture, construction, elder care, hospitality, restaurant and food services, janitorial and cleaning services, manufacturing, door-to-door sales, and beauty services. Victims of labor trafficking include adults, minors, men, women, foreign nationals, and U.S. citizens. Lack of awareness makes it difficult to recognize victims.

Traffickers rarely tell their victims where they are located, being taken, or even what job they will have. Often victims don't have the means to get home or pay for things like food; they have to rely on traffickers in order to get by, forcing them to comply with the traffickers' demands and stay in their situations. They always seem in a hurry, nervous, and looking over their shoulders. They also seem afraid of losing their job and being deported or being sent home, if they contact the authorities and cooperate with the authorities.[51] In some cases, they may get injured at the workplace or may fall sick. In such cases, they may require medical care at hospitals and domestic violence shelters. Since they seek relationships with people of the same religious, ethnic, and cultural groups, they may attend places of worship and go to community centers. Knowing the contexts and situations in which the victims are often trapped helps educate the public and service providers about what clues to look for and identify. Understanding the warning signs and cues can help prepare customized training for the law enforcement officers, airline staff, and other service providers. Based on the existing literature, some of the cues that may indicate the presence of suspicious activity and possible human trafficking are discussed here.

A trafficked person may seem disoriented, nervous, and confused. The victims may not speak or understand English or may just be extraordinarily quiet and unresponsive. Often they are constantly watched and their activities are monitored, so they may seem nervous and concerned. The victims may not have any identification or may be unwilling to show it. They may appear malnourished and may have visible injuries and signs of physical abuse. They may exhibit anxiety at the sight of any police officer or security guard. They may not know or refuse to tell their address, who lives with them, or where they work. Research also indicates that traffickers brand their victims using tattoos with different names, signs, or barcodes.

To accommodate the demand for their services, victims are often transported from one place to another. They may use public transportation for land and air travel. In such places, the cues to look for the suspicious activity include their demeanor, dress, and activities during travel. They often are unaware or refuse to provide details of their departure location, destination, or flight information. They may be travelling either with too much luggage or too few personal items. Their movements are often monitored and they are under a close watch during their travel to ensure that the victim does not escape, or reach out to authorities for help, so they may be looking around all the time.

Health professionals may come across victims of trafficking when they seek medical care. The physicians, nurses, and support staff should watch for cues that may indicate that the injuries are the result of victimization and not accident. The clues, such as patients not wanting to identify themselves, not presenting any identification documents or money, not knowing the name of the city and hospital they are in, or not having any home address, should raise suspicion and should be paid attention to. The health professionals are in a unique position to identify and alert the service providers to come and rescue the victims.

Traffickers often use fear and intimidation to control their victims. Often traffickers coach their victims not to speak with anyone and if they have to speak then they are allowed only certain responses to avoid suspicion. So, even when the victims interact with anyone, their communication seems rehearsed and scripted. The signs to look for are the scripted or inconsistent responses. In the case of trafficked children for sexual exploitation, they seem to be under the influence of drugs or alcohol. They may also seem sleepy, tired, malnourished, and actually exhibit some signs of physical or sexual abuse, such as bruises, scars, or cigarette burns.

Some of the agencies offer programs to educate and train their staff and personnel. For example, Airline Ambassadors International offers a human trafficking awareness program to educate airport staff about the problem. Polaris runs programs to combat and prevent modern-day slavery and human trafficking. Free the Slaves campaigns against modern slavery around the world. International Justice Mission offers services and programs to protect the poor from violence in the developing world. More detailed and comprehensive information locating the services and other useful information in identifying and combating trafficking in persons can be found at www.traffickingresourcecenter.org. The National Human Trafficking Resource Center (NHTRC) provides services for tracking victims too.[52]

Carefully observing children's behavior can also provide general indicators and signs of a child being victimized. For example, if the child is being secretive about his/her activities and exhibits signs of physical/sexual assault (including STD's), low self-esteem, signs of embarrassment and shame, and an eating disorder, then it is important to pay more attention to the child and identify the causes of such behavior. If the child is experimenting with drugs/alcohol and generally associates with older people and has relationships with significantly older people, then that may be an indication that the child is being exploited.

Many times, young children are recruited and forced/deceived into conducting some form of criminal activity such as selling and delivering drugs, pick pocketing, begging, cannabis cultivation, and benefit fraud. Another place where victims can be found are residential places and homes where they work as nannies, au pairs, house servants, butlers, cooks, and perform other related work in the homes. They work long hours in horrendous working conditions. The signs that may indicate exploitation include living and working for a family in a private home, having no private space or even bedroom or proper sleeping place, working long hours 7 days a week, being "on call" 24 hours a day, and high security measures entering the home/place they work. They always look and seem fearful, anxious, depressed, submissive, tense, or nervous. When asked about their residence, they often claim that they are just visiting and are unable to clarify where they are staying or what is their permanent address.

Table 1 provides some cues/indicators to look for to determine that someone is the victim of trafficking. It also provides some advice on what to do, if someone has suspected or identified a victim of human trafficking.

Arrest and Prosecution of Traffickers

During the period of 2001–2007, after the TVPA came into effect, the government has successfully prosecuted human trafficking crimes in agricultural fields, sweatshops, suburban mansions, brothels, escort services, bars, and strip clubs. In 2007, the Human Trafficking Prosecution Unit (HTPU) within the Criminal Section of the Department of Justice was created by the Civil Rights Division. The HTPU consolidates the expertise of some of the nation's top human trafficking prosecutors. HTPU prosecutors work closely with Assistant United States Attorneys (AU.S.As) and law enforcement agencies to streamline fast-moving trafficking investigations to ensure consistent application of trafficking statutes and identify multijurisdictional trafficking networks. Human trafficking crimes, like other civil rights crimes, require notification to the Criminal Section pursuant to §§8-3.120 and 8-3.140 of the *United States Attorneys' Manual* (Department of Justice, Human Trafficking Prosecution Unit, 2015). Early notification of any case with potential human trafficking indicators allows the HTPU to provide timely victim assistance resources, legal guidance, and coordination between districts prosecuting overlapping criminal networks.[53]

Despite these federal and state laws there are only a few successful prosecutions. According to the Attorney General's Report (2016), there have been 1,876 suspects prosecuted for federal human trafficking offenses and roughly 450 suspects prosecuted for state-level human trafficking crimes since the passage of the TVPA in 2000 (Bouche, et al., 2016). According to the HTPU (2015), the numbers of trafficking investigations and prosecutions and sustained dedication to combating human trafficking have increased dramatically due to the enhanced criminal statutes, victim-protection provisions, and public awareness programs introduced by the Trafficking Victims Protection Act of 2000.[54]

Following the model of the TVPA, and creation of HTPU, as of 2015, all fifty states have also passed laws criminalizing acts of human trafficking, resulting in the enhanced penalties for perpetrators and better and more pro-

Table 1: Cues/Indicators That Someone Is the Victim of Trafficking

- Unexplained absences from school for a period of time
- History of running away from home or current status as a runaway
- References to frequent travel to other cities
- History or signs of emotional, sexual, or other physical abuse
- Inexplicable appearance of expensive gifts
- Communication with an older "boyfriend" or "girlfriend"
- Withdrawal or lack of interest in previous activities
- Significant substance abuse
- Submissive or fearful behavior
- Living with employer
- Poor living conditions
- Multiple people living in a cramped space
- Inability to speak to you privately
- Answers that seem scripted and rehearsed
- Assuming you can speak with someone you suspect is a victim of trafficking privately and without jeopardizing that person's safety because the trafficker is watching, these sample questions can help you follow up on the red flags you become aware of:
- Can you leave your job if you want to?
- Can you come and go if you please?
- Have you been hurt or threatened if you tried to leave?
- Has your family been threatened?
- Do you live with your employer?
- Where do you sleep and eat?
- Are you in debt to your employer?
- Do you have your passport/identification? If not, who has it?

If you think you have identified a victim of trafficking, do not attempt to rescue that person yourself. Instead, report it:

- In immediate emergencies, call 911.
- To report suspected trafficking crimes, call the National Human Trafficking Resource Center Hotline, which is open 24/7: 888-373-7888. The center can help you determine whether you have encountered a victim of trafficking and can coordinate with law enforcement and social service agencies to help the victim. Another option is to contact the U.S. Justice Department's Human Trafficking Office: 888-428-7581.
- To report sexually exploited or abused minors, call the National Center for Missing & Exploited Children: 800-THE-LOST (843-5678).

Sources: U.S. Department of State, https://www.state.gov/j/tip/id/; and U.S. Department of Education, http://www2.ed.gov/about/offices/list/oese/oshs/factsheet.html.

tections for victims.[55] Many states have created task forces to assist the law enforcement and service providers in locating and identifying human trafficking crimes at the community level. The TVPA clearly establishes that some of its main purposes are to prosecute and punish human traffickers, protect the identified human trafficking victims, and prevent human trafficking.

Here is the actual excerpt from the TVPA (2000):

> ... to combat trafficking in persons, a contemporary manifestation of slavery whose victims are predominantly women and children, to ensure just and effective punishment of traffickers, and to protect their victims.

The inter-agency Anti-Trafficking Coordination Team Initiative has been formulated by coordinating efforts of Immigration and Customs Enforcement (ICE), the Office of Homeland Security Investigations, the Federal Bureau of Investigation (FBI), and the Department of Labor. These partnerships have proven effective. For example, a domestic servitude conviction that resulted in payment of $80,000 in restitution to two Filipina victims in Kansas City, Missouri, and in another case, ten defendants were indicted and charged in a combined forced labor and sex trafficking scheme in El Paso, Texas. In 2015, labor traffickers who exploited victims in restaurants, bars, and cantinas on Long Island, New York, and in massage parlors in Chicago, Illinois, were identified, prosecuted, and convicted. In Seattle, a couple who held a young Micronesian woman in domestic servitude was convicted. Another trafficker who held two young Nigerian women in domestic servitude in Georgia was convicted and sentenced to 14 months in federal facility.[56] Other cases include indictment of labor traffickers who exploited Vietnamese victims in bridal shops in Arizona. The coordinated efforts of the inter-agency initiative have dismantled organized criminal networks that held Dominican, Filipino, and Jamaican workers in forced labor on cleaning crews.

Conclusion

Despite the challenges encountered in the identification of victims and prosecution of offenders, the criminal justice system's response to the crime of trafficking in persons is commendable and the efforts of law enforcement and service providers across the country to "rescue and restore" victims have resulted in several promising strategies and practices to address these challenges. With a legal and uniform definition of the crime and its victims, identifying victims is a little easier, though not without challenges. The hidden nature of the crime, the lack of awareness and understanding of human trafficking among the general public and organizations coming in contact with victims, misperceptions of who is a victim, and limited resources to devote to the investigation and identification of these cases are significant challenges that still need to be overcome. Administration of well-designed and delivered training and education, targeted outreach, and use of task forces, coalitions, and/or other multidisciplinary teams that are working together to combat this crime are some of the successful measures adopted to combat the crime of trafficking in persons. Despite enormous successes in prosecuting many of the traffickers and rescuing and restoring many victims, a great deal still needs to be done as trafficking in humans perpetuates.

The Department of Justice and the Department of State suggest 15 ways a person can help fight human trafficking. These are presented in Table 2 below.

Table 2: 15 Ways You Can Help Fight Human Trafficking

1. Learn the indicators of human trafficking so you can help identify a potential trafficking victim. Human trafficking awareness training is available for individuals, businesses, first responders, law enforcement, educators, and federal employees, among others.
2. If you are in the United States and believe someone may be a victim of human trafficking, report your suspicions to law enforcement by calling 911 or the 24-hour National Human Trafficking Resource Center line at 1-888-373-7888. Trafficking victims, including undocumented individuals, are eligible for services and immigration assistance.
3. Be a conscientious and informed consumer. Discover your slavery footprint, ask who picked your tomatoes or made your clothes, or check out the Department of Labor's "List of Goods Produced by Child Labor or Forced Labor." Encourage companies to take steps to investigate and prevent human trafficking in their supply chains and publish the information for consumer awareness.
4. Volunteer and support anti-trafficking efforts in your community.
5. Meet with and/or write to your local, state, and federal government representatives to let them know you care about combating human trafficking, and ask what they are doing to address it.
6. Host an awareness event to watch and discuss films about human trafficking. For example, learn how modern slavery exists today; watch an investigative documentary about sex trafficking; or discover how human trafficking can affect global food supply chains. Also, check out CNN's Freedom Project for more stories on the different forms of human trafficking around the world.
7. Organize a fundraiser and donate the proceeds to an anti-trafficking organization.
8. Encourage your local schools to partner with students and include modern slavery in their curricula. As a parent, educator, or school administrator, be aware of how traffickers target school-aged children.

Table 2 *cont'd*

9. Be well-informed. Set up a web alert to receive current human trafficking news. Become familiar with public awareness materials available from the Department of Health and Human Services or the Department of Homeland Security.
10. Work with a local religious community or congregation to help stop trafficking by supporting a victim service provider or spreading awareness of human trafficking.
11. Businesses: Provide jobs, internships, skills training, and other opportunities to trafficking survivors.
12. Students: Take action on your campus. Join or establish a university club to raise awareness about human trafficking and initiate action throughout your local community. Consider doing one of your research papers on a topic concerning human trafficking. Request that human trafficking be included in university curricula.
13. Health Care Providers: Learn how to identify the indicators of human trafficking and assist victims. With assistance from anti-trafficking organizations, extend low-cost or free services to human trafficking victims.
14. Journalists: The media plays an enormous role in shaping perceptions and guiding the public conversation about human trafficking. Here are some media best practices on how to effectively and responsibly report stories on human trafficking.
15. Attorneys: Offer human trafficking victims legal services, including support for those seeking benefits or special visas. Resources are available for attorneys representing victims of human trafficking.

Source: U.S. Department of State, http://www.state.gov/j/tip/id/help/.

Chapter Review

In this chapter, we have discussed the complex history and current status of criminal justice responses to trafficking in persons and anti-trafficking legislation in the U.S. as well in the other parts of the world. This chapter examined some of the legal issues related to human trafficking and the criminal justice response to trafficking. It reviewed trafficking in persons' legislation and discussed the United States' legal response in confronting the crime of trafficking in persons. Then, the chapter reviewed the development of strategies, including trainings provided to the law enforcement officers, educational and awareness trainings, and campaigns for identification of victims and offenders. The chapter discussed warning signs of trafficking and criminal justice endeavors to control and prevent trafficking. It also presented information on the recommended processes for the arrest, prosecution, and punishment of the traffickers.

This chapter expanded the discussions on historical and global perspectives on human trafficking started in Chapters 2 and 6. In essence, we discussed the following:

The Criminal Justice Response to Trafficking in Persons

- The United States and Human Trafficking Legislation
- Challenges in Identification of Trafficking Victims
- Trainings/Strategies for Identification of Victims and Offenders
- Awareness and Educational Campaigns
- Task Forces
- Warning Signs of Trafficking and Plans
- Arrest and Prosecution of the Traffickers

Discussion Questions

1) List the name of the federal statute that was passed in 2000.

2) What is the purpose of the Trafficking Victims Protection Act?

3) Discuss at least three challenges in identifying victims of trafficking in persons. Give examples.

4) What are the warning signs that indicate that a person may be a victim of trafficking?

5) How does law enforcement address the problem of trafficking in persons? Give two examples.

6) Identify two of the most recent pieces of legislation that have been passed or processed for passing by the United States Congress between January 2015 and January 2016.

References

Alvarez, Maria Beatriz, and Edward J. Alessi. "Human Trafficking Is More Than Sex Trafficking and Prostitution: Implications for Social Work." *Affilia* 27, no. 2 (2012): 142–152.

Andrees, Beate. *Forced Labour and Trafficking in Europe: How People Are Trapped in, Live through and Come out.* International Labour Organization, 2008.

Annison, Rachel. *In the Dock: Examining the UK's Criminal Justice Response to Trafficking.* Anti-Slavery International for The Anti-Trafficking Monitoring Group, 2013.

Antonopoulos, Georgios A., and John Winterdyk. "The Smuggling of Migrants in Greece: An Examination of Its Social Organization." *European Journal of Criminology* 3, no. 4 (2006): 439–461.

Aronowitz, A., G. Theuermann, and E. V. Tyuryukanova. "Analysing the Business Model of Trafficking in Human Beings to Better Prevent the Crime." Vienna: Organization for Security and Co-operation in Europe, Office of the Special Representative and Co-ordinator for Combating Trafficking in Human Beings, 2010. http://www.osce.org/files/documents/c/f/69028.pdf.

Askola, Heli. "Violence against Women, Trafficking, and Migration in the European Union." *European Law Journal* 13, no. 2 (2007): 204–217.

Balch, Alex, and Andrew Geddes. "Opportunity from Crisis? Organisational Responses to Human Trafficking in the UK." *The British Journal of Politics and International Relations* 13, no. 1 (2011): 26–41.

Balch, Alex, and Glynn Rankin. (2014). *UK Hotels Policy Guide: How to Protect Your Business against Human Trafficking, Forced Labour and Labour Exploitation.* Liverpool: Centre for the Study of International Slavery, http://www.gla.gov.uk/media/1588/uk-hotels-policy-guide.pdf.

Baye, Eneze Modupe-Oluwa, and Silke Heumann. "Migration, Sex Work and Exploitative Labor Conditions: Experiences of Nigerian Women in the Sex Industry in Turin, Italy, and Counter-Trafficking Measures." *Gender, Technology and Development* 18, no. 1 (2014): 77–105.

Berman, Jacqueline. "(Un)Popular Strangers and Crises (Un)Bounded: Discourses of Sex-Trafficking, the European Political Community and the Panicked State of the Modern State." *European Journal of International Relations* 9, no. 1 (2003): 37–86.

Bouche, Vanessa, Amy Farrell, and Dana Wittmer. "Identifying Effective Counter-Trafficking Programs and Practices in the U.S.: Legislative, Legal, and Public Opinion Strategies that Work." U.S. Department of Justice: NCJRS, 2016.

Bovenkerk, Frank, and Marion van San. "Loverboys in the Amsterdam Red Light District: A Realist Approach to the Study of a Moral Panic." *Crime, Media, Culture* 7, no. 2 (2011): 185–199.

Busch-Armendariz, Noël, Maura Busch Nsonwu, and Laurie Cook Heffron. "A Kaleidoscope: The Role of the Social Work Practitioner and the Strength of Social Work Theories and Practice in Meeting the Complex Needs of People Trafficked and the Professionals that Work with Them." *International Social Work* 57, no. 1 (2014): 7–18.

Cejp, Martin. "Research into Organised Crime in the Czech Republic: Solved Topics, Methodology, Basic Results." *Publication Series: European Institute for Crime Prevention and Control* (2004): 16–26.

The Centre for Social Justice (Slavery Working Group). It Happens Here: Equipping the United Kingdom to Fight Modern Slavery. 2013. http://www.centreforsocialjustice.org.uk/publications/it-happens-here-equipping-the-united-kingdom-to-fight-modern-slavery.

Christian Brothers Investment Services, Inc. "Corporate Strategies to Address Human Trafficking. Investor Recommendations for London Olympic Sponsors and Hospitality Companies." 2012. http://cbisonline.com/us/wpcontent/uploads/sites/2/2012/09/FINAL_OlympicsReport_9_28.pdf.

Clawson, Heather J., Nicole Dutch, Amy Solomon, and L. Goldblatt Grace. "Human Trafficking into and within the United States: A Review of the Literature." Washington, DC: Office of the Assistant Secretary for Planning and Evaluation, U.S. Department of Health and Human Services, 2009.

Coghlan, Deirdre, and Gillian Wylie. "Defining Trafficking/Denying Justice? Forced Labour in Ireland and the Consequences of Trafficking Discourse." *Journal of Ethnic and Migration Studies* 37, no. 9 (2011): 1513–1526.

Cohen, Desmond, and Elizabeth Reid. "The Vulnerability of Women: Is This a Useful Construct for Policy and Programming?" *Issues Paper* 28 (1999).

Craig, Gary. "Modern Slavery in the UK: The Contribution of Research." *Journal of Poverty and Social Justice* 22, no. 2 (2014): 159–164.

Cree, Viviene E. "Confronting Sex Trafficking: Lessons from History." *International Social Work* 51, no. 6 (2008): 763–776.

Di Tommaso, Maria L., Isilda Shima, Steinar Strøm, and Francesca Bettio. "As Bad as It Gets: Well-Being Deprivation of Sexually Exploited Trafficked Women." *European Journal of Political Economy* 25, no. 2 (2009): 143–162.

Drumea, Mihnea Claudiu. "Stopping Forced Labor." *Economics, Management, and Financial Markets* 2 (2011): 839–842.

Dutch National Rapporteur on Trafficking in Human Beings and Sexual Violence against Children. *Trafficking in Human Beings: Visible and Invisible II*. Summary of the Quantitative Report 2008–2012. 2014. http://www.

dutchrapporteur.nl/current/news/archief/a-reportof-modern-forms-of-slavery-in-the-netherlands.data-on-human-trafficking-2008-2012.aspx?cp=64&cs=16855.

Efrat, Asif. "Professional Socialization and International Norms: Physicians against Organ Trafficking." *European Journal of International Relations* (2014): 1354066114542664.

Ekberg, Gunilla. "The Swedish Law that Prohibits the Purchase of Sexual Services: Best Practices for Prevention of Prostitution and Trafficking in Human Beings." *Violence against Women* 10, no. 10 (2004): 1187–1218.

European Federation of Food, Agriculture and Tourism Trade Union. "Social Justice from Farm to Fork. Fight Precarious Work!" EFFAT Charter on Precarious Work, 2009. http://www.precarious-work.eu/.

European Union. The EU Rights of Victims of Trafficking in Human Beings. 2013. http://ec.europa.eu/dgs/home-affairs/elibrary/docs/thb_victims_rights/thb_victims_rights_en.pdf.

EUROSTAT. *Trafficking in Human Beings.* 2014 edition. Luxemburg: European Union Publications Office, Statistical Working Papers, 2014. http://ec.europa.eu/dgs/home-affairs/what-isnew/news/news/docs/20141017_working_paper_on_statistics_on_trafficking_in_human_beings_en.pdf.

Faraday, Fay. *Made in Canada: How the Law Constructs Migrant Workers' Insecurity.* Metcalf Foundation, 2012.

Farrell, Amy, Monica J. DeLateur, Colleen Owens, and Stephanie Fahy. "The Prosecution of State-Level Human Trafficking Cases in the United States." *Anti-Trafficking Review* 6 (2016).

Friedman, Sara Ann. *Who Is There to Help Us?: How the System Fails Sexually Exploited Girls in the United States: Examples from Four American Cities.* ECPAT-U.S.A, Incorporated, 2005.

Graham, Nanette, and Eric D. Wish. "Drug Use among Female Arrestees: Onset, Patterns, and Relationships to Prostitution." *Journal of Drug Issues* 24, no. 2 (1994): 315–329.

Haynes, Dina Francesca. "Lessons from Bosnia's Arizona Market: Harm to Women in a Neoliberalized Postconflict Reconstruction Process." *University of Pennsylvania Law Review* 158, no. 6 (2010): 1779–1829.

House of Commons, Home Affairs Committee. *The Trade in Human Beings: Human Trafficking in the UK.* London: The Stationary Office Limited, 2009. http://www.publications.parliament.uk/pa/cm200809/cmselect/cmhaff/23/23i.pdf.

Hughes, Donna M. "The Role of 'Marriage Agencies' in the Sexual Exploitation and Trafficking of Women from the Former Soviet Union." *International Review of Victimology* 11, no. 1 (2004): 49–71.

Human Smuggling and Trafficking Center. *Domestic Human Trafficking: An Internal Issue*. December 2008. https://www.state.gov/documents/organization/113612.pdf.

Icduygu, Ahmet. "Transborder Crime between Turkey and Greece: Human Smuggling and Its Regional Consequences." *Southeast European and Black Sea Studies* 4, no. 2 (2004): 294–314.

Institute for Human Rights and Business. *The Future of the Gangmasters Licensing Authority and the Employment Agencies Standards Inspectorate*. 2010. http://www.ihrb.org/pdf/Proposal-Future_of_the_Gangmasters_Licensing_Authority.pdf.

Inter-Departmental Ministerial Group (IDMG). *First Annual Report of the Inter Departmental Ministerial Group on Human Trafficking*. 2012. https://www.gov.uk/government/uploads/system/uploads/attachment_data/file/118116/humantrafficking-report.pdf.

International Labour Office (ILO). *Profits and Poverty: The Economics of Forced Labor*. Special Action Programme to Combat Forced Labour (SAP-FL). Fundamental Principles and Rights at Work Branch (FPRW). 2014.

International Labour Organization (ILO). Abolition of Forced Labor Convention. Convention Concerning the Abolition of Forced Labor. Adoption: 25 Jun 1957. Entry into force: 17 Jan 1959. http://www.ilo.org/dyn/normlex/en/f?p=1000:12100:0::NO::P12100_ILO_CODE:C105.

International Labour Organization (ILO). "The Impact of New Ownership of Accommodation, Operations and Consumption on Types of Employment, Industrial Relations, HRD and Qualification Needs in the Accommodation and Hospitality Sector." Geneva: International Labour Organization, 2010.

International Tourism Partnership. "Guidelines for Checking Recruitment Agencies." July 2013. http://tourismpartnership.org/human-trafficking/.

International Tourism Partnership. "Human Trafficking Position Statement." http://tourismpartnership.org/human-trafficking/.

International Tourism Partnership. "Know How Guide. Addressing Human Trafficking in the Hospitality Industry." Green Hotelier, 2013. http://www.greenhotelier.org/know-howguides/addressing-human-trafficking-in-the-hospitality-industry/.

Jackson, Keith, J. Jeffery, and George Adamson. "Setting the Record: The Trafficking of Migrant Women in the England and Wales Off-Street Prostitution Sector." Association of Chief Police Officers, August 2010.

Joseph Rowntree Foundation. "Forced Labour's Business Models and Supply Chains." 2013. http://www.jrf.org.uk/sites/files/jrf/forced-labour-regulation-full.pdf.

Kalayaan. *Slavery by Another Name: The Tied Migrant Domestic Worker Visa.* 2013. http://www.kalayaan.org.uk/documents/Slavery%20by%20a%20new%20name-%20Briefing%207.5.13.pdf.

Kara, Siddharth. *Sex Trafficking: Inside the Business of Modern Slavery.* Columbia University Press, 2009.

Lazar, Ioan. "Different Forms of Compensation Available for Damages Caused to the Victims of Human Trafficking." *Official Journal L* 203 (2002): 1–4.

Lebov, Korin. "Human Trafficking in Scotland." *European Journal of Criminology* 7, no. 1 (2010): 77–93.

Leman, Johan, and Stef Janssens. "The Albanian and Post-Soviet Business of Trafficking Women for Prostitution: Structural Developments and Financial Modus Operandi." *European Journal of Criminology* 5, no. 4 (2008): 433–451.

Lundin, Susanne Maria. "Organ Economy: Organ Trafficking in Moldova and Israel." *Public Understanding of Science* (2010).

Mantouvalou, Virginia. "Modern Slavery: The UK Response." *Industrial Law Journal* 39, no. 4 (2010): 425–431.

Marriott. "Supplier Conduct Principles: Business Conduct and Ethics." 2012. http://www.marriott.com/Multimedia/PDF/CorporateResponsibility/Marriott_Supplier_Conduct_Principles.pdf.

McIntyre, Bonnie L. "More Than Just Rescue: Thinking Beyond Exploitation to Creating Assessment Strategies for Child Survivors of Commercial Sexual Exploitation." *International Social Work* 57, no. 1 (2014): 39–63.

Miko, Francis T. "Trafficking in Women and Children: The U.S. and International Response—Updated March 26, 2004." Cornell University ILR School, 2004.

National Crime Agency (NCA). "NCA Strategic Assessment: The Nature and Scale of Human Trafficking in 2013." 2014. http://www.nationalcrimeagency.gov.uk/publications/399-ncastrategic-assessment-the-nature-and-scale-of-human-trafficking-in-2013/file.

Okech, David, Whitney Morreau, and Kathleen Benson. "Human Trafficking: Improving Victim Identification and Service Provision." *International Social Work* 55, no. 4 (2012): 488–503.

Pajnik, Mojca, and Matthieu Renault. "The (Re)Making of Sexualities on the Web." *Social Science Information* 53, no. 4 (2014): 462–482.

Papanicolaou, Georgios. "The Sex Industry, Human Trafficking and the Global Prohibition Regime: A Cautionary Tale from Greece." *Trends in Organized Crime* 11, no. 4 (2008): 379–409.

Parmentier, Stephan. "Epilogue: Human Trafficking Seen from the Future." *European Journal of Criminology* 7, no. 1 (2010): 95–100.

Petrunov, Georgi. "Managing Money Acquired from Human Trafficking: Case Study of Sex Trafficking from Bulgaria to Western Europe." *Trends in Organized Crime* 14, no. 2–3 (2011): 165–183.

Poelmans, Jonas, Paul Elzinga, Dmitry I. Ignatov, and Sergei O. Kuznetsov. "Semi-automated Knowledge Discovery: Identifying and Profiling Human Trafficking." *International Journal of General Systems* 41, no. 8 (2012): 774–804.

Raphael, Jody. *Listening to Olivia: Violence, Poverty and Prostitution.* Northeastern University Press, 2004.

Rice, K. "The War on Human Trafficking." *Travel Weekly*, May 7, 2014. http://www.travelweekly.com/Travel-News/Travel-Agent-Issues/The-war-on-human-trafficking/.

Roby, Jini L. "Women and Children in the Global Sex Trade." *International Social Work* 48, no. 2 (2005): 136–147.

Scheper-Hughes, Nancy. "Mr. Tati's Holiday and João's Safari: Seeing the World through Transplant Tourism." *Body & Society* 17, no. 2–3 (2011): 55–92.

Shelley, Louise. *Human Smuggling and Trafficking into Europe: A Comparative Perspective.* Transatlantic Council on Migration, 2014. http://www.migrationpolicy.org/research/human-smugglingand-trafficking-europe-comparative-perspective.

Simeunovic-Patic, Biljana, and Sanja Copic. "Protection and Assistance to Victims of Human Trafficking in Serbia: Recent Developments." *European Journal of Criminology* 7, no. 1 (2010): 45–60.

Stephen-Smith, Sarah. "Routes In, Routes Out: Quantifying the Gendered Experience of Trafficking to the UK." London: POPPY Project, Eaves Housing, 2008.

Stiles, Siobahn. "'I Am Elena': Rhetorical Analysis as the First Step to a 'Best Practices' Formula for Sex Trafficking Public Service Announcements." *Visual Communication* 11, no. 2 (2012): 185–206.

Suchland, Jennifer. "Double Framing in *Lilya 4-Ever*: Sex Trafficking and Postsocialist Abjection." *European Journal of Cultural Studies* 16, no. 3 (2013): 362–376. 1367549413476008.

Surtees, Rebecca. "Traffickers and Trafficking in Southern and Eastern Europe: Considering the Other Side of Human Trafficking." *European Journal of Criminology* 5, no. 1 (2008): 39–68.

Tepelus, Camelia M. "Social Responsibility and Innovation on Trafficking and Child Sex Tourism: Morphing of Practice into Sustainable Tourism Policies?" *Tourism and Hospitality Research* 8, no. 2 (2008): 98–115.

Truong, Thanh-Dam. "Gender, Exploitative Migration, and the Sex Industry: A European Perspective." *Gender, Technology and Development* 7, no. 1 (2003): 31–52.

TUC Commission on Vulnerable Employment. "Hard Work, Hidden Lives: The Full Report of the Commission on Vulnerable Employment." 2007. http://www.vulnerableworkers.org.uk/files/CoVE_full_report.pdf.

Turner-Moss, Eleanor, Cathy Zimmerman, Louise M. Howard, and Siân Oram. "Labour Exploitation and Health: A Case Series of Men and Women Seeking Post-trafficking Services." *Journal of Immigrant and Minority Health* 16, no. 3 (2014): 473–480.

United Nations Global Initiative to Fight Human Trafficking (UN.GIFT). www.ungift.org/.

United Nations Human Rights Office of the High Commissioner. The 1956 Supplementary Convention on the Abolition of Slavery, the Slave Trade, and Institutions and Practices Similar to Slavery. Entry into force: 30 April 1957, in accordance with Article 13. http://www.ohchr.org/EN/ProfessionalInterest/Pages/SupplementaryConventionAbolitionOfSlavery.aspx.

United Nations Office on Drugs and Crime (UNODC). "Fact Sheet on Human Trafficking." 2006. http://www.unodc.org/unodc/en/trafficking_victim_consents.html#how.

United Nations Office on Drugs and Crime (UNODC). *Global Report on Trafficking in Persons: Executive Summary*. 2014. http://www.unodc.org/documents/data-and-analysis/glotip/GLOTIP14_ExSum_english.pdf.

United Nations Office on Drugs and Crime (UNODC). *Global Report on Trafficking in Persons 2014*. http://www.unodc.org/documents/data-and analysis/glotip/GLOTIP_2014_full_report.pdf.

United Nations Office on Drugs and Crime (UNODC). "Trafficking in Human Beings." 2006. http://www.unodc.org/unodc/en/trafficking_human_beings.html.

United Nations Secretariat. "United Nations Convention against Transnational Organized Crime and the Protocols Thereto." 2005.

United States Attorney General. "Attorney General's Annual Report to Congress and Assessment of U.S. Government Activities to Combat Trafficking in Persons: Fiscal Year 2009." Washington DC: Department of Justice, 2010.

United States Congress. Mann Act, 18 United States Code §§. 1581–1588.

United States Congress. Trafficking Victims Protection Act (TVPA). Pub. L. No. 106-386, 114 Stat. 1473. 2000.

United States Congress. Trafficking Victims Protection Reauthorization Act (TVPRA). Pub. L. No. 108-193, 117 Stat. 2875. 2003.

United States Congress. Trafficking Victims Protection Reauthorization Act (TVPRA). Pub. L. No. 109-164. 2005.

United States Department of Justice (U.S.DOJ). "Assessment of U.S. Government Efforts to Combat Trafficking in Persons in Fiscal Year 2006." 2007. http://www.usdoj.gov/ag/annualreports/tr2007/assessment-of-efforts-to-combat-tip0907.pdf.

United States Department of Justice (U.S.DOJ). "Report on Activities to Combat Human Trafficking: Fiscal Years 2001–2005." 2006. http://www.usdoj.gov/crt/crim/trafficking_report_2006.pdf.

United States Department of State, Office to Monitor and Combat Trafficking in Persons. *Trafficking in Persons Report*. Washington, DC: U.S. Department of State, 2004. http://www.state.gov/g/tip/rls/tiprpt/2004/34021.htm.

United States Department of State, Office to Monitor and Combat Trafficking in Persons. *Trafficking in Persons Report*. Washington DC: U.S. Department of State, 2005. http://www.state.gov/g/tip/rls/tiprpt/2005/.

United States Government Accounting Office (U.S.GAO). "Human Trafficking: Better Data, Strategy, and Reporting Needed to Enhance U.S. Antitrafficking Efforts Abroad." *Trends in Organized Crime* 10, no. 1 (2006).

Van Selm, Joanne. *Evaluation of the Effectiveness of Measures for the Integration of Trafficked Persons*. International Organization for Migration (IOM), 2013.

Vital Voices Global Partnership. "Stateless and Vulnerable to Human Trafficking in Thailand," Washington, DC, June 2007, p. 13. www.vitalvoices.org.

Viuhko, Minna. "Human Trafficking for Sexual Exploitation and Organized Procuring in Finland." *European Journal of Criminology* 7, no. 1 (2010): 61–75.

Weitzer, Ronald. "Moral Crusade against Prostitution." *Society* 43, no. 3 (2006): 33–38.

Wennerholm, Carolina Johansson. "Crossing Borders and Building Bridges: The Baltic Region Networking Project." *Gender & Development* 10, no. 1 (2002): 10–19.

Wilkinson, Mick, Gary Craig, and Aline Gaus. *Forced Labour in the UK and the Gangmasters Licensing Authority*. University of Hull, Wilberforce Institute for the Study of Slavery and Emancipation, 2010.

Wilson, Deborah G., William F. Walsh, and Sherilyn Kleuber. "Trafficking in Human Beings: Training and Services among U.S. Law Enforcement Agencies." *Police Practice and Research* 7, no. 2 (2006): 149–160.

Winterdyk, John, and Philip Reichel. "Introduction to Special Issue: Human Trafficking Issues and Perspectives." *European Journal of Criminology* 7, no. 1 (2010): 5–10.

Women's Commission for Refugee Women and Children. *Displaced Women and Girls.* 2016.

Wright, Tessa, and Anna Pollert. "The Experience of Ethnic Minority Workers in the Hotel and Catering Industry: Routes to Support and Advice on Workplace Problems." Working Paper 1. Working Lives Research Institute, London Metropolitan University, 2005.

Zimmerman, Cathy, Katherine Yun, Inna Shvab, Charlotte Watts, and Luca Trappolin. "The Health Risks and Consequences of Trafficking in Women and Adolescents: Findings from a European Study. London: London School of Hygiene & Tropical Medicine (LSHTM), 2003.

Zimmerman, Cathy, Mazeda Hossain, Katherine Yun, Vasil Gajdadziev, Natalia Guzun, Maria Tchomarova, Rosa Angela Ciarrocchi et al. "The Health of Trafficked Women: A Survey of Women Entering Posttrafficking Services in Europe." *American Journal of Public Health* 98, no. 1 (2008): 55–59.

Further Suggested Readings

Adelson, W. J. (2008). Child Prostitute or Victim of Trafficking?. *University of St. Thomas Law Journal, 6*(1).

Annitto, M. (2011). Consent, coercion, and compassion: Emerging legal responses to the commercial sexual exploitation of minors. *Yale Law & Policy Review, 30*(1), 1–70.

Bernstein, E. (2010). Militarized humanitarianism meets carceral feminism: The politics of sex, rights, and freedom in contemporary anti-trafficking campaigns. *Signs, 36*(1), 45–71.

Boxill, N. A., & Richardson, D. J. (2007). Ending sex trafficking of children in Atlanta. *Affilia, 22*(2), 138–149.

Bruch, E. M. (2004). Models wanted: The search for an effective response to human trafficking. *Stan. J. Int'l L., 40*, 1.

Capous Desyllas, M. (2007). Critique of the Global Trafficking Discourse and U.S. Policy, A. *J. Soc. & Soc. Welfare, 34*, 57.

Chacón, J. M. (2010). Tensions and trade-offs: Protecting trafficking victims in the era of immigration enforcement. *University of Pennsylvania Law Review, 158*(6), 1609–1653.

Chuang, J. A. (2010). Rescuing trafficking from ideological capture: prostitution reform and anti-trafficking law and policy. *University of Pennsylvania Law Review, 158*(6), 1655–1728.

David, F. (2007). *ASEAN and trafficking in persons: Using data as a tool to combat trafficking in persons.* International Organization for Migration.

David, F. M. (2007). Law enforcement responses to trafficking in persons: challenges and emerging good practice. *Trends and issues in crime and criminal justice, 347.*

Demleitner, N. V. (2001). 10.... The Law at a Crossroads: The Construction of Migrant Women Trafficked into Prostitution. *Global human smuggling: Comparative perspectives, 257.*

Feingold, D. A. (2010). Trafficking in numbers: The social construction of human trafficking data. *Sex, drugs and body counts: The politics of numbers in global crime and conflict*, 46–74.

Friesendorf, C. (2007). Pathologies of security governance: Efforts against human trafficking in Europe. *Security Dialogue*, *38*(3), 379–402.

Gallagher, A., & Holmes, P. (2008). Developing an effective criminal justice response to human trafficking lessons from the front line. *International criminal justice review*, *18*(3), 318–343.

Gallagher, A. T. (2011). Improving the effectiveness of the international law of human trafficking: A vision for the future of the U.S. Trafficking in Persons reports. *Human Rights Review*, *12*(3), 381–400.

Halley, J., Kotiswaran, P., Shamir, H., & Thomas, C. (2006). From the international to the local in feminist legal responses to rape, prostitution/sex work, and sex trafficking: Four studies in contemporary governance feminism. *Harv. JL & Gender*, *29*, 335.

Haynes, D. F. (2004). Used, abused, arrested and deported: Extending immigration benefits to protect the victims of trafficking and to secure the prosecution of traffickers. *Human Rights Quarterly*, *26*(2), 221–272.

Heiges, M. (2009). From the Inside Out: Reforming State and Local Prostitution Enforcement to Combat Sex Trafficking in the United States and Abroad. *Minn. L. Rev.*, *94*, 428.

Herzog, S. (2008). The lenient social and legal response to trafficking in women: An empirical analysis of public perceptions in Israel. *Journal of Contemporary Criminal Justice.*

Hodge, D. R., & Lietz, C. A. (2007). The international sexual trafficking of women and children a review of the literature. *Affilia*, *22*(2), 163–174.

Hoyle, C., Bosworth, M., & Dempsey, M. (2011). Labelling the victims of sex trafficking: Exploring the borderland between rhetoric and reality. *Social & Legal Studies*, *20*(3), 313–329.

Jahic, G., & Finckenauer, J. O. (2005). Representations and misrepresentations of human trafficking. *Trends in Organized Crime*, *8*(3), 24–40.

Jordan, A. D. (2002). Human rights or wrongs? The struggle for a rights-based response to trafficking in human beings. *Gender & Development, 10*(1), 28–37.

Kapur, R. (2005). Cross Border Movements and the Law. *Trafficking and Prostitution Reconsidered–new perspectives on migration, sex work and human rights*, 25–41.

Kelly, L. (2005). "You can find anything you want": A critical reflection on research on trafficking in persons within and into Europe. *International Migration, 43*(1 2), 235–265.

Mattar, M. Y. (2002). Trafficking in persons, especially women and children, in countries of the Middle East: the scope of the problem and the appropriate legislative responses. *Fordham Int'l LJ, 26*, 721.

McClain, N. M., & Garrity, S. E. (2011). Sex trafficking and the exploitation of adolescents. *Journal of Obstetric, Gynecologic, & Neonatal Nursing, 40*(2), 243–252.

Munro, V. E. (2006). Stopping traffic? A comparative study of responses to the trafficking in women for prostitution. *British Journal of Criminology, 46*(2), 318–333.

Munro, V. E. (2008). Of rights and rhetoric: Discourses of degradation and exploitation in the context of sex trafficking. *Journal of Law and Society, 35*(2), 240–264.

Reid, J. A. (2010). Doors wide shut: Barriers to the successful delivery of victim services for domestically trafficked minors in a southern U.S. metropolitan area. *Women & Criminal Justice, 20*(1–2), 147–166.

Schauer, E. J., & Wheaton, E. M. (2006). Sex trafficking into the United States: A literature review. *Criminal Justice Review, 31*(2), 146–169.

Siskin, A., & Wyler, L. S. (2012). *Trafficking in persons: U.S. policy and issues for congress*. Congressional Research Service.

Stolz, B. (2005). Educating policymakers and setting the criminal justice policymaking agenda Interest groups and the 'Victims of Trafficking and Violence Act of 2000'. *Criminal Justice, 5*(4), 407–430.

Stolz, Barbara Ann (2007). Interpreting the U.S. human trafficking debate through the lens of symbolic politics. *Law & Policy, 29*(3), 311–338.

Surtees, R. (2008). Traffickers and trafficking in Southern and Eastern Europe considering the other side of human trafficking. *European Journal of Criminology, 5*(1), 39–68.

Wilson, J. M., & Dalton, E. (2008). Human Trafficking in the Heartland Variation in Law Enforcement Awareness and Response. *Journal of Contemporary Criminal Justice, 24*(3), 296–313.

Winterdyk, J., & Reichel, P. (2010). Introduction to Special Issue: Human Trafficking Issues and Perspectives. *European Journal of Criminology, 7*(1), 5–10.

Zhang, S. X. (2009). Beyond the 'Natasha's story'—a review and critique of current research on sex trafficking. *Global crime, 10*(3), 178–195.

Table 3: Selected Cases Investigated by Department of Justice (FBI) between 2013–2015

CASE 1

Department of Justice
Office of Public Affairs
FOR IMMEDIATE RELEASE
Monday, January 26, 2015

Mexican National Sentenced to 15 Years for Participating in a Brutal Family-Run Sex Trafficking Organization

The Department of Justice today announced a sentencing and guilty plea for two members of a family run sex trafficking organization based in southern Florida. Rafael Alberto Cadena-Sosa was sentenced by U.S. District Court Judge Joes E. Martinez to serve 15 years in prison and Carmen Cadena pleaded guilty before U.S. District Court Judge Jose Martinez for participating in a brutal family-run sex trafficking organization.

CASE 2

FOR IMMEDIATE RELEASE—Department of Justice
U.S. Attorney's Office
Western District of Texas

Wednesday, November 13, 2013
Ringleader Of El Paso And Baltimore-based Federal Human Trafficking Investigation Sentenced To 17 1/2 Years In Federal Prison

In El Paso, 45-year-old Alarcon Allen Wiggins (aka "Alarcon Tha Don"), the C.E.O. of 424 Records, 1 Team 1 Family Entertainment, DBD TV and DBD Productions in Baltimore, MD, was sentenced yesterday to 212 months in federal prison for his leadership role in a forced prostitution scheme based in El Paso and Baltimore announced United States Attorney Robert Pitman and FBI Special Agent in Charge FBI Special Agent in Charge Douglas E. Lindquist.

In addition to the prison term, United States District Judge Frank Montalvo ordered that Wiggins pay $24,879.83 restitution and be placed under supervised release for a period of ten years after completing his prison term. On August 8, 2013, Wiggins pleaded guilty to conspiracy to commit human trafficking and conspiracy to transport women for purposes of prostitution.

Alarcon and nine other Baltimore residents have been convicted and sentenced as part of this investigation. Sentences for the other defendants ranged from probation to 186 months incarceration.

According to court records, the defendants were involved in a scheme from January 2009 until their arrests in October 2011 which included human trafficking; transport via interstate commerce for prostitution; coercing and enticing for prostitution; and the concealing, removing or confiscating identification documents—all for financial benefit. Wiggins and other defendants used their ties to the music industry to recruit young women then force them to work as strippers and prostitutes while confiscating all means of communication from the victims, namely cell phones and laptop computers; confiscating all identification documents from victims; prohibiting any communication by the victims and personal interaction with anyone outside the group without the defendants' permission or in their presence; and collecting all victims' earnings for the benefit of the defendants.

This case was investigated by the Federal Bureau of Investigation. Assistant United States Attorneys J. Brandy Gardes and Daniel Crumby prosecuted this case on behalf of the government.

CASE 3

FOR IMMEDIATE RELEASE
Tuesday, January 6, 2015 Department of Justice
U.S. Attorney's Office
Western District of Texas
El Paso Couple Sentenced To Federal Prison For Inducing Foreign Or Interstate Travel For Prostitution

In El Paso today, 45-year-old Maria Blake (aka "Jessica", "Yvonne") and her 45-year-old husband, Ronald, were sentenced to 30 months and six months in federal prison respectively for inducing foreign or interstate travel for prostitution announced Acting United States Attorney Richard L. Durbin, Acting Homeland Security Investigations (HSI) Special Agent in Charge Tom Hernandez and Federal Bureau of Investigation (FBI) Special Agent in Charge Douglas E. Lindquist.

In addition to the prison terms, United States District Judge Kathleen Cardone ordered that Maria Blake pay a $1,000 fine and be placed under supervised release for a period of ten years after completing her prison term. Judge Cardone also ordered that Ronald Blake pay a $500 fine, remain under home confinement for six months and be placed under supervised release for a period of ten years after completing his prison term. Furthermore, Judge Cardone ordered that the defendants' residence located in the 2400 block of Tierra Nueva in El Paso be forfeited to the Government as it was used to facilitate their prostitution scheme.

Notes

1. UN General Assembly. (2000). Protocol to prevent, suppress and punish trafficking in persons, especially women and children. Supplement to the United Nations convention against transnational organized crime. Resolution 55, 25.

2. Miller, E. (2015, January 27). Man sentenced to 15 years for role in 1990s sex-trafficking ring. Miami *Sun Sentinel*. http://www.sun-sentinel.com/local/palm-beach/fl-palm-beach-sex-trafficking-20150126-story.html.

3. Fried, J. P. (1998, December 2). Mastermind of Golden Venture smuggling ship gets 20 years. *The New York Times*. http://www.nytimes.com/1998/12/02/nyregion/mastermind-of-golden-venture-smuggling-ship-gets-20-years.html?_r=0.

4. U.S. Department of Justice, U.S. Attorney's Office, Northern District of Florida. (2015, October 30). Nine charged in interstate human trafficking conspiracy. https://www.fbi.gov/contact-us/field-offices/jacksonville/news/press-releases/nine-charged-in-interstate-human-trafficking-conspiracy.

5. United Nations Global Initiative to Fight Human Trafficking. www.ungift.org/.

6. International Labor Organization. (2014). *Profits and Poverty: The economics of forced labour*. http:// http://www.ilo.org/wcmsp5/groups/public/—ed_norm/—declaration/documents/publication/wcms_243391.pdf.

7. Kara, S. (2009). Sex trafficking: Inside the business of modern slavery. Columbia University Press.

8. United Nations Secretariat. (2005). United Nations Convention Against Transnational Organized Crime and the Protocols Thereto.

9. Trafficking Victims Protection Act (TVPA). (2000). Pub. L. No. 106-386, 114 Stat. 1473.

10. S.178—Justice for Victims of Trafficking Act of 2015. 114th Congress (2015–2016).

11. H.R.296—Justice for Victims of Trafficking Act of 2015. 114th Congress (2015–2016).

12. H.R.460—Human Trafficking Detection Act of 2015. 14th Congress (2015–2016).

13. S.166—Stop Exploitation Through Trafficking Act of 2015. 114th Congress (2015–2016).

14. H.R.500—Survivors of Human Trafficking Empowerment Act. 114th Congress (2015–2016).

15. H. Rept. 109-345—Border Protection, Antiterrorism, and Illegal Immigration Control Act of 2005. 109th Congress (2005–2006).

16. H.R.159—Stop Exploitation Through Trafficking Act of 2015. 114th Congress (2015–2016).

17. H.R.181—Justice for Victims of Trafficking Act of 2015. 114th Congress (2015–2016).

18. H.R.515—International Megan's Law to Prevent Child Exploitation and Other Sexual Crimes Through Advanced Notification of Traveling Sex Offenders. 114th Congress (2015–2016).

19. H.R.246—To improve the response to victims of child sex trafficking. 114th Congress (2015–2016).

20. H.R.350—Human Trafficking Prevention, Intervention, and Recovery Act of 2015. 114th Congress (2015–2016).

21. H.R.398—Trafficking Awareness Training for Health Care Act of 2015. 114th Congress (2015–2016).

22. H.R.469—Strengthening Child Welfare Response to Trafficking Act of 2015. 114th Congress (2015–2016).

23. H.R.468—Enhancing Services for Runaway and Homeless Victims of Youth Trafficking Act of 2015. 114th Congress (2015–2016).

24. H.R.514—Human Trafficking Prioritization Act. 114th Congress (2015–2016).

25. H.R.61—Securing the Assistance of Victims of Exploitation Act of 2015 (SAVE Act). 114th Congress (2015–2016).

26. S.205—Trafficking Awareness Training for Health Care Act of 2015. 114th Congress (2015–2016).

27. H.R.63—CATCH Traffickers Act of 2015. 114th Congress (2015–2016).

28. S.140—Combat Human Trafficking Act of 2015. 114th Congress (2015–2016).

29. S.44—A bill to provide for the expedited processing of unaccompanied alien children illegally entering the United States, and for other purposes. 114th Congress (2015–2016).

30. H.R.4383—DHS Human Trafficking Prevention Act of 2016. 114th Congress (2015–2016).

31. Lebov, K. (2010). Human trafficking in Scotland. *European Journal of Criminology*, *7*(1), 77–93.

32. This endnote has two references:

1) U.S. Department of Homeland Security. (2015). Identify and Assist a Trafficking Victim. https://www.state.gov/j/tip/id/.

2) Lebov, K. (2010). Human trafficking in Scotland. *European Journal of Criminology*, *7*(1), 77–93.

33. U.S. Department of State. (2015). Identify and Assist a Trafficking Victim. https://www.state.gov/j/tip/id/.

34. Surtees, R. (2008). Traffickers and trafficking in Southern and Eastern Europe: Considering the other side of human trafficking. *European Journal of Criminology*, *5*(1), 39–68.

35. Stephen-Smith, S. (2008). Routes in, routes out: Quantifying the gendered experience of trafficking to the UK. London: POPPY Project, Eaves Housing.

36. Jackson, K., J. Jeffery, & G. Adamson. (2010, August). Setting the record: The trafficking of migrant women in the England and Wales off-street prostitution sector. ACPO.

37. Clawson, H. J., N. Dutch, A. Solomon, & L. Goldblatt Grace. (2009). Human trafficking into and within the United States: A review of the literature. Washington, DC: Office of the Assistant Secretary for Planning and Evaluation, U.S. Department of Human and Health Services.

38. Lazăr, I. (2002). Different forms of compensation available for damages caused to the victims of human trafficking. *Official Journal L*, *203*, 1–4.

39. The U.S. Department of Health and Human Services. (2015). Identify and Assist a Trafficking Victim. https://www.state.gov/j/tip/id/.

40. Leman, J., & S. Janssens. (2008). The Albanian and post-Soviet business of trafficking women for prostitution: Structural developments and financial modus operandi. *European Journal of Criminology*, *5*(4), 433–451.

41. This endnote has two references:

1) Coghlan, D., & G. Wylie. Defining trafficking/denying justice? Forced labour in Ireland and the consequences of trafficking discourse. *Journal of Ethnic and Migration Studies*, *37*(9), 1513–1526.

2) International Labor Office (ILO). (2014). *Profits and poverty: The economics of forced labor.*

42. Lebov, K. (2010). Human trafficking in Scotland. *European Journal of Criminology, 7*(1), 77–93.

43. Surtees, R. (2008). Traffickers and trafficking in Southern and Eastern Europe: Considering the other side of human trafficking. *European Journal of Criminology, 5*(1), 39–68.

44. Graham, N., & E. D. Wish. (1994). Drug use among female arrestees: Onset, patterns, and relationships to prostitution. *Journal of Drug Issues, 24*(2), 315–329.

45. Raphael, J. (2015). *Listening to Olivia: Violence, poverty, and prostitution.* Northeastern University Press.

46. Friedman, S. A. (2005). Who is there to help Us?: How the system fails sexually exploited girls in the United States: Examples from four American cities. ECPAT-U.S.A, Incorporated.

47. U.S. Department of Health and Human Services. (2015). Identify and Assist a Trafficking Victim. https://www.state.gov/j/tip/id/.

48. Clawson, H. J., N. Dutch, A. Solomon, & L. Goldblatt Grace. (2009). Human trafficking into and within the United States: A review of the literature. Washington, DC: Office of the Assistant Secretary for Planning and Evaluation, U.S. Department of Human and Health Services.

49. Clawson, H. J., N. Dutch, A. Solomon, & L. Goldblatt Grace. (2009). Human trafficking into and within the United States: A review of the literature. Washington, DC: Office of the Assistant Secretary for Planning and Evaluation, U.S. Department of Human and Health Services.

50. U.S. Department of Justice. (2015). Identify and Assist a Trafficking Victim. https://www.state.gov/j/tip/id/.

51. Faraday, F. (2012). *Made in Canada: How the law constructs migrant workers' insecurity.* Metcalf Foundation.

52. www.traffickingresourcecenter.org.

53. "In 2007, the Civil Rights Division created the Human Trafficking Prosecution Unit (HTPU) within the Criminal Section to consolidate the expertise of some of the nation's top human trafficking prosecutors. HTPU prosecutors work closely with Assistant United States Attorneys (AU.S.As) and law enforcement agencies to streamline fast-moving trafficking investigations, ensure consistent application of trafficking statutes, and identify multijurisdictional trafficking networks. Human trafficking crimes, like other civil rights crimes, require notification to the Criminal Section pursuant to §§8-3.120 and 8-3.140 of the *United States Attorneys' Manual.* Early notification of any case with potential human trafficking angles allows the HTPU to provide victim assistance resources, legal guidance, and coordination between districts prosecuting overlapping criminal networks on a timely basis." https://www.justice.gov/crt/human-trafficking-prosecution-unit-htpu.

54. Bouche, V., A. Farrell, & D. Wittmer. (2016). *Identifying effective counter-trafficking programs and practices in the U.S.: Legislative, legal, and public opinion strategies that work.* U.S. Department of Justice: NCJRS.

55. Farrell, A., M. J. DeLateur, C. Owens, & S. Fahy. (2016). The prosecution of state-level human trafficking cases in the United States. *Anti-Trafficking Review, 6.*

56. These cases are in Table 3 at the end of the chapter.

Chapter 8

Human Trafficking and Technology

Chapter Objectives

This chapter provides a comprehensive understanding of the following:

- Human Trafficking and Technology
  - Use of Technology by the Traffickers for the Proliferation of Trafficking Business
  - Use of Technology for Combating Trafficking
  - Use of Technology for Providing Information and Support to Trafficking Victims

Introduction: Human Trafficking and Technology

Human trafficking—also known as trafficking in persons, modern slavery, and by many other names—is a grim reality of the contemporary global landscape in developed as well as emergent developing countries. It reflects the dark side of civilization, modern economics, and globalization, where illegal enterprises trade people through a rapidly growing network of electronic communication and transport.[1] While traditional channels of trafficking remain in place, online technologies give traffickers an unprecedented ability to exploit a greater number of victims and advertise their services across geographic boundaries.[2] As Malika Saada Saar, stated, technology "has created an easy and accessible venue for the commercial sexual exploitation of children..., young girls are the new commodities that traffickers and gangs are selling. And, there isn't a culture of crime and punishment for selling girls as there is for selling illegal drugs. It is less risky, and more profitable (the girls are 'reusable') to traffic girls, instead of meth or crack."[3] Technological advances in general and online technologies in particular have opened up new vistas for traffickers—allowing them to recruit and exploit a greater number of victims across geographic boundaries. It has expanded their recruitment and supply market. More and more traffickers use Internet technology and social media to recruit and advertise victims on online classified and social networking sites. Access to mobile devices has become easy and cheap. Use of mobile technologies in the form of devices and networks has expanded from a few privileged persons having access to easy and inexpensive access by the masses. It has risen in prominence and is now at the epicenter of sex and labor trafficking enterprises in the United States. Online platforms offer profitable venues for exploitation of trusting and unsuspecting individuals all over the world, including within the United States.[4]

In the contemporary "network society," technology and the flow of information are strategic forces of global social change. Mobile technology has shattered traditional boundaries created by borders and geographical locations. In contrast to the traditional channels of trafficking, online technologies give traffickers an unprecedented ability to recruit and exploit a greater number of victims from a vaster market, and advertise their services to a larger number of potential consumers and buyers with immunity.[5]

Online technology eliminates all boundaries, making instant, real-time communication and coordination a reality. Advances in technology have made it easy and cheap to connect people globally in a matter of seconds. According to the World Bank (2012), 75 percent of the global population has access to mobile phones and other modes of instant mobile communications. Traffickers exploit this mobile technology to recruit, advertise, organize, and communicate. They use mobile phones exclusively, "effectively streamlining their activities and expanding their criminal networks."[6]

The technology that has connected the world and trade and made progress possible, is also used by the traffickers to exploit human beings for sex and labor. Advances in information and communication technologies play an integral part in the proliferation of supply and demand market in the trafficking business of all types—including sex and labor. The advent of mobile communication technology in the form of mobile phones, the Internet, and social media networks has facilitated recruitment of unsuspecting job seekers and exploitation of their trust through isolation, fraud, force, and/or coercion. It has impacted social, economic, and political life at an exceptional scale. Networked technologies alter the method of receiving and disseminating information as well as communication. Technology has become fundamental instrument in the practices and processes surrounding human trafficking—the illegal trade of people for commercial sexual exploitation, forced labor, and other forms of modern-day slavery.

Mobile technology is used by the traffickers and victims to connect and disconnect with recruiters, employers, family, friends, social services, and other positive as well negative entities.[7] In this chapter, we examine the relationship between technology and human trafficking in three basic spheres of business: (1) use of technology by traffickers for the proliferation of trafficking business; (2) use of technology by the authorities for prosecution of traffickers and to prevent, expose, and monitor trafficking; and (3) use of technology as an informational tool to provide information and support for trafficking victims and at-risk groups.

Use of Technology by the Traffickers for the Proliferation of Trafficking Business

The use of Internet technologies in people's daily lives has dramatically increased in recent years. In 2010, the number of Internet users worldwide exceeded an estimated 2 billion.[8] Hundreds of millions of individuals use social networking sites,[9] and approximately half of all online adults in America have used online classified advertising sites[10] and this number increases by every second. Although technology, especially the Internet and online technologies, have provided many social benefits, the flip side of it is pretty dark. While facilitating economic and global growth, technology has also brought in a number of social ills. Traffickers make use of social networks and online classified sites to market, recruit, sell, and exploit for criminal purposes. Many of these sites are explicit in nature and some are underground. Yet, evidence from legal cases demonstrates that mainstream sites such as Craigslist, Backpage, and Myspace have already been used for trafficking.[11] Facebook, Twitter, and other social networking sites are susceptible to similar uses.[12]

The extant reports and literature are replete with examples where traffickers have used network technology to expand trafficking business beyond global boundaries and human imagination. Traffickers have exploited online technologies for both sex and labor trafficking business. Owens, Dank & Farrell (2014) report that the most common industries using trafficked labor in the United States include construction, agricultural, hospitality, domestic, and service industries. Results of their study suggest that fraud and coercion are often used as means by the domestic and overseas recruitment agencies to facilitate trafficking of individuals. Once in the destination country, the traffickers restrict victims' ability to communicate with friends and family through monitoring, surveillance, debt bondage, and physical, psychological, and sexual abuse.[13]

The Internet has dramatically changed human trafficking business landscape globally. Over the last ten years, trafficking business has migrated to an online marketplace and operates without walls. Online classified advertising for jobs serves as a vehicle for recruiting and soliciting potential victims. Traffickers use online classified websites for recruitment as well as for the sale of services. Average advertisements for service providing jobs are used by unscrupulous traffickers as a façade for recruiting trafficking victims. The unsuspecting job seekers apply and fall prey to the fraudulent tactics of traffickers who reap enormous profits at the expense of the victims. Traffickers use various forms of technology to advertise, recruit, and connect with potential victims.[14] Some of these means are newsgroups, web messaging, bulletin boards, websites, search engines, chatrooms, file transfer protocol (FTP), peer to peer networks, and file swapping programs. Traffickers use encryption to disguise the content of files, emails, web TV, and mobile Internet systems. Table 1 presents a list of online technologies most commonly used by traffickers.

Traffickers, unlike perpetrators of garden-variety crimes, are conversant with technology. Majority of them are educated, carry cell phones, video cameras, and have manners that make them appear respectable, cultured, and trustworthy. In many cases, they are respected members of the community as well as clandestine members of highly sophisticated crime syndicates.[15] They have the means and resources to remain on the "crest of technological advances."[16] Their demeanor and wealth give an appearance of being trustworthy and sophisticated—allowing them to prey upon unsuspecting job seekers.

Technology: Recruitment and Job Offers

With the advent of high-speed online and mobile technology, recruiting and offering employment in both formal and informal settings seems to be the main modus operandi. "The Internet offers a wide variety of possible approaches to recruitment; from offers aimed at a broad audience, such as employment opportunities (essentially abroad), through the use of search engines or pop-ups to publicize tempting offers, all the way to more targeted spaces, e.g., chatrooms, spam mail and Internet dating, where victims can be recruited."[17] Online and mobile technology provides traffickers with an unbridled means of recruiting their victims. Online employment agencies (particularly

Table 1: Some of the Online Technologies Most Commonly Used by Traffickers

Technology	*Purpose*
Virtual Advertising	Space rented to advertise jobs and services.
Newsgroups	Sites used to disseminate and exchange information.
Chatrooms	Virtual meeting places where people can log in and provide and exchange information in real time. No record is kept of conversations or messages. No log files are maintained, archived, or stored. Chat rooms provide complete anonymity.
Search Engines and Websites	A single web domain serving and maintaining a set of related webpages and programs that search documents or files from a database or network.
File Transfer Protocol (FTP)	This allows users remote and direct access to another's computer hard drive to upload and download files.
Peer to Peer Networks and File Swapping Programs	These programs allow users to share illegal material by finding and downloading files on online networks without leaving traceable transmissions.
Encryption	This program is used to disguise the content of files.
Mobile Internet Systems	A device that provides mobile access and cannot be traced.
SMS Messaging	The program is used to send short text messages.
Camera Phone	The device is used to take and transmit pictures, videos etc.

those ostensibly seeking fashion or artists' models) and marriage agencies can all be facades to lure victims. Internet chatrooms are also used to "befriend" and ensnare potential victims.

Most trafficking cases begin with the trafficker advertising jobs for nannies, waitresses, models, technology experts, dancers, and the like on social media.

Chatrooms and online advertisements are the two principal methods used by traffickers to recruit. Other types of sites used by traffickers for the recruitment may include: matrimonial sites of marriage agencies (that could act as mail-order bride agencies or dating clubs), escort services' sites, dating clubs, and various job offering sites including those for nannies, home assistance, waitressing, bartending, au pair, child care, modeling, the entertainment industry (dancers/hostesses), construction, hotels and restaurants, factories, agriculture, admission to universities, tourism, and the sex industry, among other commercial sites. The contact is usually required to be via mobile phone or email addresses.

The trafficking incident is often initiated by unsuspecting job seekers who are surfing the Internet, looking for jobs. Once they come upon genuine looking and sounding advertisements, they inquire and establish contact with the traffickers to apply for the advertised jobs. Traffickers use various techniques to gain trust, including offering a high salary with generous package of health, retirement, accommodation, transportation, and other benefits, expressing love and admiration for the victim, promising to make the victim a star, and providing a ticket to a new location away from the victim's home. The unsuspecting job seeker who initiated an online employment search could easily be enticed by the promise of a job with a high salary and attractive benefits. After the victim has joined the offender, various techniques are used to restrict the victim's access to communication with family and friends, including threats of physical punishment and threats of harm and even death to the victim and her family unless the victim complies with the trafficker's demands.[18]

Traffickers consider online technology an ideal instrument to use for deception and exploitation in labor and sex trafficking. It is universally accessible, cheap, and fast. More importantly, it leaves little traceable evidence and thus is virtually anonymous. Traffickers do not need any offices—they can work from homes, coffee shops, or other undisclosed locations and can have access to their clients from anywhere in the world. Owing to the use of disposable mobile technology, their location and identity is difficult to trace. The business is highly profitable and does not require a large investment. Typically, a small investment in a phone and a computer can rake in millions of dollars. Very low probability of being detected or apprehended also plays a significant role in encouraging traffickers to be bold and expand their criminal enterprise.[19]

"Technology can create or dissolve gaps in information that leave individuals vulnerable. Traffickers can exploit such vulnerabilities when one party has more knowledge or access to information than another. In this respect, network technology is an integral component of a socio-technical system that shapes such issues as exploitation, recruitment, employment, supply chains, and migration."[20] Trafficking is an enterprise that requires a high order of coordination throughout the process. It requires planning, advertising, recruiting, transporting, meeting, and transferring/transporting victims at various times and locations. Traffickers use a combination of new technologies in complex ways to avoid detection and interception of their communications. Thriving online business has enabled eager clients seeking to "shop" and "buy" services online with ease, anonymity, and immunity. Traffickers are able to send their communications through a series of carriers. Advances in communication technologies have enabled criminals to leave no traces for detection and apprehension. The technologies provide them an enhanced degree of anonymity, giving them a free pass to engage in human trade without any fear of detection and/or apprehension. The rapid development in the use of information technologies, in particular the Internet, has opened new possibilities for the traffickers.

Mobile technologies in particular play an important role in contemporary mobility and migration.[21] "Electronic and digital information and communication technology (ICT) play a central role in the network society by altering individual users' sense of time and space. Communication can be instantaneous over telecommunication systems, and information can be easily shared across vast distances."[22] For example, a migrant from Southeast Asia might take up employment in North America by coordinating in real time with a network of recruiters, agents, government officials, and employers both locally and internationally, using email, mobile phones, and/or social media. Easy and cheap access to mobile communication technology has revolutionized the trafficking business. Traffickers buy, use, and dispose of their phones and other devices after a short period of use or after a particular act has been committed to avoid being traced. Mobile phones can be programmed to transmit false identification and traffickers can get as many mobile phone service lines as desired. Pre-paid and disposable phones have provided a booming environment for trafficking business without any fear of apprehension.

Advanced mobile technology is also used for money laundering. The mobile technology allows traffickers to transfer capital and assets swiftly from place to place in such a way that they ultimately appear to be legitimate assets. These assets are then available to traffickers and criminal organizations anywhere in the world to finance further criminal operations. Electronic forms of business are exploited by traffickers to reap enormous profits. E-business offers the possibility of having "virtual identities" on the Internet. It facilitates and disguises financial activities and allows the exchange of money and services with a high level of anonymity.

Advances in computer and printer technology have facilitated production of counterfeit documents of all kinds. This has made it easy for traffickers, and criminal organizations they work with, to conduct their illegal business disguised as something legal—making apprehension and detection even harder. The advances in online technology have created new forms of crime, such as "spoofing," "phishing," "hacking," "page-jacking," "mouse-trapping," etc.

Another common and legal sounding method to ensnare females is the mail-order bride offer: International matchmaking organizations, sometimes also known as "marriage agencies," operating online can be used as a cover for the recruitment of potential victims of trafficking. Some research suggests that mail-order bride sites may involve the sale and purchase of trafficked victims online by credit card, while marriage agency sites may be offering sexual services.[23] The "mail-order bride" industry is not regulated. Businesses can advertise for marriage and require the women and young girls they attract to disclose sometimes highly personal details. The clients buying services are not screened and there are no background checks and no formal means of ascertaining whether clients are already married. During a United States Senate hearing (2004), it was disclosed that the "mail-order bride" industry (or international matchmaking organizations) have been linked to trafficking in persons.[24] "Mail-order bride" agencies online can be fronts for trafficking organizations in which adults and girls are offered as "brides" but sold privately into sexual exploitation, forced into marriage with men (some of whom will then prostitute them), or held in domestic slavery. A study conducted by Caldwell (1997) reported that the Global Survival Network (GSN) found that most mail-order bride agencies in Russia expanded their activities to include trafficking for prostitution. European embassies reported that a number of international matchmaking agencies conceal organized prostitution rings victimizing newly arrived Filipina women.[25] Asian organized crime groups used fiancée visa and marriage to bring women across the U.S. border for purposes of sexual exploitation, often with the help of U.S. nationals.[26]

The following is a case of technology and transnational trafficking. It is an illustration of how traffickers manipulate technology to circumvent both borders and national laws. In 2000, Japanese women were trafficked to Hawaii in the United States for the purposes of sexual exploitation. The traffickers intended to use their victims to do live performances, which would be shown to Japanese audiences via the Internet. Since Japanese laws concerning pornography are strict, the traffickers decided to conduct their operation in Hawaii. The traffickers advertised in Japan for "nude models"; the women were used to make pornography and perform live Internet sex shows upon their arrival in Hawaii. The operation was entirely aimed at a Japanese market with all website material written in Japanese. The women performed strip shows by web cam and responded to requests from men watching in Japan. They used wireless keyboards for live sex chat with the men at a rate of $1 per minute. The Japanese men, operating as Aloha Data, used digital cameras to capture the live video chat, then transmitted it to a server in California run by a "not respectable, but not illegal" Internet service provider called Lucy's Tiger Den. Japanese viewers accessed the performance through the California server. In this case, women were trafficked from Japan into the United States and exploited for viewers in Japan—a classic case where traffickers used technology to circumvent both borders and national laws and succeeded in conducting illegal business legally.[27]

The Internet and online technologies have facilitated buying, selling, and distributing child pornography anonymously at lightning speed. The buyers do not need to go and look for such materials in dingy and hidden places far away from their residence and watch in secret. Technology has facilitated instant access to such images and materials through anonymous online payment system offers. Information sharing platforms enable the rapid exchange of materials. Basic technology can be used to create numerous still images from footage, and small files (both images and short movie clips) can be traded on the Internet. Technology has facilitated anonymous trade in humans with immunity.

Use of Technology for Combating Trafficking

International and United States' Efforts to Combat Human Trafficking Using Technology

Online trafficking is an emerging and a complex form of crime. This section provides an overview of the international and United States efforts to combat human trafficking using technology. This multifaceted crime problem requires a coordinated and collaborative global effort at the international level as well as an individual effort at the individual state's level. It is a technological problem that invites collaborative anti-trafficking solutions.[28] Here we discuss some such efforts being made using technology as a means of global cooperation to combat human trafficking.

Article 27(3) of the Transnational Organized Crime Convention provides that member states:

> endeavor to conduct law enforcement cooperation in order to respond to transnational organized crime committed through the use of modern technology.

This provision calls upon states to make collaborative efforts to work towards law enforcement cooperation in order to respond to transnational organized crimes committed through the use of modern technology.[29]

The Convention on Cybercrime is the first international treaty seeking to address Internet and computer crime by harmonizing national laws, improving investigative techniques, and increasing cooperation among nations was drawn up during 109th Session on 8th November 2001 by the Council of Europe in Strasbourg, France. The Council of Europe's observer states—Canada, Japan, South Africa, and the United States—participated in it and was signed in Budapest on the 23rd of November 2001. This treaty came into force on the 1st of July 2004. As of March 2016, 49 states have ratified the convention. This treaty provides procedural and investigative tools to enable law enforcers around the world to cooperate to prevent and combat all types of crimes committed on or through the Internet, including trafficking.[30]

Another international entity intended to address international crime is known as **INTERPOL**. This was conceived in 1914 at the first International Criminal Police Congress, held in Monaco. It was officially created in 1923 as the International Criminal Police Commission as an organization and became known as INTERPOL in 1956. INTERPOL enables police in 190 member countries to work together to fight international crime and provides a range of policing expertise and capabilities, supporting three main crime programs: counter-terrorism, cybercrime, and emerging organized crime. In 1926, the General Assembly, held in Berlin, proposed that each country should establish a central point of contact within its police structure: the forerunner of the National Central Bureau (NCB). The NCB was established in 1927. In 2002, the I-24/7 web-based communication system was launched. This significantly improved NCBs' access to INTERPOL's databases and services. Since its establishment, INTERPOL has been working to combat human trafficking. The most recent news release on its success is appended here.

> More than 2,700 human trafficking victims rescued in INTERPOL-coordinated operation
> Results mark INTERPOL support for World Day against Trafficking in Persons—July 28, 2016.
> An operation targeting human trafficking in South and Central America has resulted in the rescue of more than 2,700 victims, 134 arrests and the dismantling of at least seven organized crime networks. Coordinated by INTERPOL's Regional Bureau for South America, Operation Intercops—Spartacus III was conducted in two parts, initially concentrating on three of South America's busiest international airports

> thought to be hubs for human trafficking networks: Ministro Pistarini (Buenos Aires, Argentina), Guarulhos (São Paulo, Brazil) and El Dorado (Bogotá, Colombia). Through access to INTERPOL's global databases, frontline police at these key locations were able to check travelers' names and documents to help identify potential traffickers and their victims. Based on the arrests made and intelligence gathered during this first phase (1–10 June), police across the 25 involved countries conducted follow-up investigations to identify and dismantle the networks involved. The results, published ahead of the World Day against Trafficking in Persons on 30 July, underline INTERPOL's ongoing commitment in supporting national law enforcement address this modern-day form of human slavery.
>
> Among the victims rescued were 27 teenage girls trafficked into different countries for sexual exploitation and as cheap labor. Several girls in Ecuador who had been contacted through social media were snatched from outside their schools, before being drugged and transported out of the country. In Peru, some 900 police officers took part in an operation targeting sexual exploitation and forced labor in the gold-mining town of La Rinconada, arresting five suspects and rescuing 190 women and 250 men.[31]

The **G8 Sub-group on High-Tech Crime** is another global effort to use technology in combating human trafficking. The Group of 8 countries (Canada, France, Germany, Italy, Japan, Russia, the United States, and the United Kingdom) was established in 1997. It adopted Ten Principles to combat computer crime to ensure that there were no "safe havens" for criminals anywhere in the world and established various subgroups to achieve forty recommendations adopted by G8 heads of state. One of those recommendations is the Subgroup on High-Tech Crime, originally mandated to strengthen the ability of G8 countries to prevent, investigate, and prosecute crimes involving computers, networked communications, and other new technologies. Countries are represented in the subgroup by multi-disciplinary delegations that include cybercrime investigators and prosecutors and experts on legal systems, forensic analysis, and international cooperation agreements.[32]

The Virtual Global Taskforce (VGT)[33] was established in 2003. The main objective of the VGT is to build an effective, international partnership of law enforcement agencies that help to protect children from online child abuse. It is currently comprised of law enforcement agencies from around the world, including the Australian High Tech Crime Centre, the Child Exploitation and Online Protection Centre in the UK, the Royal Canadian Mounted Police, the

U.S. Department of Homeland Security, Colombian National Police, Europol, Indonesian National Police, Interpol, Italian Postal and Communication Police Service, Korean National Police Agency, New Zealand Police, and the Ministry of Interior for the United Arab Emirates. The three main objectives of this co-operative group are: (1) to make the Internet a safer place; (2) to identify, locate, and help children at risk; and (3) to apprehend perpetrators and hold them accountable.

Since its establishment in 2003, the VGT has rescued hundreds of children around the world from sexual abuse and conducted numerous targeted law enforcement operations into online and offline offending. It has investigated over 1,000 suspects and identified and held hundreds of child sex offenders worldwide accountable. One recent success story is included here:

> Operation Endeavour (Jan 2014)—an organized crime group that facilitated the live streaming of on-demand child sexual abuse in the Philippines was dismantled after a joint investigation by the U.K.'s National Crime Agency (NCA), the Australian Federal Police (AFP) and U.S. Immigration and Customs Enforcement (ICE). Operation Endeavor which began in 2012, has to date resulted in: 29 international arrests, of which 11 were part of the facilitation group in the Philippines; 15 children in the Philippines aged between 6–15 identified and safeguarded from sexual abuse; and over £37,500 ($60,000) identified as having been paid for the live abuse of children by the customer network.[34]

The United Kingdom's **Internet Watch Foundation (IWF)** is an Internet "hotline" for Internet users to report their exposure to potentially illegal content online. The IWF was established in 1996 to fulfill an independent role in receiving, assessing, and tracing public complaints about child sexual abuse content on the Internet and to support the development of website rating systems. Since its formation, the IWF has been actively engaged in operating this hotline service for the public to report potentially criminal content and providing a "notice and takedown" service to advise ISPs in partnership with the police services in the UK to effect its removal.[35] The most recent success includes:

> In 2015, the IWF processed 112,975 reports and a total of 68,092 reports were confirmed as containing child sexual abuse images or videos. That's a 118% increase on 2014.
> A new "game changing" service, to help in the fight against child sexual abuse imagery: the IWF Image Hash List was created. The IWF's work

has expanded globally and it has begun developing new international Reporting Portals for countries without a reporting hotline.[36]

The **Interpol Child Image Database** (ICAID) is a system maintained and housed at the Interpol General Secretariat. The image banks of law enforcement agencies around the world contribute images to facilitate global investigations of child sexual exploitation. In 2006, police were able to identify and rescue 131 victims of child sexual abuse using ICAID; in five years, more than 500 victims have been rescued in 29 countries. The International Child Sexual Exploitation Database is available to member countries directly through I-24/7. The Image Analysis Resource Centre (funded by the U.S. National Center for Missing & Exploited Children from a U.S. Department of State grant) was initiated in 2006. The Image Analysis Resource Center also created an "Expertise Reference Database."[37]

In 2003, Microsoft established the **Child Exploitation Tracking System** (CETS)—a collaborative global law enforcement program for child pornography investigations. This system enables law enforcement officers from different departments in different countries to collaborate in the pursuit of pedophiles and in the rescue and repatriation of abused children. CETS helps law enforcement agencies follow hundreds of suspects at a time and eliminate duplication, making it more efficient for the agencies to follow up on leads, collect evidence, and build cases against suspected child pornographers.[38] CETS is currently used by agencies in Australia, Brazil, Belgium, Canada, Italy, the United Kingdom, and the United States. PhotoDNA was integrated into CETS in 2012.

PhotoDNA is another example of technology used to fight trafficking. This Microsoft program creates something similar to a fingerprint of an image, which can be compared with the signatures of other images to find copies. The National Center for Missing & Exploited Children (NCMEC) and online service providers such as Microsoft and Facebook currently use PhotoDNA to help find, report, and eliminate some of the worst known images of child pornography online.[39]

Computer-Based Training (CBT) for law enforcement delivers high-quality instructional material to the law enforcement work force by using multimedia computer technology. It enhances the quality of a training program while reducing some of the associated administrative hassles. Current technology provides realistic simulations. It is a form of e-learning that harnesses technology to strengthen law enforcement response against trafficking. Programs are tailored for domestic legal circumstances, emphasizing the regional and global impact of transnational organized crime. A training module on human trafficking provides basic understanding of human trafficking to enable law enforcement to better detect and respond to the crime.[40]

Another international effort includes **NATO Advanced Distributed Learning (ADL)** through the NATO School. The NATO School and ISN in Zurich have produced two courses covering different dimensions of human trafficking. The courses are available free of charge via the Learning Management System hosting the Advanced Distributed Learning (ADL) program. The self-paced courses are undertaken independently without the support or involvement of any tutor or professor. Advanced Distributed Learning (ADL) offers two courses for Trafficking in Persons: (1) Human Trafficking: Causes, Consequences, Counter-strategies and (2) Combating Trafficking in Human Beings.[41]

Forgery and falsification of all kinds of legal and travel documents are some of the other significant contributors that facilitate trafficking enterprises with ease and immunity. Advances in technologies make production of genuine-looking, false documents easy. Traffickers and criminal networks are able to provide trafficking victims with false passports and other travel documents such as visas.

Article 12 of the Trafficking in Persons Protocol addresses security and control of documents. Trafficking in Persons Protocol, Article 12 states that

> Each State Party shall take such measures as may be necessary, within available means: (a) To ensure that travel or identity documents issued by it are of such quality that they cannot easily be misused and cannot readily be falsified or unlawfully altered, replicated or issued; and (b) To ensure the integrity and security of travel or identity documents issued by or on behalf of the State Party and to prevent their unlawful creation, issuance and use.[42]

During the negotiation of Article 12 of the Trafficking in Persons Protocol, all countries agreed to the development of systems and technologies that minimize the amount of sophisticated maintenance and high-technology infrastructure needed to support and maintain such systems. This was critical to the success of deployment in developing countries who may not have enough resources to implement highly technological systems.

In order to make it difficult for the traffickers to falsify, forge, or alter documents, advanced technical measures are required. Advanced technology and advanced administrative and security elements are crucial to protect the production and issuance process against corruption, theft, or other means of diverting documents. New technological advances offer considerable potential for the creation of new types of documents that identify individuals in a unique manner. These advanced technologies can authenticate and separate the fake from the authentic with speed and accuracy. These advanced technologies have the ability to verify and identify forgeries with precision.

False and Authentic Documents Online (FADO)—a European image-archiving system was enacted in 1998. It was established by a Joint Action of the Council of the European Union to help combat illegal immigration and organized crime. It is a computerized system with restricted access providing fast and secure information exchange between the General Secretariat of the Council of the European Union and between document experts in the European Union member states, Iceland, Norway, and Switzerland. FADO stores data on images of genuine documents, security techniques (security features), typical false and forged documents, forgery techniques, and statistics on detected false and falsified documents and identity fraud. It is a useful database in apprehending traffickers.[43]

High Tech Passports is another measure that can be used to apprehend traffickers and other criminals. Falsified or forged documents are often used in the commission of transnational crime. This technology ensures that passports, visas, and other travel documents are not easy to forge or falsify. Use of this technology can be instrumental in combating trafficking as many a time, traffickers provide fake/forged passports and travel documents to bring in victims.[44] The **International Civil Aviation Organization** (ICAO) sets standards for travel documents and passports. The old passports contained hand-written information that facilitated forgery and falsification. The modern technology—including special dye, a particular seal, and data imprinting—have made forgery or falsification of passports and other travel documents substantially more difficult. Passports contain identifying numbers repeated on each page by laser, a machine-readable code, and a digital image of the passport holder. Special paper is used to make the passports, containing fibers only visible by ultraviolent light. All passports are issued from a centralized center where information is stored in a database which can be checked at borders.[45]

Currently, **biometric technology** is used to ensure that documents are unforgeable. These measures use physical characteristics of a person to verify their identity. The most common biometrics include fingerprints, iris scans, hand geometry, voice recognition, and face recognition. Face recognition technology uses a formula to determine whether a live image of a face matches the electronically stored image of that person.[46]

Frontex is another agency of the European Union established in 2004 to manage the cooperation between national border guards securing its external borders. It has undertaken many collaborative initiatives with Interpol to ensure border integrity. On December 15, 2015, the European Commission presented its proposal for a new European Border and Coast Guard Agency that would replace and succeed Frontex.[47]

The **Virtual Global Taskforce (VGT)** is an effective, international partnership of law enforcement agencies, non-government organizations (NGOs), and industry. Its purpose is to help protect children from online child abuse and other forms of transnational child sexual exploitation. "The VGT focuses on making the Internet a safer place, identifying, locating and helping children at risk and holding perpetrators appropriately to accountable and apprehending them. The VGT logo reaffirms the VGT's purpose that the child is the key focus of the VGT and the eye is always roaming the Internet, across international borders, watching over our children to keep them safe online."[48]

Some of the operations carried out by VGT are presented below.

> **Operation Endeavour** (Jan 2014): An organized crime group that facilitated the live streaming of on-demand child sexual abuse in the Philippines was dismantled after a joint investigation by the U.K.'s National Crime Agency (NCA), the Australian Federal Police (AFP) and U.S. Immigration and Customs Enforcement (ICE). Operation Endeavor which began in 2012, has to date resulted in: 29 international arrests, of which 11 were part of the facilitation group in the Philippines; 15 children in the Philippines aged between 6–15 identified and safeguarded from sexual abuse; and over £37,500 ($60,000) identified as having been paid for the live abuse of children by the customer network.
>
> **Operation Rescue** (March 2011): A global pedophile network consisting of thousands of online members was shattered, resulting in more than 200 children being safe-guarded and 184 offenders arrested across the globe. This operation started in 2007 and involved cooperation between seven of the VGT member agencies, including the Australian Federal Police, the Child Exploitation and Online Protection (CEOP) Centre in the United Kingdom, the New Zealand Police, U.S. Immigration and Customs Enforcement, The National Child Exploitation Coordination Centre, as part of the Royal Canadian Mounted Police, the Italian Postal and Communications Police Service and Europol.
>
> **Operation Basket** (December 2010): This operation resulted in approximately 230 commercial child sexual exploitation websites being taken down and five key members of the criminal organization behind these web sites being arrested in the Ukraine.

> **Operation Elm** (August 2008): Through this "operation" over 360 suspects were identified worldwide, over 50 UK arrests [were made] and at least 15 children safeguarded.
>
> **Operation Chandler** (June 2007): Through this operation more than 700 suspects were identified worldwide and more than 40 children safeguarded worldwide.[49]

Operation Pin is an initiative of the Virtual Global Taskforce launched in 2003. It consists of the UK's National Crime Squad, the FBI, Interpol, the Royal Canadian Mounted Police, and the Australian High Tech Crime Centre/Australian Federal Police (AFP). Under this initiative, Operation PIN created a website that purports to contain images of child abuse but is in fact a law enforcement site. Individuals accessing the site are confronted with an online law enforcement message, informing them they have entered a law enforcement website and committed an offense. They are also informed that their identifying details have been captured and provided to relevant national authorities. It is designed to capture the details of individuals who actively seek images of child abuse and deter individuals from seeking images of child abuse, by reducing their confidence in the Internet as an anonymous, risk-free arena.

In 2014, Thorn: Digital Defenders developed and introduced **the Spotlight tool**. This is designed to aggregate data from online commercial sex advertisements. Spotlight takes this massive amount of data and turns it into an asset for law enforcement. The objective of Spotlight is to improve the effectiveness and efficiency of domestic sex trafficking investigations and increase the number of women and children who are identified and connected with help resources. Spotlight is a web-based tool that provides law enforcement with intelligence and leads about suspected human trafficking networks and individuals in order to identify and assist victims. "The tool helps prioritize leads by leveraging machine learning algorithms and insight from officers in the field, and connects disparate data sources to provide deep investigative tools to help officers understand the historical and full geographical reach of a victim's trafficking situation." The Spotlight Tool is available to law enforcement across the nation and law enforcement agencies using Spotlight have seen a 43 percent reduction in their investigation time.[50]

In 2014, another technological advance—the Memex program—was launched by the Defense Advanced Research Projects Agency (DARPA) to combat human trafficking through an advanced search engine. Although this tool is not widely available, DARPA has fostered research that focuses on revolutionizing technology in the anti-trafficking space. DARPA comprises approximately 220 government employees in six technical offices, including nearly 100 program managers, who together oversee about 250 research and development programs.

> The Defense Advanced Research Projects Agency was created with a national sense of urgency in February 1958 amidst one of the most dramatic moments in the history of the Cold War and the already-accelerating pace of technology. In the months preceding the official authorization for the agency's creation, Department of Defense Directive Number 5105.15, the Soviet Union had launched an Intercontinental Ballistic Missile (ICBM), the world's first satellite, Sputnik 1, and the world's second satellite, two months after Sputnik 1, resulted in a spectacular fiery failure. Finally, at the end of January 1958, a stunned United States became the second nation to place an object in orbit when it successfully launched the Explorer 1 satellite.
>
> Out of this traumatic experience of technological surprise in the first moments of the Space Age, U.S. leadership created DARPA, initially with the shorter name Advanced Research Projects Agency (ARPA). In the nearly 60 years since it was established, DARPA has owned the critical mission of keeping the United States out front when it comes to cultivating breakthrough technologies for national security rather than in a position of catching up to strategically important innovations and achievements of others.
>
> With no research and development facilities of its own, DARPA has become known as a laboratory and incubator of innovation by providing thought leadership, community-building frameworks, technology challenges, research management, funding, and other cultural and infrastructural support elements that it takes to usher transformative ideas toward consequential new realities.[51]

Polaris operates the National Human Trafficking Resource Center (NHTRC). This toll-free hotline operates 24 hours a day, 7 days a week in over 200 languages to assist victims and community members. The hotline services can also be accessed via email and an online tip reporting form. Polaris's Global Hotline Program also supports other countries looking to set up.

"The Global Missing Children's Network is a multilingual database featuring photos of and information about missing children from around the world. It was launched in 1998 as a joint program of the National Center for Missing & Exploited Children and International Centre for Missing & Exploited Children. Photos are one of the most effective tools in the search for missing children. Rapidly distributing a child's photo can make the difference between a fast recovery and prolonged search."[52]

The National Center for Missing & Exploited Children (NCMEC) began operating CyberTipline in 1998. Using this CyberTipline, anyone who suspects exploitation of children can call and provide information and call for help anonymously. Since 1998, the CyberTipline has received over 4.3 million tips.

In 2013, Polaris and Thorn partnered with Twilio and Salesforce Foundation to develop the NHTRC SMS-based text-line. Using this testing mechanism, victims can text the short code "BeFree" for a discreet and time-efficient way to access the hotline.

The following section provides an overview of the United States laws to determine their relevance to this multifaceted crime problem. Most states have recognized and criminalized sex and labor trafficking and there are individual states that have passed laws to address trafficking at the state level. However, state laws vary in terms of definitions, penalties, and enforcement priorities. Federal laws that address human trafficking can be applied across the country.

There are some federal laws that could be applied to prosecute human trafficking cases. The 18 U.S.C. § 1591 criminalizes sex trafficking, making it illegal to recruit, entice, provide, harbor, maintain, or transport a person or to benefit from involvement in causing the person to engage in a commercial sex act, knowing that force, fraud, or coercion was used or that the person was under the age of 18.[53] Under this law, traffickers exploiting humans for sex may face charges under other federal statutes applicable to sex trafficking, such as 18 U.S.C. § 2423(a), which prohibits transportation of a minor with intent that the individual engages in criminal sexual activity.[54]

The 18 U.S.C. §§ 1589–1590 can be used to prosecute traffickers who exploit humans for labor. This law makes it illegal for anyone to knowingly provide or obtain the labor of a person by force or threats of force, or to traffic a person for labor or services by means of force, coercion, or fraud for the purpose of subjecting the person to slavery, involuntary servitude, debt bondage, or peonage.[55]

Both 18 U.S.C. § 1591 and 18 U.S.C. §§ 1589–1590 address the criminalization of a trafficker's conduct but neither addresses the victim protection. Thus, potentially a trafficked victim can face criminal charges. For example, under federal law, a 16-year-old who is found engaging in commercial sex acts is a trafficking victim, regardless of whether the minor appears to have participated willingly in said acts, because the law presumes that an underage victim cannot provide legal consent. However, the protections available to trafficking victims vary between states. In some state courts, minor victims of sex trafficking can face prostitution charges. Minor victims of human trafficking are forced, induced, or coerced into providing labor, services, or commercial sex. A trafficked child may be compelled to engage in illegal activities such as prostitution or the selling of drugs, and instead of being treated as victims, many are treated as criminals and are prosecuted accordingly.[56]

The state of New York became the first state to pass legislation addressing this issue, with the passing of the Safe Harbor for Exploited Children Act in 2010. The act prohibits prosecution of minors for prostitution. Several states have subsequently passed similar legislation. Prior to the act's passage, sexually exploited youth involved in illegal activities did not receive the protection of the Family Court and were instead prosecuted criminally, which did little more than to re-traumatize these victims. Furthermore, once incarcerated, sexually exploited youth had no access to services that could address their specific social and emotional needs, and thus they often would return to a life on the streets once released. The passage of the act guaranteed that sexually exploited youth would be treated as child victims and be offered services that could pave the way for better outcomes. As of December 2015, thirty-four states have passed safe harbor laws. However, these state legislations vary significantly from state to state. Most states that have passed safe harbor legislation have limited the scope of the protections provided to children that have been commercially sexually exploited (CSEC). In some states, safe harbor provisions are applicable only to children that have engaged in commercial sex, thus the legal protections offered apply to prostitution and prostitution-related crimes. More recently, a growing number of states is including non-commercial sex and non-violent crimes in their version of safe harbor for minor trafficking victims. Most states provide services to CSEC victims through the state child welfare system. Typically, children identified as victims of commercial sexual exploitation are designated as children in need of supervision or dependent children, allowing the state child welfare system to intervene and provide assistance to the children. In other states the agency that oversees juvenile justice is designated to provide assistance to victims of CSEC (Polaris, 2015).

In 2013, the Uniform Law Commission (ULC) released the Uniform Act on Prevention of and Remedies for Human Trafficking (Uniform Act). This act offers guidance to state legislators and provides language drafted and adopted by lawyers from across the country that can serve as a basis for state legislation.[57] The Uniform Act clearly and unequivocally recommends the immunity model for child victims of trafficking. Shortly after it was adopted, the American Bar Association (ABA) House of Delegates endorsed the Uniform Act. The Uniform Act on Prevention of and Remedies for Human Trafficking (Act): Section 15 provides immunity to a minor. It states that "(a) An individual is not criminally liable or subject to [juvenile delinquency proceeding] for [prostitution] and [insert non-violent offenses] if the individual was a minor at the time of the offense and committed the offense as a direct result of being a victim." The

Uniform Act also broadens the scope of safe harbor to protect not only children who have been commercially sexually exploited, but also recognizes that child victims of labor trafficking are forced to commit crimes during the course of their exploitation and should be provided with the same protections as victims of CSEC.[58]

Additionally, some states have enacted laws that address the role of technology in facilitating and disrupting human trafficking. For example, in Maryland, Md. Code Ann. §15-207 (S.B. 542), and in Vermont, 13 V.S.A. §2661 (H.B. 153), require their state Departments of Labor to post the NHTRC hotline information on their websites. Other states' laws, such as Texas's Tex. Civ. Prac. & Rem. Code §125.045 (S.B. 1288), Vermont's 13 V.S.A. §2661 (S.B. 153), and Washington's Wash. Rev. Code §47.38.080 (S.B. 6330) require businesses to post signs with a trafficking hotline number, and Oklahoma's 21A O.S. §748.2 (S.B. 2258) requires the state departments to establish a trafficking hotline. Other states such as Hawaii's Haw. Rev. Stat. §803-44 (H.B. 141), Maryland's, Md. Code Ann., Cts. & Jud. Proc. §10.402 (H.B. 345), and Ohio's Or. Rev. Stat. Ann. §2933.51 *et seq.* (S.B. 235) have authorized electronic surveillance of suspected traffickers.

A majority of the state laws criminalize the use of technology in sexual exploitation of a minor and generally the focus is on the use of computers to "either provide or solicit a minor for sex, the definitions of technology-assisted exploitation vary. Use of other devices capable of electronic data storage are also criminalized. Virginia explicitly includes 'any common carrier or communication common carrier ... or any telecommunications, wire, computer network, or radio communication systems' in its statutes."[59]

Additional resources and universal legal additional amendments is presented in Appendix 2.

Use of Technology for Providing Information and Support to Trafficking Victims

Just as online technologies, mainly the Internet, provide an easy and efficient vehicle to the traffickers for conducting their business, the same can be used to address the multifaceted aspects of human trafficking. Technology can be used to disseminate and share information as well as raise awareness by collaborative and individual actions of a variety of actors—individuals, communities, groups, organizations, government, the private sector, NGOs, service providers, and academia. This section reviews the potential for such action. The Trafficking Victims Protection Reauthorization Act of 2011 includes a new section titled "Creating, building, and strengthening partnerships against significant trafficking in persons." The intent of such an inclusion is to promote cooperation between the federal government and the private sector to ensure that: "(1) United States citizens do not use any item, product, or material produced or extracted with the use and labor from victims of severe forms of trafficking; and (2) such entities do not contribute to trafficking in persons involving sexual exploitation."[60]

Websites can be created and used to describe the issue and provide information on the list of resources and services available for survivors. The global scope of the Internet allows anyone with access to view these websites. Here is one example: https://www.acf.hhs.gov/sites/default/files/orr/traffickingservices_0.pdf. This website is maintained by the Department of Health and Human Services. It provides information on services available to the victims of human trafficking.

The Internet can also be used to publicize and disseminate public **education and awareness campaigns**. It can be used to set up online training initiatives on human trafficking. Not for Sale[61] is one of such initiatives. It raises global awareness on the issue of trafficking and educates the general public. The objective of this campaign is to increase awareness and knowledge about human trafficking through a variety of materials available for download from the website, including a map which allows website visitors to document cases of known human trafficking around the world.

A very common form of social activism is the use of **petitions**. The Internet can be used to connect with a larger audience to identify social activists, people who have similar beliefs and ideals, and people willing to engage in tactics used to voice their opinion and endeavor to bring change. One popular social activist site is Change.org. With millions of users, this website provides a platform for people to gather together behind a cause to demand accountability and inspire change. Many of the online petitions on Change.org relate to human trafficking and it ranks among the 12 "top causes" featured. In 2010, Craigslist shut down its "adult services" section in response to pressures from several anti-trafficking organizations, including a petition signed by more than 10,000 Change.org members.

Mobile phones can also be used in creating social awareness about human trafficking and engage communities in preventing human trafficking. A most recent example of such an effort is the **Rapid Report & Response** (**R3**) mobile system created by Prevent Human Trafficking.[62] Anyone suspecting human trafficking incident can text a message. The message is received and securely routed to the nearest first responder who will go to the site of the report and look for evidence of the incident. If the first responder confirms that the trafficking incident occurred, she/he will send a text that will create a red dot on a digital map and alert the nearest enforcement agents. The agents will then attempt to intervene in the potential human trafficking incident. The intervention will be digitally mapped by a blue dot. This map will appear on the Prevent Human Trafficking website to allow for people to track human trafficking cases. If the enforcement agents are not successful in their attempt to intervene, they can text a message and the blue dot will be replaced with a black dot. However, if the enforcement agents are able to successfully resolve the incident, the black dot will be replaced with a green dot. The R3 has the potential to generate useful tracking data that will help NGOs and government agencies intervene and prevent human trafficking more effectively. The R3 is being tested in Thailand with the intention of expanding it to other countries in Southeast Asia, South Asia, India, and eventually other parts of the world.[63]

Campaigns using mobile phones are another way mobile phones can be used to raise awareness, educate people, and engage communities to speak out against human trafficking. An example of such a campaign is Free2Work, developed by the Not for Sale Campaign (www.free2work.org). Free2Work is a mobile phone application that provides information on forced and child labor related to particular companies and brands. Specifically, Free2Work rates companies on how labor trafficking relates to their supply chain practices in terms of company policies, transparency and traceability, monitoring and training, or worker rights. Free2Work assigns each company a grade based on the found rating. The Free2Work app allows consumers to look up the overall grade of specific companies and support those that have zero tolerance for forced labor.

To fully understand the role of technology and create an effective intervention plan to address trafficking, concerted and collaborative efforts by the policy makers, governments, NGOs, researchers, and the private sector are needed. Technology-minded interventions could provide significant help to the individuals who are at the highest risk of being trafficked. The private sector is developing technologies to gather business intelligence on the web of contractors and suppliers that make up modern supply chains. NGOs are examining how global supply chains can also be the source of data that reveals labor trafficking risks to corporations and governments. NGOs and Internet companies are providing required training to migrant workers in the use of social media to connect with family, friends, and support networks.[64]

Conclusion

This chapter has presented an overview of the role of online technologies in addressing human trafficking. The discussions and data included in this chapter have demonstrated that the online technologies have contributed substantially in enhancing the global landscape. Society has reaped many social, economic, informational, educational, and cultural benefits due to the advancement in technology. Our imagination is no longer bound by traditional boundaries created by borders and geographical locations. Technology has brought the world closer and allowed people from different parts of the world to work together. However, the research and discussions presented in this chapter have also exhibited that the progress, the togetherness, and the change in social and global landscape came with a price.

The chapter also discussed the negative consequences of advances in technology and the societal reliance on technology. The same advances that brought progress and made our lives interesting, easy, and colorful also brought the ugly consequences with them—human trafficking being one of these. Technology has allowed people to be as creative and imaginative as possible. In some cases, greed and hunger for power have taken over the conscience. Technology has been used to earn exponential profits through force, fraud, and coercion. It has facilitated exploitation of human beings by other human beings for sex and cheap labor with immunity. Technology has provided mechanisms to trade humans as commodities.

Online technologies—including Internet and other mobile communication technologies—have played a significant role in both enabling and combating human trafficking. Technological advancements hold consequences and applications for both traffickers and those working to counter trafficking alike. Technology—such as use of social media, websites, and anonymizing apps—has been used by traffickers and networks to contact and recruit their victims. As discussed throughout the chapter, traffickers have used technology to entice potential victims and entrap them in this web of crime through deception, coercion, and force. However, as discussed in the chapter, the same technological advancements also have the potential to assist law enforcement and service providers to monitor illicit activity, locate and rescue victims, collect and analyze data leading to the prosecution of traffickers, and streamline communication between anti-trafficking actors and agencies.[65]

Chapter Review

This chapter has examined the relationship between technology and human trafficking in three basic spheres of business: (1) use of technology by the traffickers for proliferation of trafficking business; (2) use of technology for prosecution of traffickers to prevent, expose, and monitor trafficking; and (3) use of technology to provide information and support for trafficking victims and at-risk groups.

Discussion Questions

1) Identify three uses of mobile technology that have facilitated traffickers in carrying out their business easily.

2) Discuss three ways technology can help law enforcement officers to identify and apprehend traffickers.

3) List three international laws that provide guidance on how to address the crime of trafficking in persons.

4) Discuss the contributions of the Convention on Cybercrime—the first international treaty for addressing Internet and computer crime.

5) What is "ICAID"? Discuss its role in apprehending traffickers.

References

Aromaa, Kauko. "Trafficking in human beings: uniform definitions for better measuring and for effective counter-measures." In *Measuring Human Trafficking*, pp. 13–26. Springer New York, 2007.

"Attorney General Kamala D. Harris Teams with Yahoo! and Polaris Project to Fight Human Trafficking, Help Victims Online." Office of the Attorney General. June 18, 2012. Accessed September 23, 2016.

Baker, Linda, and Marcie Campbell. "Information Communication Technologies and Trafficking in Persons. Learning Network Brief (7). London, Ontario: Learning Network, Centre for Research and Education on Violence Against Women and Children. (2013).

Bang, Naomi Jiyoung. "Justice for Victims of Human Trafficking and Forced Labor: Why Current Theories of Corporate Liability Do Not Work." *U. Mem. L. Rev.* 43 (2012): 1047.

Banks, Duren, and Tracey Kyckelhahn, "Characteristics of Suspected Human Trafficking Incidents, 2008–2010" U.S. Department of Justice, Bureau of Justice Statistics. by NCJ 233732, April 2011, 5.

Coleman, Gabriella. "Hacker, hoaxer, whistleblower, spy: The many faces of Anonymous." *Verso Books*, 2014.

Convention on Cybercrime—ETS No.185, Budapest, 23/11/2001—Treaty open for signature by the member States and the non-member States which have participated in its elaboration and for accession by other non-member States.

Council of Europe, Group of Specialists on the Impact of the Use of New Information Technologies on Trafficking in Human Beings for the Purpose of Sexual Exploitation, February 17, 2003, 107.

Dixon Jr, Herbert B. "Human Trafficking and the Internet (and Other Technologies, Too)." *Judges J.* 52 (2013): 36.

"Domestic Sex Trafficking of Minors—2010 State by State Cases Reported by Media". Women's Funding Network. Last Updated December 17, 2010. http://www.womensfundingnetwork.org/ sites/wfnet.org/files/AFNAP/CSECState-byStateDec2010.pdf.

Federal Bureau of Investigation. "Innocence Lost/Operation Cross-Country Press Conference," Washington, D.C., June 25, 2008, http://www.fbi.Gov/news/speeches/combatting-the-sex-trafficking of-children.

Gozdiak, Elzbieta M. *Data and research on human trafficking: Bibliography of research-based literature.* DIANE Publishing, 2011.

Hampton, Keith, Lauren Sessions Goulet, Lee Rainie, and Kristen Purcell. "Social networking sites and our lives." *Retrieved July 12, 2011 from* (2011).

Heeks, Richard. "Do information and communication technologies (ICTs) contribute to development?" *Journal of International Development* 22, no. 5 (2010): 625–640.

Hughes, Donna M. "Use of New Communications and Information Technologies for Sexual Exploitation of Women and Children, The." *Hastings Women's LJ* 13 (2002): 127.

International Labour Organization (ILO). ILO Action Against Trafficking in Human Beings, 2008, 3.

"ITU StatShot, Issue 5." *ITU Newsroom.* January 2011, http://www.itu.int/net/pressoffice/stats/2011/01/index.aspx.

Jones, Steve, Camille Johnson Yale, Sarah Millermaier, and Francisco Seoane Perez. "U.S. college students' Internet use: Race, gender and digital divides." *Journal of Computer Mediated Communication* 14, no. 2 (2009): 244–264.

Kara, Siddharth. "Designing more effective laws against human trafficking." *Nw. UJ Int'l Hum. Rts.* 9 (2010): 123.

Laczko, Frank. "Data and research on human trafficking." *International Migration* 43, no. 1 2 (2005): 5–16.

Laczko, Frank. "Enhancing data collection and research on trafficking in persons." In *Measuring human trafficking*, pp. 37–44. Springer New York, 2007.

Latonero, Mark, Bronwyn Wex, and Meredith Dank. "Technology and Labor Trafficking in a Network Society: General Overview, Emerging Innovations, and Philippines Case Study." *Emerging Innovations, and Philippines Case Study (March 6, 2015)* (2015).

Latonero, Mark. "Human trafficking online: The role of social networking sites and online classifieds." *Available at SSRN 2045851* (2011).

Lenhart, Amanda, Kristen Purcell, Aaron Smith, and Kathryn Zickuhr. "Social Media & Mobile Internet Use among Teens and Young Adults. Millennials." *Pew internet & American life project* (2010).

"Mobile Phone Access Reaches Three Quarters of Planet's Population." *World Bank Group Press Release* 15 (2012).

Musto, Jennifer, and danah boyd. 2014. "The Trafficking-Technology Nexus." Social Politics 21 (3): 461–83.

News Services, "2 charged with using Craigslist to offer underage girls for sex," Chicago Tribune, January 12, 2007, http://articles.chicagotribune.com/2007-01-12/news/0701120390_1_prostitution-craigslist-ceo-jimbuckmaster-young-teens.

"Oakland Man Indicted for Sex Trafficking of Kids," ABC7 News, August 19, 2006, http://abclocal.go.com/kgo/story?section=news/local&id=4477027.

Owens, Colleen, Meredith Dank, Justin Breaux, Isela Bañuelos, Amy Farrell, Rebecca Pfeffer, Katie Bright, Ryan Heitsmith, and Jack McDevitt. "Understanding the organization, operation, and victimization process of labor trafficking in the United States." (2014).

Pornographic Statistics, Family Safe Media, http://familysafemedia.com/pornography_statistics.html#anchor6.

Poulsen, Kevin. "Pimps Go Online to Lure Kids Into Prostitution." *Wired. com, February* 25 (2009).

Prevention, Child Exploitation. "The National Strategy for Child Exploitation Prevention and Interdiction." (2010).

Qiu, Jack Linchuan. 2009. Working-Class Network Society. Cambridge, Massachusetts: The MIT Press.

Quirk, Joel. *The anti-slavery project: From the slave trade to human trafficking.* University of Pennsylvania Press, 2011.

Richard, Amy O'Neill. International Trafficking in Women to the United States: A Contemporary Manifestation of Slavery and Organized Crime. Center for the Study of Intelligence, November 1999.

Rodham Clinton, Hillary "Remarks on the Release of the 2011 Trafficking in Persons Report," June 27, 2011, U.S. Department of State, http://www.state.gov/secretary/rm/2011/06/ 167156.htm.

Saada Saar, Malika. "Girl Slavery in America," Huffington Post, April 20, 2010.

Sheldon Zhang, "Beyond the 'Natasha' story—a review and critique of current research on sex trafficking," Global Crime 10, no. 3 (August 2009): 178.

Smoot, Jeanne L. "Marriage Broker Law Seeks to Protect Readily Exploited Women," *Cumberland Times News*, July 11, 2006.

The Social Lives of Networked Teens (New Haven: Yale University Press, forthcoming 2012). 15 U.S. Department of State, Trafficking in Persons Report, June 2011, 35.

"Starting out young in the world's oldest profession: children prostitutes in L.A.," Patt Morrison, Southern California Public Radio, October 21, 2010, http://www.scpr.org/programs/patt-morrison/2010/10/21/starting-out-youngin-the-worlds-oldest-profession/.

Stefanizzi, Sonia. "Measuring the Non-Measurable: Towards the Development of Indicators for Measuring Human Trafficking." In *Measuring Human Trafficking*, pp. 45–53. Springer New York, 2007.

Steinfatt, Thomas M. And Simon Baker. "Measuring the Extent of Sex Trafficking in Cambodia—2008". United Nations Interagency Project on Human Trafficking, January 2011.

Sykiōtou, Athanasia. *Trafficking in Human Beings: Internet Recruitment: Misuse of the Internet for the Recruitment of Victims of Trafficking in Human Beings.* Directorate General of Human Rights and Legal Affairs, Council of Europe, 2007.

United Nations Convention against Transnational Organized Crime—General Assembly resolution 55/25 of 15 November 2000.

United Nations Office on Drugs and Crime (UNODC) and the United Nations Global Initiative to Fight Human Trafficking (UN.GIFT), Global Report on Trafficking in Persons, February 2009, 6.

United States Department of State. Trafficking in Persons Report, June 2011, 372. 31 International Labour Organization, ILO Action Against Trafficking in Human Beings, 2008, 3.

United States Senate, "Human Trafficking: Mail Order Bride Abuses." *Hearing before the Subcommittee on East Asian and Pacific Affairs of the Committee of Foreign Relations. 108th Cong., 2nd sess., July* 13 (2004).

Vaknin, Sam. "Corruption and financial crime." *Skopje: A Narcissus Publications Imprint* (2010).

Further Suggested Readings

Aronowitz, A. A. (2001). Smuggling and trafficking in human beings: the phenomenon, the markets that drive it and the organisations that promote it. *European Journal on Criminal Policy and Research*, *9*(2), 163–195.

Brunovskis, A., & Surtees, R. (2008). Agency or Illness—The Conceptualization of Trafficking Victims' Choices and Behaviors in the Assistance System. *Gender, Technology and Development, 12*(1), 53–76.

Chuang, J. A. (2014). Exploitation creep and the unmaking of human trafficking law. *American Journal of International Law, 108*(4), 609–649.

Chung, R. C. Y. (2009). Cultural perspectives on child trafficking, human rights & social justice: A model for psychologists. *Counselling Psychology Quarterly, 22*(1), 85–96.

Dalrymple, J. K. (2005). Human Trafficking: Protecting Human Rights In The Trafficking Victims Protection Act: Human Traffic: Sex, Slaves & Immigration. By Craig McGill. *BC Third World LJ, 25*, 451–499.

Dixon Jr, H. B. (2013). Human Trafficking and the Internet (and Other Technologies, Too). *Judges J., 52*, 36.

Ekberg, G. (2004). The Swedish Law that Prohibits the Purchase of Sexual Services Best Practices for Prevention of Prostitution and Trafficking in Human Beings. *Violence against women, 10*(10), 1187–1218.

Emmers, R., Greener-Barcham, B., & Thomas, N. (2006). Institutional arrangements to counter human trafficking in the Asia Pacific. *Contemporary Southeast Asia: A Journal of International and Strategic Affairs, 28*(3), 490–511.

Finckenauer, J. O., & Schrock, J. (2000). Human trafficking: A growing criminal market in the U.S.

Friesendorf, C. (2007). Pathologies of security governance: Efforts against human trafficking in Europe. *Security Dialogue, 38*(3), 379–402.

Hodge, D. R. (2008). Sexual trafficking in the United States: A domestic problem with transnational dimensions. *Social Work, 53*(2), 143–152.

Huda, S. (2006). Sex trafficking in South Asia. *International journal of gynecology & obstetrics, 94*(3), 374–381.

Joshi, A. (2002). Face of Human Trafficking, The. *Hastings Women's LJ, 13*, 31.

Kleemans, E. R. (2009). Human smuggling and human trafficking.

Kyle, D., & Koslowski, R. (2011). *Global human smuggling: Comparative perspectives.* JHU Press.

Latonero, M., Musto, J., Boyd, Z., Boyle, E., Bissel, A., Gibson, K., & Kim, J. (2012). *The rise of mobile and the diffusion of technology-facilitated trafficking* (p. 43). University of Southern California, Center on Communication Leadership & Policy.

Latonero, M. (2011). Human trafficking online: The role of social networking sites and online classifieds. *Available at SSRN 2045851.*

Lindquist, J. (2010). Images and evidence: Human trafficking, auditing, and the production of illicit markets in Southeast Asia and beyond. *Public Culture, 22*(2), 223–236.

Makisaka, M. (2009). Human trafficking: A brief overview.

Mameli, P. A. (2002). Stopping the illegal trafficking of human beings. *Crime, law and social change, 38*(1), 67–80.

Orlova, A. V. (2004). From social dislocation to human trafficking: the Russian case. *Problems of Post-Communism, 51*(6), 14–22.

Perrin, B. (2010). *Invisible chains: Canada's underground world of human trafficking.* Penguin Canada.

Potts Jr, L. G. (2003). Global trafficking in human beings: assessing the success of the United Nations Protocol to Prevent Trafficking in Persons. *Geo. Wash. Int'l L. Rev., 35*, 227.

Rizer, A., & Glaser, S. R. (2011). Breach: The national security implications of human trafficking. *Widener L. Rev., 17*, 69.

Scarpa, S. (2008). *Trafficking in human beings: modern slavery.* Oxford University Press.

Shifman, P. (2003). Trafficking and women's human rights in a globalised world. *Gender & Development, 11*(1), 125–132.

Sigmon, J. N. (2008). Combating modern-day slavery: Issues in identifying and assisting victims of human trafficking worldwide. *Victims and Offenders, 3*(2–3), 245–257.

Skrivankova, K. (2006). Combating trafficking in human beings. *International Review of Law Computers & Technology, 20*(1–2), 229–232.

Skilbrei, M. L., & Tveit, M. (2008). Defining Trafficking through Empirical Work Blurred Boundaries and their Consequences. *Gender, Technology and Development, 12*(1), 9–30.

Snajdr, E. (2013). Beneath the master narrative: human trafficking, myths of sexual slavery and ethnographic realities. *Dialectical Anthropology, 37*(2), 229–256.

Truong, T. D. (2001). Human trafficking and organised crime. *ISS Working Paper Series/General Series, 339*, 1–30.

Turner, J., & Kelly, L. (2009). Trade Secrets Intersections Between Diasporas and Crime Groups in the Constitution of the Human Trafficking Chain. *British Journal of Criminology, 49*(2), 184–201.

Viuhko, M. (2010). Human trafficking for sexual exploitation and organized procuring in Finland. *European Journal of criminology, 7*(1), 61–75.

Notes

1. Bang, N. J. (2012). Justice for victims of human trafficking and forced labor: Why current theories of corporate liability do not work. *U. Mem. L. Rev.*, *43*, 1047.

2. Latonero, M. (2011). Human trafficking online: The role of social networking sites and online classifieds. SSRN 2045851.

3. Saada Saar, M. (2010, April 20). Girl slavery in America. *Huffington Post.*

4. Latonero, M. (2011). Human trafficking online: The role of social networking sites and online classifieds. SSRN 2045851.

5. Baker, L., & Campbell, M. (2013). Information communication technologies and trafficking in persons. Learning Network Brief (7). London, Ontario: Learning Network, Centre for Research and Education on Violence Against Women and Children.

6. Bank, T. W. (2012). Mobile phone access reaches three quarters of planet's population. World Bank Group Press Release, 15.

7. Latonero, M., B. Wex, & M. Dank. (2015, March 6). *Technology and labor trafficking in a network society: General overview, emerging innovations, and Philippines case study.* Los Angeles: U.S.C Annenberg, Center on Communication Leadership & Policy.

8. This endnote has two references:

   1) International Telecommunication Union. (2010). The world in 2010: ICT facts and figures.

   2) Heeks, R. (2010). Do information and communication technologies (ICTs) contribute to development? *Journal of International Development*, *22*(5) 625–640.

9. ITU. (2010, July–August). The rise of social networking. ITU News, http://www.itu.int/net/itunews/ issues/2010/06/35.aspx.

10. Jones, S. (2009, May 22). Online classifieds. Pew Internet & American Life Project.

11. U.S. Immigration and Customs Enforcement. (2009, July 16). Maryland man pleads guilty in sex trafficking conspiracy involving 3 minor girls. http://www.ice.gov/news/releases/0907/090716baltimore.htm.

12. Federal Bureau of Investigation. (2010, November 8). Sacramento man sentenced to 12 years and seven months for sex trafficking of a minor. Department of Justice. http://sacramento.fbi.gov/dojpressrel/pressrel10/sc110810.htm.

13. Owens, C., M. Dank, J. Breaux, I. Bañuelos, A. Farrell, R. Pfeffer, K. Bright, R. Heitsmith, & J. McDevitt. (2014). *Understanding the organization, operation, and victimization process of labor trafficking in the United States.* Urban Institute.

14. Hughes, D. M. (2002). The use of new communications and information technologies for sexual exploitation of women and children. *Hastings Women's LJ*, *13*, 127.

15. Coleman, G. (2014). *Hacker, hoaxer, whistleblower, spy: The many faces of Anonymous.* Verso Books.

16. Sinkevich, K., & Dashutina, K. (2008). Technology and human trafficking.

17. Sykiōtou, A. (2007). *Trafficking in human beings: Internet recruitment: Misuse of the internet for the recruitment of victims of trafficking in human beings.* Directorate General of Human Rights and Legal Affairs, Council of Europe.

18. Dixon Jr, H. B. (2013). Human trafficking and the Internet (and other technologies, too). *Judges J.*, *52*, 36.

19. Vaknin, S. (2010). Corruption and financial crime. Skopje: A Narcissus Publications Imprint.

20. Latonero, M., B. Wex, & M. Dank. (2015, March 6). *Technology and labor trafficking*

in a network society: General overview, emerging innovations, and Philippines case study. Los Angeles: U.S.C Annenberg, Center on Communication Leadership & Policy.

21. Qiu, J. L. (2009). *Working-class network society*. Cambridge, Massachusetts: The MIT Press.

22. Latonero, M., B. Wex, & M. Dank. (2015, March 6). *Technology and labor trafficking in a network society: General overview, emerging innovations, and Philippines case study*. Los Angeles: U.S.C Annenberg, Center on Communication Leadership & Policy.

23. Sykiōtou, A. (2007). *Trafficking in human beings: Internet recruitment: Misuse of the internet for the recruitment of victims of trafficking in human beings*. Directorate General of Human Rights and Legal Affairs, Council of Europe.

24. U.S. Senate. (2004, July 13). Human trafficking: Mail order bride abuses. Hearing before the Subcommittee on East Asian and Pacific Affairs of the Committee of Foreign Relations. 108th Congress, 2nd session.

25. Caldwell, G., producer. (1997). *Bought and sold*. Washington, DC: Global Survival Network. (documentary film).

26. Richard, A. O. (1999, November). International trafficking in women to the United States: A contemporary manifestation of slavery and organized crime. Center for the Study of Intelligence.

27. This endnote has two references:

 1) Family Safe Media. Pornographic statistics. http://familysafemedia.com/pornography_statistics.html#anchor6.

 2) Dixon Jr, H. B. (2013). Human trafficking and the Internet (and other technologies, too). *Judges J.*, *52*, 36.

28. Musto, J., & d. boyd. (2014). The trafficking-technology nexus. *Social Politics*, *21*(3), 461–83.

29. UN General Assembly. (2000, November 15). United Nations Convention against Transnational Organized Crime. Resolution 55/25.

30. Convention on Cybercrime. (2011, November 23). ETS No.185, Budapest. "Treaty open for signature by the member States and the non-member States which have participated in its elaboration and for accession by other non-member States." https://www.coe.int/en/web/conventions/full-list/-/conventions/treaty/185/signatures.

31. Interpol. (2016, July 28). More than 2,700 human trafficking victims rescued in Interpol-coordinated operation. http://www.interpol.int/en/News-and-media/News/2016/N2016-098.

32. "**2011** The G-8 Group had the meeting in Deauville, France. The Deauville Declaration included had [sic] a section on Internet. **2010** The G-8 Group had the meeting in Muskoka, Canada. The Muskoka Declaration included statements on terrorism and organized crime. **2009** The Ministers of Justice and Home Affairs met in Rome on May 28–30 in conjunction with the G8 Summit 2009 in Italy. A statement was made including Cybercrime and Cybersecurity. It referred to the report from the Roma/Lyon Group provided to the UN Commission on Crime Prevention and Criminal Justice.

The statement made remarks on the technological progress, including as follows:

> 'Criminal misuse of social networks, encryption services, VoIP services, the Domain Name System, and other new and evolving criminal attacks on information systems, pose increased challenges to law enforcement and are spreading.'"

http://www.cybercrimelaw.net/G8.html.

33. "**Virtual Global Taskforce** (VGT) is a group of law enforcement agencies from around the world who operate together to stop child pornography online." https://en.wikipedia.org/wiki/Virtual_Global_Taskforce.

34. U.S. Immigration and Customs Enforcement. (2014, January 15). 29 arrested in international case involving live online webcam child abuse. https://www.ice.gov/news/releases/29-arrested-international-case-involving-live-online-webcam-child-abuse.

35. Internet Watch Foundation. https://www.iwf.org.uk/.

36. Internet Watch Foundation. https://www.iwf.org.uk/

37. Child Exploitation Prevention. (2010). The national strategy for child exploitation prevention and interdiction.

38. Child Exploitation Tracking System (CETS): "Developed by Microsoft, CETS is a repository that can be filled with records pertaining to child pornography and child exploitation cases. It is designed to streamline investigations and integrate with other CETS operations so that law enforcement agencies can enhance their cooperation and efficiently move their cases forward." http://www.iacpcybercenter.org/labs/child-exploitation-tracking-system-cets-2/.

39. "Microsoft began sharing the first release of PhotoDNA as an on-premise technology in 2009. Since then, this technology has helped curb the exploitation of children around the world by detecting millions of illegal images for reporting to the National Center for Missing & Exploited Children (NCMEC) and other appropriate authorities." https://www.microsoft.com/en-us/PhotoDNA/Default.

40. "Computer-Based Training (CBT) involves the use of a personal or networked computer for the delivery and access of training programs. CBT can be synchronous and asynchronous, as well as online, web-based, mobile, and distance learning. CBT is particularly useful when training learners on a specific computer application, but can also be built to train learners on general knowledge or skills. The greatest disadvantage of CBT is that it is expensive to develop and deliver, especially for smaller groups of students. CBT can be more cost efficient when designed to train a larger number of students." https://www.trainingindustry.com/taxonomy/c/computer-based-training-(cbt).aspx.

41. "One of the capabilities under the e-Learning umbrella and the most common form of e-Learning at NATO is Advanced Distributed Learning (ADL), which features educational or training courses delivered over a network using a standard web browser. NATO offers ADL courses on its two major networks, one with access to the Internet. ADL follows a collection of standards and specifications for e-Learning known as the Sharable Content Object Reference Model (SCORM). The term ADL is used synonymously with the term web-based training. SACT ADL courses are located at: https://jadl.act.nato.int." http://www.act.nato.int/advanced-distributed-learning.

42. United Nations. (2000, November 15). Protocol to Prevent, Suppress and Punish Trafficking in Persons Especially Women and Children, supplementing the United Nations Convention against Transnational Organized Crime. Resolution 55/25.

43. "FADO (False and Authentic Documents Online) is the acronym used to refer to the European System of online exchange of information on false and authentic documents.

Under the terms of Council Joint Action 98/700/JHA was decided to create a central computerized system, within the General Secretariat of the Council, which was intended to allow rapid exchange of information between Member States on genuine and false documents, to Given the growing frequency and increasing sophistication of the techniques used to produce genuine documents or their counterfeits.

The system database contains not only false and forged documents to images, as well as authentic document images and summary information about techniques of forgery and security. Thus, the system will provide documents controllers of the Member States information on newly discovered forgery methods and on genuine documents that are in circulation." (Originally written in Spanish and translated by Google). http://euroogle.com/dicionario.asp?definition=539.

44. "HighTech Passport, Ltd. (known in the industry as HTP) was created in April 1992 in San Jose, California, by two localization experts from Silicon Valley.

Today, a high-quality full-service language provider and a major player in the localization field, HTP is still privately owned and proud to be. It offers 22 years of technical and linguistic experience through an exhaustive range of language-related services available in over 80 languages and counting." http://www.htpassport.com/about-us.

45. "The International Civil Aviation Organization (ICAO) is a UN specialized agency, established by States in 1944 to manage the administration and governance of the Convention on International Civil Aviation (Chicago Convention).

ICAO works with the Convention's 191 Member States and industry groups to reach consensus on international civil aviation Standards and Recommended Practices (SARPs) and policies in support of a safe, efficient, secure, economically sustainable and environmentally responsible civil aviation sector. These SARPs and policies are used by ICAO Member States to ensure that their local civil aviation operations and regulations conform to global norms, which in turn permits more than 100,000 daily flights in aviation's global network to operate safely and reliably in every region of the world." http://www.icao.int/about-icao/Pages/default.aspx.

46. "The mission of the Biometrics Institute is to promote the responsible use of biometrics as an independent and impartial international forum for biometric users and other interested parties." "It was founded in July 2001 responding to an industry need for an independent and impartial forum for sharing knowledge and information about biometrics." It has offices in London and Sydney and has created a global biometrics network. You can listen to an introduction to the Biometrics Institute in the podcast from October 2012. http://www.biometricsinstitute.org/pages/mission.html; http://www.biometricsinstitute.org/pages/about-us.html.

47. "Fostering the free movement of people has been an important objective of European integration since the 1950s. Free movement of goods, persons, services and capital were identified as foundations of the Community in the Treaty of Rome (1957). During the 1980s five Member States (Belgium, France, Germany, Luxembourg and the Netherlands) decided to create a territory without internal borders. They signed the first agreements in a small town in Luxembourg called Schengen, hence the 'Schengen area'—a territory in which the free movement of persons is guaranteed. The original agreement was complemented in 1990 by a convention. When this convention entered into force in 1995 it abolished checks at the internal borders and created a single external border. Whatever their location, officers working at the external border perform border checks in accordance with identical procedures. The rules governing visas and the right to asylum are also common for all Schengen countries." http://frontex.europa.eu/about-frontex/origin/.

48. The Virtual Global Taskforce (VGT). http://virtualglobaltaskforce.com/.

49. http://virtualglobaltaskforce.com/what-we-do/.

50. Go to www.htspotlight.com or spotlight@wearethorn.org.

51. http://www.darpa.mil/about-us/timeline/where-the-future-becomes-now.

52. http://www.missingkids.org/GMCN.

53. 18 U.S. Code § 1591—Sex trafficking of children or by force, fraud, or coercion.

54. 18 U.S. Code § 2423—Transportation of minors.

55. 18 U.S. Code § 1590—Trafficking with respect to peonage, slavery, involuntary servitude, or forced labor.

56. 18 U.S. Code § 1592—Unlawful conduct with respect to documents in furtherance of trafficking, peonage, slavery, involuntary servitude, or forced labor.

57. "The Uniform Law Commission (ULC, also known as the National Conference of Commissioners on Uniform State Laws), established in 1892, provides states with non-partisan, well-conceived and well-drafted legislation that brings clarity and stability to critical areas of state statutory law." http://www.uniformlaws.org/Narrative.aspx?title=About%20the%20ULC.

58. "The Uniform Act on Prevention of and Remedies for Human Trafficking (UAPRHT) will help ensure effective action by the fifty states, District of Columbia, Puerto Rico, and the U.S. Virgin Islands, against those who force human beings into labor or sexual servitude against their will. States have an increasingly important role to play in what is now a worldwide movement to end this modern-day slavery and will benefit in that effort from harmonized legislation that encourages coordination both within a state and across state lines." http://www.uniformlaws.org/shared/docs/Prevention%20of%20and%20Remedies%20for%20Human%20Trafficking/2013_UPRHT_Final%20Act.pdf.

59. Latonero, M. (2011). Human trafficking online: The role of social networking sites and online classifieds. SSRN 2045851.

60. 22 U.S. Code § 7103(b)(1)–(2).

61. www.notforsalecampaign.org.

62. "Prevent Human Trafficking (PHT) is a Washington, DC, based nonprofit organization working to build a bridge between South East Asia and the United States to prevent human trafficking. PHT empowers individuals, organizations and governments to tackle the root causes of human trafficking through direct support and technical assistance. PHT uses its expertise and networks to promote best practice and inspire sustainable solutions in the movement to prevent human trafficking." www.preventhumantrafficking.org.

63. http://preventhumantrafficking.org/mobileapp.

64. Latonero, M., B. Wex, & M. Dank. (2015, March 6). *Technology and labor trafficking in a network society: General overview, emerging innovations, and Philippines case study.* Los Angeles: U.S.C Annenberg, Center on Communication Leadership & Policy.

65. Sadwick, R. (2016, January 11). 7 ways technology is fighting human trafficking. *Forbes.* http://www.forbes.com/sites/rebeccasadwick/2016/01/11/tech-fighting-human-trafficking/#3f98873f49b1.

Chapter 9

Protections for the Victims of Trafficking in Persons

Chapter Objectives

This chapter provides a comprehensive understanding of the following:

- Who Are the Victims?
  - Needs of the Victims of Human Trafficking
  - Protection, Support, and After Care of the Victims of Trafficking
    - Trafficking in Persons Protocol: The Requirement for Victims' Protection and Support
    - Trafficking in Persons Protocol: The Requirement for the Provision of Physical, Psychological, and Social Recovery of Victims
  - Comprehensive, Coordinated, and Integrated Response: Support and Protection to the Victims
  - International and the United States' Response to the Victims and Survivors
  - Federal Programs to Provide Support and Protection for the Victims
  - Community Programs and Resources for the Victims of Trafficking
  - After Care of the Victims of Trafficking in Humans

Introduction: Who Are the Victims?

Needs of the Victims of Human Trafficking

Virtually every corner of the world is touched by the crime of human trafficking. Almost all countries participate in perpetuation of this crime in one form or another. Some countries serve as destinations for the trafficked persons and goods, others as originators, yet others serve as transit points, while others serve in a combination of all three capacities. Eventually all countries consume goods and services shaped, produced, or manufactured as a result of trafficking in persons crime. Perpetrators and victims of this crime can be located in almost all countries of the world.[1] Often the crime of "trafficking in persons" has been associated with transnational criminal organizations, small criminal networks and local gangs, violations of labor and immigration codes, and government corruption.[2]

Trafficking in persons, besides being a crime, also entails a range of human rights violations. Its classification as a crime and a human right violation renders it a multifaceted problem requiring a multidimensional response. This complex issue requires a multilinear and well-coordinated international and national response. Otherwise, the crime is likely to regenerate and transmute itself into a more complex problem. The identified victims need an adequate and appropriate response in the form of protection and services. Trafficked persons who escape their situations often find themselves victimized again as a result of the treatment they receive at the hands of the authorities.[3] Its pervasiveness and prevalence in all parts of the world as well as its multidimensional nature denote that its aftermath is also massive. In order to address the aftermath of human trafficking, it is incumbent upon the states (both origin and destination) to address the needs of victims and survivors. Victims of human trafficking (adults and children) require emergency, short-term, and long-term services.[4]

The extant literature suggests that basic needs such as food, shelter, and clothing may be the most primary needs for virtually all victims of trafficking—international and domestic. In addition to these basic needs, the victims may require language interpretation, legal assistance, or legal representation in the case of the victims being from a different country and brought into the destination country illegally. Victims of human trafficking suffer similar problems as torture victims, victims of domestic violence/sexual assault, battered immigrant women, migrant workers, refugees, and asylum seekers. So, their needs may be very similar to those victims.[5] They may experience post-traumatic stress disorder (PTSD), depression, other anxiety disorders, and substance abuse.[6] They may also experience nightmares, cognitive difficulties, anger, sadness, impulsiveness, and other physical maladies such as headaches, chest pain, shaking, sweating, and dizziness. Survivors of trafficking may also need housing, legal assistance, job training, job placement, education, family reunification (for domestic victims), and repatriation (for international victims). Labor trafficking victims may suffer physical maladies and disabilities as a result of exploitation and harsh working environment. They may require long-term medical care (Bales, 2004; Caliber Associates, 2007).[7] Unaccompanied and accompanied minor international trafficking victims may need intensive case management and medical, mental health, and social services. They may experience depression and feelings of isolation, psychosomatic symptoms, "experience high levels of anxiety, survivor guilt (victims feel they do not deserve to be alive and in a safe place when friends, siblings, or other family members are suffering); exhibit behavioral problems, including aggression; and question their ethnic identity."[8]

Victims of human trafficking are often viewed as criminals (e.g., undocumented immigrants, prostitutes) and subject to arrest, detention, and/or deportation—making it more challenging to address the aftermath of human trafficking in the context of it being a human rights violation. However, several laws, treaties, conventions, protocols, acts, taskforces, and other legal documents have been created and implemented—both at international as well as at individual state level in all parts of the world—that offer advice on addressing the needs of victims and providing them protection. Victims receive some sort of protection and help, if they are identified. Here, we discuss some of these significant treaties, conventions, protocols, acts, taskforces, and other legal documents that make provisions for allocating resources to identify and provide services to the victims of human trafficking.

Protections, Support, and after Care for the Victims of Human Trafficking

Trafficking in Persons Protocol: The Requirement for Victims' Protection and Support

The first internationally recognized protocol that defined trafficking in persons and documented the process to identify, address, and deal with the perpetrators and victims is known as the Trafficking in Persons Protocol that came into effect in 2000. Since then several laws, treaties, conventions, protocols, acts, taskforces, and other legal documents have been in effect both at an international as well as an individual state level in all parts of the world. Below is the discussion of the pertinent articles and sections of this protocol that address providing protection and services to the victims.

Article 6, paragraph 2, of the Trafficking in Persons Protocol creates an obligation for states (both origin and destination) to provide victims with information and an opportunity for their views and concerns to be presented at criminal proceedings against offenders. (The basic obligation to ensure that victims are permitted an opportunity to participate is set out in Article 25 of the Transnational Organized Crime Convention). Such presentation could be in the form of either written submissions or oral statements and is to be done in a manner that is not prejudicial to the rights of the defense. The Trafficking in Persons Protocol also requires states to provide trafficking victims with information on relevant court and administrative proceedings and with counselling and information. Victims need to be advised about their legal rights in a language they can understand.

Article 6, paragraph 2 states that:

> Each State Party shall ensure that its domestic legal or administrative system contains measures that provide the victims of trafficking in persons, in appropriate cases, with:
> (a) Information on relevant court and administrative proceedings; and
> (b) Assistance to enable their views and concerns to be presented and considered at appropriate stages of criminal proceedings against offenders, in a manner not prejudicial to the rights of the defense.[9]

The Declaration of Basic Principles of Justice for Victims of Crime and Abuse of Power (General Assembly resolution 40/34, annex)

This declaration states that victims of crime should be informed of their rights to seek redress; of the role of judicial and administrative processes; of "the scope, timing, and progress of the proceedings; and of the disposition of their cases, especially where serious crimes are involved and when they have requested such information," and of the availability of health and social services and other relevant assistance.[10] It discusses the process through which victims should be provided access to justice and fair treatment. Pertinent clauses of the Declaration of Basic Principles of Justice for Victims of Crime and Abuse of Power (Adopted by General Assembly resolution 40/34) are listed below. The following sections provide information on providing victims access to justice and fair treatment.

This section clearly states:

4) Victims should be treated with compassion and respect for their dignity. They are entitled access to the mechanisms of justice and to prompt redress, as provided for by national legislation, for the harm that they have suffered.
5) Judicial and administrative mechanisms should be established and strengthened where necessary to enable victims to obtain redress through formal or informal procedures that are expeditious, fair, inexpensive and accessible. Victims should be informed of their rights in seeking redress through such mechanisms.
6) The responsiveness of judicial and administrative processes to the needs of victims should be facilitated by:
(a) Informing victims of their role and the scope, timing and progress of the proceedings and of the disposition of their cases, especially where serious crimes are involved and where they have requested such information;
(b) Allowing the views and concerns of victims to be presented and considered at appropriate stages of the proceedings where their personal interests are affected, without prejudice to the accused and consistent with the relevant national criminal justice system;
(c) Providing proper assistance to victims throughout the legal process;
(d) Taking measures to minimize inconvenience to victims, protect their privacy,
when necessary, and ensure their safety, as well as that of their families and witnesses
on their behalf, from intimidation and retaliation;
(e) Avoiding unnecessary delay in the disposition of cases and the execution of orders or decrees granting awards to victims.

It is suggested that informal mechanisms for the resolution of disputes, including mediation, arbitration, and customary justice or indigenous practices, should be utilized where appropriate to facilitate conciliation and redress for victims.[11]

Trafficking in Persons Protocol: The Requirement for the Provision of Physical, Psychological, and Social Recovery of Victims

The Trafficking in Persons Protocol requires states parties of origin and of destination to consider implementing measures to provide for the physical, psychological, and social recovery of trafficked victims. Governments should, in collaboration with non-governmental organizations, provide the following types of support: (a) medical; (b) psychological; (c) language and translation; (d) rehabilitation, skill training, and education; and (e) shelter.

Trafficking in Persons Protocol specifically addresses the need for comprehensive and coordinated intervention to protect victims of human trafficking and offer them practical assistance. Article 6, paragraph 1, of the Trafficking in Persons Protocol supplements the provisions of the Organized Crime Convention and requires that measures are taken to protect the privacy and identity of victims, including by making legal proceedings confidential, to the extent that this is possible under domestic law. The article states that where a state's procedural laws may require amendment to ensure that courts have the authority to shield the identities or otherwise protect the privacy of victims in appropriate cases, states should do so. This may include keeping the proceedings confidential, for example by excluding members of the public or media representatives, or by imposing limits on the publication of specific information, such as details that would permit identification of the victim.

Trafficking in Persons Protocol creates an obligation for states to provide victims with information and an opportunity to present their views and concerns during all proceedings. According to the TIP Protocol, states have an obligation to allow concerns to be presented, which could include either written submissions or oral statements. The Protocol requires this to be done in a manner non-prejudicial to the rights of the defense.

The basic obligation to ensure that victims are permitted an opportunity to participate is set out in Article 25, paragraph 3, of the Organized Crime Convention. That requirement applies to all offenses covered by the convention, which includes the trafficking offense under the protocol.

Article 6 stipulates the process and obligation for providing assistance to and protection of victims of trafficking in persons. It states that:

> 1) in appropriate cases and to the extent possible under its domestic law, each State Party shall protect the privacy and identity of victims of trafficking in persons, including, inter alia, by making legal proceedings relating to such trafficking confidential.
>
> 2) Each State Party shall ensure that its domestic legal or administrative system contains measures that provide to victims of trafficking in persons, in appropriate cases: (a) Information on relevant court and administrative proceedings; (b) Assistance to enable their views and concerns to be presented and considered at appropriate stages of criminal proceedings against offenders, in a manner not prejudicial to the rights of the defense.

> 3) Each State Party shall consider implementing measures to provide for the physical, psychological and social recovery of victims of trafficking in persons, including, in appropriate cases, in cooperation with non-governmental organizations, other relevant organizations and other elements of civil society, and, in particular, the provision of: (a) Appropriate housing; (b) Counselling and information, in particular as regards their legal rights, in a language that the victims of trafficking in persons can understand; (c) Medical, psychological and material assistance; and (d) Employment, educational and training opportunities.
>
> 4) Each State Party shall take into account, in applying the provisions of this article, the age, gender and special needs of victims of trafficking in persons, in particular the special needs of children, including appropriate housing, education and care.
>
> 5) Each State Party shall endeavor to provide for the physical safety of victims of trafficking in persons while they are within its territory.
>
> 6) Each State Party shall ensure that its domestic legal system contains measures that offer victims of trafficking in persons the possibility of obtaining compensation for damage suffered.

Article 6 of the Trafficking in Persons Protocol supplements the provisions of the Organized Crime Convention concerning the provision of assistance and protection to victims to ensure the physical safety of victims. Article 24 of the convention refers to the dangers represented by "retaliation or intimidation" for those who cooperate with authorities, whereas Protocol Article 9, subparagraph (1)(b), also refers to protection from the risk of "re-victimization."[12]

Existing studies and reports have demonstrated that victims may refuse or be reluctant in cooperating with the authorities and testifying against the offenders for the fear of retaliation against them and/or their families if they assist the authorities. The current data suggests that re-victimization and retaliation of victims are real possibilities and the victims' fears are often fully justified. Thus, it is imperative that the states make provisions for affording protection and support to the victims during and after their cooperation and testimony. Support and protection should include: (a) physical protection, such as relocation and permitting limitations on the disclosure of information concerning identity and whereabouts; and (b) providing evidentiary rules to permit witness testimony to be given in a manner that ensures the safety of the witness. Under the convention and the Trafficking in Persons Protocol, the basic obligation to protect victims applies to any state party in which the victims are found, including origin, transit, destination, and repatriation states. Contacts with state authorities are usually very problematic for the victims, especially when traffickers have used fear of such authorities to intimidate victims. In such cases, non-governmental organizations may play an important role as intermediaries.[13]

Article 25 also discusses the process and states' obligation for providing assistance to and protection of victims of trafficking in persons. It states that:

1) Each State Party shall take appropriate measures within its means to provide assistance and protection to victims of offenses covered by this Convention, in particular in cases of threat of retaliation or intimidation.
2) Each State Party shall establish appropriate procedures to provide access to compensation and restitution for victims of offenses covered by this Convention.
3) Each State Party shall, subject to its domestic law, enable views and concerns of victims to be presented and considered at appropriate stages of criminal proceedings against offenders in a manner not prejudicial to the rights of the defense.

Article 6, paragraph 6, of the protocol refers to the need to provide the possibility for victims to seek and obtain compensation. When the possibility of obtaining compensation does not exist under national law, legislation may be required to establish appropriate schemes. The protocol does not specify any potential source of compensation. Consequently, any or all of the following general options would probably meet the requirements of the protocol:

- Provisions allowing victims to sue offenders or others under statutory or common-law torts for civil damages.
- Provisions allowing criminal courts to award criminal damages (i.e., to order for that compensation to be paid by offenders to victims) or to impose orders for compensation or restitution against persons convicted of offenses.
- Provisions establishing dedicated funds or schemes whereby victims can claim compensation from the state for injuries or damages suffered as the result of a criminal offense.

Article 6, paragraph 3, of the protocol contains an extensive list of support measures intended to reduce the suffering and harm caused to victims and to assist in their recovery and rehabilitation.[14]

In addition to complying with the international guidelines and meeting the humanitarian goals of reducing the effects on victims, there are other reasons for providing support and protection to the victims. For example, providing support, shelter, and protection for victims may increase the probability of victims' willingness to cooperate and assist investigators in successful apprehension and prosecution of the offenders. Often traffickers intimidate victims by inciting fear of authorities in victims' minds. The literature suggests that traffickers advise human trafficking victims to stay out of sight of law enforcement and other service providers and avoid speaking to them under all circumstances. They are told that if they are found by law enforcement or service providers, they will be incarcerated, punished, and deported, in the case of international victims, and sent home in case of domestic victims–which many victims do not want. If the victims are under age, they are coached by traffickers, pimps, and brothel keepers to lie about their age. Regardless of age, they are taught to state that they are participating willingly. If the law enforcement and service providers can win victims' trust by providing support and protection and are able to convince victims that the authorities are genuinely concerned about their welfare, the probability that the traffickers will be successfully apprehended and punished increases.

Comprehensive, Coordinated, and Integrated Response: Support and Protection to the Victims

To address the aftermath of human trafficking victimization, it is essential that the response is comprehensive, coordinated, and integrated. Service providers and service providing agencies should collaborate and formulate partnerships with law enforcement, medical and mental health providers, immigration attorneys, and local ethnic community leaders to work together in coordinated and participative manners to provide support and protection services for the victims of trafficking in persons. The ultimate goal of providing support and protection to the victims should be driven by the best interests of the victims.[15] Victims of trafficking in persons have unique needs and may require an enormous range of services. The United Nations High Commissioner for Human Rights suggests some guidelines and principles for the physical, psychological, and emotional recovery of trafficking victims.[16]

International and the United States' Responses to the Victims and Survivors

Trafficking in Persons Protocol proposes that states of origin and of destination should consider implementing measures to provide for the physical, psychological and social recovery of trafficked victims. The protocol suggests that state governments should collaborate with non-governmental organizations and provide support in the areas of medical care; counseling and psychological care; interpretation, language, and translation; rehabilitation; skill training; education; and shelter. Pursuant to the protocol's proposal, the international community endeavors to provide support and assistance to the victims. Efforts made and services provided by the state vary by the state laws and political and social ideologies as well as resources available to the states. Here we discuss the United States' response to the victims. This section provides an overview of services and protections provided to the victims and survivors in various sectors.

The Trafficking Victims Protection Act of 2000 (TVPA) authorizes the United States Department of Health and Human Services to certify foreign victims of a severe form of trafficking in persons, making these individuals eligible for federally funded benefits and services to the same extent as refugees. Victims of human trafficking are subjected to force, fraud, or coercion for the purpose of commercial sex or labor. Victims can be young children, teenagers, men, and women.[17] Pursuant to the Trafficking Victims Protection Act of 2000, the United States provides support and protection to the international trafficking victims in a variety of spheres—including through financial, medical, housing, and legal assistance. In addition to the protection and support provided by the federal programs, there are also state programs that provide and supplement the federal programs. There are also various community organizations and non-governmental organizations that offer services and protections to the victims.

Federal Programs to Provide Support and Protection for the Victims

Following the provisions set forth in the Trafficking Victims Protection Act (TVPA), the United States federal government and all fifty states passed new laws that criminalize human trafficking and support the identification and prosecution of human trafficking perpetrators.[18] In order to facilitate recovery of the victims of trafficking in persons, the U.S. federal government has passed many laws, developed several federal programs, made federal funds available, and created several agencies.

Department of Health and Human Services

The U.S. federal government offers several Health and Human Services Grants. The U.S. Committee for Refugees and Immigrants (U.S.CRI) and other federal agencies provide grants to facilitate provision of comprehensive case management services to current and potential victims of trafficking seeking HHS certification in any location in the United States. Through a network of nongovernmental service organizations, sub-awardees assist victims of trafficking to become certified and be eligible for other necessary services after "certification." The agencies receiving grants ensure the provision of efficient, high-quality services to victims of human trafficking. They help victims of human trafficking apply for and receive housing, legal assistance, medical and other necessary services, and job training. They also provide assistance and services to ensure a life free of violence and exploitation.

The **National Human Trafficking Resource Center** (NHTRC) is a national, toll-free hotline for the human trafficking field in the United States. The center is operational 24 hours a day, seven days a week, every day of the year. This center provides comprehensive services to the victims. Some examples of these services include crisis intervention, urgent and non-urgent referrals, tip reporting, and comprehensive anti-trafficking resources and technical assistance. The center also works to improve the national response to protect victims of human trafficking in the United States from further exploitation and violence. The center works to raise awareness and connect community members with service providers and law enforcement personnel to identify and create a coordinated response to human trafficking in their local areas. The NHTRC functions as a national database of organizations and individuals working in the anti-trafficking field, as well as a library of available anti-trafficking resources and materials. It serves as a clearinghouse to maintain and disseminate educational and awareness materials, and online trainings.[19]

The United States Department of Justice's (U.S.DOJ) **Office for Victims of Crime** (OVC) provides services such as housing or shelter; food; medical, mental health, and dental services; interpreter/translator services; criminal justice victim advocacy; legal services; social services advocacy; literacy education; and/or employment assistance to the trafficking victims. OVC also maintains an online directory of crime victim services that identifies local organizations providing services for crime victims.[20]

In addition to the federal agencies providing services to the victims, there are also state and other community agencies that respond to the needs of the victims of human trafficking. Below is the discussion of community programs and resources available for the victims of trafficking in persons.

Community Programs and Resources for the Victims of Trafficking

Community Resources: Every state maintains service programs that are made available to the victims of human trafficking. Some of these programs are state funded and others are funded privately. The state service providing agencies as well as non-governmental organizations (NGOs) have access to these resources to assist the victims of trafficking in persons. Following are the types of community resources available to the victims of trafficking in persons.

Food: Victims of trafficking can receive food through food pantries; soup kitchens; faith-based food programs; and supermarkets/restaurants/bakeries providing day-old, slightly damaged, or leftover food items to charitable organizations.

Shelter: Victims of trafficking are eligible for a place to stay. They can seek temporary shelter in domestic violence/women's shelters; runaway and homeless youth shelters; transitional housing programs; shelters for undocumented immigrants (usually for men); and faith-based housing programs, such as the Catholic Worker Movement that provides housing opportunities in many U.S. communities. Some faith-based organizations also provide rent money or identify church members who can offer temporary housing or offer temporary shelter in seminaries, convents, or school dorms. Children who are victims of trafficking can be housed in state foster homes. Other state or local housing and community development agencies also maintain lists of affordable housing projects and nonprofit organizations. These resources can be accessed and utilized to provide shelter and housing to the victims of trafficking.

Clothing and Goods: Most often, victims of trafficking also need clothing and other necessary items to live normally. Local chapters of national organizations—such as Goodwill, Salvation Army, St. Vincent de Paul, and AMVETS Thrift Stores—can provide clothing and goods to the victims. Additionally, many nonprofit organizations such as operating thrift stores offer free clothing giveaways and professional clothing donation services, such as local Dress for Success affiliates, and are often available. Locally operated, privately funded, and charity programs can be found through Internet search engines. Some churches, schools, universities, and hospitals operate clothing drives/clothing banks. Refugee resettlement agencies provide donated goods and yard sales are excellent sources for inexpensive used clothing and household goods. Many department stores also give away damaged and out-of-season clothing to charitable organizations. Community dry cleaners may operate as clothing donation drop-off sites and some hotels also donate old furniture when renovating or they may be willing to provide shampoo and other toiletries. Sexual assault crisis center clothing collections are another resource. Churches, businesses, and civic organizations may be willing to donate gift cards for grocery stores or discount department stores.

Medical: Victims of trafficking go through a tumultuous time during victimization, and they may suffer from physical and mental health problems. They generally need medical and mental health services. Community health centers, migrant health clinics, city clinics, homeless clinics, free clinics at universities or in communities, health fairs at community hospitals (for preventive services), county mental health clinics, health programs operated out of NGOs, substance abuse services, and maternal and child health programs can be accessed and victims can receive needed medical, mental health, and drug rehabilitative services.

Legal: Victims of trafficking often need legal services to understand their status and rights in the destination country. They need legal advice in understanding their plight, filling forms to receive services, obtaining their identification and travel documents, etc. Local legal aid clinics/agencies/foundations, law school clinics, pro bono services offered by law firms, and employment law centers can be accessed by the victims. The community organizations and NGOs can connect victims with other community-based legal service providers including those serving particular ethnic communities, immigration rights clinics, nonprofit organizations providing legal assistance to immigrants, and faith-based immigration relief organizations, such as the Catholic Legal Immigrant Network, Inc. (CLINIC). These organizations can be accessed to receive legal support services.

Job Training Programs: Community organizations also offer job training programs for the victims. Local affiliates of Goodwill Industries offer job training programs and Career-One-Stop lists local contacts for apprenticeships and employment assistance. Community organizations and some community colleges and immigrant or refugee assistance organizations also offer vocational training and job placement assistance to the victims.

Education Services: Victims are also provided educational services. Many local adult education centers, immigrant community organizations, and neighborhood community centers offer GED assistance and general educational assistance programs. Local churches, schools, libraries, and community colleges offer ESL (English as a second language) classes to the victims. Local community resource centers also offer translation/interpreting services (both as written/ live language assistance and native tongue literacy).

Transportation: Some local programs offer lower fares for public transportation to clients enrolled in education programs. Some churches and other charitable organizations also offer voluntary driver programs offering free transportation to the victims.

Crime Victim Compensation: Some city or county level community programs offer victims compensation for relocation and other expenses.

After Care for the Victims of Trafficking in Humans

Under the provisions provided by the TVPA, victims of severe forms of trafficking who are also potential witnesses are granted Continued Presence (CP) by the Department of Homeland Security's Immigration and Customs Enforcement (ICE). Continued Presence (CP), is a one-year form of immigration relief that federal law enforcement officials request on behalf of the victim. Continued Presence allows the victim to remain in the United States during the course of an investigation or prosecution as well as obtain an Employment Authorization Document (EAD), which provides the victim with the documentation required to work legally in the United States.

Victims of severe forms of trafficking who are also potential witnesses, can also apply for a non-immigrant visa (T visa), also called the U.S. Citizen and Immigration Services Form I-914. Under this visa, a foreign victim of human trafficking is granted up to four years of stay in the United States. The victim must apply directly to DHS for non-immigrant status by filing an application for a T visa.

Victims of trafficking needing Continued Presence (CP) and T visa may not understand the forms and application process. To assist them with the process of completing the application, they are provided assistance from an immigration attorney or other legal service provider. National Human Trafficking Resource Center and/or local service providers listed in the OVC online directory with experience in working with trafficking victims can assist victims in completing the application, obtaining the visa, and acquiring other legal assistance as needed.[21]

As described in the U.S. Department of Homeland Security's Instructions for Completing Form I-914, a federal law enforcement officer endorsement is strongly advised. If a victim does not submit a federal law enforcement endorsement as a part of his or her T visa application, then the victim must submit an explanation describing attempts to obtain the endorsement and accounting for the lack of or unavailability of the endorsement. Alternately, the victim must submit an explanation describing why he or she did not attempt to obtain the federal law enforcement endorsement. There are several benefits to a T visa, including: legal non-immigrant status in the United States for a period of four years; employment authorization; the possibility of adjusting status to Lawful Permanent Resident; and immediate family members may obtain non-immigrant status as T visa derivatives.

Another type of visa available to the victims is U visa. The U visa is valid for up to four years. It is not specific to trafficking cases, but is available to victims of a number of crimes, including trafficking. It is available to immigrants who: (a) are victims of a violation of federal, state, or local criminal laws against rape, torture, trafficking, incest, domestic violence, sexual assault, abusive sexual contact, prostitution, sexual exploitation, female genital mutilation, being held hostage, peonage, involuntary servitude, slave trade, kidnapping, obstruction of justice, abduction, unlawful criminal restraint, false imprisonment, blackmail, murder, extortion, manslaughter, felonious assault, witness tampering, perjury or attempt, conspiracy, or solicitation to commit any of the above crimes; (b) have suffered severe physical or mental abuse as a result; and (c) have been helpful, are being helpful, or are likely to be helpful in the investigation or prosecution of the criminal activity.

Victims with a U visa can receive a work permit but they are not eligible for publicly funded programs for which T visa recipients are eligible. Both T and U visa recipients may eventually adjust to lawful permanent resident status and citizenship if they qualify.[22]

However, when the victims are from across the border and do not have any legal status in the destination country, they may need immediate legal assistance/representation to handle issues related to immigration status, documents to return back to their homes, legal representation that may be required in an ongoing investigation and prosecution of the trafficking case, or counsel in a civil lawsuit against the trafficker or in a potential custody case.[23]

To control and prevent the perpetuation of trafficking in persons, the traffickers need to be apprehended, prosecuted, and sentenced. To successfully prosecute and punish the traffickers, states need the victims to testify—in most cases, victims are the only witnesses of the crime and they may not be willing to cooperate due to the intimidating threats by traffickers. In order to succeed in prosecution, the states should not only encourage but also facilitate trafficking victims' participation in the criminal proceedings against the trafficker. The states should make provisions for providing support and protection to the victims and encourage them to participate in the judicial process through direct and indirect means.

Conclusion

Despite the Trafficking Protocol, the Transnational Crime Convention, and the adoption of several international and national laws, protocols, conventions, and policies to punish the perpetrators and to protect the rights of trafficked persons, there is still a tremendous need to address the aftermath of the crime of trafficking in persons. Victims suffer in various spheres—including physical, mental, psychological, social, and moral. Several entities (national and international) must cooperate to facilitate victims' recuperation and restoration to the mainstream society. The national and international entities need to ensure uniform implementation of the law and provide clear guidelines. In addition to the awareness and educational campaigns, providing services and protections to the victims, restore their full identity should be the priority.

Chapter Review

In this chapter, we have discussed the needs of the victims of human trafficking. We have discussed some of the laws and available services and protections provided to the victims. In essence, we discussed the following:

Protections for the Victims

- Protection, Support, and After Care of the Victims of Trafficking
  - Trafficking in Person Protocol: The Requirement for Victims' Protection and Support
  - Trafficking in Persons Protocol: The Requirement for the Provision of Physical, Psychological, and Social Recovery of Victims
- Comprehensive, Coordinated, and Integrated Response: Support and Protection to the Victims
- International and the United States' Response to the Victims and Survivors
- Federal Programs to Provide Support and Protection for the Victims
- Community Programs and Resources for the Victims of Trafficking
- After Care of the Victims of Trafficking in Humans

Discussion Questions

1) List at least three aspects in which aftermath of trafficking is manifested in victims. Give examples.

2) Identify reasons why the victims of trafficking may not report the crime or accept any services.

3) Find out what community resources exist in your community. List at least three organizations that cater to the needs of the trafficking victims in your neighborhood.

4) What legal remedies are available to the trafficking victims? List at least three.

5) Identify the type of services needed to address the aftermath of trafficking in persons. Give reasons why these services are essential.

References

Bales, Kevin. "Slavery and the Human Right to Evil." *Journal of Human Rights* 3, no. 1 (2004): 53–63.

Bales, Kevin, & Steven Lize. "Trafficking in Persons in the United States." National Institute of Justice. Washington, DC: Government Printing Office, 2004.

Bruckert, Chris, Colette Parent, and Royal Canadian Mounted Police. *Trafficking in Human Beings and Organized Crime: A Literature Review*. Research and Evaluation Branch, Community, Contract and Aboriginal Policing Services Directorate, Royal Canadian Mounted Police, 2002.

Caliber Associates. *Evaluation of Comprehensive Service for Victims of Trafficking: Key Findings and Lessons Learned*. Final report submitted to the National Institute of Justice, U.S. Department of Justice, 2007.

Clawson, Heather J., K. M. J. D. Small, Ellen S. Go, and Bradley W. Myles. "Needs Assessment for Service Providers and Trafficking Victims." Fairfax, VA: Caliber, 2003.

Clawson, Heather J., and Mary Layne. *Estimating Human Trafficking into the United States: Development of a Methodology: Final Phase Two Report*. Fairfax, VA: ICF International, 2007.

Clawson, Heather J., and Nicole Dutch. "Addressing the Needs of Victims of Human Trafficking: Challenges, Barriers, and Promising Practices." Department of Health and Human Services, Office of the Assistant Secretary for Planning and Evaluation, 2008.

Clawson, Heather J., Nicole Dutch, Amy Solomon, and L. Goldblatt Grace. "Human Trafficking into and within the United States: A Review of the Literature." Washington, DC: Office of the Assistant Secretary for Planning and Evaluation, U.S. Department of Health and Human Services, 2009.

De Jong, Joop T. V. M., Ivan H. Komproe, Mark Van Ommeren, Mustafa El Masri, Mesfin Araya, Noureddine Khaled, Willem van De Put, and Daya Somasundaram. "Lifetime Events and Posttraumatic Stress Disorder in 4 Postconflict Settings." *Journal of the American Medical Association (Jama)* 286, no. 5 (2001): 555–562.

Europol. Legislation on Trafficking in Human Beings and Illegal Immigrant Smuggling. Europol Public Information, 2005.

Farrell, Amy, Monica J. DeLateur, Colleen Owens, and Stephanie Fahy. "The Prosecution of State-Level Human Trafficking Cases in the United States." *Anti-Trafficking Review* 6 (2016).

Florida Coalition against Domestic Violence. *Domestic & Sexual Violence Advocate Handbook on Human Trafficking*. 2004.

Florida Coalition against Domestic Violence. "Florida Coalition Against Domestic Violence." 2002.

Florida University Center for the Advancement of Human Rights. *Florida Responds to Trafficking*. 2003. http://www.cahr.fsu.edu/the%20report.pdf

Richard, Amy O. "International Trafficking in Women to the United States: A Contemporary Manifestation of Slavery and Organized Crime." Washington, DC: Bureau of Intelligence and Research, 1999.

Ryan, Angela Shen. "Lessons Learned from Programs for Unaccompanied Refugee Minors." *Journal of Multicultural Social Work* 5, no. 3–4 (1997): 195–205.

Shrestha, Nirakar Man, Bhogendra Sharma, Mark Van Ommeren, Shyam Regmi, Ramesh Makaju, Ivan Komproe, Ganesh B. Shrestha, and Joop T. V. M. de Jong. "Impact of Torture on Refugees Displaced within the Developing World: Symptomatology among Bhutanese Refugees in Nepal." *Journal of the American Medical Association (Jama)* 280, no. 5 (1998): 443–448.

United Nations General Assembly. Declaration of Basic Principles of Justice for Victims of Crime and Abuse of Power. A/RES/40/34, 29 November 1985.

United Nations General Assembly. Protocol to Prevent, Suppress and Punish Trafficking in Persons Especially Women and Children, supplementing the United Nations Convention against Transnational Organized Crime. Resolution 55/25. 15 November 2000.

United Nations General Assembly. Report of the United Nations the High Commissioner for Human Rights. Sixty-Fifth Session, Supplement No. 36, A/65/36. New York: United Nations, 2010.

United Nations Office on Drugs and Crime (UNODC), and Global Programme Against Trafficking in Human Beings. *Toolkit to Combat Trafficking in Persons*. United Nations Publications, 2008.

United Nations Secretariat. United Nations Convention against Transnational Organized Crime and the Protocols Thereto. 2005.

United States Congress. "Victims of Trafficking and Violence Protection Act of 2000." Public Law 106 (2000): 386. Florida Immigrant Advocacy Center. http://www.fiacfla.org/.

United States Government Accounting Office (U.S.GAO). *Human Trafficking: Better Data, Strategy, and Reporting Needed to Enhance U.S. Anti-trafficking Efforts Abroad*. GAO-06-825: Published: Jul 18, 2006. Publicly Released: Aug 14, 2006. http://www.gao.gov/products/GAO-06-825.

Further Suggested Readings

Anderson, B., & Andrijasevic, R. (2008). Sex, slaves and citizens: the politics of anti-trafficking. *Soundings*, (40), 135.

Barone, T. (2003). Trafficking Victims Protection Act of 2000: Defining the Problem and Creating a Solution, The. *Temp. Int'l & Comp. LJ*, *17*, 579.

Brennan, D. (2008). Competing claims of victimhood? Foreign and domestic victims of trafficking in the United States. *Sexuality Research & Social Policy*, *5*(4), 45–61.

Chacón, J. M. (2010). Tensions and trade-offs: Protecting trafficking victims in the era of immigration enforcement. *University of Pennsylvania Law Review*, *158*(6), 1609–1653.

Chapkis, W. (2003). Trafficking, migration, and the law protecting innocents, punishing immigrants. *Gender & Society*, *17*(6), 923–937.

Cooper, B. (2002). New Approach to Protection and Law Enforcement under the Victims of Trafficking and Violence Protection Act, A. *Emory LJ*, *51*, 1041.

Davidson, J. O. C. (2006). Will the real sex slave please stand up?. *Feminist review*, *83*(1), 4–22.

Dalrymple, J. K. (2005). HUMAN TRAFFICKING: PROTECTING HUMAN RIGHTS IN THE TRAFFICKING VICTIMS PROTECTION ACT: HUMAN TRAFFIC: SEX, SLAVES & IMMIGRATION. By Craig McGill. *BC Third World LJ*, *25*, 451–499.

Doezema, J. (1999). Loose women or lost women? The re-emergence of the myth of white slavery in contemporary discourses of trafficking in women. *Gender issues*, *18*(1), 23–50.

Doezema, J. (2002). Who gets to choose? Coercion, consent, and the UN Trafficking Protocol. *Gender & Development*, *10*(1), 20–27.

Fitzpatrick, J. (2002). Trafficking and a human rights violation: The complex intersection of legal frameworks for conceptualizing and combating trafficking. *Mich. J. Int'l L.*, *24*, 1143.

Fitzgibbon, K. (2003). Modern-day slavery? The scope of trafficking in persons in Africa. *African Security Studies*, *12*(1), 81–89.

Gallagher, A. (2001). Human rights and the new UN protocols on trafficking and migrant smuggling: A preliminary analysis. *Human Rights Quarterly*, *23*(4), 975–1004.

Gallagher, A. M. (2004). Triply Exploited: Female Victims of Trafficking Networks-Strategies for Pursuing Protection and Legal Status in Countries of Destination. *Geo. Immigr. LJ*, *19*, 99.

Haynes, D. F. (2006). (Not) Found Chained to a Bed in a Brothel: Conceptual, Legal, and Procedural Failures to Fullfill the Promise of the Trafficking Victims Protection Act. *Geo. Immigr. LJ*, *21*, 337.

Holman, M. (2008). Modern-Day Slave Trade: How the United States Should Alter the Victims of Trafficking and Violence Protection Act in Order to Combat International Sex Trafficking, More Effectively, The. *Tex. Int'l LJ*, *44*, 99.

Hyland, K. E. (2001). The impact of the protocol to prevent, suppress and punish trafficking in persons, especially women and children. *Human Rights Brief*, *8*(2), 12.

Hyland, K. E. (2001). Protecting human victims of trafficking: An American framework. *Berkeley Women's LJ*, *16*, 29.

Jordan, A. D. (2002). Human rights or wrongs? The struggle for a rights-based response to trafficking in human beings. *Gender & Development*, *10*(1), 28–37.

Kandathil, R. (2005). Global sex trafficking and the Trafficking Victims Protection Act of 2000: Legislative responses to the problem of modern slavery. *Mich. J. Gender & L.*, *12*, 87.

Kim, K., & Hreshchyshyn, K. (2004). Human trafficking private right of action: Civil rights for trafficked persons in the United States. *Hastings Women's LJ*, *16*, 1.

Patel, A. (2010). Back to the drawing board: rethinking protections available to victims of trafficking. *Seattle J. Soc. Just.*, *9*, 813.

Pearson, E. (2002). Half-hearted protection: what does victim protection really mean for victims of trafficking in Europe? *Gender & Development*, *10*(1), 56–59.

Piotrowicz, R. (2002). European initiatives in the protection of victims of trafficking who give evidence against their traffickers. *International Journal of Refugee Law*, *14*(2 and 3), 263–278.

Potts Jr, L. G. (2003). Global trafficking in human beings: assessing the success of the United Nations Protocol to Prevent Trafficking in Persons. *Geo. Wash. Int'l L. Rev.*, *35*, 227.

Reauthorization, V. P. (2008). William Wilberforce Trafficking Victims Protection Reauthorization Act of 2008. *Public law*, *110*, 457.

Raymond, J. G. (2002, October). The new UN trafficking protocol. In *Women's studies international forum* (Vol. 25, No. 5, pp. 491–502). Pergamon.

Riegler, A. (2007). Missing the mark: Why the Trafficking Victims Protection Act fails to protect sex trafficking victims in the United States. *Harv. JL & Gender*, *30*, 231.

Ryf, K. C. (2002). First Modern Anti-Slavery Law: The Trafficking Victims Protection Act of 2000, The. *Case W. Res. J. Int'l L., 34*, 45.

Sadruddin, H., Walter, N., & Hidalgo, J. (2005). Human trafficking in the United States: expanding victim protection beyond prosecution witnesses. *Stan. L. & Pol'y Rev., 16*, 379.

Sangalis, T. R. (2011). Elusive empowerment: Compensating the sex trafficked person under the trafficking victims protection act. *Fordham L. Rev., 80*, 403.

Sanghera, J. (2005). Unpacking the trafficking discourse. *Trafficking and prostitution reconsidered: New perspectives on migration, sex work, and human rights, 3*, 14.

Sharma, N. (2005). Anti-trafficking rhetoric and the making of a global apartheid. *NWSA Journal, 17*(3), 88–111.

Stolz, B. (2005). Educating policymakers and setting the criminal justice policymaking agenda Interest groups and the 'Victims of Trafficking and Violence Act of 2000'. *Criminal Justice, 5*(4), 407–430.

Tiefenbrum, S. (2002). Saga of Susannah—A U.S. Remedy for Sex Trafficking in Women: The Victims of Trafficking and Violence Protection Act of 2000, The. *Utah L. Rev.*, 107.

Tiefenbrun, S. W. (2006). Updating the domestic and international impact of the U.S. Victims of Trafficking Protection Act of 2000: Does law deter crime. *Case W. Res. J. Int'l L., 38*, 249.

Van Impe, K. (2000). People for sale: The need for a multidisciplinary approach towards human trafficking. *International Migration, 38*(3), 113–191.

Weitzer, R. (2007). The social construction of sex trafficking: Ideology and institutionalization of a moral crusade. *Politics & Society, 35*(3), 447–475.

Notes

1. This endnote has two references:
   1) Europol. (2005). Legislation on trafficking in human beings and illegal immigrant smuggling. Europol Public Information.
   2) Miko, F. T., & G. Park. (2001). Trafficking in women and children: The U.S. and international response—Updated August 1, 2001. *Federal Publications*, 55.
2. Richard, A. (1999). International trafficking in women to the United States: A contemporary manifestation of slavery and organized crime. The Center for the Study of Intelligence.
3. Pearson, E. (2002). *Human traffic, human rights: Redefining victim protection*. Anti-Slavery International.
4. This endnote has two references:

1) Caliber Associates. (2007). *Evaluation of comprehensive service for victims of trafficking: Key findings and lessons learned.* Final report submitted to the National Institute of Justice. U.S. Department of Justice.

2) Clawson, H., Layne, M., & Small, K. (2006). Estimating human trafficking into the United States: Development of a methodology. Washington, DC: National Institute of Justice.

5. Clawson, H., Small, K., Go, E., & Myles, B. (2004). Needs assessment for service providers and trafficking victims. National Institute of Justice, Washington, DC: Government Printing Office. Clawson, H., Layne, M., & Small, K. (2006). Estimating human trafficking into the United States: Development of a methodology. Washington, DC: National Institute of Justice.

6. For more detailed discussion of these symptoms, see: De Jong, J. T. V. M., Komproe, I. H., Van Ommeren, M., Masri, M.E., Araya, M., Khaled, N., van de Put, W., & Somasundaram, D. (2001). Lifetime events and posttraumatic stress disorder in four post conflict settings. *Journal of the American Medical Association, 286*, 555–562; and Shrestha, N. M., Sharma, B., Van Ommeren, M., Regmi, S., Makaju, R., Kompro, et al. (1998). Impact of torture on refugees displaced within the developing world: Symptomatology among Bhutanese refugees in Nepal. *Journal of the American Medical Association, 280*(5), 443–448.

7. This endnote has two references:

1) Bales, K. (2004). Slavery and the human right to evil. *Journal of Human Rights, 3*(1), 53–63.

2) Caliber Associates. (2007). *Evaluation of comprehensive service for victims of trafficking: Key findings and lessons learned.* Final report submitted to the National Institute of Justice, U.S. Department of Justice.

8. Shen Ryan, A. (1997). Lessons learned from programs for unaccompanied refugee minors. *Journal of Multicultural Social Work, 5*(3–4), 195–205.

9. Protocol to Prevent, Suppress and Punish Trafficking in Persons Especially Women and Children, supplementing the United Nations Convention against Transnational Organized Crime. (2000, November 15). Adopted and opened for signature, ratification and accession by General Assembly Resolution 55/25.

10. UN General Assembly. (1985). Declaration of basic principles of justice for victims of crime and abuse of power. UNGA Resolution 40, 34.

11. Report of the United Nations the High Commissioner for Human Rights. (2010). General Assembly, Sixty-Fifth Session, Supplement No. 36. New York: United Nations.

12. Protocol to Prevent, Suppress and Punish Trafficking in Persons Especially Women and Children, supplementing the United Nations Convention against Transnational Organized Crime (2000, November 15). Adopted and opened for signature, ratification and accession by General Assembly Resolution 55/25.

13. United Nations Office on Drugs and Crime (UNODC) and Global Programme Against Trafficking in Human Beings. (2008). *Toolkit to Combat Trafficking in persons.* United Nations Publications.

14. United Nations Office on Drugs and Crime (UNODC) and Global Programme Against Trafficking in Human Beings. (2008). *Toolkit to Combat Trafficking in persons.* United Nations Publications.

15. Florida Coalition Against Domestic Violence. (2002). https://www.fcadv.org/.

16. Report of the United Nations the High Commissioner for Human Rights (2010). General Assembly, Sixty-Fifth Session, Supplement No. 36. New York: United Nations.

17. U.S. Code. (2000). Victims of trafficking and violence protection act of 2000. Public Law 106, 386.

18. Farrell, A., M. J. DeLateur, C. Owens, & S. Fahy. (2016). The prosecution of state-level human trafficking cases in the United States. *Anti-Trafficking Review*, 6.

19. The National Human Trafficking Resource Center (NHTRC) "is a national anti-trafficking hotline [and resource center] serving victims and survivors of human trafficking and the anti-trafficking community in the United States. The toll-free hotline is available to answer calls from anywhere in the country, 24 hours a day, 7 days a week, every day of the year in more than 200 languages. The [NHTRC] can also be accessed by emailing nhtrc@polarisproject.org, submitting a tip through the online tip reporting form, and visiting the web portal at www.traffickingresourcecenter.org. [The NHTRC provides] human trafficking victims and survivors with access to critical support and services to get help and stay safe, and to equip the anti-trafficking community with the tools to effectively combat all forms of human trafficking. [The NHTRC offers] round-the-clock access to a safe space to report tips, seek services, and ask for help." "The NHTRC provides innovative anti-trafficking trainings, technical assistance, and capacity building support." "The [NHTRC] has been in operation since December 7th, 2007, by Polaris, a nonprofit, non-governmental organization that is a leader in the global fight to eradicate modern slavery and restore freedom to survivors of human trafficking. [It is] not a government entity, law enforcement, or immigration. Funding is provided by the Department of Health and Human Services (HHS) and other private donors and supporters." https://traffickingresourcecenter.org/mission; https://humantraffickinghotline.org/sites/default/files/NHTRC%20AAG%202015.pdf.

20. "The Office for Victims of Crime Resource Center (OVCRC) is part of the National Criminal Justice Reference Service (NCJRS), a federally sponsored information clearinghouse that provides information on crime, victim assistance, substance abuse, and public safety to support research, policy, and program development worldwide." http://www.ovc.gov/.

21. http://ovc.ncjrs.gov/findvictimservices/.

22. "U.S.CIS helps protect victims of human trafficking and other crimes by providing immigration relief. Human trafficking, also known as trafficking in persons, is a form of modern-day slavery in which traffickers lure individuals with false promises of employment and a better life. Individuals and their families may also fall victim to many other types of crime in the United States. These crimes include: rape, murder, manslaughter, domestic violence, sexual assault, and many others. There are two types of immigration relief we provide to victims of human trafficking and other crimes: T Nonimmigrant Status (T visa)—T nonimmigrant status provides immigration protection to victims of trafficking. The T visa allows victims to remain in the United States and assist law enforcement authorities in the investigation or prosecution of human trafficking cases. U Nonimmigrant Status (U visa)—U nonimmigrant status provides immigration protection to crime victims who have suffered substantial mental or physical abuse as a result of the crime. The U visa allows victims to remain in the United States and assist law enforcement authorities in the investigation or prosecution of the criminal activity." https://www.uscis.gov/humanitarian/victims-human-trafficking-other-crimes.

23. This endnote has two references:

1) Caliber Associates. (2007). *Evaluation of comprehensive service for victims of trafficking: Key findings and lessons learned*. Final report submitted to the National Institute of Justice. U.S. Department of Justice.

2) Florida University Center for the Advancement of Human Rights. (2003). *Florida responds to trafficking.* http://www.cahr.fsu.edu/the%20report.pdf.

Chapter 10

Future Directions: Current State and Future of Trafficking in Persons

Chapter Objectives

This chapter discusses:

- The Current State and Future of Trafficking in Persons
    - Definitional Controversy
- Where Does It Happen? International as well as Domestic
- Who Are the Victims of Trafficking in Persons?
- The Trafficking Process: How It Happens
- Estimates of Trafficking in Persons: Prevalence and Incidence
    - Who Are the Traffickers?
- Effects of Human Trafficking and Needs of Victims
    - Anti-Trafficking Efforts
    - Future of Human Trafficking

The Current State and Future of Trafficking in Persons

Preceding chapters examined various aspects of trafficking in persons as a crime such as its nature and extent; historical, local, and global perspectives; differences and similarities between human trafficking and similar crimes;

various forms of trafficking; and human trafficking as a form of human trade and exploitation for the purpose of commercializing humans for labor, sex, organs, and other profit-producing practices. The preceding chapters also discussed conceptual frameworks, international and United States' efforts, international and domestic laws, effectiveness of laws, and use of technology in human trafficking, as well as criminal justice approaches to human trafficking, legal protections for victims, and penalties for the perpetrators.

The nucleus of this chapter is to depict the current state of our understanding of trafficking at a domestic and international level, trends, and its aftermath. The discussion focuses on the state of general understanding of trafficking and its precursors and emergent environments and conditions that allow its conception, manifestation, and perpetuation despite international and domestic endeavors to curb its proliferation.

Current State of Trafficking

Based on the extant literature, laws, reports, and discussions presented in the preceding chapters, certain assumptions can be made regarding the current state of developments in the area of trafficking in persons. This chapter summarizes these improvements as well as areas that need further examination and future challenges to address this crime.

Since the Palermo Protocol and the Trafficking Victims Protection Act became effective, a tremendous amount of attention has been directed towards understanding this crime. Subsequently, several efforts have been made to curb its progression. These efforts have been in the form of raising public awareness, providing education and training to the first line responders—such as law enforcement officers at all levels, attorneys, and court personnel—new laws and policies or revising existing ones to address this crime, prosecuting the offenders, and providing support to the victims. Efforts have also been made in making public and private funds available for public awareness campaigns, research, training, and education. Some of these efforts include anti-trafficking campaigns through government and non-governmental organizations. All these efforts have one goal: to address this multifaceted problem of trafficking in persons that keeps morphing itself and re-emerging in one form or another. These endeavors have concentrated on creating a general understanding of what is "trafficking" and how it is different from other similar acts. Often it is confused with other acts that are closely associated with trafficking such as smuggling, illegal immigration, prostitution, and sex crimes. Such awareness campaigns have led to a great deal of media campaigns, anti-trafficking activism, and involvement of governments at a national as well as international level. In addition to the Palermo Protocol from the United Nations and the United States Trafficking Victims Protection Act in 2000, most countries have created new policies, laws, and enforcement mechanisms to address trafficking in persons. Accordingly, literature on trafficking has burgeoned, leading to some remarkable accomplishments in our understanding of trafficking in persons as a crime. Below is the discussion of some of these accomplishments and improvements as well as efforts to address this multifaceted problem.

Uniform Definition

The first and one of the most important accomplishments is a legal definition of trafficking in persons that is universally accepted. Prior to the adoption of the United Nations Trafficking Protocol and of the United States Trafficking Victims Protection Act (TVPA), there was no uniform definition. The field had been strewn with inconsistencies and disagreements regarding the definition of human trafficking among politicians, practitioners, and scholars.[1] Trafficking in persons (TIP) was conceptualized, described, and understood differently by different organizations and entities. It was interpreted differently and interchangeably used with terms such as "slavery," "modern slavery," "illegal migration," "smuggling," "under-age prostitution of foreigners," "facilitated irregular migration," "sex-slavery," "servitude," and "child labor" among others. Such an interchange of different terms made it difficult to address this problem and created an almost unsurmountable challenge in estimating how much of this crime exists, how injurious it is to the social fabric, and how to address it. Each organization and entity involved in addressing this problem estimated its magnitude based on the definition used to identify it. Consequently, estimates varied from a handful of victims to several thousands, from economic loss of a few thousands to billions of dollars. Several other assertions regarding the extent and manifestation of this crime were made, based on the definitions that no two organizations agreed upon. Such an array of affairs confounded the manner in which victims, perpetrators, and communities understood this crime. It also affected the manner in which media propagated it and policy makers addressed it.

In 2000, the United Nations Organization developed and agreed to a definition for trafficking in persons. This came to be known as United Nations or Palermo Protocol. Approximately at the same time, the U.S. Congress also defined human trafficking by passing the Trafficking Victims Protection Act of 2000 (TVPA). Since the ratification of the UN Protocol and TVPA, there is a legal definition that is accepted as a standard definition. This definition identifies what activities can be classified as trafficking. Trafficking in Persons Protocol (Article 3) provided a uniformity in describing the phenomenon of trafficking in persons. Article 3, paragraph (a) of the Protocol to Prevent, Suppress and Punish Trafficking in Persons emphasized that when the recruitment, transportation, transfer, harboring, or receipt of persons is coupled with the threat or use of force, coercion, fraud, or deception as means of achieving consent of the affected person, then that act becomes an act of trafficking. The emphasis is on the "threat or use of force, coercion, fraud, or deception" as means of achieving consent. This definition provided basic elements essential to distinguish it from other crimes that may look and sound similar such as smuggling and illegal immigration, but are fundamentally different. It demonstrated that trafficking is a process and provided a clear and consistent overview of elements that must be present to consider it a crime. According to this definition, the elements of human trafficking include act, means, and purpose, where act refers to the "recruitment, transportation, transfer, harboring or receipt of persons," means refers to "use of force, coercion, fraud, or deception" and purpose refers to "for the purpose of exploitation." The definition provided a clear distinction of the acts that are trafficking acts. The Trafficking in Persons (TIP) Protocol also provided guidance on the acts that should be criminalized as trafficking. According to Article 5 of Trafficking in Persons Protocol, the conduct set out in Article 3 to be criminalized in domestic legislation includes "attempts to commit a trafficking offense," "participation as an accomplice in such an offense," and "organizing or directing others to commit trafficking." The article also defined "exploitation" and explicated that exploitative acts are not limited to sexual exploitation but inclusive of "forced labor or services, slavery or practices similar to slavery, servitude or the removal of organs." This transformed our understanding of trafficking which for a long time had only been perceived and propagated in terms of sexual exploitation of young girls and women transported to rich countries from poor countries. No attention was paid to other victims or other forms of exploitation.

Where Does It Happen? International as Well as Domestic

The extant literature demonstrates that, contrary to common misperceptions, it is a crime that has penetrated almost every corner of the world in one form or another. Almost all countries participate in perpetuation of this crime. Some countries are the origin, others are the destination, while others are the countries that serve as interim place holders when the victims are in transit. Regardless of their role served, as origin, destination, or place holder, all countries consume goods and services shaped, produced, or manufactured by the victims of trafficking in persons. Thus, everyone participates in its conception, manifestation, and perpetuation, making it more challenging to effectively address. Both the perpetrators and victims of this crime can be located in almost all countries of the world.[2,3] Often the crime of "trafficking in persons" has been associated with transnational criminal organizations, small criminal networks and local gangs, violations of labor and immigration codes, and government corruption.[4]

Who Are the Victims of Trafficking in Persons?

As discussed throughout the book in various chapters, our understanding regarding the act of trafficking as a crime has considerably increased during the last 20 years. We now understand and address trafficking in persons as exploitation of human beings for labor, sex, servitude, and removal of body organs. It has expanded from only sexual exploitation of women and little girls to exploitation of men, women, boys, and girls with the threat or use of "force," "fraud," or "coercion" to obtain victims' consent. It is not limited to only sexual exploitation but encompasses other acts of exploitation, such as various types of labor, servitude, forced removal of body organs, etc. It refers to the situations where victims are trapped and cannot or are not allowed to leave their exploitative situations. It is understood now that a victim cannot consent to human trafficking. Even if the victim initially consented to commercial sex or a labor setting prior to acts of force, fraud, or coercion (or if the victim is a minor in a sex trafficking situation), which may have been given or obtained using manipulation, false promises, and or other tactics such as playing on the victims' desperate situation, it is not relevant to the crime, nor is the payment.

It is also clearly understood that victimization is not limited to women and young girls but is inclusive of adult men and women as well male and female children. Victims are no longer only poor, naïve, unemployed, and uneducated humans. Rather they come from all walks of life, including middle and high socioeconomic status, people with varied levels of education and professional degrees, the employed looking for better paying jobs and advancement, or the unemployed looking for jobs. Almost anybody can be victimized and trapped in a trafficking web. In general, traffickers seek to target those who are most vulnerable—the young and the desperate who can be easily manipulated[5] regardless of their citizenship, immigration status, socioeconomic status, or education level. They are indiscriminative in their selection of targets and victimize anybody who is vulnerable and can be easily manipulated. Their only motivation is greed.

The Trafficking Process: How It Happens

It is widely accepted and understood now that trafficking can be an international as well as a domestic enterprise. Though transportation across borders may be an important element in many cases, it by no means is an essential element of trafficking. Contrary to commonly held perceptions that trafficking is exploitation of foreign nationals, especially illegal and undocumented immigrants from other countries (mainly from poor and developing nations), it is now believed that trafficking can happen within the same country. Victims do not have to be illegal immigrants. Legal immigrants and/or indigenous citizens of a nation are equally vulnerable to trafficking. It does not necessarily have to involve transportation of foreigners across borders, rather citizens of a country can be trafficked within the same country. It does not have to happen in poor and developing countries only, rather it happens in all countries—including the developed and rich countries.

Estimates of Trafficking in Persons: Prevalence and Incidence

Presently, as a result of the legal definition provided by the UN Protocol and TVPA, there is some distinction between trafficking, smuggling, migration, illegal migration, forced migration, or slavery. Twenty years of research, laws, protocols, and conventions have identified each of these acts and demonstrated their unique attributes that distinguish one from the other. Though there may be some overlap in some cases, generally trafficking as a crime can be isolated from other crimes. Our understanding of who are the trafficking victims has also improved. Our ability to isolate trafficking victims from victims of other crimes has resulted in better and more reasonable estimates.

Who Are the Traffickers?

As compared to twenty years ago—prior to the ratification of TIP Protocol and TVPA—today there is a little bit more clarification on who the traffickers are. It is now understood that trafficking can and does occur in legal and legitimate business settings as well as underground markets. Contrary to the commonly held perceptions that it is an underground industry organized and run by some big criminal organizations, such as "the mafia," it is an industry that is run as an organized crime as well as a small business—the kind of "mom and pop" operation run by two or more people in a small rural or urban neighborhood. It is an intricate and multifaceted crime that many times occurs right in front of our eyes but remains hidden. It is often cloaked and presented as a legitimate normal business. Traffickers can be big criminal organizations, or your neighborhood store owners, your neighbors, or respected doctors in reputed hospitals—just to name a few. Just as anybody can be a victim, anybody can also be a trafficker. All that is needed is greed and motivation. Trafficking as a business is run similarly to a regular business enterprise. It can be run as a small business or a large, complex, corporate business. "Traffickers could range from small-time, solo operators to loose networks of criminals, to highly sophisticated criminal organizations that operate internationally."[6] Exploitation of trafficking victims occurs in many different forms and settings. According to the UNICEF (2016), labor trafficking occurs in a wide variety of industries—such as restaurants, bars, hotels, agriculture, construction, traveling sales crews—and sex trafficking is facilitated in numerous ways through brothels, strip clubs, escort and message services, pimp controlled prostitution on the streets and on the internet.[7]

Effects of Human Trafficking and Needs of Victims

Twenty years of research and reports have also made us aware of the aftereffects of victimization manifested in victims. These effects expand beyond physical health. These include psychological, psychiatric, and emotional health problems. The survivors require various types of services. All victims need assistance with basic needs, such as safe environment, food, shelter, and clothing. In addition to these basic needs, they may require emotional and moral support, legal assistance, and physical and mental health services. Victims go through traumatic experiences and may suffer from depression and other related disorders. They may need assistance with finding employment and reintegrating in society. Thus, programs and policies are needed to cater to the victims' needs.

In sum, our current knowledge of trafficking in persons ascertains the following:

1) It permeates all corners of virtually every country in every region of the world. It is a global crime that is not bound by any geographical or demographic boundaries. Both the perpetrators and victims of this crime can be located in almost all countries of the world.[8,9]
2) It engenders conditions of exploitation and severe human rights violations. Greed—not human welfare, rights, or compassion—drive this enterprise, and victims are exploited for economic gain. It is an enterprise that violates basic human rights and deprives victims of their rights to life and liberty in order to make profits. Its classification as a crime and a human right violation renders it a multifaceted problem requiring a multidimensional response.
3) Socially, economically, and politically marginalized individuals are especially vulnerable to the fraudulent, cruel, and innovative ploys of the traffickers.
4) It has the ability to morph itself into forms that are difficult to recognize and allow it to stealthily and legally penetrate society. Its pervasive and multifaceted nature allows its existence without being identified or recognized. It adapts to the existing social and economic environment so as to remain hidden or rematerialize in a new and more forceful form.
5) It's aftereffects are manifested in all aspects of victims' lives—including their physical and mental health.
6) Victims' needs expand beyond basic needs of safety, food, shelter, and clothing. They need assistance in almost all aspects of life to become whole and be integrated in society.
7) Despite many laws, protocols, anti-trafficking campaigns, and other significant efforts, its presence is felt everywhere.
8) It is a such a complex and multifaceted crime that international communities have to combine and coordinate their efforts to address it. Due to its complexity, no single state or agency can respond effectively to this population.

Such is the state of our understanding of this crime.

Anti-Trafficking Efforts

Development in the current understanding of trafficking has made it clear that it is a complex and multifaceted crime that mandates a comprehensive, coordinated, and multidisciplinary response at the international as well as state level.[10] Consequently, various agencies from the fields of criminal enforcement, labor enforcement, victim outreach and services, public awareness, education, trade policy, international development and programs, immigration, intelligence, and diplomacy have coordinated their efforts to address the challenges created by this crime.

Legal efforts to prosecute and punish offenders and protect victims can be found in international and national laws related to human trafficking. The international community (UN) and United States, as well as almost every country in the world, have some laws prohibiting and outlawing human trafficking. According to the United Nations, 134 countries have criminalized trafficking.[11] The UN Protocol, TVPA, and other similar laws provide guidance and facilitate prosecution and punishment of offenders and protection of victims. Every country has laws condemning this crime. The United States has a separate office—the Office to Monitor and Combat Trafficking in Persons (OMCTIP)—that provides assistance in combating trafficking and monitors efforts made to combat it. This office coordinates anti-trafficking efforts and partners with foreign governments, international organizations, civil societies, and the private sector to develop and implement effective strategies. The OMCTIP is responsible for bilateral and multilateral diplomacy, targeted foreign assistance, and public engagement on trafficking in persons.[12] The OMCTIP pursues policies, partnerships, and practices that uphold the 3P paradigm of prosecuting traffickers, protecting victims, and preventing trafficking in accordance with the United Nations Palermo Protocol to Prevent, Suppress and Punish Trafficking in Persons.[13] As set forth in the UN Protocol, authorized by the UN, and mandated by the TVPA, the United States has created an evaluation system called the Tier System. The U.S. Department of State evaluates each country's efforts towards controlling and preventing trafficking in persons and places each country onto one of the tiers, as mandated by the TVPA.

Other efforts include several campaigns, initiatives, and programs in different countries. All these efforts are based on the principles of the Palermo Protocol and the TVPA. These efforts have been discussed in detail in Chapter 6. The coordinated efforts of the inter-agency initiative have dismantled organized criminal networks to a great extent.

Future of Human Trafficking

As discussed above, although enormous anti-trafficking efforts have resulted in remarkable accomplishments, this crime of trafficking continues to progress and remerge in different forms. Traffickers find more ways to exploit human beings for profit. Elderly guardianship and trafficking pregnant women to sell babies are some of the new forms of trafficking. Thus, a great deal still needs to be done.

Significant issues related to human trafficking that still need to be addressed are discussed below.

A significant fact to be noted is that although there exists an enormous amount of written materials on human trafficking, there is a lack of evidence-based empirical research. The majority of the extant literature on this topic is anecdotal or sensationalistic, scholarly articles in form of general overviews of the problem, or critiques of the literature.[14] Many of the estimates on the extent of trafficking and aftermath originate and are based on the information extracted from the assertions of government agencies and international organizations without any substantiation.[15,16,17] Future efforts should focus on evidence-based and methodologically sound empirical research. The estimates should also be based on evidence and officially substantiated sources.

Another issue in need of attention is the focus of anti-trafficking efforts. These efforts need to focus on all types of trafficking—including labor and other newly emerging forms of trafficking. So far, the majority of anti-trafficking efforts, policies, and media, as well as law enforcement tactics have focused on the problem of sexual exploitation (Chuang 2010; UNODC 2006, 2012). As discussed throughout the book, humans are trafficked for exploitation in all kinds of services—sex is only one type. Prevention and control efforts should include all other types of exploitations.

Future efforts should also interpret trafficking in the context of human rights. Besides being a violation of state and international law, trafficking also entails a range of human rights violations. It should be classified as a crime and a human right violation. Efforts need to be made to understand its multifaceted nature and its ability to morph itself. Trainings for the first line responders (such as local law enforcement, immigration and border authorities, transportation and aviation authorities, and social workers, as well as others) should include cues to recognize and identify victims of various forms of exploitation that remain hidden as they exist as routine service providers.

Future efforts should include strategies that will prevent regeneration and transmutation of trafficking into a more complex problem. The identified victims should be provided adequate protection and services and traffickers should be prosecuted and punished severely. Lack of such response will re-victimize the individuals who escape trafficking situations.[18]

It should also be noted that future response to trafficking as a crime and human rights violation should be comprehensive, coordinated, and integrated. It needs to be recognized that no one agency or one state can tackle a multifaceted problem like human trafficking. The governmental and non-governmental agencies need to cooperate, collaborate, and share information as well as resources in order to respond to the challenges posed by trafficking. Service providers and service providing agencies should collaborate and formulate partnerships with law enforcement, medical and mental health providers, immigration attorneys, and local ethnic community leaders to confront this problem. There should be a united, not fragmented, front to undertake the task of eradicating this crime.

The ultimate goal of future efforts should be identifying underlying causes that force humans to become sources of surplus supply and easy targets for trafficking. Strategies should be to confront the social, political, and economic environments that are conducive to the conception, manifestation, and perpetuation of trafficking. The focus of eradication should begin with the extinction of circumstances that create high demand and surplus supply. The international community should come together and confront trafficking on a united front.

Discussion Questions

1) Discuss future strategies to curb trafficking.

2) Identify at least two aspects of human trafficking that need to be addressed.

3) Find a local, national, or international newspaper that has discussed the newest forms of trafficking tactics traffickers use to trap victims. Write your opinion on these new forms and bring to class to discuss.

References

Adelman, M. R. (2003). International Sex Trafficking: Dismantiling the Demand. *S. Cal. Rev. L. & Women's Stud.*, *13*, 387.

Bales, K., & Lize, S. (2005). Trafficking in persons in the United States. *Croft Institute for International Studies, University of Mississippi.*

Barnhart, M. H. (2009). Sex and slavery: An analysis of three models of state human trafficking legislation. *Wm. & Mary J. Women & L.*, *16*, 83.

Green, P., & Grewcock, M. (2002). War against Illegal Immigration: State Crime and the Construction of a European Identity, The. *Current Issues Crim. Just.*, *14*, 87.

Heiges, M. (2009). From the Inside Out: Reforming State and Local Prostitution Enforcement to Combat Sex Trafficking in the United States and Abroad. *Minn. L. Rev.*, *94*, 428.

Kim, K. (2007). Psychological coercion in the context of modern-day involuntary labor: Revisiting United States v. Kozminski and understanding human trafficking. *University of Toledo Law Review*, *38*(3).

Kotrla, K. (2010). Domestic minor sex trafficking in the United States. *Social work*, *55*(2), 181–187.

Kutnick, B., Belser, P., & Danailova-Trainor, G. (2007). *Methodologies for global and national estimation of human trafficking victims: current and future approaches.* ILO.

Raymond, J. G., Hughes, D. M., & Gomez, C. J. (2001). Sex trafficking of women in the United States. *International sex trafficking of women & children: Understanding the global epidemic*, 3–14.

Richard, S. (2004). State legislation and human trafficking: Helpful or harmful. *U. Mich. JL Reform*, *38*, 447.

Schauer, E. J., & Wheaton, E. M. (2006). Sex trafficking into the United States: A literature review. *Criminal Justice Review*, *31*(2), 146–169.

Further Suggested Readings

Brennan, D. (2005). Methodological challenges in research with trafficked persons: Tales from the field. *International Migration*, *43*(1 2), 35–54.

Bush, G. W. (2009). *The national security strategy of the United States of America.* Wordclay.

Flowe, M. (2009). International Market for Trafficking in Persons for the Purpose of Sexual Exploitation: Analyzing Current Treatment of Supply and Demand, The. *NCJ Int'l L. & Com. Reg.*, *35*, 669.

Logan, T. K., Walker, R., & Hunt, G. (2009). Understanding human trafficking in the United States. *Trauma, Violence, & Abuse*, *10*(1), 3–30.

Overbaugh, E. (2009). Human trafficking: The need for federal prosecution of accused traffickers. *Seton Hall L. Rev.*, *39*, 635.

Patrick, S. (2006). Weak states and global threats: Fact or fiction?. *Washington Quarterly*, *29*(2), 27–53.

Piper, N. (2005). A Problem by a Different Name? A Review of Research on Trafficking in South East Asia and Oceania. *International migration*, *43*(1 2), 203–233.

Potts Jr, L. G. (2003). Global trafficking in human beings: assessing the success of the United Nations Protocol to Prevent Trafficking in Persons. *Geo. Wash. Int'l L. Rev., 35*, 227.

Shanty, F., & Mishra, P. P. (2008). *Organized crime: from trafficking to terrorism* (Vol. 1). Abc-clio.

Sharma, N. (2005). Anti-trafficking rhetoric and the making of a global apartheid. *NWSA Journal, 17*(3), 88–111.

Smith, H. M. (2011). Sex trafficking: trends, challenges, and the limitations of international law. *Human Rights Review, 12*(3), 271–286.

Truong, T. D. (2006). Poverty, gender and human trafficking in Sub-Saharan Africa: Rethinking best practices in migration management.

Vance, C. S. (2011). States of contradiction: Twelve ways to do nothing about trafficking while pretending to. *social research, 78*(3), 933–948.

Weitzer, R. (2011). Sex trafficking and the sex industry: The need for evidence-based theory and legislation. *The Journal of Criminal Law and Criminology (1973–), 101*(4), 1337–1369.

Wilson, D. G., Walsh, W. F., & Kleuber, S. (2006). Trafficking in human beings: Training and services among U.S. law enforcement agencies. *Police Practice and Research, 7*(02), 149–160.

Notes

1. This endnote has two references:
1) Laczko, F., & M. A. Gramegna. (2003). Developing better indicators of human trafficking. *The Brown Journal of World Affairs, 10*(1), 179–194.
2) Richard, A. (1999). International trafficking in women to the United States: A contemporary manifestation of slavery and organized crime. The Center for the Study of Intelligence.

2. Europol. (2005). Legislation on trafficking in human beings and illegal immigrant smuggling. Europol Public Information.

3. Miko, F. T., & G. Park. (2001). Trafficking in women and children: The U.S. and international response—Updated August 1, 2001. *Federal Publications*, 55.

4. Richard, A. (1999). International trafficking in women to the United States: A contemporary manifestation of slavery and organized crime. The Center for the Study of Intelligence.

5. U.S. Department of State. (2015). What is modern slavery? http://www.state.gov/j/tip/what/.

6. Shelley, L. (2010). *Human trafficking: A global perspective*. Cambridge University Press.

7. UNICEF, United States Fund. Children First. (2016). End Trafficking, Fast Facts. https://www.unicefusa.org/sites/default/files/End%20Trafficking%20OnePager-%202016.pdf.

8. Europol. (2005). Legislation on trafficking in human beings and illegal immigrant smuggling. Europol Public Information.

9. Miko, F. T., & G. Park. (2001). Trafficking in women and children: The U.S. and international response—Updated August 1, 2001. *Federal Publications*, 55.

10. U.S. Department of State. (2016). Review of the 2016 Trafficking in Persons Report. State Department Testimony of Ambassador Susan Coppedge for the Senate Foreign Relations Committee.

11. UNODC. (2012). *Global report on trafficking in persons*. Vienna: United Nations.

12. Office to Monitor and Combat Trafficking in Persons, U.S. Department of State. http://www.state.gov/j/tip/.

13. UN General Assembly. (2000). Protocol to prevent, suppress and punish trafficking in persons, especially women and children, supplementing the United Nations convention against transnational organized crime. Resolution 55, 25.

14. Weitzer, R. (2014). New directions in research on human trafficking. *The ANNALS of the American Academy of Political and Social Science*, *653*(1), 6–24.

15. Zhang, S. X. (2009). Beyond the 'Natasha' story–a review and critique of current research on sex trafficking. *Global crime*, *10*(3), 178–195.

16. Zhang, S. X. (2012). Measuring labor trafficking: A research note. *Crime, Law and Social Change*, *58*(4), 469–482.

17. Gozdziak, E. M., & E. A. Collett. (2005). Research on human trafficking in North America: A review of literature. *International Migration*, *43*(1 2), 99–128.

18. Pearson, E. (2002). *Human traffic, human rights: Redefining victim protection*. Anti-Slavery International.

Glossary and Acronyms

Abuse of Power: Exert undue influence on someone because of one's position of power. Exploit and/or take undue advantage of someone with less power by a person who has a position of authority.

Airline Ambassadors International: A program that offers a human trafficking awareness program to educate airport staff about the problem of human trafficking.

American Bar Association (ABA): A voluntary bar association of lawyers and law students, which is not specific to any jurisdiction in the United States. It was founded August 21, 1878.

Anomie: Chaotic and lawlessness.

Anomie Theory: A theory that purports that the common individualistic goal of "monetary success at all costs" encourages and facilitates an environment conducive to developing and using innovative ways of making a profit. Often this innovation manifests in the form of criminal enterprises—such as trafficking.

Arbitration: The settling of disputes (especially labor disputes) between two parties by an impartial third party, whose decision the contending parties agree to accept.

The Arizona League to End Regional Trafficking: A coalition representing partnerships with law enforcement, faith-based communities, nonprofit organizations, social service agencies, attorneys, and concerned citizens.

Biometric Technology: The type of technology that measures and analyzes physical attributes such as facial features and voice or retinal scans. Currently, biometric technology is used to ensure that documents are unforgeable. These measures use physical characteristics of a person to verify their identity. The most common biometrics include fingerprints, iris scans, hand geometry, voice recognition, and face recognition.

Black Market: Refers to businesses that run illegally and are kept secret from legal entities such as government so as to conduct business that is prohibited by the law, avoid following business laws, exploit people and their situations, and make enormous profits with the least cost or investment.

Bondage: Situations in which individuals are forced, coerced, or compelled to continue providing services without adequate remuneration. It is very similar to slave-like services.

Bonded Labor: A form of slavery where a person becomes a bonded laborer when their labor is demanded as a means of repayment for a loan which he/she or the family had taken. The person is coerced, forced, or defrauded into providing services without any wages as a repayment of a debt taken.

Brokering Functions: Refers to the function of advertising and spreading the word about the benefits of organ sales among possible organ suppliers and recipients and establishing contacts with organ brokers.

Brokers: People who work in finding, recruiting, and matching a vulnerable, inadequately informed, or totally uninformed organ donor to a recipient.

Capitalism Theory: This theory is based on the principles of capitalism. In the context of globalization, it demonstrates the normalcy of exploitation of labor by justifying the inception, existence, perpetuation, and proliferation of trafficking in persons as an act as well as a process.

Charter of Fundamental Rights of the European Union, (2000/C 364/01) Article 1 on Human Dignity and Article 3 on the Right to the Integrity of the Person: Prohibition on making the human body and its parts as such a source of financial gain.

Child Exploitation Tracking System (CETS): A collaborative global law enforcement program for child pornography investigations. This system enables law enforcement officers from different departments in different countries to collaborate in the pursuit of pedophiles and in the rescue and repatriation of abused children.

Child Labor: Refers to the employment of a child in a business or industry especially in violation of state or federal statutes prohibiting the employment of children under a specified age. It is the work that harms children or keeps them from attending school.

Coercion: Forcing someone to comply through the threat of serious harm or physical restraint against the person.

Commercial Sex Act: Any sex act on account of which anything of value is given to or received by any person.

Commodification of Humans: Treating human beings as commodities with the objective of making a profit. Human beings are considered property-like commodities to be bought and sold like inanimate objects.

Communications Technology: Information technology which stresses the role of unified communications and the integration of telecommunications (telephone lines and wireless signals) and computers.

Compelled Service: Refers to servitude. The Palermo Protocol describes compelled service using a number of different terms, including involuntary servitude, slavery or practices similar to slavery, debt bondage, and forced labor.

Compulsory Labor: All work or service which is exacted from any person under the menace of any penalty and for which the said person has not offered himself voluntarily.

Conceptual Framework: Refers to an analytical tool with several variations and contexts. It is used to make conceptual distinctions and organize ideas. Strong conceptual frameworks capture something real and do this in a way that is easy to remember and apply.

Conflict Theory: Power and control create conflict between those who have power and control and those who do not. Social, political, or material inequality among different groups allows the powerful to control activities and movements of those without any or with little power. Social inequality is created by the rich and powerful in order to maintain their own power and wealth. They create social structures that are geared towards maintaining the unequal distribution of power and wealth and blocking all possibilities of exit or upward mobility for poor classes.

Conspiracy: A secret plan by a group to do something unlawful or harmful.

Contemporary Slavery: Refers to the contemporary situations where people are exploited and forced to work through violence for the most minimum or no pay.

Continued Presence: A one-year form of immigration relief that federal law enforcement officials request on behalf of the victim.

Council of Europe (CoE) Convention against Trafficking in Human Organs: This is the only international treaty that specifically deals with trafficking in human organs, seeking to prevent and combat trafficking in human organs, to protect the rights of victims and to facilitate co-operation at both national and international levels.

Council of Europe (CoE) Convention on Action against Trafficking in Human Beings: A regional human rights treaty of international human rights law. Its main functions are: to prevent and combat all forms of human trafficking, to protect and assist victims and witnesses of trafficking, to ensure effective investigation and prosecution, and to promote international co-operation against trafficking.

Council of Europe (CoE) Convention on Cybercrime: The first international treaty that sought to address Internet and computer crime by harmonizing national laws, improving investigative techniques, and increasing cooperation among nations. This was drawn up during 109th Session on November 8, 2001, in Strasbourg, France.

Council of Europe (CoE) Convention on Human Rights and Biomedicine (the Oviedo Convention): CETS 165 (4 April 1997); prohibits sale and purchase of organs. Article 21 of the Convention states that "the human body and its parts shall not, as such, give rise to financial gain."

Covert: Not in plain view. Hidden and deceptive.

Criminal Code: Also known as penal code. It is a document which compiles all, or a significant amount of, a particular jurisdiction's criminal law.

Criminal Networks: Groups or organizations involved in crime.

Cybercrime: Crime conducted via the Internet or some other computer network.

Dark Side: Negative or bad side often not known or noticed.

Debt Bondage: A pledge by a debtor of his personal services or of those of a person under his control as security for a debt.

Debt Repayment Schemes: A plan or action of repaying debts, or a single payment made towards paying off a debt.

Deceased Donor Programs: Programs that organize organ donations from the deceased and live donors.

Deception: Making someone believe something that is not true.

Declaration of Independence: One of the founding documents of the United States, proclaiming that "all men are created equal, [and] that they are endowed by their Creator with certain unalienable rights."

Declaration of Istanbul on Organ Trafficking and Transplant Tourism (2008): According to this declaration, member states are advised to take measures to protect the poorest and vulnerable groups from "transplant tourism" and the sale of tissues and organs, including attention to the wider problem of international trafficking in human tissues and organs.

Defraud: To take something illegally from a person or company, to trick or cheat someone or something in order to get money: to use fraud in order to get money from a person, an organization, etc.

Department of Homeland Security (DHS): The new agency into which INS was folded effective March 1, 2003. The benefits functions of the former INS transferred to USCIS, while the enforcement functions transferred to Customs and Border Protection and Immigration and Customs Enforcement.

Deportation: The formal removal of an immigrant from the United States when the immigrant has been found removable for violating immigration law. Deportation is ordered by an immigration judge without any punishment being imposed or contemplated. Prior to April 1997, deportation and exclusion were separate removal procedures. The Illegal Immigration Reform and Immigrant Responsibility Act of 1996 consolidated these procedures. After April 1, 1997, immigrants in and admitted to the United States may be subject to removal instead of deportation.

Destination Countries: Countries where the victims are finally taken and put to work and where the exploitation takes place.

Deviant Place Theory: According to this theory, even if victims do not actively engage or solicit the help of perpetrators that may increase their chances of becoming trafficking victims, the areas they live in may increase probability of their victimization.

Discrimination: An unjust or prejudicial treatment of different categories of people or things, especially on the grounds of race, age, or sex.

Document Forgers: People who are skilled in providing falsified passports and entry visas, fake marriage certificates, false work contracts with multinational firms and shipping companies, or false documents relating to studies at universities and colleges, requests for family reunions, or visits for medical treatment.

Domestic Human Trafficking: When individuals are trafficked within a country and they do not need to cross international borders, then that is commonly referred to as domestic human trafficking.

Domestic Servitude: A form of human trafficking found in distinct circumstances—where victims are forced to perform all kinds of domestic chores (cooking, cleaning, child rearing, etc.) and they are not free to leave.

Domestic Violence: Refers to the situations where there is violence between members of a family or people living in the same home.

Duress: Refers to the unlawful pressure exerted upon a person to coerce that person to perform an act that he or she ordinarily would not perform. It can also be situations where a person is coerced by the wrongful conduct or threat of another to enter into a contract under circumstances that deprive the individual of his or her volition.

Economic Globalization: Refers to the increased flow of capital and people, and the extension of production and distribution networks around the world.

Economic Theory of Value: In this theory, profit is the driver behind capitalist production. This theory purports that a capitalist buys individual labor with an understanding that the capitalist has the right to make use of the bought labor for a particular period of time in order for the capitalist to keep making profits and ensuring that the workers receive wages.

Enslavement: The process of making someone a slave; the process of controlling someone such that the person is not free.

Exploitation: The action or fact of treating someone unfairly in order to benefit from their work.

Exploitation of Humans: Treating human beings in such a manner that their welfare is ignored and they are used to produce maximum profits for their employer/owner/master.

Face Recognition Technology: The type of technology that uses a formula to determine whether a live image of a face matches the electronically stored image of that person.

Facilitated Irregular Migration: Refers to the act of someone assisting and facilitating movement of a person or a group of persons, either across an international border, or within a state.

Faith-Based Organization: A group of individuals united on the basis of religious or spiritual beliefs.

False and Authentic Documents Online (FADO): A European image-archiving system was enacted in 1998. It was established by a Joint Action of the Council of the European Union to help combat illegal immigration and organized crime. It is a computerized system with restricted access providing fast and secure information exchange between the General Secretariat of the Council of the European Union and between document experts in the European Union member states, Iceland, Norway, and Switzerland.

False Arrests: Refers to a common law tort, where a plaintiff alleges he or she was held in custody without probable cause, or without an order issued by a court of competent jurisdiction. Although it is possible to sue law enforcement officials for false arrest, the usual defendants in such cases are private security firms.

Federal Statute: Refers to a law enacted by Congress. It is the written will of Congress as expressed formally by an act of Congress. Generally, a bill is passed by Congress and signed by the president, when it becomes a federal statute.

Forced Exploitation: Refers to the condition of a person (the victim) who is forced to provide labor or services through the use of coercion, threat, or deception. A person in such a situation does not have personal autonomy and does not have the capacity to make decisions to leave the exploitative situation.

Forced Labor: Forced labor is a situation in which victims are forced to work against their own will, under the threat of violence or some other form of punishment, their freedom is restricted and a degree of ownership is exerted. Forms of forced labor can include domestic servitude; agricultural labor; sweatshop factory labor; janitorial, food service and other service industry labor; and begging. (Labor Trafficking Fact Sheet—https://

www.acf.hhs.gov/sites/default/files/orr/fact_sheet_labor_trafficking_english.pdf)

Forced Marriage: A form of marriage where one or both of the persons getting married are coerced, forced, or deceived into marriage and the person getting married does not have the power to refuse or end the marriage. The person is maintained in marriage through coercion.

Forced Migration: Involuntary movements of refugees and internally displaced people (those displaced by conflicts) as well as people displaced by natural or environmental disasters, chemical or nuclear disasters, famine, or development projects.

Forced Prostitution: Refers to conditions of control over a person who is coerced by another to engage in sexual activity. It is also known as involuntary prostitution, prostitution, or sexual slavery that takes place as a result of coercion, force, or fraud.

Foreigners: People born in another country than the country of their residence. They are also persons not native to or naturalized in the country or jurisdiction.

Four Main Tenets of the "American Dream": Achievement, Individualism, Universalism, and Materialism.

Free2Work: A campaign developed by the Not for Sale Campaign. It is a mobile phone application that provides information on forced and child labor related to particular companies and brands.

General Strain Theory: According to general strain theory, people feel trapped in poverty and desperate situations and believe that in their local communities, they do not have any chance of ever getting out of poverty. They may experience a range of negative emotions including desperation, which leads them to traffickers. This theory hypothesizes that strains or stressors increase the likelihood of negative emotions like anger and frustration leading to crime.

Glamorous: Refers to something or someone charming, |fascinating, or attractive, especially in a mysterious or magical way. Something or someone full of excitement, adventure, and unusual activity is also known as glamorous.

Global Crime: Crime that transcends all geographical and demographic boundaries. It happens indiscriminately in all parts and all countries of the globe.

Global Health Issue: Refers to a health issue or a problem that affects people all over the world.

Global Initiative: An introductory act or step leading to global action involving all countries of the globe.

Globalization: A process of interaction and integration among the people, companies, and governments of different nations, a process driven by international trade and investment and aided by information technology.

Global Missing Children's Network: A multilingual database featuring photos of and information about missing children from around the world. It was launched in 1998 as a joint program of the National Center for Missing & Exploited Children and the International Centre for Missing & Exploited Children.

Global Perspectives: Refers to situations believed to be related to the rest of the entire world rather than limited to one nation.

Global Poverty: A general scarcity of material possessions or money around the globe.

Guest Worker Programs: Refers to those programs under which employers are authorized to import unskilled labor from other countries for temporary or seasonal work lasting less than a year.

Guiding Principles for Human Cell, Tissue and Organ Transplant: Refers to the first WHO "Guiding Principles on Transplantation," endorsed by the Assembly in 1991 in Resolution WHA 44.25. These guiding principles have greatly influenced professional codes and practices as well as legislation around the world during almost two decades. These guidelines were endorsed and updated by the 63rd World Health Assembly in May 2010 through resolution WHA 63.22 and identifying areas of progress to optimize donation and transplantation practices. These principles govern the removal of organs from both deceased and living donors for the purpose of transplantation. They provide key international standards.

Hacking: Use of a computer to gain unauthorized access to data in a system.

Hidden in Plain Sight: Crime that happens right in the open yet generally goes undetected or documented.

High-Risk Lifestyles: These refer to lifestyles that enhance the victimization risk. Addiction to drugs or alcohol or being a runaway, homeless, or easily tempted by a glamorous lifestyle are indicative of a high-risk lifestyle.

Human Exploitation: Taking advantage of one human being by another for the purposes of making a profit.

Human Rights Violation: Refers to the violation of basic rights and freedoms to which all humans are considered to be entitled, such as the rights to life, liberty, equality, and a fair trial, freedom from slavery and torture, and freedom of thought and expression.

Human Trafficking: A process by which people are recruited in their community and exploited by traffickers using deception and/or some form of coercion to lure and control them.

Human Trafficking Legislation: Laws, bills, statutes, rules, decrees, conventions, protocols, treaties and similar regulations that address human trafficking.

Human Trafficking Prosecution Unit: This unit was created within the Criminal Section the Civil Rights Division. This consolidates the expertise of some of the nation's top human trafficking prosecutors and these prosecutors work closely with Assistant United States Attorneys and law enforcement agencies to streamline fast-moving trafficking investigations.

Human Trafficking Ring: Refers to a group of people engaged in trafficking of people for exploitation. A group of people engaged in the trade and exploitation of people as well as movement of the person from one place to another for the purposes of exploitation.

Human Trafficking Task Force: A group of experts working together to investigate and submit a formal report on trafficking.

Illegal Migration: Refers to the migration of people across borders in a way that violates the immigration laws of the destination country.

Illicit: Unlawful, not legally permitted or authorized; unlicensed; disapproved of or not permitted for moral or ethical reasons.

Immigration and Customs Enforcement (ICE): Responsible for enforcement within the interior of the nation, and includes functions of the Customs Service, Federal Protection Service, and the investigative and enforcement functions of the former INS (other than those border functions assumed by CBP).

Individual Liberty: A state of being free; enjoying various social, political, or economic rights and privileges.

Industrial Capitalism: Refers to an economic and political system characterized by a free market for industrial goods and services and private control of production and consumption.

Industrialization: A process by which an economy is transformed from primarily agricultural to one based on the manufacturing of goods. Individual manual labor is often replaced by mechanized mass production, and craftsmen are replaced by assembly lines.

Inhumane Living Conditions: Refers to the substandard living conditions that lack basic standards and compassion. Such living conditions pose grave risks to the health and safety of the humans subjected to such conditions.

Interagency Task Force: A task force made up of representatives of more than one agency to coordinate federal efforts to combat trafficking in persons.

International Campaigns: A series of coordinated international activities, designed to achieve a social, political, or commercial goal.

International Justice Mission: This program offers services and programs to protect the poor from violence in the developing world.

International Organization for Migration (IOM): This organization was established in 1951. It is the leading inter-governmental organization in the field of migration and works closely with governmental, intergovernmental, and non-governmental partners. It works in the four broad areas of migration management: (1) migration and development; (2) facilitating migration; (3) regulating migration; and (4) forced migration.

International Protocol: An international agreement that supplements or amends a treaty.

International Treaties: Series of formal written agreements between two or more nations.

INTERPOL: The world's largest international police organization, with 190-member countries today. It was officially created in 1923 as the International Criminal Police Commission. The organization became known as INTERPOL in 1956. Its main function is to facilitate international police cooperation even where diplomatic relations do not exist between particular countries.

Interpol Child Image Database (ICAID): A system maintained and housed at the Interpol General Secretariat. The image banks of law enforcement agencies around the world contribute images to facilitate global investigations of child sexual exploitation.

Intra-State Domestic Trafficking: Transportation of people within states for exploitation through by force, fraud, or coercion.

Investigation: A formal and official systematic, minute, and thorough attempt to learn the facts about something complex or hidden.

Involuntary Servitude: A form of exploitation in which unscrupulous employers exploit workers and treat them as servants. A scheme, plan, or pattern is intended to convince a person that if the person did not comply, that person or another person would suffer serious harm. It is a form of human trafficking found in distinct circumstances—working in an environment against one's will and without any compensation—that creates unique vulnerabilities for victims.

Justice for Victims of Trafficking Act of 2015 (S 178): Passed by the US Senate with a vote of 99–0 on April 22, 2015. This section expands the definition of "child abuse" under the Victims of Child Abuse Act of 1990.

Labor Certification: All foreigners are required to be eligible to work in the United States. Labor Certification is a requirement for the employers seeking to employ foreigners whose immigration to the United States is based on job skills or nonimmigrant temporary workers coming to perform services for which qualified United States citizens and authorized workers are not available.

Labor Trafficking: Exploitation of people in providing services in various types of industries, including the sex industry, by the use or threat of force, fraud, or coercion.

Language Barrier: Difficulties faced when communicating with others while speaking different languages.

Lawful Permanent Resident: Immigration status of a person authorized to live and work legally in the country of residence.

Legal Permanent Resident (LPR): An immigrant who has the right to live permanently in the US "Green Card" holders are LPRs. LPRs are also called permanent residents or resident aliens.

Legal Transplantation: Transplanting organs legally.

Life Style Theory: This theory purports that one's lifestyle enhances or diminishes victimization probability. Victims' lifestyle, absence of capable guardians, the environment with which the potential victims interact and their routine activities determine their risk of being trafficked.

Living Donors: Live persons donating their organs.

Living Organ Donation Guidelines: Living organ donation guidelines mandate that living donors should be related to their recipients (unless such related persons and recipients do not match well immunologically). Living donors are required to give informed and voluntary consent and act willingly—free of any undue influence or coercion. The living donors are required to be informed of the probable risks, benefits, and consequences of the donation in a complete and understandable fashion.

Lucrative Criminal Enterprise: A criminal enterprise that generates enormous amount of profits at almost negligible cost. It is a business, where the business owner makes a one-time small investment and keeps making inordinate amounts of profit through recycling the one-time small investment.

Mail-Order Bride: A woman who lists herself in catalogs and is selected by a man for marriage.

Marginalized People: These are the people who have no resources and no power. So they are excluded from many of the opportunities otherwise available. They do not have resources to move out of desperate social and economic situations. They feel trapped in poverty and desperate situations. These are groups of people that are excluded from full participation in society. They are excluded from the main group and relegated to a lesser group due to socioeconomic status, race, ethnicity, or immigration status.

Marriage Agencies: A business that endeavors to introduce men and women for the purpose of marriage or dating.

Means: A method, action, or system by which a result is obtained.

Medical Wonder: Significant medical invention that has saved or prolonged the lives of thousands of patients worldwide. For example, advancement in medicine and technology has made the transplantation of organs, cells, and tissues viable and effective therapies across a wide range of both fatal and non-fatal diseases, saved many lives, and prolonged life span and provided quality of life to many patients.

Metamorphosis: The process of a change or transformation of the form or nature of a thing or person into a completely different one.

Migrant Laborers: Persons who move from place to place to get work, especially a farm laborer who harvests crops seasonally. Generally, these are illegal immigrants, who cross borders illegally in search of seasonal work.

Migrant Workers: These are workers who move from place to place to do seasonal work.

Minders: Persons who accompany organ suppliers and recipients, who are from countries that are different from the country in which the removal and transplantation take place, during their travel to and from the transplant operations.

Misperception: A mistaken belief, idea, or interpretation about something.

Mobile Technology: The technology used for cellular communication.

Modern Slavery: Defined by 1956 UN Supplementary Convention on the Abolition of Slavery, the Slave Trade, and Institutions and Practices Similar to Slavery, which says: "debt bondage, serfdom, forced marriage and the delivery of a child for the exploitation of that child are all slavery-like practices and require criminalization and abolishment."

Mouse-Trapping: Technique used by some websites to keep visitors from leaving their website, sometimes by launching an endless series of pop-up ads.

Multidimensional Crime: Crime that has many dimensions and is occurring both between and within nations. Almost all countries in every region of the world are affected by it.

Multilateral Response: A response having many aspects involving more than two nations or parties.

Multilateral Treaty: Refers to a treaty that involves several nations.

Multinational Corporations: Large businesses and enterprises involving several nations.

Natal Alienation: The forced loss of ties of birth and blood to both ascending and descending generations.

National Center for Missing and Exploited Children (NCMEC): This center began operating CyberTipline in 1998. Using this CyberTipline, anyone who suspects exploitation of children can call and provide information and call for help anonymously.

National Human Trafficking Resource Center (NHTRC): One of the nonprofit, non-governmental organizations engaged in combating human trafficking. It works exclusively on the issue of human trafficking. The NHTRC, a Department of Health and Human Services (HHS) funded program, is operated and implemented by the Polaris Project for the purpose of providing a national, 24-hour, toll-free hotline number for the human trafficking field in the US.

Network Society: A society reflective of social, political, economic, and cultural changes caused by the spread of network, digital information, and communications technologies.

Networked Technologies: A network that connects computers and devices in a limited geographical area such as a home, school, office building, or closely positioned group of buildings.

Non-Governmental Organizations (NGOs): In general, a non-governmental organization (NGO) is any nonprofit, voluntary citizens' group which is organized on a local, national, or international level. NGOs perform a variety of services and humanitarian functions.

Non-Prejudicial: No preconceived opinion or feeling, either favorable or unfavorable.

Non-Regenerative Organs: Refers to the organs that do not regenerate or grow back.

Not-for-Profit: An entity or organization whose primary objective is to support some issue or matter of private interest or public concern for non-commercial purposes.

Objectification of Humans: Treating humans as units of production or commodities for economic ends and profit. Human beings are considered commodities to be bought and sold like inanimate objects, with a sole purpose of making profits.

Office to Monitor and Combat Trafficking in Persons (OMCTIP): The Office to Monitor and Combat Trafficking in Persons (OMCTIP) was created in October 2001 by the US Department of State. The OMCTIP leads the United States' global engagement in combating human trafficking and supporting the coordination of anti-trafficking efforts across the US government. This office partners with foreign governments, international organizations, civil societies, and the private sector to develop and implement effective strategies for confronting human trafficking. The OMCTIP is responsible for bilateral and multilateral diplomacy, targeted foreign assistance, and public engagement on trafficking in persons.

Online Chatrooms: A designated area or forum on the World Wide Web that allows users to communicate with each other through instant messaging. Text is instantly displayed in the chatroom's conversation log after a user hits enter or send.

Optional Protocol to the Convention on the Rights of the Child on the Sale of Children, Child Prostitution and Child Pornography: This optional protocol supplements the convention by providing states with detailed requirements to end the sexual exploitation and abuse of children. It also protects children from being sold for non-sexual purposes—such as for other forms of forced labor, illegal adoption, and organ donation. The protocol provides definitions for the offcences of "sale of children," "child prostitution," and "child pornography." It also creates obligations on governments to criminalize and punish the activities related to these offenses.

The Optional Protocols to the Convention on the Rights of the Child (A/54/L.84), (United Nations, Geneva; 2000): Protocols prohibit organ removal from children as they are unable to give consent or understand the benefits or problems associated with organ donation.

Organ Purchase: The act of buying organs for sale to the traffickers, laboratories, patients, and hospitals, etc.

Organ Recipients: People who are receiving the organ transplant. They are generally patients or buyers.

Organ Suppliers: People who are engaged in finding people for organ removal, recruiting them, and supplying them to the traffickers for removal of organs.

Organ Trafficking: The Istanbul Declaration on Organ Trafficking and Transplant Tourism describes organ trafficking as the "recruitment, transport, transfer, harboring, or receipt" of persons, "by means of the threat or use of force or other forms of coercion, of abduction, of fraud, of deception, of the abuse of power," of a position of vulnerability, or of the giving or receiving of payments or benefits to achieve the consent of a person having control over another person, for the purpose of exploitation "by the removal of organs[, tissues, or cells] for transplantation."

Organ Transplantation: An act of transplanting a healthy organ into a patient who had defective organ. An organ is donated by living or deceased donors.

Organ Transplant Target Audiences: The potential buyers and sellers as well as brokers, hospital and medical personnel, and others who are engaged in the purchase and sale of organs for transplant.

Organized Business: Business that is involved in organized crime to commit serious domestic and transnational crimes. It is a collaborative group of businesses, existing for a period of time and engaged in national and international criminal activities.

Organized Crime: A category of transnational, national, or local groupings of highly centralized enterprises run by criminals who intend to engage in illegal activity, most commonly for money and profit.

Organized Criminal Group: A structured group of three or more persons, existing for a period of time and acting in concert with the aim of committing one or more serious crimes.

Origin Countries: Countries where the trafficking incident begins—where the victims are recruited by the traffickers.

Outlaw of Slavery: Declaring slavery illegal by legislating so that holding a person as a slave and denying a person basic liberties and rights is against the state's laws.

Page-Jacking: Illegally copying legitimate website content (usually, in the form of source code) to another website designed to replicate the original website.

Petition: A form asking for a certain benefit. For example, an immigration form (Form I-130).

Peonage: Act of holding a person in servitude or debt. It is closely related to involuntary servitude.

Personal Autonomy: Situations where a one has the capacity to decide for oneself and pursue a course of action in one's life, often regardless of any particular moral content.

Phishing: The activity of defrauding an online account holder of financial information by posing as a legitimate company.

Physical Maladies: Physical illnesses that makes you sick and unable to have normal function. For example, headaches, chest pain, shaking, sweating, and dizziness.

Pioneer: A person, country, group, or an entity that develops or is the first to use or apply a new method, area of knowledge, or activity.

Polaris: A nonprofit, non-governmental organization. It was founded in 2002. It is one of the largest anti-trafficking organizations in the US, with programs operating at local and national levels through their offices in Washington, DC, and Newark, New Jersey. It is not a government entity, law enforcement agency, or immigration bureau.

Post-Traumatic Stress Disorder: A condition of persistent mental and emotional stress occurring because of injury or severe psychological shock.

Poverty-Stricken Areas: Refers to the areas of a city, neighborhood, or community that are besieged with poverty in all aspects.

Precursors: A person or thing that comes before another of the same kind; a forerunner.

President's Interagency Task Force to Monitor and Combat Trafficking in Persons (PITF): A cabinet-level entity was created by the TVPA to coordinate US government-wide efforts to combat trafficking in persons. The PITF functions to strengthen federal efforts to combat human trafficking by co-ordinating efforts from the government leaders, the private sector, advocates and survivors, faith leaders, law enforcement, and academia.

Prosecution Unit: A unit that is responsible for prosecuting offenders.

Process: Refers to one of the essential elements of human trafficking—the activities to achieve the consent of a person having control over another person, for the purpose of exploitation.

Psychosomatic Symptoms: When a disease indicates both mind and body symptoms.

Pull Factors: These factors represent the "demand" side of trafficking—such as the need for cheap, submissive labor; commercialization and the sex industry; and low-risk in travelling. Socially and economically marginalized people are pulled towards the offers by the traffickers and easily entrapped in the trafficking situations.

Purpose: Objective or goal.

Push Factors: These factors refer to the factors that propel potential victims towards traffickers. Social and economic vulnerabilities intensify their susceptibility. The disadvantaged or marginalized social groups are highly vulnerable to being entrapped by traffickers. These factors include poverty, marginalized social and economic status, traditional and cultural practices, lack of education, lack of employment opportunities, and political and economic instability.

Rapid Report & Response (R3): A mobile system created by Prevent Human Trafficking. Anyone suspecting human trafficking incident can text a message. The message is received and securely routed to the nearest first responder who will go to the site of the report and look for evidence of the incident.

Rational Choice Theory: According to this theory, the criminal decision making process is a function of free will and victimization is not random.

Recruitment: A process of finding, screening, interviewing, and hiring the best-qualified candidates for jobs.

Recruitment Strategies: Refers to strategies for finding, screening, and hiring the best-qualified candidates for jobs.

Refugee: Any person who is outside his/her country of nationality who is unable or unwilling to return to that country because of persecution or a well-founded fear of persecution. Persecution or the fear thereof must be based on the alien's race, religion, nationality, membership in a particular social group, or political opinion. People with no nationality must generally be outside their country of last habitual residence to qualify as a refugee. Refugees are subject to ceilings by geographic area set annually by the president of the United States in consultation with Congress and are eligible to adjust to lawful permanent resident status after one year of continuous presence in the United States.

Restitution: Restoration of something lost or stolen to its proper owner.

Risk-Taking Ability: Daring and adventurous nature. Not afraid of risks.

Runaway/Throwaway Youth: Children and young people who run away from their homes or are abandoned or are forced to leave their homes.

Safe Harbor for Exploited Children Act: The state of New York became the first state to pass the Safe Harbor for Exploited Children Act in 2010. The act prohibits prosecution of minors for prostitution.

Servitude: A state of being a slave or completely subject to someone's control.

Severe Forms of Trafficking in Persons: "Sex trafficking in which a commercial sex act is induced by force, fraud, or coercion, or in which the person induced to perform such act has not attained 18 years of age"; or labor trafficking, "the recruitment, harboring, transportation, provision, or obtaining of a person for labor or services, through the use of force, fraud, or coercion for the purpose of subjection to involuntary servitude, peonage, debt bondage, or slavery" (22 U.S.C. 7102).

Sex Industry: Any commercial enterprise offering or producing adult entertainment; a euphemism for prostitution or pornography.

Sex-Slavery: A form of slavery that limits a person's autonomy, freedom of movement, and power to decide matters relating to one's sexual activity. A person is maintained as a sex slave, providing sex on demand.

Sex Trafficking: Situations in which humans are coerced, forced, or deceived into prostitution or maintained in prostitution through coercion.

Sex Trafficking Ring: Refers to an organized group running the illegal business of recruiting, harboring, transporting, obtaining, or providing persons including minors for the purpose of sex and commercial sex including pornography.

Sexual Assaults: Attacks and/or assaults that involve sexual violence and forceful sexual acts.

Slavery: A slave is a person who has no autonomy and is forced to comply with the demands and whims of the master. Such living conditions refer to slavery.

Smuggling: Illegal and facilitated movement across an international border for profit; may involve deception and/or abusive treatment. The main objective of smuggling is to profit from the act of facilitating crossing the border (generally an international border), not exploitation.

Social Impact: Impact on society.

Social Inequality: Refers to situations where there are unequal opportunities and rewards for different social positions or statuses within a group or society.

Socioeconomic Status: The social standing or class of an individual or group. It is often measured as a combination of education, income, and occupation.

Special Assessment: To designate a unique charge that government units can assess against persons or entities.

Spoofing: Hoax, trick, or deceive.

Stateless Crime: A crime that does not fall under the purview of either international or national courts. For example, organ trafficking and trafficking in persons for the purpose of organ removal are considered stateless crimes because neither international criminal law nor individual states' domestic criminal laws address this crime or provide adequate guidelines as to how to address these crimes.

Stereotype: A widely held but an oversimplified image or idea of a particular type of person or thing.

Stockholm Syndrome: Situations in which victims begin to identify with their victimizers as a means of emotional and physical survival. In such cases, the victims do not believe that they are victims. They actually start bonding with the traffickers and feel a connection with their traffickers and any interactions with service providers, law enforcement, or others trying to convince them that they are victims and need to be rescued are ineffective.

Surplus Labor: Labor that is excess of demand; when there are more people willing to provide services and goods than are needed or demanded.

Surplus Services: The amount of services that exceed the portion that is utilized. The services that exist but are not needed.

Sweatshop: A place where people work long hours for low pay in poor working conditions. Where the safety and welfare of the workers is overlooked.

Task Force: A group of experts working together to investigate and submit a formal report on the issue they are assigned. For example, a human trafficking task force will work together to investigate and submit a formal report on human trafficking. Task forces can serve as central resources for those engaged in community organizations and can serve as means of facilitating communication, coordination, and information sharing across agencies working on a case.

Temporary Worker: An alien coming to the United States to work for a temporary period of time. The Immigration Reform and Control Act of 1986 and the Immigration Act of 1990, as well as other legislation, revised existing classes and created new classes of nonimmigrant admission. The nonimmigrant temporary worker classes of admission are as follows:

H-1B: Workers with "specialty occupations" admitted on the basis of professional education, skills, and/or equivalent experience.

H-2A: Temporary agricultural workers coming to the United States to perform agricultural services or labor of a temporary or seasonal nature when authorized workers are unavailable in the United States.

H-2B: Temporary non-agricultural workers coming to the United States to perform temporary services or labor if unemployed persons capable of performing the service or labor cannot be found in the United States.

H-3: Aliens coming temporarily to the United States as trainees, other than to receive graduate medical education or training.

H-4: Spouse and children of H visa recipients.

O-1, O-2, O-3: Temporary workers with extraordinary ability or achievement in the sciences, arts, education, business, or athletics; those entering solely for the purpose of accompanying and assisting such workers; and their spouses and children.

P-1, P-2, P-3, P-4: Athletes and entertainers at an internationally recognized level of performance; artists and entertainers under a program that is "culturally unique"; and their spouses and children.

Q-1, Q-2, Q-3: Participants in international cultural exchange programs; participants in the Irish Peace Process Cultural and Training Program; and spouses and children of Irish Peace Process participants.

R-1, R-2: Temporary workers to perform work in religious occupations and their spouses and children.

Tier System: An evaluation system is created by the Trafficking Victims' Protection Act (TVPA). It is divided into three tiers. The department evaluates each country's efforts towards controlling and preventing trafficking in persons and places each country onto one of the tiers, as mandated by the TVPA. This placement is based more on the extent of government action to combat trafficking than on the size of the country's problem. The analyses are based on the extent of governments' efforts to reach compliance with the TVPA's minimum standards for the elimination of human trafficking—consistent with the Palermo Protocol.

Trade in Humans: Engaging in the business of sale and purchase of human beings as commodities for profit.

Trafficking in Persons: The same as human trafficking—the recruitment, transportation, transfer, harboring, or receipt of persons, by means of the threat or use of force or other forms of coercion, of abduction, of fraud, of deception, of the abuse of power or of a position of vulnerability.

Trafficking in Persons Protocol (2000) and Removal of Organs: Article 3(a) of the Trafficking in Persons Protocol states: "'Trafficking in persons' shall mean the recruitment, transportation, transfer, harboring or receipt of persons, by means of the threat or use of force or other forms of coercion, of abduction, of fraud, of deception, of the abuse of power or of a position of vulnerability or of the giving or receiving of payments or benefits to achieve the consent of a person having control over another person, for the purpose of exploitation. Exploitation shall include, at a minimum, the exploitation of the prostitution of others or other forms of sexual exploitation, forced labor or services, slavery or practices similar to slavery, servitude or the removal of organs."

Trafficking Syndicates: Groups of traffickers.

Trafficking Victims' Protection Act (TVPA): In 2000, the United States Congress passed this federal statute, which offered protections for persons who may be illegally in the country and victims of human trafficking. Public Law 106–386, Oct. 28, 2000, 114 Stat. 1465 was passed: (1) to combat trafficking in persons, especially into the sex trade, slavery, and involuntary servitude, (2) to reauthorize certain federal programs to prevent violence against women, and for other purposes.

Trans-Atlantic Slavery: Refers to the segment of the global slave trade that transported between 10 million and 12 million enslaved Africans across the Atlantic Ocean to the Americas from the sixteenth to the nineteenth centuries. It was the second of three stages of the so-called triangular trade in which arms, textiles, and wine were shipped from Europe to Africa, slaves from Africa to the Americas, and sugar and coffee from the Americas to Europe.

Transfer: Move from one place to another; change ownership from one owner to another.

Transit Countries: Refers to countries where humans are held until they are ready to be transported to final destinations.

Transnational: Involving more than one nation; extending or operating across national boundaries.

Transnational Organized Crime: A consortium of self-perpetuating associations and individuals from different countries working in collaboration and operating transnationally for the purpose of obtaining power, influence, or monetary and/or commercial gains, wholly or in part by illegal means.

Transnational Trafficking: Refers to the transportation of people within nations/countries for the purpose of sexual and/or labor exploitation by the use or threat of the use of force, fraud, or coercion.

Transplant Commercialism: Refers to a policy or practice in which an organ is treated as a commodity, including by being bought or sold or used for material gain.

Transplant Tourism: Defined by the United Network for Organ Sharing as "the purchase of a transplant organ abroad that includes access to an organ while bypassing laws, rules, or processes of any or all countries involved."

Transportation: Refers to the action of transporting (moving from place to another) someone or something or the process of being transported.

Trauma Theory: This theory purports that traffickers' tactics in maintaining control over victims through the infliction of fear and trauma as well as victims' state of mind and decision making process lead victims to be entrapped in trafficking. Such control hampers victims' ability to ask for help or accept any assistance. They stay in the situation.

Travel for Transplantation: Refers to the movement of organs, donors, recipients, or transplant professionals across jurisdictional borders for transplantation purposes.

Ubiquitous in Nature: Prevalent in every country in every region of the world, transcending any and all any boundaries.

UN Convention against Transnational Organized Crime: This is the main international instrument in the fight against transnational organized crime. It was adopted by General Assembly Resolution 55/25 of 15 November 2000 and entered on 29 September 2003. The convention is supplemented by three protocols, which target specific areas and manifestations of organized crime: the Protocol to Prevent, Suppress and Punish Trafficking in Persons, Especially Women and Children; the Protocol against the Smuggling of Migrants by Land, Sea and Air; and the Protocol against the Illicit Manufacturing of and Trafficking in Firearms, Their Parts and Components and Ammunition.

Under-Age Prostitution: Children used or allowed for commercial sex.

Underground Industries: Illegal industries that ignore all laws, rules, and regulations and thrive on providing prohibited goods and services to the buyers who are willing to pay exorbitant prices for otherwise banned goods and services.

Uniform Act on Prevention of and Remedies for Human Trafficking (Uniform Act): This act was passed in 2013 by the Uniform Law Commission (ULC). This act offers guidance to state legislators and provides language drafted and adopted by lawyers from across the country that can serve as a basis for state legislation.

Uniform Crime Reports: Reports of crime collected and disseminated by the Federal Bureau of Investigation.

Universal Declaration of Human Rights: The Universal Declaration of Human Rights (UDHR), drafted by representatives with different legal and cultural backgrounds from all regions of the world, was proclaimed by the United Nations General Assembly at the Palais de Chaillot in Paris on 10 December 1948 (as General Assembly Resolution 217A) as a common standard of achievements for all peoples and all nations.

Unprecedented: Happening for the first time. Something that has never before been known or experienced.

UN Protocol to Prevent, Suppress and Punish Trafficking in Persons, Especially Women and Children: This protocol was adopted by the United Nations General Assembly in 2000 and entered into force on December 25, 2003. As of June 2015 it has been ratified by 167 parties.

Victim Precipitation Theory: According to this theory, victims are partially or wholly responsible for their victimization. This theory suggests that the victim him/herself initiates a contact and agrees to participate in the activity that may eventually lead to victimization.

Virtual Global Taskforce (VGT): The Virtual Global Taskforce (VGT) was established in 2003. Its main objective is to build an effective, international partnership of law enforcement agencies that helps to protect children from online child abuse. It is currently comprised of law enforcement agencies from around the world, including the Australian High Tech Crime Centre, the Child Exploitation and Online Protection Centre in the UK, the Royal Canadian Mounted Police, the US Department of Homeland Security, Interpol, Colombian National Police, Europol, Indonesian National Police, Interpol, Italian Postal and Communication Police Service, Korean National Police Agency, New Zealand Police, and the Ministry of Interior for the United Arab Emirates.

Vulnerability: Refers to state of being open to injury, or having the quality of being easily hurt or attacked.

White-Slave Traffic Act: Also known as Mann Act. It is the first United States law prohibiting transporting women from one state to another for the purposes of sex work.

Index